THEORY AND INTERPRETATION OF NARRATIVE

James Phelan, Peter J. Rabinowitz, and Robyn Warhol, Series Editors

Media of Serial Narrative

Edited by Frank Kelleter

THE OHIO STATE UNIVERSITY PRESS • COLUMBUS

Copyright © 2017 by The Ohio State University.
All rights reserved.

Library of Congress Cataloging-in-Publication Data
Names: Kelleter, Frank, 1965– editor.
Title: Media of serial narrative / edited by Frank Kelleter.
Other titles: Theory and interpretation of narrative series.
Description: Columbus : The Ohio State University Press, [2017] | Series: Theory and
  interpretation of narrative | Includes bibliographical references and index.
Identifiers: LCCN 2016056111 | ISBN 9780814213353 (cloth ; alk. paper) | ISBN 0814213359
  (cloth ; alk. paper)
Subjects: LCSH: Serialized fiction—History and criticism. | Comic books, strips, etc.—
  History and criticism. | Film serials—History and criticism. | Television series—History
  and criticism. | Digital media. | Digital storytelling. | Popular culture.
Classification: LCC PN3448.S48 M43 2017 | DDC 809.3—dc23
LC record available at https://lccn.loc.gov/2016056111

Cover design by Lisa Force
Text design by Juliet Williams
Type set in Minion and Avenir

∞ The paper used in this publication meets the minimum requirements of the American
National Standard for Information Sciences—Permanence of Paper for Printed Library
Materials. ANSI Z39.48-1992.

9 8 7 6 5 4 3 2 1

CONTENTS

ACKNOWLEDGMENTS vii

INTRODUCTION   About This Volume   1

CHAPTER 1   Five Ways of Looking at Popular Seriality   7
            Frank Kelleter

PART I   LITERATURE AND COMICS

CHAPTER 2   Antebellum Popular Serialities and the Transatlantic
            Birth of "American" Comics   37
            Jared Gardner

CHAPTER 3   Serial Politics in Antebellum America: On the Cultural
            Work of the City-Mystery Genre   53
            Daniel Stein

CHAPTER 4   Serial Entertainment / Serial Pleasure: The Yellow Kid   74
            Christina Meyer

PART II   CINEMA

CHAPTER 5   Inevitability of Chance: Time in the Sound Serial   93
            Scott Higgins

CHAPTER 6   Spectral Seriality: The Sights and Sounds of Count Dracula   108
            Shane Denson and Ruth Mayer

CHAPTER 7   Hollywood Remaking as Second-Order Serialization   125
            Frank Kelleter and Kathleen Loock

| CHAPTER 8 | New Millennial Remakes
CONSTANTINE VEREVIS | 148 |

PART III   TELEVISION

CHAPTER 9	The Ends of Serial Criticism JASON MITTELL	169
CHAPTER 10	Sensing the Opaque: Seriality and the Aesthetics of Televisual Form SUDEEP DASGUPTA	183
CHAPTER 11	The Inevitable, the Surprise, and Serial Television SEAN O'SULLIVAN	204

PART IV   TRANSMEDIA AND DIGITALITY

CHAPTER 12	"All Over the Map": Building (and Rebuilding) Oz HENRY JENKINS	225
CHAPTER 13	Popular Seriality in Everyday Practice: *Perry Rhodan* and *Tatort* CHRISTINE HÄMMERLING AND MIRJAM NAST	248
CHAPTER 14	Digital Seriality: On the Serial Aesthetics and Practice of Digital Games SHANE DENSON AND ANDREAS SUDMANN	261

| LIST OF CONTRIBUTORS | 285 |
| INDEX | 288 |

ACKNOWLEDGMENTS

LIKE EVERY COLLECTION, this book owes its existence to more people than are listed in the table of contents. As its editor, I wish to thank the members, associated members, and fellows of the Popular Seriality Research Unit (PSRU, 2010–16). Some of them have written essays for this volume. Others are represented more indirectly, but no less forcefully, through their far-ranging contributions to the study of seriality and popular culture. Without them, this book would not exist: Birgit Abels, Regina Bendix, Ilka Brasch, Felix Brinker, Heinrich Detering, Lukas Etter, Rita Felski, Kathleen Fitzpatrick, Fabian Grumbrecht, Christian Hißnauer, Stephanie Hoppeler, Nathalie Knöhr, Martin Lampprecht, Britta Lesniak, Julia Leyda, Tonia Sophie Müller, Kaspar Maase, John Durham Peters, Gabriele Rippl, Mark Sample, Stefan Scherer, Sabine Sielke, Bettina Soller, Claudia Stockinger, Maria Sulimma, Babette Bärbel Tischleder, William Uricchio, Robyn Warhol, and Lisanna Wiele. I furthermore wish to thank the participants of the 2011 and 2013 events on Popular Seriality in Göttingen, co-organized by Kathleen Loock. Again, some of the participants have contributed chapters to this volume; others have contributed ideas, inspiration, and critique—among them are Lorenz Engell, Oliver Fahle, Brigitte Frizzoni, Ursula Ganz-Blättler, Julika Griem, Knut Hickethier, Matt Hills, Hans-Otto Hügel, Christian Junklewitz, Judith Keilbach, Thomas Klein, Gerhard Lauer, Lothar Mikos, Ruth Page, Irmela Schneider, Ben Singer, Lynn Spigel, Carola Surkamp, and Tanja Weber.

More have joined the conversation in 2016, when this book was being prepared for publication, among them Stephanie Boluk, Will Brooker, John Caldwell, Monica Dall'Asta, Eva Geulen, Sven Grampp, Jennifer Greenhill, Helen Hanson, Ulla Haselstein, Dan Hassler-Forest, Amy Herzog, Till Heilmann, Rieke Jordan, Rob King, Amanda Klein, Frank Krutnik, Amanda Lotz, Annemarie Navar-Gill, Madita Oeming, Federico Pagello, Madleen Podewski,

Janina Rojek, Sarah Schaschek, Jeffrey Sconce, Phyll Smith, Susan Squier, Peter Stanfield, Gunter Süß, Daniela Wentz, Harald Wenzel, Linda Williams, Michaela Wünsch, Ellen Wright, and others. Those who have helped as readers, administrators, and student assistants are too numerous to list. They include Jonathan Andrews, Moritz Emmelmann, Christy Hosefelder, Karl Imdahl, Ansgar Jahn, Madita Oeming, Simon Rienäcker, Christian Voss, and Regina Wenzel. I am also grateful to my colleagues at the John F. Kennedy Institute for North American Studies who supported the PSRU's move from Göttingen to Freie Universität Berlin with enthusiasm and generous input, in particular Laura Bieger, Irwin Collier, Winfried Fluck, Jessica Gienow-Hecht, Ulla Haselstein, Christian Lammert, Martin Lüthe, Florian Sedlmeier, Alexander Starre, Sarah Wasserman, and Harald Wenzel.

At The Ohio State University Press, I wish to thank Lindsay Martin for her professional, patient, and altogether perfect supervision of this book project, as well as the series editors of Theory and Interpretation of Narrative for their intellectual hospitality—something a number of contributors were able to experience firsthand when they cooperated with the fabulous Project Narrative at The Ohio State University, Columbus. On behalf of all contributors, I would also like to thank the three reviewers of the manuscript for their comprehensive, challenging, and engaging feedback. Finally, I wish to exploit my position as editor to thank all contributors: working with you on this project has been a joy and a privilege! I never thought that editing an essay collection could be this much fun.

Frank Kelleter

INTRODUCTION

About This Volume

THIS VOLUME investigates a storytelling practice that shapes all media of popular culture: serialization. In modern entertainment formats, seriality and popularity are so obviously connected that scholarship for a long time has sidestepped questions about their specific interrelation: What are the structural conditions of serial stories? Which historical circumstances are presupposed or supported by series and serials? How do commercial types of seriality differ from serial structures in other cultural fields? The present volume addresses these issues, focusing on key sites and technologies of seriality since the mid-nineteenth century: newspapers, comics, cinema, television, and digital communication. Paying close attention to the affordances of individual media, as well as to their historical interactions, the book's fourteen chapters survey the forms, processes, and functions of popular-serial storytelling.

The first chapter provides a conceptual framework for these questions, developing a layered theory of "popular seriality." Frank Kelleter presents five interlinked ways of looking at commercial serial storytelling: (1) He argues that serial narratives are best described as *evolving* narratives, because they exist as entities that keep developing in adaptive feedback with their own effects. (2) As a result, practices of *recursivity*, such as the continual realignment of possible diegetic futures with already established pasts, are essential to serial storytelling. (3) Furthermore, commercial series need to be examined as narratives of *proliferation* that tend to expand beyond the bounds of their original media and core texts. (4) Therefore, it is helpful to think of popular-serial practice according to the Latourian model of *actor-networks*. Following this model, popular series can be analyzed as self-dynamic cultural agents, consisting of acting persons, active institutions, and action-conducting forms, objects, and technologies. (5) Consequently, a *cultural-ecological* (or systems-theoretical) approach is well suited to describing the development, since the nineteenth century, of commercial series in correlation with the coevolving conditions of their (capitalist) cultural environments.

Following this theoretical framework, four larger sections then go on to discuss central media of serial narrative with chapters on literature and comics (Part I), cinema (Part II), television (Part III), and digital forms of seriality (Part IV), the latter paying particular attention to transmedia storytelling. The first section opens with an essay by Jared Gardner, who documents the roots of popular seriality in the transatlantic magazine culture of the eighteenth century. This chapter also examines the role of print industries (Benedict Anderson's "print capitalism") in preparing, perhaps even necessitating, the birth of an entire realm of serial entertainment in the nineteenth century—what would later be called *popular culture*. Attempting a deep genealogy of comics, Gardner turns to the American 1840s to discuss how Rodolphe Töpffer's *The Adventures of Obadiah Oldbuck* was understood by contemporaries as employing an original medium of storytelling (a novel told in a series of images) that could yet be treated as something easily recognizable and long familiar. All in all, Gardner's chapter considers the unique ways in which comics have facilitated a range of experimentation with seriality, especially concerning the highly charged relationship between serial storytellers and serial audiences.

Focusing on the same period, Daniel Stein investigates another early form of popular seriality that helped to politicize national entertainment formats in the United States: antebellum "city mysteries." Published in the wake of Eugène Sue's internationally successful *Les mystères de Paris* (1842–43), these sensational newspaper novels did more than merely "represent" the conflicts of their period. As Stein argues, due to their serial production, distribution, and reception, urban mysteries literally made modern politics possible: they structured the field of political agency and (re)produced practical policies in the decades before the Civil War, thus laying the groundwork for an American popular culture that cannot be considered in isolation from its sociohistorical action possibilities.

Building on both Gardner's discussion of the media affordances of serial comics and Stein's interest in the cultural politics of nineteenth-century periodical print formats, Christina Meyer, in the fourth chapter, unfolds what she calls the *serial matrix* of the most popular comics character around the turn of the century: the Yellow Kid, who first appeared in the Sunday "Comic Weekly" supplement of Joseph Pulitzer's *New York World* in the 1890s. Analyzing the narrative structure of the Yellow Kid newspaper pages and their inherent principles of repetition and variation, Meyer demonstrates how these comics offer insight into late nineteenth-century urban discourses of race and social stratification. Moreover, the Yellow Kid's proliferation across commercial media—including advertisements, theater plays, and merchandise—provides an early example of the inherently prolific logic of popular seriality.

The second section discusses cinematic manifestations of popular seriality. Scott Higgins argues that the Hollywood sound serial (between 1930 and 1956) offered an exceptional kind of engagement for spectators and an important alternative to feature-film storytelling. In particular, this chapter illuminates the sound serial's distinctive treatment of time, analyzing it on three levels: the serial as a whole, the episode, and the cliffhanger. At all three levels, Higgins shows, sound serials managed narrative time to combine wildly incredible events with highly conventional structures. Guaranteeing "survival and success" in the face of "staggering improbability," sound serials practiced storytelling as a game in which plotting and characterization were pleasantly subordinated to the performance of technological ingenuity itself.

For Shane Denson and Ruth Mayer, such serial games of repetition and variation are always characterized by a strong sense of (media) reflexivity. The sixth chapter finds this type of serial self-performance best expressed in what it calls *iconic* serial figures, that is, persistent stock characters of popular storytelling that offer themselves to frequent makeovers and media changes, such as Tarzan or Fu Manchu. Within the "political and economic order of modernity," Denson and Mayer argue, such figures operate as "mediating instances" between the old and the new. The chapter focuses on Dracula and his relationship to modern media technologies in Bram Stoker's original novel (1897) and Tod Browning's early sound-era film (1931). In both cases, Dracula is shown to enact a "spectral" logic of serial proliferation, a ghostly wavering between presence and absence that defines the mediality of this figure and drives its repeated resurrections and transformations in and through new technologies of storytelling.

Frank Kelleter and Kathleen Loock also focus on the reflexivity of serial media, discussing the practice of film remaking as an operation that, while related to more explicit forms of narrative serialization in other media, generates specifically cinematic formats of continuation (such as the film sequel, the prequel, the trilogy, the franchise, the reboot, etc.). Compared to periodic series, these more erratic iterations—the chapter focuses on the manifold remakings of *Planet of the Apes*—provide a relatively abstract, or second-order, type of serialization: they structure media-historic sequences (rather than rhythms of everyday life), they foster far-ranging cultures of knowledge and commitment (e.g., cinephilia rather than concentrated fan cultures), and they provide expansive continuity markers that can inspire large-scale practices of cultural self-performance at the level of pop-generational identity.

In the section's final chapter, Constantine Verevis complements Kelleter and Loock's conceptualization of cinematic remaking with a detailed investigation of remaking practices in the first decades of the new millennium. Unlike in earlier periods, when remakes or sequels were widely seen as inferior formats that indicated Hollywood's waning creativity, industry discourses in the twenty-first century have come to reassess a film's remake status, identifying the transformation of already available material as the creation of additional "value." Strongly relying on postproduction and digital convergence practices, the new millennial remake, as Verevis describes it, sees its predecessor no longer as an "original" but utilizes it as "a prototype and basis for generating serial forms (sequels, series, and cycles)."

The third section, dedicated to television, opens with Jason Mittell raising a question that has often been asked in media scholarship but that has rarely been inflected by considerations of seriality: What do television narratives mean? Or, put differently, how can we talk about TV series in terms of their relation to issues of cultural politics? Using *Homeland* and *Breaking Bad* as case studies, Mittell investigates how representations of gender, ethnicity, and cultural power in these shows are contingent upon constant acts of repurposing within and without their narratives. Although television criticism aims to provide coherent readings, such assessments must remain fluid as long as the series is progressing. In this manner, Mittell argues, the various ways in which viewers, fans, or scholars revisit and revise a program's political meaning demonstrate both the challenges and the stakes of serial criticism.

Sudeep Dasgupta, in the tenth chapter, explicitly relies on Mittell's theory of televisual meaning-making. In particular, he engages with Mittell's account of "forensic" viewing and proposes to expand the attendant concept of narrative complexity to encompass the sensory presence of nonsignifying "things" in contemporary television series. For example, Dasgupta argues that in *Mad Men*, screen images of/as objects resist the forensic project of fixing meaning by force of their "sheer" materiality. According to Dasgupta, such moments of "opacity" in serial storytelling require us to do more than analyze plot and character: we also need to attend to the sensory experience of television seriality in a period after postmodernism.

Equally interested in the multifaceted nature of contemporary American television series, Sean O'Sullivan closes this section by placing shows such as *The Sopranos, Six Feet Under, Deadwood, The Wire,* and *Breaking Bad* within a spectrum of storytelling techniques that spans narratives of surprise and narratives of the inevitable. "Surprise," as O'Sullivan describes it, acts as a practice either of unexpected revelation or, more subtly, of structural unpredictability. By contrast, narrative "inevitability" privileges what cannot be avoided but which—for exactly this reason—produces suspense. Among other things, the chapter details how *Breaking Bad* reanimated surprise as a storytelling philosophy for a plot premised on inevitability, thereby expanding the use of serial surprises in ways that both draw from television's past and offer new directions for its future.

The final section of *Media of Serial Narrative* discusses the impact of digital communication and transmedia entertainment formats on serial narration. Henry Jenkins turns to the Oz universe to delineate digital-age practices of building and rebuilding serial worlds. Focusing on Disney's prequel, *Oz the Great and Powerful,* Jenkins argues that we still lack an aesthetic terminology to appropriately describe and appraise serial narratives that achieve remarkable world-building but fall short of some of the more traditional virtues of storytelling. Drawing on theories of popular seriality that stress serial narrative's tendency toward proliferation and accretion, this chapter examines the resulting tension—so characteristic of our current entertainment media— between two types of audience desire: the desire to follow a streamlined core narrative on the one hand and the desire to experience a richly populated and abundantly growing storyworld on the other.

The next chapter addresses the empirical sphere of reception. Christine Hämmerling and Mirjam Nast present the results of an ethnographic study that traced and compared reception practices for the two longest-running serial narratives in Germany: the science fiction pulp novel series *Perry Rhodan* (since 1961) and the TV procedural *Tatort* (since 1970). Focusing on what they call *quotidian integration*—that is, various ways in which recipients integrate narrative commodities into their everyday lives, making serial stories socially meaningful—Hämmerling and Nast conclude that central assumptions of contemporary media theory concerning technological convergence and participatory fan activities are in need of empirical qualification.

Finally, Shane Denson and Andreas Sudmann present a theoretical and methodological model for approaching digital seriality in its most typical manifestation: computer games and gaming cultures. Seriality, they argue, is a vital but often ignored feature of digital games and one that bridges the (alleged) conceptual opposition of narratological and ludological accounts of gaming. This is true not only for gaming software and hardware (with its numbered successions, sequels, prequels, etc.) but also for the experiential structure of iterative "levels" or "worlds" within the act of gaming itself. In fact, at the "paraludic" level of transmedia relations (to comics, films, television, and their respective storytelling cultures), digital games experimentally insert themselves into an entire ecology of serial media—the very subject matter of the present volume.

Of course, many more topics could have been included: radio, soap operas, telenovelas, sports broadcasting, and countless other types of popular seriality. By necessity, this book must make selections. But in doing so it draws on a scholarly network that has produced multiple further accounts, including studies on topics not discussed but often referenced here. Written in close collaboration by an interdisciplinary set of scholars from the United States, Germany, Australia, and the Netherlands, these fourteen chapters aim to contribute to a better understanding of the wide distribution and broad appeal of serial narratives since the nineteenth century. In their sum, they raise questions that are central to grasping the media realities of the twenty-first century: Which types of narrative practice are specific to popular series, and how are they shaped by the constraints and possibilities of their media technologies? How can we explain the progressively shrinking boundaries between storytelling and story consumption in long-running series? How do serial narratives organize time and space, and how do they contribute to larger social practices of spatiotemporality? Which transformations in the field of cultural distinctions are produced by complex commercial narratives when they are embedded in urbane or modish lifestyles, traditional canonization practices, or innovation-hungry academic knowledge cultures?

Media of Serial Narrative takes its departure from these questions, drawing a detailed image of popular seriality in print periodicals, cinema, television, and digital media.

CHAPTER 1

Five Ways of Looking at Popular Seriality

FRANK KELLETER

WHAT IS CULTURE if not a realm of repetition and variation? Without practices of continuation, modification, and expansion, we might not be able to tell stories at all. And yet reproduction is not a self-evident theme in the humanities. Almost intuitively, the study of narrative concentrates on figures of distinction, construction, or functionality: Work, Text, Structure. Even when our stories have long given up on the aura of closure—even when they deal with the blessings or perils of endless repetition, or when they apply "serial methods" (as modernist avant-gardes have done again and again, from Gertrude Stein to Andy Warhol and well on into their postmodernist self-description)—we persist in addressing these proliferating acts of sequencing as self-contained oeuvres and finished products. Even the most open work of art must apparently come to an end at some point. To exist as an artwork at all, it must find a place (perhaps distrusted but always identifiable) between two book covers or in a catalogue raisonné, under a unified title, credited to one or more human creators.[1]

---

1. My introductory paragraphs modify observations from Kelleter 2012a. On the "open" work of art, see Eco 1962. On Gertrude Stein, see Haselstein 2010a/b. The controversy surrounding the authentication of Andy Warhol's *Red Self-Portrait* highlights the aesthetic constraints of (post)modernist serialism. On this issue, see Dorment 2009. On *serialism* as a programmatic method and conceptual topos of modernist art and philosophy, see Kelleter 2012a: 13–17.

The will to formal closure probably derives, like art itself, from existential needs. What John Dewey (1934) described as *aesthetic experience* is certainly not dependent on happy endings, but every conclusion holds a promise of serendipitous coherence. Cessation makes a text look like a text, even when the story that is being told offers no solution. Of course, the study of literature and film has long known about the sensory, psychological, and even epistemological satisfaction that comes with narrative closure. The sense of an ending: entire models of society, such as systems theory, benefit from this.[2] But setting up conclusions is only part of what stories do. The other part has to do with uncertainty about final outcomes, with the postponement of a definite end, the promise of perpetual renewal. Even finished tales seek to continue and multiply themselves. Popularity and repetition have always worked hand in hand, from the daily bedtime story to such standardized entertainment formats as the detective novel or the TV medical drama. Commonly, such genres provide smooth endings, but what paradox is inherent in the fact that they do so again and again, without a redeeming overall conclusion to their perpetual acts of narrating?

True, at some point we stop telling bedtime stories to our children, but that moment usually comes when they have advanced to other narrative routines. It is also true that at the end of a detective novel, the crime is usually solved and order has been restored—but then the next misdeed is always lurking in the background of the seemingly finished tale. What if Sherlock Holmes had used his extraordinary skills to solve just one case and had then retired? Would we recognize him as the character we know today? Or would J. R. Ewing still be the same to us if he had put just one business intrigue in motion? We explicitly enjoy these characters as serial figures that recur with the same or similar— though repeatedly mutating—properties. In horror films, too, the final thrill often comes with the recognition that diegetic death only sets up diegetic resurrection.[3] Perhaps this helps explain why so many popular genres, especially crime stories and superhero comics, like to present the protagonist's opponent as his doppelgänger. Such constellations point to the knowledge that serial forms hold about their own rules and conditions. As each puzzle calls for a

---

2. On the concept of *aesthetic experience*, see Bubner 1989; specifically for popular culture, see Maase 2008. On the phrase *sense of an ending*, see Kermode 1967. To my knowledge, there is no study that relates the plausibility of Niklas Luhmann's systems theory to its aesthetic dimension.

3. See the endings of Brian De Palma's *Carrie* (1976; still reintegrating the shock of renewal into a scene of narrative closure) and John Carpenter's *Halloween* (1978; one of the first postclassical horror films that made the device of revoked closure explicit *as* a device before it became a genre convention). On undead characters as instances of serial media's self-reflexivity, see chapter 6 in this volume.

solution, so each solution calls for another puzzle. The hero requires a suitable villain as one episode requires the next. There is no end to it: the Flood is followed by another imperfect world; after the Messiah, a new Prophet arrives; one love novel is superseded by the one that comes after.

Classically, these two basic impulses of storytelling—the satisfaction of conclusion and the appeal of renewal—are balanced through suspense and resolution. Tension is built up to be released again. Anyone looking at this issue with an exclusive interest in completed individual stories (as literary scholarship has taught us with its concentration on works of art) loses sight of the fact that the tension curve rises again after a story has ended: What might be different in the next monster movie—or, for that matter, in the next book of cultural theory? To study the importance of these questions means to study the cultural work of serial narrative. It also means to study the dependency of culture on serial reproduction.

The present volume addresses these concerns with special regard to the media of serial narrative, investigating popular series in literature, comics, cinema, television, and digital technologies. The term *popular* is used here in a strictly historical sense. Thus, in the following chapters, *popular culture* describes a set of social and aesthetic practices that first surfaced in the mid-nineteenth century, closely tangled up with the logic of industrial reproduction and the technological affordances of new mass media (Hagedorn 1995, Hayward 1997, and Kelleter 2012a). As always, historical precedents can be traced back even further—say, to the early days of print capitalism—but it was in the wake of early newspaper novels such as Eugène Sue's *Les mystères de Paris* (1842–43) that mass-addressed serial narratives began to dominate Western entertainment formats. Today, they constitute a large-scale system of commercial storytelling best described as *popular seriality*—an ever more self-aware and increasingly expansive field of narrative that has been causing significant shifts in the relationship of cultural domains. This is particularly true in our own digital era, when even the capacious term *modernization* appears too old-fashioned to capture the full force of these transformations. (Both the social sciences and the humanities can hardly keep up with a process of innovative destruction that makes them produce ever new and quickly replaceable formulas for what used to be called—before it turned into a permanent experience—*cultural change*.)

It may seem unfashionable, if not covertly elitist, to distinguish popular culture in this fashion from other fields of cultural reproduction, such as a self-described "high" culture (understood as a realm of canonized aesthetics and institutionalized refinement) or "folk" culture (in the sense of a self-styled "people's culture"). But focusing on how different storytelling domains describe and perform themselves in their shifting exchanges and intermixtures allows us to take seriously the empirical reality of their self-distinctions without taking at face value the borders and hierarchies they so precariously produce.[4] From the perspective proposed here, popular culture requires no special legitimization as an object of study. In fact, the history of existing research seems to indicate that partisan advocacy of popular culture has often served to obscure the specificities of this stunningly successful field of aesthetic practice. Thus, when I now address comics, newspapers, novels, film serials, Hollywood remakes, television series, or computer games as explicitly commercial products, this implies no critique of their social standing or suspicion of their ideological motives. Instead, it accounts for how they relate (to) themselves and their specific way of doing things. Within a differentiated sphere of cultural reproduction, these entities regularly operate as *undisguised commodities*, that is, as commodities which, unlike traditional artworks, do not usually try to cover up their economic conditions and only rarely claim to have transcended them.

I should add that these are key assumptions of the Popular Seriality Research Unit (PSRU) based at the Freie Universität Berlin.[5] Distancing itself both from ideology-critical condemnations and populist or neo-vitalist endorsements of popular culture, the PSRU intends to offer a conceptual outlook situated at a respectful remove from the battle lines established between critical theory (the legacy of the Frankfurt School), cultural studies (in the wake of the Birmingham School), and cultural philosophy (following several master thinkers). Of course, this model is still far too schematic. While the Frankfurt and Birmingham schools are fairly well defined—one a neo-Marxist critique of "the culture industry" that pits the negativity of avant-garde art against illusory freedoms produced by an all-encompassing "mass culture," the other centered on populist notions of reception that put their anticapitalist hopes in acts of "participation" (understood as either countertotalitarian resistance or democratic meaning-making)—the field of "neo-vitalist" approaches

---

4. For a more detailed discussion of this heuristic model, especially concerning the pragmatic compatibility of systems theory (with its interest in self-descriptions and operational closure) and actor-network theory (with its interest in historically situated practices across cultural domains), see Kelleter 2014a. On the distinction of cultural fields (or "artistic cultures"), see Naremore/Brantlinger 1991 and Kelleter 2012a. On the term *self-description*, see especially Luhmann 1999.

5. Apart from its base in Berlin, the PSRU (2010–16), funded by the German Research Foundation (DFG), has additional subprojects at the universities of Göttingen (its original base), Hannover, Karlsruhe, Siegen, Tübingen, and Duke University. It has attracted associated projects and fellows from Bonn (Germany), Berne (Switzerland), Utrecht (Netherlands), Aix-Marseille (France), Monash University (Australia), and Middlebury College, Davidson College, MIT, The Ohio State University, New York University, and the University of Virginia (USA).

to popular seriality is less distinct. As a general tendency, these philosophies privilege motifs such as subversion and speculation, often by splitting up the concept of seriality into an emancipative ("open") and a restrictive ("closed") variety.[6] From their perspective, popular series are likely to be seen as expressions of utopian transgression or (media) philosophical conjecture, to be distinguished from the managerial, "practico-inert" seriality depicted in neo-Marxist models like Jean-Paul Sartre's (1960). Early manifestations of this argument described television series as the epitome of a postmodernist aesthetics of multiplicity (Nelson 1997, relying on Eco 1962). Following Deleuze (1968, 1969), poststructuralist and posthumanist approaches in particular have shown a strong affinity for neo-vitalist positions, portraying seriality as a fundamental life force of culture. Currently, there is an energetic intellectual market for diverse *post*-isms that value seriality as a transcendence-bound principle of nonlinear intensity or speculative temporality, sometimes with barely concealed metaphysical or religious associations.[7]

In terms of cultural history, the emergence of these and similar conceptual options is interesting, because many of them project the high-cultural serialism of modernist avant-gardes onto popular commodities—a move that would be unthinkable without concurrent shifts in the relation of commercial and canonized aesthetics. But then the analytical utility of neo-vitalist and posthumanist approaches is often limited to reproducing their own sense of philosophical charisma: economic and institutional investigations are sometimes deliberately excluded (or suspected to contain a demeaning attitude toward popular culture); studying the socially stabilizing functions of popular series or their psycho-habitual effects tends to be regarded as theoretically regressive; hybridity, self-referentiality, and sensory experientiality (*affect*) are transformed from observational results into evaluative categories.

The challenge, therefore, is to understand popular seriality not as the deceptive formalism of capitalist entertainment, or as the emancipative consequence of everyday uses, or as the articulation of elemental sensualities, but as something that emerges from situated historical actors and agencies with particular modes of describing and performing themselves. In the following sections, I will delineate five perspectives that have become central to studies of popular seriality in this vein. I should stress, however, that this theoretical

---

6. On this topic, see Denson/Mayer 2012 and Kelleter 2014b.

7. Intellectual precursors can be found in Kammerer's pseudo-biological metaphysics of seriality (1919) and Bergson's concept of *élan vital* (1907). Neoliberal versions were formulated by Johnson (2005) and, more implicitly, in the context of accelerationist philosophies (e.g., Land 2011). Religious and apocalyptic overtones abound in a number of recent ontological approaches that stress the (dark) sublimity of nonhuman scales and sensitivities.

framework does not serve as a blueprint for all the subsequent chapters in this volume, their individual outlooks remaining visible in every case.[8]

POPULAR SERIES AS EVOLVING NARRATIVES

In Anglo-American media studies, one of the oldest formalist definitions of serial storytelling distinguishes between a "series" and a "serial": the first an episodic narrative of repetitive variation and the second a narrative that works with progressing story arcs (Williams 1974). These are indeed basic manifestations of serial plotting, and their wide conceptual acceptance and safe reproduction in serial storytelling cultures—including academic accounts—has allowed for identifying and creating all kinds of formal possibilities in between. Not surprisingly, there are numerous typological systems that try to define and arrange such forms. As always, one can argue about the logic of their competing terminological decisions (e.g., Newman 2006 and Weber/Junklewitz 2008). However, when we think of commercial storytelling as a network of cultural practices rather than a set of distinct structures, we notice that all these formats have at least one thing in common. In both their self-understanding and their narrative performance, they can all be distinguished from the types of story associated with the work or oeuvre. As hinted above, this is true even for artworks that conceive of themselves as "open" structures or artworks that deliberately present themselves in fragments or segments—or, for that matter, as multipart works, released serially after composition. At the level of narrative practice, an important difference between such works and popular series (the term *series* now referring to both episodic and progressing stories, but not to so-called miniseries or other serially distributed work narratives) is that the reception of serial forms, in its initial manifestation, does not distinctly "follow" the production and publication of a finished text. Rather, serial reception first happens in interaction with the ongoing story itself. A series is being watched or read while it is developing, that is, while certain narrative options are still open or have not yet even materialized as options.[9]

---

    8. A different and much shorter presentation of these perspectives in the form of a "dossier" can be found in Kelleter 2017.

    9. At a systemic level (i.e., a level of observation that sees popular seriality reproducing itself *as* a storytelling culture), this is even true for certain oeuvre-like formats like "miniseries," novelistic "trilogy" boxes, the on-demand publication of complete seasons, or the retrospective reception of DVD sets. Re-releases, too, often provoke further formal or generic developments in the domain of serial storytelling. Thus, even expired series can act on their larger narrative environments, for example, by stimulating or discouraging self-renewals in spin-offs, reboots, generic cycles, and so forth (see Klein/Palmer 2016). As chapter 7 below argues, this

Put differently, we find a particularly close entanglement of production and reception in serial storytelling. Of course, in work-bound aesthetics, reception and production also stand in a relationship of mutual dependence, but even so they are thought to exist—and are routinely addressed and enacted—as temporally distinct areas of practice. By contrast, serial aesthetics does not unfold in a clear-cut, chronological succession of finished composition and responsive actualization. Rather, both activities are intertwined in a feedback loop. This sets the practice of watching a running series apart from the practice of reading a stand-alone novel or watching a classical feature film. Repeated temporal overlap between ongoing publication and ongoing reception allows serial audiences to become involved in a narrative's progress. In more general terms, seriality can extend—and normally *does* extend—the sphere of storytelling onto the sphere of story consumption.

Hence popular series have a special ability to generate affective bonds and to stimulate creative activities on the part of their recipients, who, for all practical purposes, operate as *agents of narrative continuation*. This is even true when readers "do" nothing but read, because the sphere of production will then automatically make inferences about their behavior as *customers*; a drop in sales thus becomes a reader's response. Beyond that, there are myriad examples of more explicit consumer reactions contributing to the developments of narrative universes (such as letters to the editor or amateur productions). In turn, the quick timing of narrative steps in commercial serial storytelling—that is, the speed with which installments follow each other, in some formats weekly, in others even daily—enables the ongoing story to respond directly to current events and become part of its recipients' daily realities and routines.[10]

Perhaps, then, popular series are not only "vast narratives" (Harrigan/Wardrip-Fruin 2009)—a term that highlights their ability to spend extended amounts of time telling potentially dense stories—but are also, even when they produce epic effects, *fast* narratives. As commodities, their prime interest is not only to attract but to durably reattract as many readers or viewers as

---

phenomenon invites us to distinguish between first-order and second-order seriality, the latter shifting serial feedback from the level of the episode or installment to some higher level of cultural continuation (and commonly requiring historical descriptions to reveal its seriality). Of course, none of this is exclusive to popular culture, but it is always distinct to it. (Traffic between cultural spheres does not nullify their operational reality.)

10. Many of these issues are discussed by Gardner (2012) with regard to comics. On fan cultures, see Hills 2002. On television, see especially Mittell 2015. On readers' affective engagement with serialized literature, see Warhol 2003. On the relationship between narrative formulas and audience-based forms of play, see Higgins 2016 and chapter 5 in this volume. On quotidian integration, see chapter 13 below.

possible by regularly exchanging recent innovations with new offerings and quickly updating past manifestations with future-bound variations. (Speed should be measured historically here to prevent the illusion that all of this begins with digital media.) What is crucial in this process of enduring auto-obsolescence is that a series can observe its own effects on reactivated or "engaged" consumers while the narrative proceeds. In other words, these are *evolving* narratives: they can register their reception and involve it in the act of (dispersed) storytelling itself. Series observe their own effects—they watch their audiences watching them—and react accordingly. They can adapt to their own consequences, to the changes they provoke in their cultural environment (which is another way of saying that there is a feedback loop). Incidentally, this explains why narrative failure is a permanent companion of serial storytelling. As in most evolutionary processes, success only means avoiding disappearance, not reaching a final state of fulfillment.

To analyze commercial series, therefore, means to focus on moving targets. These narratives exist, not so much as structures that can be programmatically designed, but as structures whose designs keep shifting in perpetual interaction with what they set in motion. Of course, this is not to say that series cannot behave like works of art or produce artful or epic results. They can and frequently do.[11] But the effect of structural unity that this requires is not in their ontological makeup. Rather, it has to be produced and reproduced by the series and its various agents of continuation in the act of (evolving) storytelling itself.

In terms of methodology, this conception of series as moving targets has far-reaching consequences. From the perspective of a narratological (or otherwise formalist) understanding of seriality, many of the points made in this chapter—and throughout this volume—will seem like a risky "broadening" of the concept of seriality, almost encompassing the notion of popular culture itself. One could claim, for instance, that numerous phenomena of commercial entertainment, such as the duplication of success formulas or the repurposing of popular material by audiences, do not "require" serial narratives (or even popular ones) but can be traced in nonserialized texts as well. Of course, this argument hinges on the assumption that seriality is a formal property of multipart texts. But once we shift our attention to networked cultural practices, seriality will become visible in ostensibly nonserialized textual

---

11. See, for instance, O'Sullivan's numerous explorations of the artistic dimension of TV seriality (e.g., 2010 and chapter 11 in the present volume). For extended case studies on HBO's *The Wire* in this context, see Kelleter 2014a and Williams 2014. On the question of popular-serial canonization, see Helms/Phleps 2008, Kelleter 2010, and Hißnauer/Scherer/Stockinger 2014.

structures as well, precisely because these structures can now be investigated as (inter)actions that have been consolidated in domain-specific forms.[12] My point, therefore, is to encourage an understanding of seriality as a practice *of* popular culture, not a narrative formalism *within* it. This is not an issue of "broad" versus "narrow" concepts but of scholastic versus systemic-praxeological modes of description. Or, in other words: one and the same text can be regarded as simultaneously serial and nonserial, depending on the perspective from which it is seen—or, more properly, depending on the historical situation in which its textual activities are mobilized in one way or another.[13]

In an important sense, this argument can be extended into a theory of popular culture itself. Of course, repetition and variation are not exclusive features of popular seriality but basic properties of almost any type of creative activity (cooking, fashion, Bach cantatas, subscription concerts, etc.). Nor is the phenomenon of audience appropriation restricted to popular-commercial material. In principle, every object, sign, or event can always be reinterpreted or diverted from its intended or original use. Nevertheless, there are obvious differences in this regard between popular seriality and serial practices in other aesthetic fields, especially concerning their respective self-understandings and self-performances. Systems-theoretical approaches remind us of the differentiating force of such auto-referential operations. Popular culture, too, in the course of its history increasingly comes to describe itself *as* popular culture, often using references to other domains as strategies of self-reevaluation. From this perspective, popular culture is indeed distinguished from "high" culture, "folk" culture, or quotidian culture, and so on, but not in its material repertory or in the social provenance of single texts or formal habits (workaday clothes can take on pop-cultural meaning; commercial products or producers can be canonized in the field of established art; canonized works or artistic practices can serve entertainment purposes, etc.). Rather, popular culture is distinguished from other aesthetic fields in the varying degrees of explicitness with which it marks its own cultural practices *as* its own, positioning them for shifting purposes of self-reproduction (i.e., providing them with emotional and pragmatic values that ultimately guide possibilities and probabilities of formal design as well).

Thus, if we take seriously the idea of narrative evolution sketched out above (in which series are seen as "moving targets"), we are bound to notice a methodological problem: describing commercial series from an immobile

---

12. See this volume's chapter on remaking as an evolving cinematic *formatting* practice (rather than a typological matrix for ideal cinematic formats). Compare also footnote 9 above.

13. Compare Mittell's contribution to this volume (chapter 9 below).

perspective—registering and comparing merely formal features, for example—captures only a modest part of their cultural productivity. Here we see a common challenge in seriality studies that is already apparent at the level of formal-narratological analysis. When we isolate individual episodes of an initially open-ended series and then analyze these selections with tools that were developed for stand-alone works, we are probably missing something important (similarly Hayward 1997). To do justice to the evolving, interactive, and auto-adaptive character of serial narratives, we need additional instruments of description.

POPULAR SERIES AS NARRATIVES OF RECURSIVE PROGRESSION

In popular series, narrative organization typically takes place on the go, while the story is moving forward, replacing itself with continual variations of itself, or—particularly in the digital age—renewing itself through more parallel-processed acts of reworking. Among other things, this means that producers cannot revise an overall narrative before final publication to get rid of inconsistencies.[14] Popular series therefore have to do their work of coordination, pruning, and coherence-building within the ongoing narrative itself. As a result, these stories will often appear more untidy than work-bound structures when they are consumed *as if they were* predesigned works. A constantly growing excess of things that have already been told—in the case of television, an excess of connecting options that increases every week—forces them to engage in incessant continuity management (especially when they tell their stories in progressing arcs). However, while the amount of narrative information that has to be arranged grows with each new installment—even in episodic series, once they understand themselves as "cumulative narratives" (Newcomb 1985, 2004)—the underlying commercial production culture all

---

14. *Star Wars* is one of the exceptions that prove the rule. It is no longer possible to watch this film as it originally appeared in 1977. Instead, viewers have access only to various enhanced, reedited, and retitled versions of *Episode IV: A New Hope*. Note, however, that these revisions themselves evolved serially—and hence recursively—after the initial film continued to require ever more sequential consistency (including media-technological updates). "Despecialized editions" which try to reconstruct the 1977 theatrical version with the use of various older sources, exist only as fanedits (e.g., Harmy 2011). Narratologically, the initial *Star Wars* movie can therefore be compared to other stand-alone works that were serialized after their success invited further acts of storytelling; in such cases, the first installment is created (*as* a "first" installment) recursively by the second installment. The expression "storytelling on the go" is borrowed from Ganz-Blättler 2012.

but prevents reliance on an overarching trajectory toward closure which would allow the narrative to systematize its innovations from the perspective of a pre-arranged ending. As commodities, popular series have a vested interest in continuing for as long as possible, even when all parties involved know that there is no such thing as real infinity, not even for very successful products. Still, the question of closure poses a fundamentally different problem for serial narratives than it does for work-bound narratives. As Jason Mittell (2015) says, narrative success for television series means being able to continue, not coming to an end.

What Knut Hickethier has described as the "double formal structure" of television series (1991, 2003)—that is, the interdependence of overall narrative and successively unfolding episodes—highlights how in serial storytelling an existing text always prepares its own variation and renewal in another text that does not yet exist. Episodic series, too, have to be told in such a fashion that audiences would like to read or watch the next episode, even when nothing is continued at the level of the plot and when the narrative world supposedly returns to its eternal point of departure. Popular series are structurally geared toward their own renewal. In this manner, they constantly suggest a narrative totality (even to themselves) that is anticipatory by definition because it must remain elusive as long as the series has not yet reached its ending. While these narratives always project a finished story-text—or, in Hickethier's words, an *overall idea* (*Gesamtvorstellung*) of what the series is about—the actuality of compositional finish must remain inaccessible at the moment of ongoing public storytelling itself. In other words, a series' overall idea *evolves* just as much as its moving parts do. This is even the case when some central author has already preplotted a narrative trajectory or planned a specific conclusion—an unlikely situation anyway, since serial narratives are typically produced by a division of labor and under conditions of intense feedback, so that preconceived endings usually exist only as precarious, highly flexible drafts or in the context of so-called miniseries (i.e., work-narratives that are being released in segments).

All these points underline the *recursive* character of serial progression. Recursivity here means the continual readjustment of possible continuations to already established information. Long-running series, in particular, are forced not only to repeatedly reinterpret and even change their pasts but to do so in the very act of continuing themselves. Thus, new elements or unexpected developments—often intruding from such presumably extranarrative realms as production economics (an actor leaving after failed contract negotiations) or the world of geopolitics (terrorist incursions that reverberate within narratives of realism)—have to be realigned again and again with previously told events. To do so plausibly is a major structural challenge for all running series; failure to do so sets up the narrative for ridicule. CBS's *Dallas* (1978–91) provided a classic example of this problem when the series declared that an entire season had never taken place. Less extreme (or more subtle) strategies of serial recursivity in the face of imminent failure include the gradual rearrangement of character constellations within a large ensemble cast; selective memory construction, for example, through flashbacks that invent a new past (a standard method of "retconning" in superhero comics); revoking the perspective of individual characters by placing them in new contexts or retrospective revelations (e.g., when a character is redefined as a lost family member so that all his or her previous actions are given new meaning); collaborative definitions, usually by engaged audiences, of a narrative "canon" that distinguishes between legitimate and illegitimate versions of a story (an almost inevitable consequence of any longer-running series, especially when it is told across media); and many other operations.

As I will argue below, what all these practices have in common is that they foster an intensive tendency toward *self-observation* in serial narratives. There is a rich body of scholarship on the high degree of self-reflection in serial forms (e.g., Engell 2004, 2006, 2009, 2012; Sconce 2004; Denson/Mayer 2012; Jahn-Sudmann/Kelleter 2012; and Jahn-Sudmann/Starre 2013). What should be stressed from the perspective proposed here is that auto-referentiality is not some gratuitous extra that a producer can choose to affix to serial texts or not, but one of their inherent (necessary) features. Precisely because they progress recursively—and because they compete with each other as commodities, that is, as competitors facing failure—serial stories are obliged to monitor their own developments. Both their (structurally) recursive operations and their (economically) competitive operations literally force them to pay attention to their own evolution and, as part of this, to the material and technological conditions of their continued existence. As entities of widely distributed intention, commercial series pay permanent attention not only to the variation possibilities of their stories but typically also to the history of popular seriality itself, including changing generic options and media affordances. And thus, at a higher level of cultural evolution they offer one of the most compelling opportunities to observe how modern popular culture observes itself.

POPULAR SERIES AS NARRATIVES OF PROLIFERATION

If a serial narrative can adjust itself to its ongoing reception, serial audiences, in turn, possess more freedom than work audiences to impact the stories they consume. As commercial culture expands, audiences become increasingly inclined to make use of this freedom. The history of popular seriality is a growing storehouse of amateur and reader productions, ranging from early unauthorized renderings of Sherlock Holmes—one of the first serial characters in a modern commercial sense—to YouTube fanvids and beyond. These constant appropriations, speculations, unofficial continuations, and so forth, tend to generate *authorization conflicts* (Kelleter/Stein 2012). Since the nineteenth century such conflicts have arisen in numerous historical and structural varieties. A random list includes mild feelings of authorial resignation, as in the case of L. Frank Baum, who after a number of Oz books came to recognize that the serial universe was in charge of its originator rather than the other way round (Kelleter 2012b); intense ownership battles among coauthors (especially in superhero comics; see Kelleter/Stein 2012); or openly hostile fights about output efficiency, usually between a single author—a rare or improbable position in serial storytelling—and highly engaged readers who regard serial authorship as a delegated office.[15]

These and similar conflicts of authorization ultimately feed into genre profusion and genre diversification. They do so via narrative traffic that renders the separating line between producers and fans permeable (fans turning into authors, official authors acting from a self-understanding as fans).[16] From a systemic standpoint, all this activity is best described as a necessary—that is, unavoidable—feature of serial aesthetics. As I will argue below, such narrative traffic expresses popular culture's inherent tendency to produce, out of itself and by itself, ever more diversified continuations, spin-offs, revisions, subgenres, and so on. At this point, let it suffice to say that the culture of serial storytelling *generates* both commitments and conflicts that serve as reliable forces of its own reproduction.[17]

Ever since the first serialized newspaper novels appeared in the wake of Eugène Sue's *Les mystères de Paris* (1842–43), popular serial storytelling has

---

15. See the authorization conflicts surrounding George R. R. Martin's *A Song of Ice and Fire* (since 1996). As early as 1987—before the advent of the Internet—Stephen King dramatized the discontent of serial authorship in *Misery*, a telling exercise in (partisan) pop-cultural self-observation.

16. I am not saying that this is true for every fan or for every author. For most of them, it is not true. But the possibility—and high likelihood—that it will always be true for some fans and for some authors is a defining feature of popular seriality.

17. As indicated by concepts such as *reproduction, self-observation, improbability*, and so forth, my conceptual framework here remains systems-theoretical (Luhmann 1999). I shall return to this point. On the compatibility of systems theory and actor-network theory (discussed below), see Kelleter 2014a.

been characterized by *proliferation*.[18] Even after just a few episodes, a series has commonly accrued so much information and so many narrative possibilities that it will sooner or later develop side formats to accommodate this diegetic overflow. Such formats can be authorized (e.g., spin-offs, tie-ins, or more recent types of transmedia storytelling) or unauthorized (e.g., letters to the editor, fan fiction, etc.). In either case, commercial series tend to proliferate beyond the bounds of their original media and core texts. Significantly, this narrative sprawl affects not only individual narratives but the development of popular seriality at large.[19] It does so because as commercial products, series operate in a storytelling market that (1) compels every single series to keep repositioning itself with an eye to its competitors and that (2) encourages the entire field of serial entertainment to maximize current and future profitability through the creation of generic repertoires, transgeneric "multiplicities" (Klein/Palmer 2016), and "serial clusters" (Mayer 2014: 9).[20] As a result, popular series exhibit a strong propensity *to serialize themselves*. In this manner, the first *Harry Potter* novel is followed not only by a second and third *Harry Potter* novel but by a multitude of competing series about young wizards and sorcerers, complete with engaged audiences and countless media transpositions in movie adaptations, games, and so on. And all of these proliferations can have an impact, in turn, on the narrative trajectory of the source series itself (if such a source can be identified at all).

Long-running episodic series are no different in this regard. Their characters—think of Superman, Popeye, or James Bond—are initially aware of past and future only in a very limited sense. Frequently, as Umberto Eco (1972) stresses, they do not even remember themselves from one installment to the next. This is what makes it so difficult to canonize them in the field of restricted production (Bourdieu 1993). Superhero comics, for example, often lack a single authoritative manifestation or text, even for their origin stories. Instead we are confronted with proliferating variations (figure 1.1).

So while it is true that Superman does not *age* as a character (Eco 1972)—that is, there is no clear sequential trajectory of his life within a coherently unfolding fictional world or work—Superman nevertheless does *develop*: as a

---

18. On newspaper novels, see this volume's chapter about "urban mysteries" in antebellum America (chapter 3). Compare also Stein's numerous studies of the generic development of superhero comics.

19. For a more detailed discussion of serial sprawl, centered on the Oz universe, see Kelleter 2012b.

20. Mayer, in one of the PSRU's most detailed case studies (2014), focuses on Fu Manchu narratives between 1913 and the 1970s; see also chapter 6 below. Narratologically minded readers should bear in mind that this is not about "extending" a text-based concept of seriality onto genres and formulas but about redescribing generic structures as consolidated serial practices.

FIGURE 1.1. Many Supermen (DC/Warner Bros. Entertainment).

figure of seriality. This is to say that we can trace countless transmutations of the character without ever being able to decide which one is definitive—a narrative of its own, evolving at a higher level of pop-cultural self-observation. Hence, after a while, the sprawling versions can also include an aged, and even a dying, Superman. But these continuations, dependent as they are on second-order observation, will always be marked as variations, that is, as temporary and revocable innovations within a storyworld that progresses more in the sense that it spreads than it unfolds.[21]

Consequently, to address such proliferating characters as serial *figures* means to recognize them as malleable and persistently shifting narrative elements. This does not mean that they always have to be stereotypical, grafting broad re-instantiations onto an essentially empty frame.[22] Rather, the more

---

21. On the term *storyworld*, see Ryan 2014. For further discussion of serial storyworlds, see Jenkins's contribution in this volume (chapter 12).

22. My paragraph here summarizes a longer examination of character reversals and changing character constellations in the TV series *Lost* (Kelleter 2015). For comparison, see Denson and Mayer's investigations of what they call *iconic* serial figures, such as Dracula or Fu Manchu, whose transmedial malleability very much depends on their "flatness" (2012 and chapter 6 below). On the difference between iconic and more explicitly serialized forms of repetition and profusion, see Gardner (2010), who argues that iconic formats (such as the single-panel comic) lend themselves to stereotypical representations, while more fully executed serial formats (such as the multipanel gutter) invite ambivalent characterizations. The ideological dimension of iconic serialities is also stressed in Mayer 2014.

their proliferation tells its own story—which can also happen *within* a series—the more these serial figures allow and indeed provoke increasingly rounded incarnations that can explore alternative shapes and nuances in great detail (Sherlock Holmes as a modern-day hipster, Dr. Watson as an Asian American woman, *Lost*'s hero Jack Shephard as an irresolute nihilist, villain Ben Linus as a harmless teacher, etc.). Perhaps this is what defines serial figures in the current media ecology: they *produce* characters at high speed; they have a marked—and often marketed—capacity for multiple characterizations.

POPULAR SERIES AS SELF-OBSERVING SYSTEMS AND ACTOR-NETWORKS

Based on the points discussed so far, Henry Jenkins's apt definition of popular culture as "participatory culture" (1992) can be rephrased here to denote a field of practice in which the responsibility for textual formats and formal developments rests in the conflictive division of labor of the production process itself—a process that increasingly comes to include readers and viewers as agents of narrative continuation and second-order self-awareness.[23] If we describe things this way, recipients appear no longer as mere "users" of prefabricated commodities. The idea of "usage" suggests the prior existence of a consensus industry that is separated by an almost ontological divide from its human subjects, while these subjects, in turn, are said to repurpose hegemonic dictates only in a secondary process of productive reception (hopefully for counterhegemonic purposes). In more familiar terms, serial acts of appropriation, extrapolation, or rewriting are likely to appear as the subversive doings of a readerly "people" resisting the impositions of a manipulative "power bloc" of industrial authorities (Hall 1981 and Fiske 1989). Or, to cite more recent versions of this constellation: audience activities are seen to *democratize* processes of meaning-making that would otherwise revert to an undesirable default position of centralized control. They allow diverse identities to articulate themselves.

This is a tempting narrative, especially if you are troubled by the high-modernist elitism of the "culture industry" paradigm (Horkheimer/Adorno

---

23. I say *increasingly* because the self-understanding of popular audiences coevolves with the self-performances of popular products. For this reason it is interesting to ask at which points in history audience members come to recognize themselves *as* members of an audience in an act of mass communication (rather than as individual readers confronted with one distinct and clearly bound text-object, such as a novel). There are obvious differences in this regard between nineteenth-century newspaper readers writing letters, twentieth-century fan communications, and twenty-first-century digital outlets for networked fan art (or, for that matter, industrial authors producing their own officially sanctioned fan fiction in *What If* and *Elseworld* spin-offs).

FIGURE 1.2. *Star Wars: Empire at War* (Petroglyph Games/LucasArts, 2006).

1947) yet want to hold on to Marxian explanatory models. In fact, 1970s scenarios such as "the people vs. the power bloc"—but also some of its critical updates, recoding subversion as democratic self-assertion—reproduce a character constellation that has itself been a mainstay of (Western, particularly Anglophone) popular storytelling ever since the nineteenth century (figure 1.2).

But there are a number of problems with this script, even in its later, more nuanced (and frequently more Americanized) manifestations that de-emphasize straightforward resistance in favor of grassroots participation. To begin with, supply and demand are more closely entangled in serial storytelling than this narrative—or better: this particular *self-description* of popular culture—suggests.[24] As we have seen, this is true in *temporal* terms

---

24. Calling theories of participation *self-descriptions* of popular culture, in Luhmann's sense of the term, is the opposite of critiquing them for some supposed "complicity" with a totalizing regime of oppression. Rather, it serves to underline the productive involvement of (chiefly Anglophone) academic modes of explanation in the reproduction of popular culture itself. This concerns the fact that scholars of contemporary media are always doing more than simply analyzing those media, especially when they operate within and on the same cultural environment as their objects of study. For example, when American television scholars examine American television series, they typically position themselves within the same narrative matrix

(a serial commodity is not supplied once and for all and *then* utilized; instead, supply and demand feed back into each other).²⁵ But also in *emotional* and *institutional* terms, descriptions of the production/reception nexus as a divide between calculating providers and intractable users fail to account for the high degree of permeability between professional and amateur practices that is such a noteworthy feature of commercial storytelling. This is not to deny that there are power relations and hierarchies in serial production cultures. On the contrary, it is to stress their full force outside the reassuring round of populist or metaphysical character constellations (rebels fighting the empire, elemental forces refusing to be named, etc.)—constellations that our critical theories have often inherited from popular storytelling itself.²⁶ So, at the very least, it can be asked where the human intentions of both resisting and participating subjects—and their academic observers—actually come from. Of course there are jealously guarded borders of access, responsibility, and ownership; countless authorization conflicts attest to this fact. But these inequalities exist and reproduce themselves through contested practices that evolve in reaction to their own results. Thus, the entire culture of serial storytelling maintains its unlikely existence via the proliferation of competing arguments, strategies, self-identifications, ideological positions, philosophical translations, attributions, negotiations, alliances, mobilities, and so on.

In other words, production and reception—or industrial and quotidian actors—are best understood as *coevolving* forces. Once we see them this way, the widespread desire for an operational space outside "the system" (conceptualized both by the Frankfurt and the Birmingham schools as a totalizing, frequently totalitarian, structure that nonetheless harbors residual spaces of

---

of democratic self-reference which their objects are also engaged in (e.g., by developing distinctively American notions of participation, anti-elitism, or commodity-based identity articulation). For a more detailed discussion of how (U.S.) media studies and (U.S.) media practices act as interdependent forces within a larger (U.S.) media and storytelling culture, see Kelleter 2014a.

25. Theories of "aesthetic experience" which try to save popular material from anticapitalist reductionism tend to turn this chronological scenario around, positing a prior sensuality that inheres in objects *before* they are commodified. Reading commercial texts thus becomes an exercise in identifying moments of transcendent "irreducibility," which can take many forms "precisely" (as the saying goes): "intensity," "mediality," "thingness," "alterity," "affect," and so forth. These philosophical models (with often European sources) share the antitotalitarian pathos of Anglophone cultural studies but prefer to project their visions of emancipation or incommensurability on nonhuman forces rather than human individuals.

26. Compare Boltanski 2014 on the parallel emergence of sociology and the detective novel. Similar investigations could be launched—with different temporal arguments—for political economy and the sentimental novel, literary phenomenology and the romance, the modern metaphysics of nonhuman being(s) and the horror film, or network philosophies and the picaresque imagination.

irreducible existence) becomes itself visible in systemic terms. In particular, the constellation of a unified center versus multitudinous peripheries—which exists in many variations and nuances, not just in its early expression of "the people vs. the power bloc"—can now be investigated as a scenario not so much *about* but *of* popular culture. The same might be true for the axiological bifurcation of the very concept of seriality into an emancipative and a repressive variant, a motif that almost comes to define philosophical storytelling after World War II. Yet analyzing something in systemic terms is not a question of uncovering totality; it is a question of tracing reproductive practices, that is, reconstructing how disparate agents coevolve while sustaining their precarious differences through interlocking self-descriptions.

But isn't this just a rhetorical sleight of hand? Couldn't it be argued that I am personifying series (perhaps seriality itself), ascribing agency to something that is really the result of deliberate human actions? It all depends on what we mean by *agency* and how we want to account for the presence of nonhuman and transhuman (institutional) factors in serial storytelling. Based on the points discussed so far, we can describe popular series as *self-observing systems,* in the sense that they are never just the "product" of intentional choices and decisions, even as they require and involve intentional agents (most notably, people) for whom they provide real possibilities of deciding, choosing, using, objecting, and so on. In shaping the self-understanding of their human contributors, series themselves attain agential status. As praxeological networks, they experiment with formal identities and think about their own formal possibilities. And they do not do so *instead* of human beings but *with* and *through* dispersed participants, employing human practitioners (who are sometimes much younger than the series in question and who will often express a sense of practical commitment to it rather than a sense of originating authorship) for purposes of self-reproduction. Series are not intentional subjects but entities of distributed intention.

Rather than raising the question of usage, therefore, it seems useful to raise the question of agencies. Scriptwriters, fans, executive boards, television scholars, cable networks, camera setups, genre conventions, program slots, canons, memes: they all *do* something in the act of serial storytelling, but their actions and inter-actions are highly specific to each evolving narrative. For the type of research advocated here, it has therefore proven valuable to think of popular-serial practice along the lines of the *actor-network* model provided by, among others, Bruno Latour (2005, 2013).[27] But the point of this reference

---

27. On the value of ANT for seriality studies, see Engell 2009, Kelleter 2014a, Mayer 2014, and chapter 14 in this volume.

does not reside in its master-theoretical charisma. The (currently) innovative flair of a philosophical name is not important here. Important are the methodological consequences of such an approach—or similar ones with perhaps less stylish appeals. What matters, in other words, is that popular series are appropriately described as active cultural institutions that consist not just of the stories they tell but also of the manifold proceedings and forces that are gathered in their acts of storytelling. These are actor-networks in the sense that they owe their existence to a (re)productive assemblage of acting persons and transpersonal institutions as well as action-conducting forms, narrative conventions and inventions, technologies with specific affordances, and nonpersonal objects and aesthetic theories about such objects.[28]

Therefore, instead of drawing an axiological distinction between production and reception in which the former is cast as manipulative, restrictive, or commercial, and the latter as liberating, critical, or wayward, it seems more promising to reconstruct how shifting positions of commercial "production" and "reception" are created, maintained, and complicated through historically specific (i.e., evolving) practices of pop-cultural self-description and self-performance. The methodological challenge of this approach is to map in dense descriptive detail the concrete actions and carriers of action that come together, however disharmoniously, in a given serial narrative. This perspective is suitable for seriality studies because commercial series are inevitably multiauthored, produced and consumed in many-layered systems of responsibility and performance, and always dependent on both the material demands of their media and the constraints of their cultural environments. In fact, series habitually reflect on these conditions in their own (acts of telling) stories, inviting us to think of serial agency as something dispersed in a network of people, roles, organizations, machineries, and forms.

POPULAR SERIES AS AGENTS OF CAPITALIST SELF-REFLEXIVITY

My fifth perspective on popular seriality builds on, and slightly modifies, Benedict Anderson's notion of the "imagined community" (1991). Often invoked, sometimes trivialized, this concept does not describe a people's shared opinions or agreed-upon fictions. Anderson's theory is not about manufacturing

---

28. For the term *affordance*, see Uricchio (2014), who refers to Norman's (1988) popular study of object design. For an ecological usage (denoting the "action possibilities" of an object or environment), see Gibson 1979.

consent but about collective interactions that channel dissent into improbable feelings of togetherness. Seen this way, antagonisms can strengthen communal cohesion if they are conducted in the context of linked communicative practices. Thus the nation—Anderson's exemplar of an implausibly large-scale, yet strangely sustainable, collective—thrives on the existence of debate, controversy, and even polemics.

Imagined communities are paradoxically unified by enduring differences. For Anderson, this concerns the curious fact that the modern nation is composed of people who never have to meet; who need not belong to the same family, ethnicity, religion, or political party; who are not required to live in the same place or even the same time zone; and who do not have to hold the same opinions but who nevertheless will recognize themselves as members of the same "community" and feel emotionally attached to it (be it positively or negatively). Why? Because they read the same newspapers, listen to the same radio programs, or watch the same sports events, even when rooting for different teams. In this sense, imagined communities are produced by a costly system of practices, institutions, and technologies. They are "imagined" in the sense that they are never given but always made. They require work more than coercion, effort more than control. Their cohesion arises, as Arjun Appadurai suggests (1996), from a million daily acts of unforced routine. Or, in the words of Bruno Latour, modern society is "not a building in need of restoration but a movement in need of continuation" (2005: 37).

Put differently, imagined communities are dependent on the operations of technological mass media. In fact, large territories became governable only with the invention of modern communication machines that were capable of binding together remote spaces through synchronized practice (Innis 1950). It is no surprise, therefore, that Anderson finds his prime example of the workings of imagined collectivization in the act of newspaper reading in the nineteenth century: a "ceremony" that is "incessantly repeated at daily or half-daily intervals throughout the calendar" (1991: 35). The result is procedural communality where dogmatic communality is no longer probable or even possible.[29]

There is an obvious connection between the reproductive practices of Western modernity observed by Anderson and the activities of popular seriality. As argued above, popular series should not be thought of as mere resources of culture that can be used freely for autonomous follow-up actions.

---

29. The preceding (as well as parts of the following) paragraphs modify a section from my essay on Franklin D. Roosevelt's Fireside Chats (2014b). For Anderson's take on seriality, see Chatterjee 1999, Denson/Mayer 2012, and Mayer 2015; compare also chapters 2, 3, 7, and 14 in this volume.

Rather, serial narratives, as actor-networks and self-observing systems, contribute to how the people who produce and consume them (sometimes doing both things at the same time!) understand themselves and proceed in these roles. Thus, while consumers, producers, media scholars, and so forth, operate as agents of narrative continuation, serial narratives in turn operate as agents of role differentiation: they produce "producers" just as they make fans or encourage people to "be" critics or scholars—that is, to *act* as such.[30] Thus, in terms of creating inhabitable fictional spaces, in terms of forging affective bonds between different and differing agents of continuation, the power of popular series resides at least as much in *how* they create storyworlds (in Ryan's and Jenkins's understanding of the concept) as it does in the types of stories they tell.

In other words, series are entities of distributed intention that are nevertheless unified *procedurally* as cultural agents. As a result, even more than work-bound narratives, they resist symptomatic readings that would seek to reveal a tightly controlled motive underlying whatever is being told. This is not to say that serial storytelling takes place in a realm beyond ideology. But popular seriality's ideological dimension seems to be little dependent on acts of encoding. Instead, it calls to mind those acts of communicative assembling that Benedict Anderson sees involved in the creation of imagined communities. In other words, the analysis of seriality requires a nonsymptomatic model of ideology.

Invoking ideology, then, to talk about popular series is not the same as advocating a "hermeneutics of suspicion" (Felski 2011) that wants to uncover questionable political positions within serial texts. The goal here is neither to expose false consciousness nor to reveal commercial interests as the hidden—hence "true"—meanings behind all other pursuits of serial stories. In fact, the very idea that depth or concealment indicates truth is best approached as one of modernity's most *popular* scenarios. If we adopt this perspective, the notion of remote or disembodied powers working behind the scenes becomes visible as the signature, not of critical thought as such but of a particular type of symptomatic reading—perhaps we should better say *symptomatic storytelling*—that borrows and continues key conventions of Western popular culture itself. Recognizing this, one will perhaps be less inclined to substitute critique—as a practice of reliable description in an imperfect world—with neo-ontological theologies of art.

---

30. This is the Latourian question: What needs to be in place—how many productions need to have already occurred—before an individual can act as a "producer" and lay claim to that title?

All of this is to say that popular series are ideological not so much by means of their narrative content (which, being the result of dispersed authorization anyway, cannot easily be pinned down to canonized propositions or unified effects) but more by means of their self-adaptive narrative operations and media procedures (which include representational inequities and activist countermeasures). Their evolving, recursive, proliferating, and multi-agential mode of storytelling enables cultures of attachment—*imagined communities*—that are all the more powerful for being held together by shared communications—shared conflicts and anxieties, too—rather than shared opinions. This helps explain why in many self-descriptions of popular seriality, including scholarly accounts, words such as *engagement* and *participation* have widely ceased to function as descriptive statements and have become value statements instead—an observation that is especially true for popular seriality's prime culture: the United States of America. In terms of its *ideological practice*, then (i.e., its practice of sustaining *ideas* rather than hidden purposes), commercial serial storytelling has widely come to understand and to perform itself as an essentially democratic culture. More importantly, it has come to configure the democratic—originally based in theories of communal and public face-to-face deliberation—as an expansive culture of (frequently commodity-based) representational struggle, mediated involvement, and ubiquitous choice.

What are the practical results of such self-descriptions? Which habits and occupations are stabilized by the expectations, gratifications, and disappointments that keep serial narratives alive? What do all these controversies about participation, authorization, canonicity, representational politics, inclusion and exclusion, and so on, bring into existence? At its most abstract, my (systems-theoretical) argument suggests that popular seriality, understood as a larger historical phenomenon that has accompanied Western modernity since the mid-nineteenth century, supports a practical *regime of continuation* itself. What is being continued here is the contingent, but historically powerful, partnership between democratic ideologies and a particular system of cultural production. It is worth remembering in this context that one of the most difficult problems of serial storytelling consists in translating repetition into difference. Following Eco (1990), this has been said so often that we sometimes like to move beyond these terms. But we ignore Eco's lesson at our own peril, because what looks like a simple matter of narrative technique on closer inspection turns out to be a core problem of modernity itself: the problem of renewing something by duplicating it. This problem lies at the heart of an entire system of cultural production that, for want of a better term—and without need for revelatory pathos—is still best described by the name it has chosen to describe itself: *capitalism*.

It is not a coincidence, then, that starting in the mid-nineteenth century, seriality has become the distinguishing mark of virtually all forms of capitalist entertainment. Serial storytelling seems to be a central praxeological hub in the shaky yet traditionally potent alliance between market modernity and the idea of popular self-rule. This is so because serial media, interactive from the start, embody what may well be the structural utopia of the capitalist production of culture at large: the desire to practice reproduction *as* innovation, and innovation *as* reproduction. Popular seriality promises to duplicate creatively, involving contributors without number to endlessly generate its own follow-up possibilities. Little wonder that commercial series have an almost innate interest in issues of renewal, expansion, and one-upmanship (Jahn-Sudmann/Kelleter 2012). No mere "illustrations" or passive mirrors of developments that are happening outside of them, they can be regarded as prime sites of *capitalist self-reflexivity*, especially concerning capitalism's increasingly tenuous association with the much older (initially premodern) notion of democracy.

Consider that capitalism, as a self-aware and self-theorizing economic system, functions only under the condition that it creates belief in its continued existence in the future (Vogl 2010). Credit transactions are possible only if everyone involved has confidence that there will be further transactions tomorrow (and the more the better).[31] Continuation is the name of the game, and serial media play an important part in creating systemic trust in the improbable reality of their own—and hence their own culture's—persistence. By packaging proliferating narratives into variation-prone structures, schedules, and genres, popular series day in, day out sustain the illusion that the unexpected always comes in a familiar format: that there will forever be something *following* from our present-day excitements and that each disaster is simultaneously a continuation of our stories and debates because the new and the unsettling always reach us in the reassuring shape of what is already known. Whatever else popular seriality tells us, whichever plots it offers us, whichever characters it lets us love or hate, it always also assures us that there will be no end to the return of our stories, no end to the multiplication of our story engagements—and thus no end to the world we know and imagine and controversially practice as our own. Serial media reproduce a sense of infinite futurity, without which capitalist market cultures would threaten to collapse at every crisis point.

Serial narratives, then, may be less hospitable to propositional persuasion than work narratives (or philosophies, for that matter); their evolving,

---

31. For a more detailed discussion of these issues, centered on American radio during the Great Depression, see Kelleter 2014b.

recursive, proliferating, and multi-authored mode of storytelling tends to neutralize—or rather to multiply and diffuse—charismatic master intentions by sheer force of dispersion.[32] But in enabling procedural communities of commitment and conflict—through what mass-addressed storytelling *does* in praxeological ensembles, not merely through what it formally *is*—popular seriality serves to shape, mobilize, and adaptively readjust modern practices of belonging and identity articulation in fast-changing market societies, not least by encouraging these societies to describe themselves as participatory cultures of engagement, debate, and choice.

BIBLIOGRAPHY

Anderson, Benedict (1991). *Imagined Communities: Reflections on the Origins and Spread of Nationalism* [1983]. London: Verso.
Appadurai, Arjun (1996). *Modernity at Large: Cultural Dimensions of Globalization*. Minneapolis: University of Minnesota Press.
Bergson, Henri (1907). *L'évolution créatrice*. Paris: Alcan.
Boltanski, Luc (2014). *Mysteries and Conspiracies: Detective Stories, Spy Novels and the Making of Modern Societies*. Cambridge: Polity.
Bourdieu, Pierre (1993). *The Field of Cultural Production*. New York: Columbia University Press.
Bubner, Rüdiger (1989). *Ästhetische Erfahrung*. Frankfurt: Suhrkamp.
Chatterjee, Partha (1999). "Anderson's Utopia." *Diacritics* 29.4: 129–34.
Deleuze, Gilles (1968). *Différence et répétition*. Paris: PUF.
——(1969). *Logique du sens*. Paris: Minuit.
Denson, Shane and Ruth Mayer (2012). "Grenzgänger: Serielle Figuren im Medienwechsel." *Populäre Serialität: Narration—Evolution—Distinktion. Zum seriellen Erzählen seit dem 19. Jahrhundert*. Ed. Frank Kelleter. Bielefeld: Transcript-Verlag. 185–203.
Dewey, John (1934). *Art as Experience*. New York: Perigee.
Dorment, Richard (2009). "What Is an Andy Warhol?" *The New York Review of Books* 56.16: 14–18.
Eco, Umberto (1962). *Opera Aperta*. Milano: Bompiani.
——(1972) "The Myth of Superman." *Diacritics* 2.1: 14–22.
——(1990). "Interpreting Serials." *The Limits of Interpretation*. Bloomington: Indiana University Press. 83–100.
Engell, Lorenz (2004). "Historizität als Serialität im Zeitalter des Fernsehens." *Die Medien der Geschichte: Historizität und Medialität in interdisziplinärer Perspektive*. Ed. Fabio Crivellari et al. Konstanz: UVK. 181–94.
——(2006). "Ein Mauerfall—von der Rückkehr zum Anfang: Umbruch und Serie in den Medien-Revolutionen des 20. Jahrhunderts." *MedienRevolutionen: Beiträge zur Mediengeschichte der Wahrnehmung*. Ed. Ralf Schnell. Bielefeld: Transcript-Verlag. 101–19.

---

32. This is most visible in series that are theoretically committed to doctrinaire systems of thought, such as Tim LaHaye and Jerry Jenkins's evangelical *Left Behind* novels (1995–2007) or the *Sun Koh* fantasy dime novels (1933–36) in Nazi Germany. The practical tension between serial sprawl and closure-bound political or religious dogmatism in such formats is described in chapter 3 below (on urban mysteries). On the *Left Behind* series, see Stein 2009b.

———(2009). "Fernsehen mit Unbekannten: Überlegungen zur experimentellen Television." *Fernsehexperimente: Stationen eines Mediums.* Ed. Michael Grisko and Stefan Münker. Berlin: Kadmos. 15–45.

———(2012). *Fernsehtheorie zur Einführung.* Hamburg: Junius.

Felski, Rita (2011). "Suspicious Minds." *Poetics Today* 32.2: 215–34.

Fiske, John (1989). *Understanding Popular Culture.* Boston: Unwin.

Ganz-Blättler, Ursula (2012). "DSDS als Reality-Serie: Kumulatives Storytelling 'on the go.'" *Populäre Serialität: Narration—Evolution—Distinktion. Zum seriellen Erzählen seit dem 19. Jahrhundert.* Ed. Frank Kelleter. Bielefeld: Transcript-Verlag. 123–41.

Gardner, Jared (2010). "Same Difference: Graphic Alterity in the Work of Gene Luen Yang, Adrian Tomine, and Derek Kirk Kim." *Multicultural Comics from Zap to Blue Beetle.* Ed. Frederick Luis Aldama. Austin: University of Texas Press. 132–48.

———(2012). *Projections: Comics and the History of Twenty-First-Century Storytelling.* Stanford: Stanford University Press.

Gibson, James J. (1979). *The Ecological Approach to Visual Perception.* Boston: Houghton Mifflin.

Hagedorn, Roger (1995). "Doubtless to Be Continued: A Brief History of Serial Narrative." *To Be Continued . . . : Soap Operas around the World.* Ed. Robert C. Allen. London: Routledge. 27–48.

Hall, Stuart (1981). "Notes on Deconstructing 'The Popular.'" *People's History and Socialist Theory.* Ed. Raphael Samuel. London: Routledge. 227–40.

Harmy (2011). "Harmy's STAR WARS Despecialized Edition HD." originaltrilogy.com (April 5). August 30, 2014. http://originaltrilogy.com/forum/topic.cfm/Harmys-STAR-WARS-Despecialized-Edition-HD-V25-MKV-IS-OUT-NOW/topic/12713/.

Harrigan, Pat and Noah Wardrip-Fruin, eds. (2009). *Third Person: Authoring and Exploring Vast Narratives.* Cambridge: MIT.

Haselstein, Ulla (2010a). "Gertrude Stein and Seriality." *Blackwell Companion to Modern United States Fiction.* Ed. David Seed. Oxford: Blackwell. 229–39.

———(2010b). "Die literarische Erfindung der Serialität: Gertrude Stein's *The Making of Americans*." *Kunst der Serie. Die Serie in den Künsten.* Ed. Christine Blättler. München: Fink. 17–32.

Hayward, Jennifer (1997). *Consuming Pleasures: Active Audiences and Serial Fictions from Dickens to Soap Opera.* Lexington: University Press of Kentucky.

Helms, Dietrich and Thomas Phleps, eds. (2008). *No Time for Losers: Charts, Listen und andere Kanonisierungen in der populären Musik.* Bielefeld: Transcript-Verlag.

Hickethier, Knut (1991). *Die Fernsehserie und das Serielle des Fernsehens.* Lüneburg: Lüneburg Universitätsverlag.

———(2003). "Serie." *Handbuch Populäre Kultur.* Ed. Hans-Otto Hügel. Stuttgart: Metzler. 397–403.

Higgins, Scott (2016). *Matinee Melodrama: Playing with Formula in the Sound Serial.* New Brunswick: Rutgers University Press.

Hills, Matt (2002). *Fan Cultures.* London: Routledge.

Hißnauer, Christian, Stefan Scherer, and Claudia Stockinger, eds. (2014). *Zwischen Serie und Werk: Fernseh- und Gesellschaftsgeschichte im "Tatort."* Bielefeld: Transcript-Verlag.

Horkheimer, Max and Theodor W. Adorno (1947). *Dialektik der Aufklärung.* In Theodor W. Adorno. *Gesammelte Schriften.* Vol. 3. Ed. Rolf Tiedemann. Frankfurt: Suhrkamp, 1981.

Innis, Harold (1950). *Empire and Communications.* Oxford: Clarendon.

Jahn-Sudmann, Andreas and Frank Kelleter (2012). "Die Dynamik serieller Überbietung: Amerikanische Fernsehserien und das Konzept des Quality-TV." *Populäre Serialität: Narration—Evolution—Distinktion. Zum seriellen Erzählen seit dem 19. Jahrhundert.* Ed. Frank Kelleter. Bielefeld: Transcript-Verlag. 205–25.

Jahn-Sudmann, Andreas and Alexander Starre (2013). "Die Experimente des 'Quality TV': Innovation und Metamedialität in neueren amerikanischen Serien." *Transnationale Serienkultur: Theorie, Ästhetik, Narration und Rezeption neuer Fernsehserien.* Ed. Susanne Eichner, Lothar Mikos, and Rainer Winter. Wiesbaden: VS. 103-19.

Jenkins, Henry (1992). *Textual Poachers: Television Fans and Participatory Culture.* New York: Routledge.

Johnson, Steven (2005). *Everything Bad Is Good for You: How Popular Culture Is Actually Making Us Smarter.* London: Penguin.

Kammerer, Paul (1919). *Das Gesetz der Serie: Eine Lehre von den Wiederholungen im Lebens- und Weltgeschehen.* Stuttgart: Deutsche Verlags-Anstalt.

Kelleter, Frank (2010). "Populärkultur und Kanonisierung: Wie(so) erinnern wir uns an Tony Soprano?" *Wertung und Kanon.* Ed. Matthias Freise and Claudia Stockinger. Heidelberg: Winter. 55-76.

——— (2012a). "Populäre Serialität: Eine Einführung." *Populäre Serialität: Narration—Evolution—Distinktion. Zum seriellen Erzählen seit dem 19. Jahrhundert.* Ed. Frank Kelleter. Bielefeld: Transcript-Verlag. 11-46.

——— (2012b). "Toto, I Think We're in Kansas Again (and Again and Again): Remakes and Popular Seriality." *Film Remakes, Adaptations, and Fan Productions: Remake/Remodel.* Ed. Kathleen Loock and Constantine Verevis. Basingstoke: Palgrave Macmillan. 19-44.

——— (2014a). *Serial Agencies: "The Wire" and Its Readers.* Washington: Zero Books.

——— (2014b). "Trust and Sprawl: Seriality, Radio, and the First Fireside Chat." *Media Economies: Perspectives on American Cultural Practices.* Ed. Marcel Hartwig, Evelyne Keitel, and Gunter Süß. Trier: wvt. 47-66.

——— (2015). "'Whatever Happened, Happened': Serial Character Constellation as Problem and Solution in *Lost*." *Amerikanische Fernsehserien der Gegenwart.* Ed. Heike Paul and Christoph Ernst. Bielefeld: Transcript-Verlag. 57-87.

——— (2017). "From Recursive Progression to Systemic Self-Observation: Elements of a Theory of Seriality." *The Velvet Light Trap* 79 (forthcoming).

Kelleter, Frank and Daniel Stein (2012). "Autorisierungspraktiken seriellen Erzählens: Zur Gattungsentwicklung von Superheldencomics." *Populäre Serialität: Narration—Evolution—Distinktion. Zum seriellen Erzählen seit dem 19. Jahrhundert.* Ed. Frank Kelleter. Bielefeld: Transcript-Verlag. 259-90.

Kermode, Frank (1967). *The Sense of an Ending: Studies in the Theory of Fiction.* London: Oxford University Press.

Klein, Amanda Ann and R. Barton Palmer, eds. (2016). *Cycles, Sequels, Spin-Offs, Remakes, and Reboots: Multiplicities in Film and Television.* Austin: University of Texas Press.

Land, Nick (2011). *Fanged Noumena: Collected Writings 1987-2007.* Falmouth: Urbanomic.

Latour, Bruno (2005). *Reassembling the Social: An Introduction to Actor-Network-Theory.* Oxford: Oxford University Press.

——— (2013). *An Inquiry into Modes of Existence: An Anthropology of the Moderns.* Cambridge, MA: Harvard University Press.

Luhmann, Niklas (1999). *Die Gesellschaft der Gesellschaft.* Frankfurt: Suhrkamp.

Mayer, Ruth (2014). *Serial Fu Manchu: The Chinese Supervillain and the Spread of Yellow Peril Ideology.* Philadelphia: Temple University Press.

——— (2015). "Die Geburt der Nation als Migrationspraxis: Benedict Andersons *Imagined Communities*." *Schlüsselwerke der Migrationsforschung: Pionierstudien und Referenztheorien.* Ed. Julia Reuter and Paul Mecheril. Berlin: Springer VS, 2015. 263-74.

Maase, Kaspar, ed. (2008). *Die Schönheiten des Populären: Ästhetische Erfahrung der Gegenwart.* Frankfurt: Campus.

Mittell, Jason (2015). *Complex TV: The Poetics of Contemporary Television Storytelling*. New York: New York University Press.

Naremore, James and Patrick Brantlinger (1991). "Introduction: Six Artistic Cultures." *Modernity and Mass Culture*. Ed. James Naremore and Patrick Brantlinger. Bloomington: Indiana University Press.

Nelson, Robin (1997). *TV Drama in Transition: Forms, Values and Cultural Change*. Basingstoke: Macmillan.

Newcomb, Horace M. (1985). *"Magnum*: The Champagne of TV?" *Channels of Communication* (May/June): 23–26.

———(2004). "Narrative and Genre." *The SAGE Handbook of Media Studies*. Ed. John D. H. Downing et al. Thousand Oaks: Sage. 413–28.

Newman, Michael Z. (2006). "From Beats to Arcs: Toward a Poetics of Television Narrative." *The Velvet Light Trap* 58: 16–28.

Norman, Donald A. (1988). *The Psychology of Everyday Things*. New York: Basic Books.

O'Sullivan, Sean (2010). "Broken on Purpose: Poetry, Serial Television, and the Season." *Storyworlds: A Journal of Narrative Studies* 2.1: 59–77.

Ryan, Marie-Laure (2014). "Story/Worlds/Media: Tuning the Instruments of a Media-Conscious Narratology." *Storyworlds across Media: Toward a Media-Conscious Narratology*. Ed. Marie-Laure Ryan and Jan-Noël Thon. Lincoln: University of Nebraska Press. 25–49.

Sartre, Jean-Paul (1960). *Critique de la raison dialectique I: Théorie des ensembles pratiques*. Paris: Gallimard.

Sconce, Jeffrey (2004). "What If? Charting Television's New Textual Boundaries." *Television after TV: Essays on a Medium in Transition*. Ed. Lynn Spigel and Jan Olsson. Durham: Duke University Press. 93–112.

Stein, Daniel (2009a). "Was ist ein Comic Autor? Autorinszenierung in autobiografischen Comics und Selbstporträts." *Comics: Zur Geschichte und Theorie eines populärkulturellen Mediums*. Ed. Daniel Stein, Stephan Ditschke, and Katerina Kroucheva. Bielefeld: Transcript-Verlag. 201–37.

———(2009b). "The *Left Behind* Series, Jerry B. Jenkins and Tim LaHaye." *The Encyclopedia of American Popular Fiction*. Ed. Geoff Hamilton and Brian Jones. New York: Facts on File.

———(2012). "Spoofin' Spidey—Rebooting the Bat: Immersive Story Worlds and the Narrative Complexities of Video Spoofs in the Era of the Superhero Blockbuster." *Film Remakes, Adaptations and Fan Productions: Remake/Remodel*. Ed. Kathleen Loock and Constantine Verevis. Basingstoke: Palgrave Macmillan. 231–47.

———(2013a). "Of Transcreations and Transpacific Adaptations: Investigating Manga Versions of Spider-Man." *Transnational Perspectives on Graphic Narratives: Comics at the Crossroads*. Ed. Shane Denson, Christina Meyer, and Daniel Stein. London: Bloomsbury. 145–61.

———(2013b). "Superhero Comics and the Authorizing Functions of the Comic Book Paratext." *From Graphic Strips to Graphic Novels: Contributions to the Theory and History of Graphic Narrative*. Ed. Daniel Stein and Jan-Noël Thon. Berlin: de Gruyter. 155–89.

Uricchio, William (2014). "Things to Come in the American Studies-Media Studies Relationship." *American Studies Today: New Research Agendas*. Ed. Winfried Fluck et al. Heidelberg: Winter. 363–82.

Vogl, Joseph (2010). *Das Gespenst des Kapitals*. Zürich: diaphanes.

Warhol, Robyn (2003). *Having a Good Cry: Effeminate Feelings and Pop-Culture Forms*. Columbus: The Ohio State University Press.

Weber, Tanja and Christian Junklewitz (2008). "Das Gesetz der Serie: Ansätze zur Definition und Analyse." *MEDIENwissenschaft* 25.1: 13–31.

Williams, Linda (2014). *On "The Wire."* Durham: Duke University Press.

Williams, Raymond (1974). *Television: Technology and Cultural Form*. London: Fontana.

PART I

Literature and Comics

CHAPTER 2

Antebellum Popular Serialities and the Transatlantic Birth of "American" Comics

JARED GARDNER

I

It is a truism that the United States is a nation born of print. Less recognized is the specific *nature* of the print with which the nation first imagined itself. Overwhelmingly, the documents that forged the nation were *serial*. American popular seriality is conventionally associated with the importation (often piratical) of serial periodical fiction from abroad (most famously that of Charles Dickens). However, as I discuss at length in *The Rise and Fall of Early American Magazine Culture* (2012), when the first installments of *The Pickwick Papers* first arrived it was received by a public already deeply acculturated to seriality—through the work of the influential serial essayists who dominated the early American magazine culture and, more famously today, through the debates surrounding the Constitutional Convention, the vast majority of which were published serially. In both of these cases from the early national period we see seriality emerging in new print media forms—magazine, newspaper—translated from European templates to a postcolonial people seeking to imagine a coherent national conversation across an impossibly complex geographic and political map. Benedict Anderson suggests that the modern nation-state came of age with the rise of the novel and its privileging of "meanwhile time"—or Benjamin's "homogenous, empty time" (Anderson 1991: 24). But it was *serial* time—fragmented, recursive, and dialogic—that came first. From the *American Magazine* in 1741 through the Federalist Papers of 1787, it was in *serial* print that the nation came first to imagine and define itself (Kelleter 2002).

The increasing marginalization of serial forms in the early decades of the nineteenth century was paralleled by the surprising rise of the novel, the form that would emerge at the center of the American literary marketplace and, later, the profession of American literary history. A generation earlier, the novel had been reviled by the ministerial class and other cultural gatekeepers as a morally corrupting entertainment, but the editors and serial essayists of early magazine culture saw the novel as a poor literary form for the new nation for other reasons. Borrowing from the spiritual godfather of all early American magazines, Addison and Steele's *Spectator*, Ben Franklin's nephew Benjamin Mecom proclaimed in his 1758 *New England Magazine* that "a great Book is a great Evil" with the potential to place tyrannical demands on the time and imagination of the reader. In its place, Mecom celebrated instead serial publication as the "noble Art" best "calculated to diffuse Good Sense through the Bulk of a People" (1758: 14). For half a century, all American magazines would make similar claims on behalf of their form, celebrating the gaps and disjunctions opened up by seriality for providing spaces in which readers could write back—literally or imaginatively—thus participating in a virtual coffeehouse the editors saw as the ideal model for the new nation.

It is therefore not surprising that ultimately the serial forms of the revolutionary and early national periods would be displaced in the counter-revolutionary nineteenth-century, the cacophonous serial coffeehouse giving way to the synchronized "meanwhile time" of the novel. While the scholars of the 1980s sought to redeem the literature of the early republic from the antiquarian backwaters in which it had wallowed for generations by identifying it as revolutionary and subversive, I argue that the rise of the novel represented not a revolutionary but a counter-revolutionary moment in American literary history (Gardner 2012). The early novels we have meaningfully linked to the revolutionary impulse are largely limited to a select body of narratives written over the course of a decade beginning in 1789, when magazine culture and the serial periodical essay were at their height—"novels" that in fact share more in common with the serial periodical than with the novel as we would define it after 1810. The challenges scholars have faced in the search for the "missing links" between early American novels like Hannah Webster Foster's *The Coquette* (1797) and the emergence of the novel at the center of American literary culture two decades later only underscores this fact. The novels of James Fenimore Cooper are simply not the same species as the "novels" of Foster, and attempts to yoke them into a continuous genealogy ultimately obscures the serial genealogies in whose current Foster's books (*The Coquette* and *The Boarding School*) do in fact swim.

II

Of course, the long history of popular seriality is one in which its impulses will often decline only to reemerge later, in new media and new forms. Thus it is not surprising that serial culture would reemerge in the United States and in Europe during a revolutionary period, first in the 1830s with the rise of *serialmania* following the international success of Dickens's early serial novels and then reaching a kind of fever pitch in the early 1840s, which arguably marks the full emergence of what we now call *popular seriality*, epitomized internationally by the urban mysteries genre initiated by Eugène Sue's *Mysteries of Paris* (*Les mystères de Paris*), serialized from 1842 to 1843.[1]

Inspired by Sue's novel and by his own early experience working in the new medium of the penny press, the American writer George Lippard began serializing *The Quaker City; or, The Monks of Monk Hall: A Romance of Philadelphia Life, Mystery, and Crime* in 1844, a work that would go on to become the biggest bestseller in America before Harriet Beecher Stowe's *Uncle Tom's Cabin* and E. D. E. N. Southworth's *Hidden Hand* (both themselves serialized). Among the many corrupt denizens of the modern city Lippard seeks to expose in *Monk Hall*—including priests, politicians, and businessmen—perhaps his most personal target are the editors of both the penny press and the contemporary literary magazine. Against those periodical forms, Lippard seeks to imagine with *Monk Hall* a new serial form that would do away with the tyranny of editors and publishers "and allow him to write directly to the people" without "these mere Agents between the author and the Reader" (*Quaker City*, January 20, 1849; quoted in Streeby 1997: 187). His desire for alternative modes of serial publication led him first to self-publish *Monks of Monk Hall* in ten installments, and then to found a story paper, *Quaker City*, which sought to bring about revolutionary change through "popular literature."[2]

That in the 1840s Lippard saw in the new periodical format of the story paper a potential for a radically new relationship between reader and publisher might at first seem surprising. After all, the story paper pioneered by *Brother Jonathan* and *New World* was not a form associated with political writing or

---

1. Compare chapter 3 in this volume. I borrow the phrase "serial-mania" from *The Spectator* of 1833, the earliest use I have found of the term describing the rising appetite for popular serial fiction ("Mrs. Bray's Historical Novels" 888).

2. For an influential account of Lippard's "subversive" agenda, see Reynolds 1988.

radical ideology. But it was not the content of the story paper to which Lippard was attracted but its form, rightly identifying it as having the potential to open up spaces for serial conversation, spaces increasingly controlled by the effective monopolies of the antebellum trade publishers. And that Lippard would make this connection had everything to do with the fact that Sue's *Mysteries of Paris* was first serialized by *New World* in 1843, beating none other than the increasingly powerful New York firm of Harper & Bros. to the punch.

Not content with getting there first, the *New World* editors would use the occasion to ridicule the respected publishing house—declaring that until their own serialization of the novel began, the Harpers had been "ignorant of its existence," lambasting the quality of the press's translation, and attempting at great length to disprove Harper's claims to having an unabridged edition of the novel ("Harpers' Translation" 538). Taking on the publishing establishment alone would have been enough to capture Lippard's attention, but that the story paper did so through the piratical (and swashbuckling) publication of *Mysteries of Paris* only strengthened the connection between the radical impulses underlying the earliest urban mysteries and the new serial print form that sought to take on the publishing establishment in the United States.

The same year Sue began serializing *Mysteries of Paris,* launching the urban mystery genre, *Brother Jonathan* published an equally remarkable import from Europe, one that would go on to exert influence on the development of popular seriality in the twentieth century even beyond those of Sue's novel. While we conventionally speak of the emergence of the comics form with the development of the modern sequential comic strip in the late nineteenth century, first in illustrated magazines and then in the new color newspaper supplements at the end of the century, we should more properly trace the origins of the intersections of graphic storytelling and popular serialities back a half century earlier to the early 1840s, to *Brother Jonathan* and *The Adventures of Obadiah Oldbuck*.

The creator of this first "American" comic was the Swiss artist Rodolphe Töpffer. Experimenting with a new form of lithography called *polyautography,* Töpffer had been producing extended visual narratives since the late 1820s. Goethe himself publically acknowledged the importance of this new approach to storytelling and encouraged Töpffer to find a publisher for his books. Beginning in 1832, these works began to be published and pirated. Despite this success, or so the story goes, it would be almost a half-century before serious experiments with sequential graphic narrative would return, and still longer before book-length experiments with the form would be published, a fact that has long mystified comics historians—especially given the popularity of the original pirated editions in the United States.

As we will see, however, between the arrival of Töpffer's work in the United States in the 1840s and the rise of the comic strip more than half a century later, there is much less a gap than our histories suggest. Making the case, however, requires attention to the broader media ecology of the early 1840s in which the first "American" comic was born.

III

As Isabel Lehuu (2003) points out, *Brother Jonathan* played an important role in the emergence of a new visual "spectacle of print" in the 1840s. Along with its rival *The New World*, *Brother Jonathan* was famous for its mammoth editions, for its promotion of serial fiction, and for being the first lavishly illustrated weekly, advertising as many as one hundred engravings in a single issue. This was especially true in its newspaper folio edition—four feet long and eleven columns wide. The quarto edition, begun in 1842 in response to demands by readers for a version of the periodical published "in a shape convenient for preservation" ("Library Edition" xxxiv), was relatively sparing in its use of images in order to make room for as much serial fiction as possible.

Initially launched in 1839 by Park Benjamin and Rufus Griswold with the printer James G. Wilson, the publication was forced to regroup after Benjamin and Griswold quickly jumped to found a rival publication, *The New World*. Both weeklies also published "extras" with their subscriptions, competing with each other at the docks for the hottest editions fresh from Britain. In truth, however, both *The New World* and *Brother Jonathan* had a more formidable, common enemy: the publishing establishment epitomized by Carey & Lea in Philadelphia and, more recently and closer to home, the rising Harper Brothers in New York.

At the time the new medium of the story papers came on the scene, trade-book publishers had been enjoying a period of profit and relative security in a traditionally volatile industry.[3] Throughout the 1820s and 1830s, a variety of forces had converged to drive down the costs and risks of printing. The introduction of stereotype printing in the 1820s freed printers from the need to tie up expensive type in plates for subsequent editions (or, alternatively, from having to reset an entire volume when demand was incorrectly predicted); now plates could be stored and reused for subsequent editions with no additional outlay beyond ink and paper. Paper costs too fell precipitously

---

3. For my history of the book trade during this period, I am indebted to Gross/Kelley 2010 and Greene 2010.

at this time, thanks to the widespread adoption of the new cylinder papermaking machines in the 1830s. These and related technological advances greatly reduced the financial risks that American publishers had long faced, and profits increased accordingly while retail prices of books remained relatively unchanged, thanks in large measure to a series of agreements between publishers dating back to the early years of the nineteenth century which had been developed to regulate pricing and avoid direct competition for specific titles and authors.

Indeed, this system might well have remained intact if not for the rise—beginning in the 1830s—of "serial-mania." Dazzled by the phenomenal success in London of Dickens's *Pickwick Papers,* Carey & Lea in Philadelphia began publishing the series in 1837 in installments, eventually (and retroactively) making arrangements with Dickens to secure American rights to his future works, starting with *Oliver Twist* (McParland 2011: 49). The temptations of this literary gold rush, however, meant that the Harpers had little incentive to respect the traditional publishing agreements; taking advantage of a one-day shorter passage to London, the New York press began to compete directly for the growing demand for serial fiction. Even as this new competition began to erode the comfortable profit margins the publishers had experienced in recent years, things took a considerable turn for the worse with the economic crash of 1837, which put new downward pressure on the relatively high retail book prices publishers had long maintained.

It was into this newly fluid print economy that the new serial form of the story paper inserted itself, deploying skills honed over the previous decade in a print culture seemingly removed from the staid economies of book publishing. The first story papers were cousins of the penny papers, which had first emerged in New York in 1833 with Benjamin Day's *Sun* and, two years later, James Gordon Bennett's *Herald*. Setting themselves up against the established six-penny papers by eschewing subscriptions in favor of street sales by an army of newsboys and highlighting sensational stories—murder, corruption, scandal—that the establishment press had politely ignored, by the end of the decade the *Sun* and the *Herald* alone had more readers than the city's nine surviving six-penny papers combined (Stevens 1991: 27).

The stories the penny press told and the space they opened up for readers to imagine themselves as inhabiting changed not only journalism but also American popular culture. Indeed, in the United States, it is following the rise of the penny press, and often in conjunction with considerations of its influence, that the term *popular culture* first came into use. Twenty years after Tocqueville's visit to the United States, the Swedish educator Per Adam Siljeström argued for "newspaper literature of the United States as contributing in a great measure to promote and extend popular culture in the country" (Siljeström/ Rowan 1853: 257). And one Judge Thomas declared in an 1854 lecture at the Young Men's Association in Albany: "The Newspaper Press is destined to be the chief instrument of popular culture" ("I Can't Afford It" 28).

Following the departure of Benjamin and Griswold for *The New World*, none other than Benjamin Day came onboard *Brother Jonathan*. Even without the presence of this founding figure, however, the influence of the penny press was everywhere in these new "mammoth weeklies." Swarming arriving ships before they had even docked, the agents of the story papers would secure the latest fictions from abroad and race them back to the offices where they would be broken up and distributed to an army of compositors (typesetters) who would set the type through the night. By morning, the street urchins who constituted the penny press's network of newsboys would fan out across the city, a complete novel from abroad in hand often less than twenty-four hours after it first touched American shores. Further, they were able to distribute their extras across the country as periodical "supplements," thereby taking advantage of a loophole in the postal codes and further undercutting the book publishers. Through these means, the New York story papers circulated inexpensive popular literature nationally, using the tricks of the trade learned from a decade in the penny press business.

In going after establishment publishers, the new weeklies had taken on a powerful enemy. By spring of 1843, the publishers had closed the loophole in the postal code that allowed the extras to travel the mails at a dramatically reduced rate. The extras quickly came to an end, but their impact is still being felt today. In the wake of this "first paperback revolution" would follow the dime novel (beginning with *Beadle's* series in the 1860s), the pulps (beginning with *Argossy* in the 1890s), and of course the paperback revolution of the 1930s and 1940s (beginning in the United States with Pocket Books).[4] The New York publishing establishment might have won the battle in 1843, but the war against the spread of popular, cheap, and serial fiction was already lost.

While the influence of *Brother Jonathan* and the story paper in shaping the popular print culture of the next century has been most often told through the genealogy of popular and serial fictions and the new literary markets and genres that emerged along the way, equally important (and ultimately inseparable from that history) is the role the story papers played in the emergence of a mass-mediated *graphic* culture, one bound to the serial forms in which it was born. In the story of *Obadiah Oldbuck* and its reception we see that fifty

---

4. To my knowledge, John Tebbel is the first print historian to label the period of the 1830s and 1840s "the first paperback revolution" (1972: 240–51).

years before it was "born," comics had already put down roots on American shores.

IV

Even as mass-mediated print was dramatically accelerating in the United States, a new practice among readers began to emerge that seems at first to be in every way opposed to the rise of an industrial print culture. Evolving out of the commonplace books of earlier generations, the communal authorship of friendship albums, and shortly thereafter the more private practice of scrapbooking, there appeared an increasingly widespread practice.[5] Before the rise of the industrial book in the 1840s, friendship albums were usually homemade or purchased at local stationers. The contents that the owners added to these books were often a collage of transcribed poetry, personal handwritten messages, and mass-produced paper ephemera: ticket stubs, newspaper clippings, and, increasingly after 1840, illustrations from story papers. The rise of scrapbooking and mass-mediated popular culture might seem to have little to do with one another, but as Cynthia Patterson (2010: 165–66) noted in her study of visual culture in the story papers of the 1840s, it was in the friendship albums and scrapbooks of the period that we see how these images were valued, curated, and recirculated.

While the quarto editions of *Brother Jonathan* and *New World* explicitly set themselves up for binding (using higher paper quality and charging a higher subscription price), the folio editions especially encouraged—even demanded—scrapbooking to preserve images to which the reader might wish to return. As a mammoth newspaper, this was ephemeral print. But whereas up to this point newspapers had few if any illustrations, the story papers were rich with images—including images that begged to be cut from their original surrounding text. One such example is found in a story printed in both the folio and quarto editions of *Brother Jonathan* in 1842, "East India Sporting: Marvellous Adventure with a Tiger," a windy and digressive account of an escape from a tiger attack through the use of a barrel. Indeed so willfully tedious is the prose account that it might seem, at least in the context of its American reprint, intended as a satire on the kind of epistolary accounts with which so many British magazines filled their pages, similar to Poe's "How to Write a Blackwood Article" from 1838.

---

5. For the practice of scrapbooking in America, especially after 1850, see Tucker/Ott/Buckler 2006 and Gruber 2013.

In contrast to the prose—overlabored with parentheticals and literary quotations—are the six accompanying illustrations, in the quarto edition each a full two-columns wide, which together sequentially tell the story infinitely more efficiently and effectively than does the copious prose. Like the vast majority of the contents of the first story papers, the piece was borrowed from an overseas source—in this case, the *Bengal Sporting Magazine,* an English-language magazine published in Calcutta and circulating back to Britain, where stories of big-game hunting in the Indian subcontinent were very much in fashion.[6] The text was reset according to the common practice, but the woodcuts had to be redrawn. To do so, *Brother Jonathan* likely deployed a printing practice similar to Töpffer's polyautography: a form of lithography allowing the artist to work directly with a pen on a specially prepared paper, in this case allowing the artist at *Brother Jonathan* to trace the printed woodcuts and quickly reproduce the image (figure 2.1). Of course, this was not an exact reproduction. In the translating of images from woodcut to paper lithography, the lines are simplified, shading is reduced, and the image is distilled toward what we might recognize as an early example of the clear line style often associated with the development of the comic strip in the pages of the illustrated magazines of the late nineteenth century.[7]

Laid out horizontally across two columns, the panels serve as an invitation to skip the tedious prose and let the images tell the story. As friendship albums and early scrapbooks were often bound at this time in oblong octavo, the layout of the individual images also serves as an invitation to recirculate the images in private albums, as *Brother Jonathan* was well aware was common practice. Indeed, in Europe, as we will see, the earliest comic albums of Töpffer were already using precisely such a format. Distilled down to their essence, the American story paper's images—which unironically foregrounded the prose and diminished the space afforded to the images—demonstrated even more efficiently than the British originals the possibilities of graphic storytelling.

It is in this context that we need to understand the seemingly surprising decision on the part of the editors to feature in their series of extras a very different kind of publication than they had up to that point. The early extras were all sensational fictions like *Gaspar; the Pirate of the Indian Seas* (Extra No. 2) or *The Tempter and the Tempted* (No. 8), novels fresh off the boats from London. With the ninth extra, however, the publishers attempted something

---

6. Without access to the original, I am relying in what follows on comparison to a London reprint in *The Sporting Review* 7 (1842), which includes the six woodcuts I discuss below.

7. Although exceeding the focus of this essay, it is worth noting that a great many of the earliest sequential comics in illustrated magazines like *Puck* and *Life* featured similar "animal adventures."

FIGURE 2.1. *Brother Jonathan* cartoon (1842).

entirely new: *The Adventures of Obadiah Oldbuck,* a story told through a series of almost 200 pictures. This book, too, was imported via England, from a British plagiary of 1841 which gave to Töpffer's *Vieux Bois* (1837) its English title and its cover by Robert Cruikshank. Robert and his more famous brother, George, had been working at this time to develop an English audience for picture stories, and the tremendous success in France of editions of works by Töpffer and his imitators (such as Cham, whose first book was published in Paris in 1839 to great success) inspired hope that this might be the key to unlocking a similar demand in Britain.

Already a celebrated caricaturist when serial-mania broke out, George Cruikshank experienced a new celebrity following his collaborations with Dickens, and most especially after his illustrations for *Oliver Twist* (1838). Cruikshank had already taken steps to open up popular print markets for comics, including, beginning in 1835, cofounding the *Comic Almanack,* an annual satire of the popular almanacs of the day. But the dream of creating a comics culture in London equivalent to what could then be found in Paris continued to elude Cruikshank when, in 1841, his partner on the *Comic Almanack,* Henry Mayhew, left to help launch *Punch,* England's first successful illustrated magazine. Subtitled "The London *Charivari,*" *Punch* was an explicit attempt to import to England the new graphic energy being unleashed in Paris following the wave of Töpffer-mania in that city. *Le Charivari* was an illustrated satirical newspaper published by Charles Philipon and Gabriel Aubert, and by the late 1830s it was increasingly featuring caricature and cartoons, including works by Töpffer and his Parisian disciples. Inspired by the success of these features, in 1839 Aubert published unauthorized editions of the three Töpffer albums currently available, including *Vieux Bois,* which soon made its way to England where it was once again plagiarized, this time by Cruikshank's publisher Tilt & Bogue. Under its new title, *The Adventures of Obadiah Oldbuck,* the book soon made its transatlantic voyage to New York, where *Brother Jonathan*'s printer, Wilson & Co., was waiting for it.

A few facts emerge from this highly compressed account of the transatlantic piracy that brought a picture book by a Geneva schoolteacher into the heart of the storm that was popular print culture in 1842 New York.[8] On Goethe's encouragement, Töpffer had in 1833 begun publishing his albums in very small print runs, largely circulated through private networks in Geneva. It was not until Töpffer's work made its way to Paris at the end of the decade that it truly took off, although most readers were encountering the work in pirated volumes. In Paris, London, and New York, in the context of the serial-mania of the late 1830s, Töpffer's approach to graphic storytelling suddenly found an appreciative audience. The three pirates who brought *Oldbuck* to America—Aubert in Paris, Tilt & Bogue in London, and Wilson & Co. in New York—were all associated with the rise of graphic seriality. While today we associate the serial literature of the 1830s and 1840s with its fiction writers, the success of serial fiction beginning in 1836 has everything to do with images as well. These images served multiple functions for readers of the day. They were tools for navigating complex plots, refreshing memory across numerous installments and interruptions; sites for individual and collaborative speculation between installments as to further adventures yet unscripted; and tokens of remembrance once the serials were complete, often relocated to an album or a scrapbook.

Indeed, it is not surprising that these publishers wondered whether graphic literature—itself a *series* of images—could not be as popular as serial

---

8. The definitive account of Töpffer's life and work is Kunzle 2007.

fiction. And in an increasingly international and multilingual marketplace, graphic literature presented several potential advantages. As highlighted by the frustrations the *New World* experienced in getting out their own translation of *Mysteries of Paris* ahead of the Harpers, typesetting and translation presented daunting challenges, especially as the competition continued to heat up. Graphic literature, like silent film a half century later, offered the possibilities for crossing international borders more fluidly, with only captions to be translated. Using a previous publisher's plates if available (as it appears they were in the case of the American edition of *Oldbuck*) or quickly producing redrawn versions of the original (as was the case in "Adventure with a Tiger"), graphic narratives presented to publishers like Wilson & Co. the dream of a global network of serial fictions ignoring the borders of language and nation as freely as it did copyright.

In London, *Obadiah Oldbuck* seems to have been largely greeted with indifference, as being too "continental," despite Cruikshank's ongoing efforts to create a comics culture in England (Kunzle 2007: 163). In America, however, he was from the start embraced as a native citizen; the reviews were surprising mostly for not being at all surprised by what they were reviewing. Comics history has granted the book a status equivalent with the appearance of the Yellow Kid in the Sunday newspaper in 1895 or Superman in comic books in 1938—something radically new that changed the form forever.[9] And yet, in notices of *Oldbuck* from 1842, we see something closer to *familiarity*. In promoting the book, *Brother Jonathan* insisted, the reader had "undoubtedly heard" of "graphic narrations," and they sold *Oldbuck* not as the *first* example but as the most "exclusively as well as eloquently graphic production it was ever any body's lot to see" ("Here Is" 90). Indeed, for readers of popular periodicals like *Brother Jonathan,* there was already a history of "graphic narrations" at whose apex *Oldbuck* positioned itself, although most American readers would have previously encountered this tradition largely through almanacs, children's books, or, more rarely given the costs, imported periodicals. But *this,* the editors insisted (shamelessly, it must be added), was the original, the thing itself.

Brother Jonathan's publishing company advertised the book as "a humorous Story, told in [a series of] 200 Engravings." To modern ears, such a description of a text we are accustomed to describe as a unified whole sounds wrong, but it was in precisely these terms that the earliest comics *and* films, two new narrative media that emerged in the late nineteenth century, were understood. In 1904, for example, Edwin S. Porter's *The Great Train Robbery*

---

9. On the Yellow Kid, see chapter 4 in the present volume.

was described as a "series of moving pictures" ("Thrilling Train Robberies" 4). It is language that would have made sense to an early filmgoing audience much more aware than present viewers of the fundamental grammar shared by both film and comics: a series of pictures. This understanding of movies as a "series" of pictures was institutionalized by copyright law, which did not acknowledge film texts as a unified whole until 1912. Instead, producers were required to file paper copies of *each* individual frame.

However, if *Obadiah Oldbuck* elicited little surprise, opportunities for *Brother Jonathan* to further experiment with this format for their extras were short-circuited soon after its publication, when the weeklies were stripped of their beneficial postal rate. Wilson & Co. did, however, republish *Oldbuck* in 1844, translating the book back to the album (oblong octavo) format used by the English plagiary and increasingly favored by the small but growing body of transatlantic comics volumes. In 1846, Wilson published a second Töpffer plagiary, titled *The Strange Adventures of Bachelor Butterfly*, but soon they had abandoned the market to Dick & Fitzgerald, which quickly made of comics literature something of a specialty. Dick & Fitzgerald republished *Oldbuck* and *Bachelor Butterfly* as well as other graphic narratives imported from England, such as *The Laughable Adventures of Messrs. Brown, Jones, and Robinson* (by Richard Doyle). By the 1850s, Dick & Fitzgerald were regularly advertising a wide range of graphic narratives, and they continued to do so up until the final decades of the century.

V

While we have remembered the appearance of the first comic in America as a moment of missed opportunities and neglect, the evidence suggests that *Oldbuck* found a welcoming audience and began to exert influence almost immediately. Here I am thinking less of the American imitators of Töpffer's books, of which there were a few.[10] Instead, the influence of Oldbuck is felt in its longevity and the fondness with which generations of readers remembered him. As early as December 1842, newspapers had already assumed so universal a familiarity with *Oldbuck* that images from the book became a reference point for description, as when the *Boston Post* described the engraving "The Fatal Mistake" in *Graham's* as "remind[ing] one of Obadiah Oldbuck on

---

10. For example, *The College Experiences of Ichabod Academicus*, almost certainly written by Yale undergraduates Hugh Florien Peters and Garrick Mallery and illustrated by William T. Peters, Hugh's father, published roughly around 1850, or *Journey to the Gold Diggins* by "Jeremiah Saddlebags," from 1849.

the sea shore" (Carlo 1842: 1). In his Civil War journals, Thomas Wentworth Higginson would compare himself to Oldbuck, and an 1877 profile of Harriet Martineau in the *Independent* analogized her dogged pursuit of her dreams to those of Oldbuck.[11]

As late as 1895, a reporter for the Kansas City *Chief* would reminisce: "Who that were boys during the early forties, will not remember a comic paper, that was quite generally circulated in Ohio, detailing the history of Obadiah Oldbuck, one of the first illustrated comic journals we ever saw" ("A Reminiscent Article" 1). A year later, the humorist Bill Arp described himself the day after a disappointing election as doing "like Obadiah Oldbuck always did when bad luck overtook him. I put on a clean shirt and went down town to rejoice with those who were rejoicing and to weep with those who wept" (Arp 1896: 1). And toward the very end of his long career, the distinguished journalist Noah Brooks would fondly recall "my boyhood's friend, Mr. Oldbuck" (1898: 221). These and numerous other examples describe a comic character whose afterlife in the American popular consciousness far exceeded those of the vast majority of the serial fictions that *Brother Jonathan* and the story papers that followed in its model were to publish.

It is worth considering *how* Oldbuck came to be remembered. Like the original from which it is pirated, *Oldbuck* tells the story of a man perpetually disappointed in love, stymied by ill fortune, and determined to end it all. But repeatedly his attempts at suicide are thwarted by his own incompetence, leaving him the next day determined to "turn[] over a new leaf" (Podgers 1862: 2). Even once he has secured the approbation of his beloved, a series of new and seemingly endless obstacles stand in his way, including tyrannous monks, highwaymen, and officers of the law. And yet, after each disappointment, each dark night of the soul or aborted suicide attempt, Oldbuck awakens prepared once again to turn over that new leaf. It is in these terms that Oldbuck is most familiarly celebrated over the course of the half century following his first arrival in America: for his ability to "turn over a new leaf" each and every day with full optimism that things would indeed turn out differently this time around. As *The Rural Repository* counseled in 1843, "If the United States Bank has played you false—if speculations have proved unprofitable—if friends have deceived you," just "take the benefit of your experience, and, like Obadiah Oldbuck, turn over a new leaf"—begin anew against all evidence that anything will change ("Ups and Downs" 110).

In the pages of the story papers and illustrated magazines that sprung up in the second half of the nineteenth century on the model of *Brother Jonathan*,

---

11. Higginson 1999: 108; and "A Literary Worker," *Independent* (March 1877), 9.

the American comic strip would take its modern shape, initially in the pages of *Puck* and *Life* in the final decades of the century. The model provided by Töpffer had maintained its currency throughout the intervening decades in reprints, it is true, but in many ways the more lasting genealogy is found in the *type* of Oldbuck himself: the gangly, hapless "hero" who faces an endless series of misfortunes only to begin again, every day. This would after all be the defining feature of the first modern comic strip generally recognized as finally bringing together all the features we associate with the form: sequential panels, dialog balloons, consistent characters, and serial storytelling.

Created in 1900 for the new newspaper Sunday supplements by Frederick Burr Opper, himself a veteran of the illustrated magazines of the previous generation, *Happy Hooligan* is in many ways an updating of *Obadiah Oldbuck*, which was "generally circulated in Ohio" ("A Reminiscent Article" 1), where Opper grew up in the 1850s and 1860s. Each week for more than three decades, Happy would encounter a series of misfortunes and misjudgments, resulting almost inevitably in Happy finding himself on the receiving end of a policeman's club or the rage of an angry mob. And yet the next week our hero Happy would return ready to try again, maintaining his seemingly indomitable faith that things would indeed turn out right this time around.

From Happy Hooligan to Krazy Kat to Charlie Brown more than a century later, Oldbuck provided the model of the serial personality who could renew himself each day in the face of inevitable defeat. Presented as a "series" of pictures, telling the story of an ill-starred man always prepared to "turn over a new leaf," and arriving in the United States as a new popular serial culture was forever transforming the media landscape, Oldbuck is a fitting godfather for American popular serialities. The serial culture that seemingly went dormant with the collapse of the early American magazine culture of the early national period was reawakened in a new form, now capable, like Oldbuck himself, of turning over a new leaf—a new form—no matter what changes might transform the media ecology going forward.

BIBLIOGRAPHY

Anderson, Benedict (1991). *Imagined Communities: Reflections on the Origins and Spread of Nationalism* [1983]. London: Verso.
Arp, Bill (1896). "Bill Arp on Elections." *Concord Times* (November 19): 1.
Brooks, Noah (1898). "My Boyhood Friend, Mr. Oldbuck." *The Book Buyer* 17: 221–22.
Carlo, Jr. (1842). "Literary." *Boston Post* (December 15): 1.
"East India Sporting: Marvellous Adventure with a Tiger." *Brother Jonathan* 1.9 (February 26, 1842): 233–37.

Gardner, Jared (2012). *The Rise and Fall of Early American Magazine Culture*. Champaign: University of Illinois Press.

Garvey, Ellen Gruber (2013). *Writing with Scissors: American Scrapbooks from the Civil War to the Harlem Renaissance*. New York: Oxford University Press.

Greene, James N. (2010). "The Rise of Book Publishing." *An Extensive Republic: Print, Culture, and Society in the New Nation, 1790–1840*. Ed. Robert A. Gross and Mary Kelley. Vol. 2 of *A History of the Book in America*. Chapel Hill: University of North Carolina Press. 75–127.

Gross, Robert A. and Mary Kelley, eds. (2010). *An Extensive Republic: Print, Culture, and Society in the New Nation, 1790–1840*. Vol. 2 of *A History of the Book in America*. Chapel Hill: University of North Carolina Press.

"Harpers' Translation of the 'Mysteries of Paris.'" *New World* (November 4, 1843): 538.

"Here Is a Curious Thing!" *Brother Jonathan* 3–4 (1842): 90.

Higginson, Thomas Wentworth (1999). *The Complete Civil War Journal and Selected Letters of Thomas Wentworth Higginson*. Ed. Christopher Looby. Chicago: University of Chicago Press.

"I Can't Afford It." *Country Gentleman* 3 (January 12, 1854): 28.

Kelleter, Frank (2002). *Amerikanische Aufklärung: Sprachen der Rationalität im Zeitalter der Revolution*. Paderborn: Schöningh.

Kunzle, David (2007). *Father of the Comic Strip: Rodolphe Töpffer*. Jackson: University Press of Mississippi.

Lehuu, Isabelle (2003). *Carnival on the Page: Popular Print Media in Antebellum America*. Chapel Hill: University of North Carolina Press.

"Library Edition—Quarto." *Brother Jonathan* (February 26, 1842): xxxiv.

"A Literary Worker." *Independent* (March 1877): 9.

McParland, Robert (2011). *Charles Dickens's American Audience*. New York: Lexington Books.

Mecom, Benjamin (1758). "The Quintessence of Books—A Great Book Is a Great Evil." *New-England Magazine* 1: 14.

"Mrs. Bray's Historical Novels." *The Spectator* 6 (1833): 888.

Patterson, Cynthia Lee (2010). *Art for the Middle Classes: America's Illustrated Magazines of the 1840s*. Jackson: University Press of Mississippi.

Podgers (1862). "Gossip from California." *New York Times* (November 14): 2.

"A Reminscent Article." *Kansas City Chief* (September 26, 1895): 1.

Reynolds, David S. (1988). *Beneath the American Renaissance: The Subversive Imagination in the Age of Emerson and Melville*. New York: Knopf.

Siljeström, Per Adam and Frederica Rowan (1853). *The Educational Institutions of the United States, Their Character and Organization*. London: J. Chapman.

Stevens, John D. (1991). *Sensationalism and the New York Press*. New York: Columbia University Press.

Streeby, Shelley (1997). "Opening Up the Story Paper: George Lippard and the Construction of Class." *boundary 2* 24: 177–203.

Tebbel, John William (1972). *A History of Book Publishing in the United States. Volume 1: The Creation of an Industry, 1630–1865*. New York: R. R. Bowker.

"Thrilling Train Robberies Are Manufactured to Your Order." *Washington Times* (May 29, 1904): 4.

Tucker, Susan, Katherine Ott, and Patricia P. Buckler, eds. (2006). *The Scrapbook in American Life*. Philadelphia: Temple University Press.

"Ups and Downs." *Rural Repository* 19 (1843): 110–11.

CHAPTER 3

Serial Politics in Antebellum America
On the Cultural Work of the City-Mystery Genre

DANIEL STEIN

I

City mysteries were serialized sensational narratives about urban vice and crime that enjoyed immense popularity in the decades before the American Civil War. During the antebellum era, novels such as George Lippard's *The Quaker City; or, The Monks of Monk Hall: A Romance of Philadelphia Life, Mystery, and Crime* (1844–45); Ned Buntline's *The Mysteries and Miseries of New York* (1847–48; published under Buntline's real name, Edward Zane Carroll Judson); and George Thompson's *City Crimes, or, Life in New York and Boston* (1849), all fascinated a broad readership and became bestsellers in a rapidly expanding print market. These novels offered prime reading entertainment for mass audiences, but at a time of heightened controversy over the fate of the nation, they also served as a medium for political agitation. As I will argue in this chapter, they produced as well as capitalized on a powerful nexus of serial entertainment and political engagement. This chapter thus aims to make sense of the serial politics performed by these narratives within the broader field of American culture. How did American city-mystery novels utilize the affordances of serial fiction to entertain *and* politicize their readers?

What kind of agency did these novels exert in the formation of early American popular culture? And what role did they play in antebellum politics?[1]

Though I will focus on the city mysteries' cultural work in antebellum America, it is vital to acknowledge the genre's transatlantic origins to understand the serial thrust of these narratives. The first city mystery was Eugène Sue's feuilleton novel *Les Mystères de Paris* (*The Mysteries of Paris*), serialized in the Parisian daily *Journal des Débats* between June 1842 and October 1843. *Les Mystères de Paris* spawned a large number of mysteries across national borders: more than one hundred novels set in places such as Paris, London, Berlin, Hamburg, Vienna, Amsterdam, Brussels, Lisbon, Milan, Melbourne, Montreal, St. Petersburg, and a host of cities in the United States.[2] Inspired by Sue's success—both in terms of increasing the *Journal*'s readership and in terms of the controversy generated by his politicized narrative about conflicts between the proletariat and the city's elites—American authors quickly adapted his plot, rhetoric, and character ensemble to homegrown contexts.[3]

Lippard's *Quaker City* was the first to do so, becoming a national bestseller (Reynolds 1995: vii). The novel utilized a sensationalist rhetoric and melodramatic plotting in its depiction of excessive sex and violence, which was intensified by the narrative's serial structure: by the incremental revelation of actions and their consequences over a period of many months and ten installments. Adding to the novel's popularity were prototypical muckraking elements that promised to expose both the brutality and the licentiousness of Philadelphia's underworld as well as the lurid crimes of the city's upper-class—its political leaders, business magnates, and clergy, with honest workers and middle-class families figuring as the victims of oppression. *Quaker City* offered readers a voyeuristic gaze at illicit scenes of sexual deviation and criminal activities, and it launched thinly disguised attacks on those in power who did not abide by the author's radical-democratic convictions and who would find themselves attacked in installment after installment.[4]

---

1. This essay is part of my book project within the Popular Seriality Research Unit (PSRU), "Serial Politicization: On the Cultural Work of American City Mysteries, 1844–1860."

2. Between 1844 and 1860, many texts depicted vice and crime in American cities. Erikson (2005) discusses about three hundred fictional and nonfictional works. Reynolds speaks of fifty city mysteries (1995: xiv). According to Zboray/Zboray, thirteen New England city mysteries appeared in 1844, and by 1860, sixty-four additional works had been published (2000: 457). On the genre's transnational scope, see Knight (2012); on the transnationalism of American serial fiction more generally, see Okker (2011).

3. The first American translations of *Les Mystères de Paris* appeared in 1843; see Jared Gardner's chapter in this volume.

4. On Lippard's "practice of seriality" and "his poetics in parts," see Looby (2015: 12); on Lippard's radical politics, see Reynolds (2015).

Quaker City was followed by a slew of city mysteries, including Buntline's *Mysteries and Miseries of New York* and Thompson's *City Crimes* as well as *The Mysteries and Miseries of New Orleans* (Buntline 1851); *Mysteries of Lowell* (Bradbury 1844); *The Knights of the Seal; or, The Mysteries of the Three Cities* (Duganne 1845); *Mysteries of Fitchburg* (Penchant 1844); *Mysteries of Salem* (Hargrave 1845); *Mysteries of Worcester* (Spofford 1846); and *Mysteries of San Francisco* (Myers 1853).[5] These novels spread the action across the country from East to West, North and South, diversifying the genre through a process of regional specification while creating the sense of a national American literature that was more than the sum of its parts. Additional regional and ethnic variants appeared in the form of non-English-language mysteries, most prominently novels by German immigrant authors that were serialized in German-language newspapers, such as August Gläser's *Geheimnisse von Philadelphia* (1850); Heinrich Börnstein's *Die Geheimnisse von St. Louis* (1851); Ludwig von Reizenstein's *Die Geheimnisse von New-Orleans* (1854–55); Rudolph Lexow's *Amerikanische Criminal-Mysteries, oder das Leben der Verbrecher in New-York* (1854); and Emil Klauprecht's *Cincinnati, oder Geheimnisse des Westens* (1854).[6]

City mysteries were perhaps the earliest example of a Western popular literary genre in the modern sense of the term: a body of serial texts written, marketed, and read *as* serial genre texts. Werner Sollors speaks of an "international vogue in urban *Mysteries*" (2001: 104), while Michael Denning describes them as "the first genre to achieve massive success and to dominate cheap fiction" (1998: 85). They laid the foundation for the more tightly organized "fiction factories" (17) of the postbellum era, facilitating the rise of dime novel series in the second half of the nineteenth century and the emergence of film serials, radio plays, and comic books in the first half of the twentieth century. These American city-mystery novels appeared at a specific time—the antebellum era—and in a specific climate—a "culture of sensation" (Streeby

---

5. As Thompson's *City Crimes* indicates, not all city mystery novels replicated the "mystery"-title formula. Once the formula had been applied to a city, authors came up with titles that announced genre affiliation but promised variation of the popular theme. Authors like Bradbury, Buntline, Lippard, and Thompson also wrote sequels that called for new titles. *City Crimes* foregrounds the genre-typical focus on urban crime and (like Duganne's *Knights of the Seal*) extends the exposure of criminal networks beyond a single city. Hargrave was the only female city-mystery writer—indicating a gendered division between the sentimentalist fiction of female writers (e.g., Susan Warner, E. D. E. N. Southworth, Harriet Beecher Stowe) and male-dominated sensationalist literature (Streeby 2002: 32–33). The genre nonetheless negotiated notions of femininity and masculinity. I have found no African American authors, but many texts dealt with racial issues (see Helwig 2006 and Ostrowski 2006).

6. On German American *Geheimnisromane*, see Herminghouse 1985; Schuchalter 2011; and Stein 2014b, 2016.

2002)—in which the national reach of bestsellers began to impart substantial political prowess to fiction writing and novel reading.[7] Most famously, Harriet Beecher Stowe's controversial antislavery novel *Uncle Tom's Cabin*, which was initially serialized in the abolitionist newspaper *The National Era* (1851–52), generated a whole industry of pro- and anti-Tom productions, providing Americans with a set of characters, scenes, and sentiments through which they could process different responses to the slave system.[8]

In this time and climate, the city mysteries pursued objectives that were fundamentally at odds: entertaining antebellum readers with sensational stories but also moving them toward political action by exposing the failures of urban elites and calling on public institutions to reform. In *The Mysteries and Miseries of New York*, for instance, Ned Buntline directly addresses mayor William Frederick Havemeyer, the Chief of Police George W. Matsell, the magistrates of the city council, and "Benevolent Associations" like the New York Hospital, criticizing the recent spike in crime, poverty, and prostitution and urging readers to demand social and political change while dramatizing this critique through his character constellation, plot development, and rhetoric. Denning thus speaks of a "paradoxical union of sensational fiction and radical politics" (1998: 87). If we want to gain a deeper sense of the genre and its texts as literary "agents of cultural formation" (Tompkins 1985: xvii) that shaped antebellum culture, we must reconstruct the breadth and diversity of the genre and read individual texts as part of a larger conversation among city-mystery authors, their narratives, and their readers. In order to do so, we must consider the city mysteries as serially produced, serially published, and serially read popular narratives whose impact on antebellum culture was not confined to their ability to propose political positions and dramatize the plight of the powerless but extended to a specific serial-political dynamic of production and reception.

II

Before I turn to the city mysteries and the politics of the genre, clarifications concerning the key concepts of my analysis—cultural work, popular seriality, serial politics—are in order. In her study of late eighteenth- and nineteenth-century fiction, Jane Tompkins suggests that a primary function of popular

---

7. For Streeby, "culture of sensation" designates a literary sphere of "low" popular narratives as well as a "wider spectrum of popular arts and practices that includes journalism, music, blackface minstrelsy, and other forms of popular theater" (2002: 27).

8. On the cultural productivity of *Uncle Tom's Cabin*, see Meer (2005).

literature was "to redefine the social order," to "articulat[e] and propos[e] solutions for the problems that shape [their] particular historical moment." As "instruments of cultural self-definition," novels such as *Uncle Tom's Cabin* or Susan Warner's *The Wide, Wide World* (1850) "have designs upon their audiences, [. . .] wanting to make people think and act in a particular way" by "providing men and women with a means of ordering the world they inhabited" (1985: xi, xvi, xi, xiii).[9] Shifting from textual exegesis to a broader perspective on the cultural effects of narratives, Tompkins proposes: "Rather than asking, 'what does this text mean?' or, 'how does it work?,' I ask, 'what kind of work is this novel trying to do?'" (1985: 38). Instead of interpreting stock figures and genre formulas as evidence of banal production and consumption, studying the cultural work of popular narratives thus means to read stereotypes and formulas as part of an ongoing conversation among authors, texts, and audiences in a marketplace of political ideas and media networks (1985: 38, 95–95).

City-mystery novels had sensational designs on their readers even though they presented "a 'low' kind of literature in relation to [the] more middlebrow popular sentimentalism" of Stowe and Warner (Streeby 2002: 27). As Buntline exclaims at the beginning of his narrative: "I wish to lay before you all the vice of the city [. . .] so that you and the good and philanthropic may see where to apply the healing balm, I wish to show where and how our young men are led away and ruined in the glittering gambling palaces, now many a poor, now wretched and degraded female, has been driven into the paths of infamy, when one kind word and one helping hand would have saved her" (1848: I.7).

Most city mysteries were serialized in periodicals or published as pamphlet series and later reprinted as books; they created a genre by reiterating its sensationalist title formula—*Mysteries of . . .*—and adapting character types, storylines, as well as narrative modes to new contexts of production and reception. Examples of character types are aristocratic or otherwise noble savior figures, ruthless rakes, female victims of sexual exploitation, wanton adulteresses, abominable Catholic priests, and human freaks of nature. Plot developments often revolve around heinous acts of seduction and rape, religious hypocrisy, as well as the exploitation of the working poor through moneyed city elites, while prominent narrative modes include sensationalism, sentimentalism, melodrama, and gothic horror. If popular narratives employ characters as "things to think with" (Tompkins 1985: 119) and use plots and modes as means to shape and organize social affects, then the city mysteries

---

9. Compare Fluck (1997: 18–20) on literature's ability to simulate the emotional experience of an unrealized imaginary and thus articulate certain options for social and political action (*Artikulationseffekt*).

clearly did not "flatten the complexities of existence" (1985: 96) in antebellum America. Indeed, they added complexity to this existence by inviting readers to empathize with storylines that claimed to recreate the urban world inhabited by their readers and conjured up in the narratives through frequent references to specific neighborhoods, streets, and establishments.

Since Tompkins does not account for the serial production and reception of popular novels, it is necessary to connect the concept of cultural work with a notion of popular seriality—that is, with an understanding of popular serial narratives as mass-addressed and explicitly commercial types of cultural production that thrive on a dialectic of schematization and variation, and standardization and innovation. Highly conducive to narrative proliferation, such series tend to generate ever new mechanisms to manage their own diversification (including generic and paratextual structures).[10] In the antebellum era, I argue, popular seriality first reached a national scale, and serial storytelling established itself as a founding principle of modern popular culture.[11] Two assumptions ground this notion of popular seriality. First, as ongoing productions that thrive in capitalist economies because they can constantly defer final closure, popular serial narratives are shaped by processes of recursivity that cut across established distinctions between production and reception (Kelleter 2012). In order to grasp the affective and evocative power of Ludwig von Reizenstein's *Die Geheimnisse von New-Orleans,* for instance, we must reinsert it into the dialogue about the nation's racial and sexual politics into which it intervenes in a concrete historical moment and within a specific media landscape. Relevant contexts include the controversy over the Kansas-Nebraska Act (1854), which triggered a vitriolic attack from Reizenstein against the politicians in Congress who betrayed the founding ideals of the Republic by voting for the act; the city's recovery from a devastating yellow fever epidemic in 1853, which underscored Reizenstein's depiction of the disease as retribution for the sins of slavery; and the prominence of taboo violations (e.g., interracial sex, homosexuality) that generated publicity by inciting negative reviews from a rival newspaper.[12]

---

10. On popular seriality, see Kelleter 2012 and chapter 1 in this volume. On the serial dialectic of repetition (or schematization) and variation, see Eco 1990. On paratexts, parodies, and genre construction as culturally productive mechanisms of serial management, see Stein 2012, 2013, and 2014a.

11. Antebellum print publications began to reach mass audiences across regions, classes, genders, and ethnicities. Industrialization and urbanization shaped a "recreational economy" in which reading was a central activity (Stewart 2011: 4). On the foundational role of eighteenth-century magazines, see Gardner 2012a.

12. Reizenstein's novel was serialized in the *Lousiana Staats-Zeitung* (January 1853–March 1854); the rival paper was the *Deutsche Zeitung* (see Rowan 2002 and Stein 2014b). In Stein

Moreover, the processes of transatlantic adaptation and regional diversification that propelled the serial evolution of the genre complicate any clear distinction between production and reception. Lippard, Buntline, Osgood Bradbury, A. J. H. Duganne, and Joseph Holt Ingraham were readers of Sue's novels as well as of each other's works; Reizenstein positioned his novel within the genre by tracing a development from Sue via Buntline to German American writers like Börnstein and Klauprecht in a statement to the reader that opens *Die Geheimnisse von New-Orleans*.[13] Lippard cited from a review of *Quaker City* when he reserialized the novel in his *Quaker City Weekly* journal in 1849: "[Lippard is t]he Eugene [*sic*] Sue of America, possessing graphic powers, which even excel those of the great French novelist." On the back pages of the original *Quaker City* installments, he even claimed that his novel had "commenced long before 'Mysteries of Paris' appeared," although he acknowledged that it "bears the same relation to Philadelphia that the 'Mysteries' do to Paris" (quoted in Ehrlich 1972: 50, 56). What we find here are two central practices of popular serial storytelling: (1) a practice of outdoing, by which every addition, be it an individual installment of an ongoing narrative or an entirely new series competing against another series, tries to tell the same basic story by increasing, heightening, or intensifying previous versions (Jahn-Sudmann/Kelleter 2012); and (b) a contravening practice of authorization, by which discourses of authorial originality and genre awareness legitimize new narratives (Kelleter/Stein 2012; Stein 2014a). *Quaker City* inscribes itself into the serial genealogy of the city-mystery genre, posing as a transatlantic continuation of Sue's initial series by claiming that it does for Philadelphia what *Les Mystères de Paris* did for Paris. Yet Lippard is careful to preclude any sense of merely copying Sue's formulas by suggesting the (temporal) primacy of his own work. In a capitalist economy, where products must be both dependable (at least as good as the last product) and newly pleasurable (ideally more satisfying than competing products), Lippard promotes himself as the "American" Sue, a more entertaining and relevant version of the French feuilleton novelist.

The second assumption is that popular series are active agents within larger networks of culture.[14] Just as they must not be approached as self-contained works, they must not be isolated from the realm of practices from which they emerge and which they impact as well. In this context, it is important to note

---

2014b, I discuss S. H. Lützen's review and Reizenstein's response, published in the following installment of *Die Geheimnisse von New Orleans*, as a paratextual discourse that exemplifies the ability of serial narratives to react to, as well as intervene in, their reception.

13. I offer close readings and historical contextualization of the German American city-mystery novels by Reizenstein, Heinrich Börnstein, and Emil Klauprecht in Stein 2016.

14. For a more detailed discussion, see the first chapter in this volume and references there.

that city mysteries appeared before there was a fully professionalized culture industry. Denning discerns an "unstable economy of formulaic narratives" and "a contested terrain, a field of cultural conflict" (1998: 81, 3), while David Stewart (2011) considers the reading of literary fiction and nonfictional texts a new and widely shared cultural practice that facilitated processes of personal and national sense-making at a time of sweeping socioeconomic and political change.[15] City mysteries depended on, interacted with, but also shaped a media ecology that went beyond the confines of print literature. They evoked this ecology by borrowing from stage melodrama (e.g., excessive action, moral dichotomies), blackface minstrelsy (songs, jokes, stock characters), religious performance (mock sermons), domestic novels (virtuous suffering, seduction plots, deathbed scenes), and the penny press (sensationalist rhetoric, scandal mongering).

This media ecology was a virtual vortex of American politics—a vortex in which political parties utilized popular rhetoric to further their goals, while popular entertainment latched onto political issues to mobilize large readerships.[16] Emil Klauprecht's *Cincinnati, oder Geheimnisse des Westens* foregrounds the spread of political rhetoric into serial newspaper fiction in scenes that mock the alcohol-soaked and cliché-saturated atmosphere at political gatherings among the city's Germans, and it expresses the author's Republican sympathies through an ongoing parody of a rival newspaper writer and editor, the comically renamed Colonel Schwappelhuber of the *Demokratische Staatstrompete von Ohio*. Significantly, the city-mystery genre and other forms of antebellum popular culture did not merely "reflect" political ideologies. Instead, they created intimate fictional worlds whose ontological and epistemological premises readers needed to share for the extended duration of periodical reading if they were to achieve the full pleasures of serial consumption. Those who invested time and money to follow Klauprechts's novel from one installment to the next were compelled to do more than merely consume the unfolding story as a form of political commentary. They may have been seduced by the twists and turns of the series, empathizing with some characters and vilifying others and thereby affirming, perhaps even adopting, a specific spectrum of social and political positions.[17] Such popular narratives were

---

15. Lehuu speaks of an "ephemeral period" characterized by "ephemeral publications" (2000: 25).

16. On these issues, see also Altschuler/Blumin 2000 and Maase 2010. Stewart underscores the physicality of reading, suggesting that antebellum readers ingested the writings of authors like Thompson to emerge from this experience with a new sense of self and their bodies (2008: 242).

17. In his study of antebellum reading practices, Stewart speaks of "books that seduce" (2011: 6).

political precisely in the sense that they kept readers in a permanent state of agitation, immersed in a gradually unfolding world that amassed one social wrong after another, pounding away at the reader's moral outrage. As such, they produced public excitements, rendered political emotions graspable, and thus made positions possible or impossible, for instance, by prodding readers to recognize themselves as members of distinct social groups with special grievances. Reading Lippard's *Quaker City* or Buntline's *Mysteries and Miseries of New York* meant gaining awareness of one's identity as one of many exploited working-class mechanics or as one of the many victims of urban crime. On a larger scale, as we see in texts such as *Quaker City* or *Die Geheimnisse von New-Orleans* which portray the failed politics of a single city as the harbinger of national demise, city-mystery novels enabled a national readership to recognize itself *as* a national readership, dramatizing what was at stake when different politicians, parties, and legislatures debated the pressing issues of the day.[18]

If city mysteries claimed to unveil the conspiracies of the wealthy and powerful against the poor and powerless, and if they gloated in the revelation of secret networks operating beneath the surface of respectability, then the pleasures of serial reading derived at least partly from the readers' feeling that these were allegorical texts—veiled commentaries on actual people and institutions. Lippard, for instance, speaks of "the administration of a certain Governor" in a footnote in *Quaker City* and complains in another footnote about the misappropriation of funds in connection with the founding of Girard College, implying that the corrupt actions of the United States Bank and its director Nicholas Biddle had prevented the college from being erected in time (1995: 269; and Reynolds 1995: xxxv). Reizenstein's depiction of characters like the German aristocratic immigrant Emil and the lesbian Orleana generated public speculation and controversy about who among the region's residents served as their inspiration (Rowan 2002). True, not all city mysteries emulated Lippard's sensationalist prose and melodramatic techniques; nor did all of them endorse his understanding of popular literature as a battering ram for a nationwide project of social reform.[19] But as texts that placed themselves—in various ways and with different degrees of explicitness—within a serial genre of public interest, they offered their readers powerful fictions to

---

18. Emerson emphasizes the novel's "agency at the local level" and its efforts to reenergize "localized democracy" (2015: 104), which can be viewed as part of a local-national dialectic that depends on the serial format to perform its cultural work.

19. As Lippard wrote in his *Quaker City Weekly* (February 10, 1849): "a literature which does not work practically for the advancement of social reform [...] is just good for nothing at all" (quoted in Reynolds 1995: viii).

understand themselves as American citizens with distinct, if potentially competing, identities and urgent duties as political subjects. It is no coincidence that these political subjects then voiced their opinions on the pages of print publications like the sensationalist penny press, abolitionist papers, and cheap popular fiction. As Benedict Anderson argues, it was the serial publication of the newspaper—"one-day best-sellers" (1991: 35)—that enabled the emergence of the modern nation-state because it offered readers a recurring encounter with themselves as newspaper-reading citizens within a larger collective. But the American nation in the nineteenth century did not only rely on newspapers as media of national or regional incorporation and sense-making; it also depended on a modern popular culture in which city mysteries were among the most widely read, most controversial, and most politicizing narratives.

III

Most intriguing about the city-mystery genre is the inherent tension at its core: the radicalism of dogmatic ideologies aimed at immediate and fundamental political action (and, thus, closure), on the one hand, and the necessities of popular serial storytelling, including the establishment of divergent viewpoints, sprawling character constellations, ambiguous plot developments, and an open-ended narrative trajectory that gains traction from the very denial—or at least continuing delay—of story closure, on the other. Any series intending to bring about political change, and especially the kind of populist grassroots democratization envisioned by Lippard, had to appeal to large audiences. Yet large audiences in the American 1840s and 1850s were made up of male and female; young and old; working-class, middle-class, and upper-class; and rural and urban readers from various national backgrounds and religious affiliations.[20] City mysteries had to account for, and appeal to, this heterogeneity, ensuring a degree of inclusiveness that complicated any radical dogmatism. Lippard thus developed braided strains of narrative and a broad selection of characters from different social spheres, connecting them via the secret chambers of Monk Hall. Moreover, he created "two seemingly conflicting voices" that displayed the outrage of the social critic and reformer as well as the gaze of the "sensationalist quasi-pornographer who revels in [...] the very vices and depravities he professes to deplore." *Quaker City* (but also Buntline's *Mysteries and Miseries of New York* and Thompson's *City*

---

20. The readership of some city mysteries was more localized due to limited distribution (New England mysteries) or language restrictions (German American *Geheimnisromane*).

Crimes) oscillates between "righteous indignation" toward political corruption and the cruelties of moneyed socialites against the urban poor, on the one hand, and the "ghoulish appreciation" of sex and crime in the darkest corners of American cities, on the other (Ashwill 1994: 293, 313). Rather than diminishing the political efficacy of these novels, this oscillation was actually their greatest political ploy. It politicized urban bodies, spaces, and social spheres by connecting the reader's somatic pleasures of serial consumption with national conflicts over slavery, capitalism, and expansion.

One way in which city-mystery writers sought to manage this inherent tension was to make the serial format work to their advantage: inviting ongoing scandal and controversy, such as when George Thompson infuses *City Crimes* with repeated violations of dominant norms (for instance, Miss Fairfield's sexual encounters with a black servant simultaneously crossing boundaries of race and class); creating charismatic authorial personas by stylizing themselves as champions of the virtuous poor and valiant exposers of political corruption in and outside of their novels; and using endless "suspense and surprise" cycles (Looby 2004: 184), cliffhangers, and action sequences to gain and maintain control over their readers' emotions. A second way was to publish more overt political writings in weekly and monthly journals: Lippard wrote serialized novels and political essays for his *Quaker City Weekly*; Buntline published his own journal, *Ned Buntline's Own*; and Thompson was a contributor and part-time editor of magazines such as *Venus' Miscellany* and *The Broadway Belle*. While Lippard's journal aimed at "social reform through the medium of popular literature" (quoted in Reynolds 1995: xvii), Thompson's mostly pornographic writings sought to reform readers by appealing to a sexuality devoid of conventional moral constraints (Reynolds and Gladman 2002), thus extending, and indeed serializing, his depictions of sexuality from *City Crimes* into other types of publication. A third way was to become politically active beyond the realm of publishing: Lippard founded the benevolent society Brotherhood of the Union and worked as a labor organizer; Buntline joined the Know-Nothing Party; Bradbury was a Whig representative in the Maine State Legislature; and Börnstein founded the Verein freier Männer (Association of Free Men) in order to join (German) residents of St. Louis into a political bloc (Rowan 1990: xi–xii). Denning thus distinguishes between the "politics of the genre" and the "politics of its audience and authors" (1998: 86); in the case of the American city mysteries, both types of politics were integrally connected. In the antebellum years, newspapers and especially their editors were political power players with substantial clout over public opinion. For example, as the editor of *Anzeiger des Westens* and author of *Die Geheimnisse von St. Louis*, Börnstein was able to orchestrate a shift among German Americans in the Midwest from the Democratic Party toward the new Republican Party over issues such as slavery (abolitionism), religion (anti-Catholicism), and immigration (anti-nativism).

An all-encompassing analysis of the city mysteries would have to account for the novels' "local paratext[s]" (Looby 2004: 186), that is, their embeddedness in carrier media such as story paper, newspaper, periodical pamphlet, and bound book. These media featured editorial statements, responses from readers, reviews, critical essays, nonfiction coverage, other fictional texts, illustrations, and advertisements. Examining this material would allow us to view the city mysteries within their immediate textual, discursive, and medial universe and to read them as part of a larger discourse about the literary meanings and politics of popular fiction. *Quaker City,* for instance, uses footnotes that function as authorial asides through which Lippard annotates the narrative, often to elaborate on a plot point or make a political reference, thereby conflating the roles of narrator and author. The book version of Buntline's *The Mysteries and Miseries of New York* features an appendix that extends the series beyond the narrative into the paratextual realm by printing a selection of letters Buntline had received from readers, as well as statements by New York mayor Havemeyer, a passage from New York police law, excerpts from newspaper articles about the situation of the urban poor, statistics from the New York State Asylum, and a lengthy attack on the competing author Harrison Gray Buchanan, whose *Asmodeus; or, Legends of New York: Being a Complete Exposé of the Mysteries, Vices and Doings, as exhibited by the Fashionable Circles of New York* (1848) Buntline accused of plagiarism (a special case of popular seriality). Moreover, Buntline uses "prefatorials" at the beginning of each new installment to make use of, and intervene into, the public reception of his narrative, repeatedly emphasizing his political integrity ("Th[is] writer is one who can neither be bribed from his duty, or frightened from his course") and assuring readers that their investment in, and support of, the narrative is already being rewarded ("deeper gratification fills his heart when he [i.e., Buntline] knows from proofs, which cannot be doubted, that it [the novel] has been already influential in pointing the benevolent and good of our city to a field where their labors and kindnesses cannot be misplaced") (1848: II.4, III.4).

For the remainder of my argument, I will, however, concentrate on the ways in which individual texts negotiate the tension between a moral absolutism geared toward the politicization of readers and the narrative demands of serial storytelling. As ongoing stories tied closely to their reception, serial narratives are well-equipped to involve authors and readers in political debates that are anchored in the depicted storyworld but ultimately encourage readers "to turn outward" (Ashwill 1994: 296) to the world at large: to urban spaces "in our very midst," such as the Bowery or Five Points, as Buntline writes in *Mysteries and Miseries of New York* (1848: I.5). We know that popular series sanction the transition from passive reading to active authorship, often turning readers into letter writers, critics, or even authors of competing stories (Lund 1993, Hayward 1997, Gardner 2012b, and Stein 2013). As a reader named Isaac N. Walter writes in a letter to Buntline appended to *The Mysteries and Miseries of New York*: "I could furnish you with several instances if you should ever desire them, that you could do well with in writing some other publication. I will furnish them if you wish." Buntline reprints his response letter and states, "Any information which our reverend, and esteemed correspondent will send us will be thankfully received, and used" (1848: Appendix 111). Yet active readers also create challenges for serial narratives, and perhaps even greater challenges for politically radical narratives. They tend to question, undermine, attack, or parody a series' politics, and they often make story suggestions and advocate character modifications that will complicate any rigorous politics. As we know from other popular forms of narrative—such as superhero comics (Kelleter/Stein 2012 and Stein 2013, 2014a)—successful genres generate diversity and manage sprawling significances rather than propose monolithic meanings; they must be malleable in order to survive in changing social, cultural, and political circumstances.

City-mystery writers generally emphasized the topicality of their stories by addressing specific legislation (from tariffs, corruption, and urban reform to bank regulation or the fugitive slave law) and by attacking particular politicians, parties, and elected authorities. Many writers insisted that their shocking tales of vice and crime in high places rested on a factual basis. Thompson claimed that his work was "founded on fact" and that he was writing romances of the real (2002: 310, and Looby 1993: 651); Buntline claimed that he had done extensive research that distinguished his work from fanciful novels and classified the text as "a *history* more than [. . .] a romance" (1848: I.5); Lippard's *Quaker City* begins with an origin tale that legitimizes the story as being based on trustworthy information that Lippard had received from a recently deceased Philadelphia lawyer. Claims of verisimilitude were staples of the genre, capitalizing on the gossip factor promised by revelations about the sexual deviance; economic scheming; and hypocrisy of social, political, and religious elites. Yet such claims did not express any single politics. As Ronald J. Zboray and Mary Saracino Zboray have shown, New England mysteries by authors such as Justin Jones, Joseph Holt Ingraham, and Osgood Bradbury were not only shorter than their New York and Philadelphia counterparts; they also expressed a Whiggish politics that largely rejected the artisan republicanism of many New York and Philadelphia mysteries and substituted Sue's aristocratic figures with "provincial types (and stereotypes)" from "crafty Yankee peddlers" to "African American fiddle players at harvest fairs, [...] Lowell mill operatives, and upwardly mobile clerks" (2000: 462). German American writers pursued their own local politics in cities such as St. Louis, Cincinnati, and New Orleans. In Reizenstein's *Die Geheimnisse von New-Orleans*, aristocratic German émigrés from the failed 1848 revolution encounter a Southern society on the brink of death and destruction, threatened by yellow fever and impending slave revolts, while the virtuous Böttcher and Steigerwald families in Börnstein's *Die Geheimnisse von St. Louis* and Klauprecht's *Cincinnati* serve as a refutation of anti-German sentiments (Stein 2016).

City mysteries frequently used paratexts to formulate these and other political objectives. Buntline's *Mysteries and Miseries of New York* addresses itself to the hypocritical and corrupt New York clergy and signals its missionary motivation in the opening "prefatorial," which announces that the narrative "will offend" readers and will "strike at vice in every garb and station." The "aim in this work [...] is to do good" and "lay open [the] festering sores" of political corruption Buntline claims to have witnessed during his research in the city's underworld (1848: I.6–7). The stated goal is to move readers toward philanthropy, to pummel them into rethinking social injustices and show empathy toward the exploited populace. Buntline's "pictures of real life" (1848: IV.3) emerge from the detailed portrayal of actual urban spaces and the representation of characters whose true-to-lifeness is foregrounded in the dialects, sociolects, and jargon they speak. Furthermore, *Mysteries and Miseries of New York* includes authorial asides and explicit moralizing that relate Buntline's political convictions directly to readers.

Buntline's prefatorials speak of his novel's "unexampled and heart-cheering success" as well as the "unexpected and unparalleled patronage" it received from readers, but also of threats and anonymous letters attacking its politics. They paint Buntline as a fearless agitator, who exclaims, "We cannot be bought" (1848: II.4). More important than the author's popularity and financial success, the prefatorials state, is his gratitude that his writing has motivated philanthropic acts and encouraged readers to fight the betrayal of republican values by capitalist greed. In addition, Buntline claims to have sent copies of his narrative to the mayor and police of New York, threatening to publicize the names of those who neglect their republican duties: "We have to stand *alone* in this warfare," he writes in populist terms and then promotes his political independence: "We have no political prejudices, and belong to no party," but "[we will] give all the little influence which we may possess" (1848: Appendix 101). His ultimate aim is to change urban politics through the evocative power of serial storytelling. It is not enough to identify the city's political evildoers on only one occasion. Only if the accusations are presented again and again will the narrative acquire sufficient force to convince readers that they must fulfill their republican duty by voting the delinquents out of office.

We must, however, be careful to distinguish such promotional rhetoric from the actual political effects that Buntline's and other city mysteries may have had (or not). Writing about Thompson's *The House Breaker; or, The Mysteries of Crime* (1848), Looby maintains that such novels enact a serial dialectic of pleasurable entertainment and political enragement that was not necessarily progressive or even revolutionary. Thompson does not "confront [. . .] systemic injustices of the social world" but "attend[s] obsessively to spectacular excesses that evoke in readers a futile moral indignation, class resentment, and scandalized voyeurism" (1993: 653). It would be mistaken, then, to read city mysteries simply as subversive texts that undermined the foundation of American society and mobilized readers against local and national governments. They could be affirmative of bourgeois values precisely because they denounced the violation of these values and enabled readers to exhaust their political frustrations in the act of reading. Moreover, Buntline ends his attack on the exploitation of the working poor in *Mysteries and Miseries of New York* with a list of characters who will reappear in the sequel *B'hoys of New York* (1850) and with a statement about another upcoming narrative, *G'hals of New York* (1850). Thus, the commercial interests of a celebrity author seem to override the novel's anticapitalist theme.

Achieving literary fame and attracting a broad range of readers also meant competing for audience attention. As active participants in a larger field of commercial media, city mysteries sought to win readers by capitalizing on their own specific mediality. They were relatively cheap, could be materially owned (and thus reread, collected, and treasured) and perused in the private confines of the home. Spreading out consumption across many months and even years, inserting regular gaps in the narrative that left time for reflection, speculation, and anticipation, they created a particularly intimate relationship between author, reader, and text.[21] Yet antebellum readers sensed that they were part of a readership that extended beyond their immediate social environment and constituted an interpretive community whose consumption of serial texts was structured by shared rhythms of reading, waiting, and often actively responding to the ongoing narrative (Okker 2003: 10, 15–16). In addition, city mysteries exulted in the crossing of social and geographic boundaries, taking their readers on slumming tours into the seedy sections of the

---

21. Compare Smith on "the intimacy of serialized publication" (1995: 71).

city and lifting the veil (or bedsheet) from the illicit sexual pleasures of the rich and famous as well as exposing the depravities of degenerate men, seductive adulteresses, lewd prostitutes, and freakish creatures. The voyeuristic pleasures offered by such material enabled audiences to experience erotic stimulation through vicarious participation in outré behavior, allowing them to imaginatively transgress boundaries of race, gender, sexuality, and class (often all at once) at a time when these boundaries were coming under increasing pressure.

City mysteries sought to curb the challenges of competing print publications by absorbing much of their rhetoric and some of their style, often adding a satirical slant, ironic commentary, or caricature in order to establish themselves as the superior form. As Reynolds suggests, Lippard's *Quaker City* not only parodies the sensationalist press, but it was "itself a kind of massive penny paper" (1995: xxv), reporting on the most shocking criminal endeavors and indecencies with righteous indignation. In addition, city mysteries utilized intertextual and intermedial references to align themselves with the racial, sexual, economic, and religious politics of the popular theater. One chapter of *Quaker City* begins with the words "We open this scene with a picture" (1995: 281), and many scenes in this and other novels mimic theatrical tableaux. Depictions of melodramatic heroines and "fallen women" further weave these narratives into the intermedial fabric of the times, while *Quaker City* is filled with racially ambiguous characters—Devil-Bug's two black helpers, Glow-worm and Musquito, but also the cunning servant Endymion—that owe much to blackface minstrelsy. The novel also includes scenes of exuberant dancing and singing, references to the black dancer Juba, and to Jim Crow entertainment; and it also features black dialect.[22] In addition to this minstrel discourse, graphic illustrations placed city mysteries within the increasingly visual politics of antebellum culture.

IV

While the city-mystery genre began in France and spread throughout Europe, it was especially productive in the United States. Here, it fell on fertile ground, filling a cultural void with stories about rapidly growing cities that mystified urban dwellers of different classes, ethnicities, genders, and religions at a time when American society was changing more rapidly and more fundamentally than its European counterparts. If we follow Kelleter's (2002) view of

---

22. For a recent rereading of *Quaker City*'s racial politics, see Altschuler (2015).

the United States as an unlikely and implausibly diversified (multicultural, multireligious, and multiregional) society whose political stability has always hinged on the ability of media and narratives to incorporate citizens procedurally where they can no longer be incorporated dogmatically, then it is no surprise that the antebellum era saw the emergence of a popular serial genre dealing with some of the most pressing political questions of the day: black slavery in the South vs. worker's rights in the North, gender relations, class conflicts, religious cleavages, social reform, westward expansion, and manifest destiny. For the expanding United States, the project of a national culture—James Madison's extended republic of the *Federalist Papers*—depended on the ability of people and institutions to communicate with and about themselves. If modern media had a role to play in the construction, negotiation, and maintenance of the nation as an "imagined community" (Anderson 1991), their task was to organize a diversifying population into a self-aware body politic. That the city mysteries did so in part by playing the game of body politics—by depicting human bodies of all shapes, sizes, and colors and by relishing in fantasies of body violation (rape, incest, torture, murder)—underscores their relevance for a national popular culture. Devising an unconventional politics of the body and utilizing an extreme rhetoric of affect (sentimentalism, sensationalism, melodrama; Stewart 2011: 3) that was intensified through serial delivery and consumption, the city mysteries embodied a society that was indeed trying to come to grips with massive strains on the assumed integrity of its national body.[23]

As serialized narratives, city mysteries offered readers the repeated return to a known storyworld with familiar characters and an increasingly intimate narrative voice at a time when the actual world seemed more and more ephemeral. The daunting city is transformed here into a recognizable place, but this is also a fictional space loaded with controversial social and political significances: a space where few can be trusted and where treachery, seduction, and financial ruin are always just one plot turn away. This type of seriality—tenuous at best, since things could always change and readers were compelled to bridge temporal intervals between issues—promised shared pleasure and comfort in times of economic crisis, social unrest, and political turmoil. Ultimately, it performed its cultural work through practicing the nation itself as an open-ended serial narrative, involving readers in politicized processes of local, regional, and national meaning-making. Yet such imagined collectivization was a double-edged sword. What drew readers together into a community

---

23. On the nexus of literary body politics and the expanding national body politic, see Streeby 2002: 27–28.

of consumers of sensational stories also fed into an emotionalized political discourse that pitted proponents of different visions for the nation's future against each other and that climaxed, less than two decades after the genre's appearance in the United States, in the Civil War. Several city mysteries register the looming failure of national politics to achieve sectional reconciliation by failing to provide narrative closure. Lippard's *Quaker City* and Reizenstein's *Die Geheimnisse von New-Orleans* cannot provide viable solutions for the violations of republican values they have amassed over the course of several hundred pages, and both end in apocalyptic scenarios of ultimate retribution. The serial form, with its demand for ever more drastic depictions of evil acts, moral debauchery, and political corruption, thus determines the political solutions—or rather the lack thereof—imagined by these novels (Fluck 1997: 143). Lippard's Philadelphia has been ravaged by so much corruption, violence, and abuse of power that, in a particularly dismal dream sequence, it appears as a modern-day Sodom far beyond repair. *Die Geheimnisse von New-Orleans* kills off most of its central characters, who are murdered or taken by yellow fever as punishment for their support of the slave system, and the novel imagines two possible futures for the American nation that will each prove destructive. One is a violent slave revolt that will massacre the nation's white population, and the other is a secret lesbian society that may function as a bastion of true love but will ultimately fail to secure the survival of the republic (Stein 2014b).

Quaker City, like so many popular series, is also a meta-reflexive text, formulating its own theory of seriality. Early on, Gus Lorrimer, Lippard's stereotypical rake, exclaims in a drunken reverie: "Every thing fleeting and nothing stable, every thing shifting and changing, and nothing substantial! A bundle of hopes and fears, deceits and confidences, joys and miseries, strapped to a fellow's back like Pedlar's wares" (1995: 23). Lorrimer is referring to the instability of antebellum urban life, but his words also reveal the novel's conflicted self-understanding as a serial commodity. In the antebellum era, popular serial literature offered authors and readers an uncertain footing, but a footing nonetheless: a set of authorial and readerly practices that may always be *in medias res* ("fleeting," "[un]stable," "shifting," "changing," "[in]substantial") and always subject to change—because every new installment or every new generic variation must do things differently, even if only slightly so—but nonetheless ongoing and hence potentially pleasurable and self-reinforcing. Lorrimer's ambiguous sentiments ("hopes and fears, deceits and confidences, joys and miseries") describe modern urban experience in terms that evoke the serial dialectic of seductive promise and addictive curse: on the one hand, better and better stories, increasing aesthetic pleasures; on the other hand, the need to invest more and more time, money, and emotions in the consumption of a serial text that may never provide a gratifying sense of closure ("strapped to a fellow's back"). In such an uncertain state, all that is left to do is purchase more entertainment and enjoy the ephemeral gratification it offers. In the case of Lippard, a prime peddler of literary wares even though he professed to abhor "heartless monopoly and godless capital" (*New York: Its Upper Ten and Lower Million* [1970: 165]), this type of self-destructive consumption threatened to outmatch the political thrust of his fiction. If readers really enjoyed his novel "till the last nerve loses its delicacy of sense," then there was little hope that they would join the struggle for social reform and political change. For the development of American popular culture, however, this type of consumption was anything but destructive. While the political impact of the city mysteries waned with the onset of the Civil War, the narrative forms and literary practices they initiated remain effective to this day.

BIBLIOGRAPHY

Altschuler, Glenn C. and Stuart M. Blumin (2000). *Rude Republic: Americans and Their Politics in the Nineteenth Century*. Princeton: Princeton University Press.
Altschuler, Sari (2015). "'Picture it all, Darley': Race Politics and the Media History of George Lippard's *The Quaker City*." *Nineteenth-Century Literature* 70.1: 65–101.
Anderson, Benedict (1991). *Imagined Communities: Reflections on the Origin and Spread of Nationalism* [1983]. London: Verso.
Ashwill, Gary (1994). "The Mysteries of Capitalism in George Lippard's City Novels." *ESQ* 40.4: 293–317.
Börnstein, Heinrich (1853). *Die Geheimnisse von St. Louis* [1851]. St. Louis: Verlag des Anzeigers des Westens.
Buntline, Ned (1848). *Mysteries and Miseries of New York: A Story of Real Life*. New York: Berford.
Denning, Michael (1998). *Mechanic Accents: Dime Novels and Working-Class Culture in America*. New York: Verso.
Eco, Umberto (1990). "Interpreting Serials." *The Limits of Interpretation*. Bloomington: Indiana University Press. 83–100.
Ehrlich, Heyward (1972). "The 'Mysteries' of Philadelphia: Lippard's *Quaker City* and 'Urban' Gothic." *ESQ* 18: 50–65.
Emerson, D. Berton (2015). "George Lippard's *The Quaker City*: Disjointed Text, Dismembered Bodies, Regenerated Democracy." *Nineteenth-Century Literature* 70.1: 102–31.
Erikson, Paul J. (2005). PhD Diss. Welcome to Sodom: The Cultural Work of City-Mystery Fiction in Antebellum America. Austin: University of Texas Press.
Fluck, Winfried (1997). *Das kulturelle Imaginäre: Eine Funktionsgeschichte des amerikanischen Romans, 1790–1900*. Frankfurt: Suhrkamp.
Gardner, Jared (2012a). *The Rise and Fall of Early American Magazine Culture*. Urbana: University of Illinois Press.
——— (2012b). *Projections: Comics and the History of Twenty-First-Century Storytelling*. Stanford: Stanford University Press.
Hayward, Jennifer (1997). *Consuming Pleasures: Active Audiences and Serial Fictions from Dickens to Soap Opera*. Lexington: University Press of Kentucky.

Helwig, Timothy (2006). "Denying the Wages of Whiteness: The Racial Politics of George Lippard's Working-Class Protest." *American Studies* 47.3/4: 87–111.
Herminghouse, Patricia (1985). "Radicalism and the 'Great Cause': The German-American Serial Novel in the Antebellum Era." *America and the Germans: An Assessment of a Three-Hundred-Year History*. Vol. 1. *Immigration, Language, Ethnicity*. Ed. Frank Trommler and Joseph McVeigh. Philadelphia: University of Pennsylvania Press. 306–20.
Jahn-Sudmann, Andreas and Frank Kelleter (2012). "Die Dynamik serieller Überbietung: Amerikanische Fernsehserien und das Konzept des Quality-TV." *Populäre Serialität: Narration—Evolution—Distinktion. Zum seriellen Erzählen seit dem 19. Jahrhundert*. Ed. Frank Kelleter. Bielefeld: Transcript-Verlag. 205–24.
Kelleter, Frank (2002). *Amerikanische Aufklärung: Sprachen der Rationalität im Zeitalter der Revolution*. Paderborn: Schöningh.
———, ed. (2012). *Populäre Serialität: Narration—Evolution—Distinktion. Zum seriellen Erzählen seit dem 19. Jahrhundert*. Bielefeld: Transcript-Verlag.
Kelleter, Frank and Daniel Stein (2012). "Autorisierungspraktiken seriellen Erzählens: Zur Gattungsentwicklung von Superheldencomics." *Populäre Serialität: Narration—Evolution—Distinktion. Zum seriellen Erzählen seit dem 19. Jahrhundert*. Ed. Frank Kelleter. Bielefeld: Transcript-Verlag. 259–90.
Klauprecht, Emil (1854). *Cincinnati, oder Geheimnisse des Westens*. Cincinnati: Schmidt.
Knight, Stephen (2012). *The Mysteries of the Cities: Urban Crime Fiction in the Nineteenth Century*. Jefferson: McFarland.
Lehuu, Isabelle (2000). *Carnival on the Page: Popular Print Media in Antebellum America*. Chapel Hill: University of North Carolina Press.
Lippard, George (1970). *New York: Its Upper Ten and Lower Million* [1853]. Upper Saddle River: Gregg Press.
———(1995). *The Quaker City; or, The Monks of Monk Hall: A Romance of Philadelphia Life, Mystery, and Crime* [1844–45]. Ed. David S. Reynolds. Amherst: University of Massachusetts Press.
Looby, Christopher (1993). "George Thompson's 'Romance of the Real': Transgression and Taboo in American Sensation Fiction." *American Literature* 65.4: 651–72.
———(2004). "Southworth and Seriality: *The Hidden Hand* in the *New York Ledger*." *Nineteenth-Century Literature* 59.2: 179–211.
———(2015). "Lippard in Part(s): Seriality and Secrecy in *The Quaker City*." *Nineteenth-Century Literature* 70.1: 1–35.
Lund, Michael (1993). *America's Continuing Story: An Introduction to Serial Fiction, 1850–1900*. Detroit: Wayne State University Press.
Maase, Kaspar (2010). *Was macht Populärkultur politisch?* Wiesbaden: VS.
Meer, Sarah (2005). *Uncle Tom Mania: Slavery, Minstrelsy and Transatlantic Culture in the 1850s*. Athens: University of Georgia Press.
Okker, Patricia (2003). *Social Stories: The Magazine Novel in Nineteenth-Century America*. Charlottesville: University of Virginia Press.
———, ed. (2011). *Transnationalism and American Serial Fiction*. London: Routledge.
Ostrowski, Carl (2006). "Slavery, Labor Reform, and Intertextuality in Antebellum Print Culture: The Slave Narrative and the City-Mysteries Novel." *African American Review* 40.3: 493–506.
Reizenstein, Ludwig Freiherr von (2002). *Die Geheimnisse von New-Orleans* (1854–55). Ed. Steve Rowan. Shreveport: Éditions Tintamarre.
Reynolds, David S. (1995). "Introduction." George Lippard, *The Quaker City; or, The Monks of Monk Hall: A Romance of Philadelphia Life, Mystery, and Crime*. [1844–45] Ed. David S. Reynolds. Amherst: University of Massachusetts Press. vii–xliv.
———(2015). "Deformance, Performativity, Posthumanism: The Subversive Style and Radical Politics of George Lippard's *The Quaker City*." *Nineteenth-Century Literature* 70.1: 36–64.

Reynolds, David S. and Kimberly R. Gladman (2002). "Introduction." *Venus in Boston and Other Tales of Nineteenth-Century City Life*. Ed. David S. Reynolds and Kimberly R. Gladman. Amherst: University of Massachusetts Press. ix–liv.

Rowan, Steven (1990). "The Return of Henry Boernstein." *The Mysteries of St. Louis*. Ed. Steven Rowan and Elizabeth Sims. Chicago: Kerr. vii–xv.

Rowan, Steven (2002). "Introduction: Searching for a Key to *The Mysteries*." Baron Ludwig von Reizenstein. *The Mysteries of New Orleans*. Ed. Steven Rowan. Baltimore: Johns Hopkins University Press. xiii–xxxiii.

Schuchalter, Jerry (2011). "*Ja, die Wirklichkeit ist oft grausamer [. . .] als die schreckenvollste Phantasie*: Amerika und der deutsche Geheimnisroman." *Amerika im europäischen Roman um 1850: Varianten transatlantischer Erfahrung*. Ed. Alexander Ritter. Wien: Praesens. 327–42.

Smith, Susan Belasco (1995). "Serialization and the Nature of *Uncle Tom's Cabin*." *Periodical Literature in Nineteenth-Century America*. Ed. Kenneth M. Price and Susan Belasco Smith. Charlottesville: University Press of Virginia. 69–89.

Sollors, Werner (2001). "German-Language Writing in the United States: A Serious Challenge to American Studies?" *The German-American Encounter: Conflict and Cooperation between Two Cultures, 1800–2000*. Ed. Frank Trommler and Elliott Shore. New York: Berghahn. 103–14.

Stein, Daniel (2012). "Spoofin' Spidey—Rebooting the Bat: Immersive Story Worlds and the Narrative Complexities of Video Spoofs in the Era of the Superhero Blockbuster." *Film Remakes, Adaptations and Fan Productions: Remake/Remodel*. Ed. Kathleen Loock and Constantine Verevis. Basingstoke: Palgrave Macmillan. 231–47.

——— (2013). "Superhero Comics and the Authorizing Functions of the Comic Book Paratext." *From Comic Strips to Graphic Novels: Contributions to the Theory and History of Graphic Narrative*. Ed. Daniel Stein and Jan-Noël Thon. Berlin: De Gruyter. 155–89.

——— (2014a). "Popular Seriality, Authorship, Superhero Comics: On the Evolution of a Transnational Genre Economy." *Media Economies: Perspectives on American Cultural Practices*. Ed. Marcel Hartwig, Evelyne Keitel, and Gunter Süß. Trier: WVT. 143–67.

——— (2014b). "Race, Gender, Sex, Class, Nation: Serienpolitik zwischen Sehnsucht und Heimsuchung in Ludwig von Reizensteins *Die Geheimnisse von New-Orleans* (1854–1855)." *Sehnsucht suchen? Amerikanische Topographien aus komparatistischer Perspektive*. Ed. Simone Sauer-Kretschmer and Christian A. Bachmann. Berlin: Bachmann. 39–69.

——— (2016). "Transatlantic Politics as Serial Networks in the German-American City Mystery Novel, 1850–1855." *Traveling Traditions: Nineteenth-Century Cultural Concepts and Transatlantic Intellectual Networks*. Berlin: De Gruyter. 247–65.

Stewart, David M. (2008). "Consuming George Thompson." *American Literature* 80.2: 233–63.

——— (2011). *Reading and Disorder in Antebellum America*. Columbus: The Ohio State University Press.

Streeby, Shelley (2002). *American Sensations: Class, Empire, and the Production of Popular Culture*. Berkeley: University of California Press.

Thompson, George (2002). *City Crimes; or Life in New York and Boston* [1849]. *Venus in Boston and Other Tales of Nineteenth-Century City Life*. Ed. David S. Reynolds and Kimberly R. Gladman. Amherst: University of Massachusetts Press. 105–310.

Tompkins, Jane (1985). *Sensational Designs: The Cultural Work of American Fiction, 1790–1860*. New York: Oxford University Press.

Zboray, Ronald J. and Mary Saracino Zboray (2000). "The Mysteries of New England: Eugène Sue's American 'Imitators,' 1844." *Nineteenth-Century Contexts* 22.3: 457–92.

CHAPTER 4

Serial Entertainment / Serial Pleasure
The Yellow Kid

CHRISTINA MEYER

INTRODUCTION

"Dear Santa Claus: Bring me some houses, a little table and dishes and a yellow kid" (Dillon 1898: 8). This chapter will put into the spotlight the comic figure—the Yellow Kid—mentioned by a reader of the *Omaha World-Herald* in a letter to the editor from 1898. The Yellow Kid figure first appeared in early 1893 in the newly introduced colored Sunday newspaper supplements. It then rapidly developed from an occasional into a regular, weekly feature (in color and as a half-page or full-page comic-tableau or spread) in the Sunday "Comic Weekly" supplement of Joseph Pulitzer's New York *World* from late 1895 onwards.[1] This chapter aims to decode the serial logic of the

---

1. On comic "tableaux" see Blackbeard 1995: 36; on "spreads" see Soper 2005: 275. The first colored Sunday supplement of Pulitzer's *World* was printed in 1893; it contained illustrations, short human-interest stories, and other prose miscellanea, as well as a number of one-panel and multipanel cartoons. A year later, Pulitzer printed a separate "Comic Weekly" section in his Sunday *World*. From 1896 onwards, this originally four-page section was increased to eight pages filled with single-panel or multipanel comics, full-page or half-page comic-tableaux, other forms of graphic comic art, and short prose texts. The Sunday comic sections were, to borrow from Tom De Haven's novel *Funny Papers* (1985), "color wraparound[s]," into which the news and other parts of the newspapers were embedded (see De Haven 1985: 93, Baker/Brentano 2005: 31, and Harvey 2009: 38). Their impact was enormous. Circulation figures of

Yellow Kid and to situate this comic figure in the larger research field and theoretical framework of popular seriality. To do so, it will first flesh out the serial-consuming practices and the aesthetic patterns of the Yellow Kid comic-tableaux. Second, since the Yellow Kid quickly started to circulate in all kinds of formats (e.g., merchandise, posters, and advertisements), this chapter will broaden its analysis to include the figure's proliferation into areas other than the Sunday supplements and in embodiments other than two-dimensional newspaper drawings.

The story of the "birth" of Mickey Dugan—as the Yellow Kid is officially called—is well-known and shall thus be recounted only briefly. The Yellow Kid is a bald, round-headed child with jug ears and buck teeth, who walks barefoot through the streets of New York City, clothed in a long, yellow nightshirt emblazoned with words in dialect spelling. Together with an entourage of animals (a goat, a green parrot, a black cat, and a dog) and other children (Liz, Kitty Dugan, and Molly Brogan among others), he lives in the middle of the fictitious tenement district "Hogan's Alley." Each Sunday, the readers of Pulitzer's colored comic supplement in *The World* encountered a new event in the life of Mickey Dugan. A few months after the American cartoonist and illustrator Richard Felton Outcault had started this Sunday comics series, he left Pulitzer's paper to work for Pulitzer's rival, William Randolph Hearst, the owner of the *New York Journal*. Following Outcault's departure from *The World*, however, the Yellow Kid "community" did not disappear from the Sunday comic supplement.[2] Instead, there were now two versions of the serialized Yellow Kid tableaux that New York residents were met with each Sunday.[3] Outcault produced Yellow Kid pages for Hearst's Sunday supplement, which was titled "American Humorist," and George Benjamin Luks (remembered today as one of "The Eight" Ashcan artists) was assigned by Pulitzer to continue the successful Yellow Kid series in the Sunday *World*. While Pulitzer's paper published each Yellow Kid adventure under the heading "Hogan's Alley,"

New York newspapers are listed in Ayer & Son's *American Newspaper Annual* (1896: 507–76). On the "discrepancy between reported circulation and the actual readership," see Johanningsmeier 1997: 17. Overviews of the emergence of the Yellow Kid are provided by Blackbeard 1995, Gordon 1998, Wood 2004, and Balzer/Wiesing 2010.

2. I should mention here that Outcault stopped drawing "Hogan's Alley" episodes, but he still penned one-panel cartoons for Pulitzer's Sunday comic supplement. Outcault's name thus did not entirely disappear from *The World*.

3. The Yellow Kid pages were consumed not only by New Yorkers but also by readers outside the city. The comics were disseminated in other newspapers as well, though often with a week delay; see, for example, Outcault's first episode for Hearst's *Journal* (October 18, 1896), which appeared a few days later in *The Denver Evening Post* (with minor changes in the narrative columns in the background; compare Outcault/Townsend 1896a: 9).

the episodes of Outcault's Yellow Kid pages in Hearst's Sunday comic supplement carried the title "McFadden's Row of Flats." The collaboration between Outcault and the author Edward Waterman Townsend began with the first "McFadden's Row" episode. In the "McFadden's Row" series, Townsend, who was well known for his serialized "Chimmie Fadden" stories (published in the *New York Sun*), wrote short narrative columns, and Outcault contributed the illustrations.[4] Just three months later, in January 1897, Outcault/Townsend stopped working on the "McFadden's Row" series, and Outcault started to create another Yellow Kid series (in collaboration with Rudolph Edgar Block, then editor of the Sunday supplement), which depicted the Kid and his friends on a number of adventures abroad in the serial "Around the World with the Yellow Kid" (January to May 1897).[5] Parallel to his work on the Yellow Kid spin-off, Outcault continued to contribute one-panel, self-contained Yellow Kid pages as well as half-page panel sequences (usually made up of two rows) to the "American Humorist." The protagonist of the Sunday pages also soon appeared on weekdays, in "Leaflets from the Yellow Kid's Diary" in the editorial page of the main news section in Hearst's *New York Journal*. Furthermore, Outcault illustrated the so-called Huckleberry Volunteers, a short-running Yellow Kid series for Hearst's *Evening Journal*, which contributed to the war effort against Cuba.[6] In Luks's "Hogan's Alley" series for Pulitzer's *World*, the kid branched out even further; from December 1896 onwards, it was joined by the "yellow twins" Alex and George (Luks 1896a: 4).[7] As Robert Gambone states, "This background" of two (at times three) simultaneous and competing Yellow Kid series in two competing newspapers "raises a host of complex issues," involving "the relationship between style, aesthetic, and originality, technological innovation, and the market context of the comics" (2009: 131).

Against this backdrop, this chapter will unfold the serial logic of the Yellow Kid, developing a twofold argument: My contention is that the Yellow Kid's success and popularity hinge on the figure's seriality—and *serial* here does not only refer to the comic figure's cyclic repetition in the Sunday supplement

---

4. Townsend and Outcault worked together again when they published the fictional autobiography of the Yellow Kid, an illustrated story of the kid's "sweet young life" (Townsend/Outcault 1897).

5. I call Outcault/Block's "Around the World" a comics serial instead of a series because even though the episodes are self-contained, they narrate a linear, chronological story, with a clear beginning (departure from New York) and end (return to New York).

6. "The Huckleberry Volunteers" pages were published Fridays on the final page of Hearst's *Evening Journal* (April 8, 1898, to April 22, 1898); the text columns were written by Paul West. Copies of this series are reproduced in Blackbeard 1995: 118–25.

7. These yellow twins later appeared in their own comics series titled "Little Nippers" in Pulitzer's newspaper.

comics and its expansive, nationwide dissemination, but *serial* also means proliferation across media. I furthermore argue that the Yellow Kid's serial logic—a logic of sprawl and proliferation, and a logic of multiplication and replication—is embedded in and spawned by the economic structures, technologies, and ideologies of capitalist culture.[8]

THE YELLOW KID—SERIAL ENTERTAINMENT?

"Capitalism and modern industrial technology," writes Dana Brand, "produce an immense and perpetually renewing spectacle of commodities and images. [. . .] There is a surplus of signifiers and a dearth of signification." She continues that while "it is possible to bathe in such a world, to collect images, or to enjoy the way in which they rapidly succeed each other, [. . .] it is harder to be oriented, rooted, or convinced of the solidity or permanence of anything one believes or observes." Thus, "the paradoxical nature of modern experience, understood in this way, has had an inevitable impact on the way in which art is produced and perceived" (1991: 2–3). This essay will build on these observations and argue that the Yellow Kid comic-tableaux responded to needs and offered consumption practices that the products and practices of other cultural fields of modernity did not afford, or rather afforded in ways other than those of the Yellow Kid pages. Against the backdrop of Jared Gardner's claim that comics are "the most important of the new vernacular modernisms [. . .] [which] diagram the serial complexities of modern life and fix the fragments of modernity on the page [. . . to be] repeatedly viewed and analyzed" (2012: 7, 19), my contention is that the visual and verbal "signs" in the Yellow Kid comic pages enabled new reading practices and offered different platforms of identification.

For example, in the context of continued serial narration in periodic media, the Yellow Kid pages in the Sunday supplements played a special role: apart from being huge, colorful, and eye-catching, newspaper comic pages were cheaper than established magazines and six-cent dailies. In addition, they were widely available (including outside New York), and they catered to a heterogeneous readership encompassing different social, ethnic, and economic backgrounds.[9] Illiteracy, for instance, was no impediment to enjoying

---

8. On serial figures, see Denson/Mayer 2012 and Mayer 2014: 7–12.

9. On consumption practices and target audiences of serialized narratives in nineteenth-century periodicals, see Hayward 1997: 21–83. For other forms of mass entertainment in the late nineteenth century, for example, vaudeville or early cinema, see Allen 1980 (especially chapters 2–4).

newspaper comics. The pages invite visual scanning and searching without necessarily forcing consumers to delve into compositional details or read the words. Readers with both visual and verbal literacy could filter the pages according to their preferences and needs. This was due to the tableaux' heterogeneous composition, meaning, on the one hand, their combination of competing modal elements (e.g., words, pictures, and lines to indicate spatial relationships). On the other hand, or rather in addition to that, the heterogeneous composition included diverse, at times conflicting, political messages and ideological disputes, which offered different forms of reader engagement, for example, identification, distancing, confirmation, and criticism. In short, there is something for everybody—or to quote Lisa Yaszek: "Audiences coming from various discursive formations may all laugh at the Yellow Kid, but the joke may be different for these various readers, depending on their sociohistorical positions" (1994: 30). Yasek's claim is echoed in Blackbeard's study, in which he speaks about the accessibility of the pages to "a wide spectrum of readers" and their "operat[ing] on multiple levels" (1995: 72). This ambivalence, or rather this coexistence of manifold reading possibilities, is crucial for understanding the meaning-making processes of early comics series.[10] In a different context, Charles Hatfield reflects on comics as the "art of tensions" and succinctly states that comics "are always characterized by a plurality of messages": they are "composed of several kinds of tension, in which various ways of reading—various interpretative options and potentialities—must be played against each other" (2009: 132).

Yet, in order to reach large audiences, the mass-produced colored comics in the Sunday supplements also relied on highly standardized, formulaic elements which readers would re-encounter every week with only slight variations. In the Yellow Kid comics, it is mostly the protagonist that establishes coherence between episodes. In his semibiographical account "How the Yellow Kid Was Born," Outcault explains: "He never grows up, or, if he does, he immediately reincarnates himself in his old form and goes through the same programme again" (1898: 7).[11] Interestingly, the Yellow Kid himself comments on his status as a recurrent, easily recognizable serial comic figure.

---

10. The audiences addressed in the Yellow Kid tableaux are diffuse. In Outcault and Townsend's "McFadden's Row" series, for example, the artists offer multiple identificatory choices not only by means of the visual representations in the individual episodes but also through a diversity of voices and perspectives in the narrative depictions. In a larger project still in progress, I will offer case studies to demonstrate the multiple reading options in the Yellow Kid comic-tableaux.

11. This essay was also printed in Pulitzer's *St. Louis Post-Dispatch* (same day, page 7 in the comic supplement).

In the fictional autobiography *The Yellow Kid in McFadden's Flats* (1897), the first-person narrator explains to his readers: "If I didn't [remove all the dirt from the yellow dresses so often] you wouldn't know they were yellow, and if you didn't know that I'd have to be introduced to you every time I met you, dear reader, unless you might remember me by me sweet and innocent smile" (Townsend/Outcault 1897: 16).[12] Apart from that, coherence is established by what we might call *serial surroundings*: the Yellow Kid's entourage, that is, the stock figures who resurface each week (such as Molly, Liz, and Slippy Dempsey) and recurring animals (such as the goat, the parrot, and the cat). In more general terms, Gardner speaks of the *"repeated* interaction of *fixed* and *predictable* 'types' within the new urban environment, bounded by a crowded visual plane and within a *limited* narrative time" (2012: 7; emphases added). Such schematized repetitions are, of course, intimately tied to the production culture of nineteenth-century newspapers, including the technological capabilities of the printing press and the working conditions of newspaper artists. As journalist George Clark summarized it in 1902:

> Hasty and necessarily coarse engraving, stereotyping on the eight-minute-per-plate order, cylinder presses run at high speed, poor paper, and cheap, gray ink are the bugbears of the newspaper artist's existence. These are the factors over which he has no control. They are determined by the very nature of the newspaper business, and the artist is forced to bow to the inevitable and adapt himself to the conditions imposed upon him. (70)

It should be noted here that it was not only the periodicity of mass papers (or the serial mode of their publication) that allowed newspaper comics to spread throughout the country. The rapid and extensive dissemination of the Yellow Kid pages outside New York was also made possible by an elaborate distribution system (e.g., syndication and street sales) dependent on modern transportation infrastructure (the transcontinental railroad, extended postal service, even telegraphy).[13]

The "repetitive redundancy" on which Yellow Kid episodes are founded—their inherent principle of "serialized, ritualized disorder"—explains what

---

12. On the "iconic simplicity" of this comic figure, see Soper 2005: 289.

13. On newspaper syndication, see Johanningsmeier 1997. Henkin (2006) offers an overview of postal services in the nineteenth century. On services to rural areas, see Fuller 1964. On the "special trains" delivering the Sunday editions to readers not living in rural areas or smaller towns, see Johanningsmeier 1997: 23. On telegraphic services, see Nalbach 2003. Hearst's *Journal*, on October 25, 1896, proudly announced the transmission of pictures via telegraph, one of which was a picture of the Yellow Kid ("Here Are" 31).

Gardner calls the "recursive seriality of the comic" (2012: 21).[14] This is important: the newspaper comic pages were based on a noncontinuous, nonlinear type of "discontinuous seriality" (Gardner 2012: 24), and it was because (and not despite) of this that the Yellow Kid gained in popularity. However, repetitive redundancy, availability, accessibility, and readability tell only half the story. The other half concerns the intramedial competition between two series in two different newspapers, which tended to increase aesthetic and narrative complexity rather than standardize narrative and visual strategies. Among other things, this complexity manifests itself in the ways in which the comic pages engage in self-reflexivity.[15] Both Outcault and Luks turned their rivalry into a recurrent and very visible topic of their comics, for example, by reciprocally poking fun at each other in caricatured portraits or by implicitly commenting on issues of copyright and plagiarism (Meyer 2012a/b). Moreover, the artists stylize themselves as participants in their own stories, both in "Hogan's Alley" and "McFadden's Row." An example of this comes in the "Football" episode of Outcault/Townsend, where the narrative voice in the text columns explains: "Outcault was there with me, and his pencil caught the scene just at that exciting moment when the Kid finished a run [...] and made a touchdown, which won the game. The picture shows the glory of that moment" (1896c: 5). In addition, the periodicity and the material constraints of newspapers are alluded to at both the level of plot and visual (self-)representation. For example, at the bottom of Luks's "New Year's Celebration in Hogan's Alley" there is a character whose body is only partially visible to the reader. In the accompanying speech balloon, the words read: "I'M SO FAT DEY KUD ONEY GIT HAF OF ME ON DIS PAGE" (Luks 1896b: 4).[16] Of course, the illustration is funny because the visual representation of the cut-off body mimics the verbal comment using abbreviated speech in the speech balloon, but to see this as simply an entertaining gimmick would miss the whole truth. Both verbally and visually, the tongue-in-cheek comment draws attention to the size and the borders of a newspaper page, that is, the constraints of the tableau's medium. Aesthetic operations are marked as such (Kelleter 2012, on self-observational principles of serial narratives). Such "self-referential loops" (Mayer 2014: 13) illustrate that the serial mode of the Yellow Kid comic-tableaux is defined not only by a formula of repetition (recurrent protagonist and entourage) and variation (different settings or themes) but also, and more

---

14. On recursive seriality, see also Kelleter/Stein 2009 and Kelleter 2012: 21–28.

15. For a discussion of self-reflexivity as self-observation, see Kelleter/Stein 2009.

16. This is not the only "Hogan's Alley" episode in which the unnamed male figure appears to comment both on his own physical status and on the materiality of the newspaper page; compare also Luks 1897a: 5; and Luks 1897c: 4.

importantly, by medial self-reflexivity and the multimodal tensions built into the pages.[17]

However, when we speak about the serial logic of the Yellow Kid, we need to look not only at the Sunday pages but also at the figure's numerous other two- and three-dimensional manifestations which spread throughout the country. What happens when a serial figure exits its original space—in this case, the Sunday newspaper page—and "emancipates itself from the literary grid [in this case, the newspaper comic grid, C. M.] from which it emanates" (Mayer 2014: 8)? This is the next section's main focus of inquiry.

PROLIFERATIONS OF THE YELLOW KID, OR HOW IT WENT VIRAL

The serial pleasures of the Yellow Kid have everything to do with the prolific, unstoppable proliferation of the figure outside the Sunday supplement pages. In the conservative press, the Sunday supplement child was (unsurprisingly) viewed with suspicion due to its rapid and widespread invasion into various spheres of public and private life, seemingly threatening to influence audiences negatively. The Yellow Kid was considered contagious, an "epidemic," "more violent than the small-pox, and almost as far-reaching in its results" (Slocum 1903: 491).[18]

Next to weekly Sunday comic-tableaux, copies of Yellow Kid pictures appeared in newspapers in the wanted ads sections; in announcements promoting the next Sunday edition of *The World* and the *Journal*; and in advertisements for clothes, watches, and many other products (Ingersoll 1896: 8). Altered yet recognizable versions of the Yellow Kid appeared in paneled cartoons and comic-tableaux penned by other artists (Shultz 1897: 5). Furthermore, the kid was utilized as a foil for caricatures of politicians, social reformers, and bosses in magazines such as *Judge* or *Vim*, and he had guest appearances in political cartoons and other publications.[19] In 1897,

---

17. Mayer's study focuses on the serial figure of Fu Manchu.

18. In my current research project, I will discuss in greater detail the public debates (in books, pamphlets, magazine essays, and newspaper articles) that accompanied the transmedial spread of the Yellow Kid.

19. In Pulitzer's *World*, the artist Walt McDougall produced cover-page illustrations for the Sunday "Comic Weekly." In McDougall's "New York's Great Reform Freak Show" (1897), Republican Senator Thomas Collier Platt is represented as an elderly (white-bearded) "Yellow Kid of Parkhurst Alley" with the typical features of the Yellow Kid: the big, round head, ears that stick out, a boyish physique, and a yellow nightshirt emblazoned with words. For Hearst's *Journal*, the artist Cory drew a number of political cartoons in 1896, with Yellow Kid versions

a forty-eight-page magazine titled *The Yellow Kid* was in circulation, providing even more illustrations of the kid for readers and fans.[20] Additional versions of the figure could be found on posters promoting the Sunday supplement, which were plastered throughout the city. The Yellow Kid also appeared as a character onstage in theater adaptations (e.g., Frank Dumont's "The Yellow Kid Who Lives in Hogan's Alley, A Burlesque," a play first performed in Philadelphia and New York in 1896, which then ran successfully throughout the country), and the figure adorned music sheet covers and was celebrated in songs such as "The Dugan Kid Who Lives in Hogan's Alley" (words by Wm. H. Friday Jr.; music by Homer Tourjée) or in C. E. Vandersloot's two-step piano play "Yellow Kids on Parade" (1897). And there is more: merchandise featuring the comics hero included pet-shaped chewing gum, Yellow Kid candy, Yellow Kid pin-back buttons (often as giveaways distributed by tobacco companies introducing a new cigarette brand), wooden cigar boxes, puzzles, dolls, trade-cards, and many more commercial "things."[21]

This is how the Yellow Kid became one of the first crossmedia, "transregional" celebrities and national icons, as well as one of the first mass-merchandised products in the final decade of the nineteenth century.[22] Outcault had no control over this process, because his request for copyright protection of the Yellow Kid—he sent a letter to the librarian A. R. Spofford at the Library of Congress on September 7, 1896—did not grant him "any rights over, or protections from, other artists who chose to draw the characters," since "copyright protected specific drawings but did not protect an artist/creator from the use by someone else of established characters in their original

---

at their center. Mutated versions of the kid also appeared on the cover pages of *Judge* magazine in November and December 1896 (e.g., Hamilton 1896).

20. The full title reads *The Yellow Kid. A Semi-Monthly Magazine of Wit, Fiction and Illustration*; the magazine was launched on March 20, 1897. Outcault contributed Yellow Kid drawings for the cover of the first couple of issues.

21. See Mel Birnkrant's website which features a collection of Yellow Kid merchandise (my thanks to Corey Creekmur for pointing this out to me); see also Richard Olson's website with pictures of Yellow Kid collectibles and paraphernalia.

22. I borrow the term *transregional* from Mayer 2014: 16; see also Meyer 2016. The mass-marketing of popular characters in the nineteenth century had begun before the Yellow Kid rose to fame in the 1890s. Examples include the so-called Brownies (created by Canadian-born artist Palmer Cox), who first appeared in the *St. Nicholas* magazine in February 1883. The serialized stories of the Brownies characters were later reprinted in book form. They were also used as advertising tools and became popular children's toys (see Morgan 2003 and Olivier 2011). Before the Yellow Kid and the Brownies, a character named Ally Sloper, who originated in the British humor magazine *Judy,* rose to stardom in England in the 1860s. He was not only popular among working-class readers but also, as Bailey writes, "a cult figure in 'upper Bohemia'" (1983: 4, 9). On Ally Sloper's life outside the print medium, see Sabin 2009.

drawings" (Winchester 1995: 19).²³ Apart from that, the lack of control over plurimedial embodiments of the Yellow Kid had to do with the dynamics of serial proliferation which always involve multiple, interconnected agents.²⁴ In his own account of the Yellow Kid's rapid and ultimately unstoppable rise to fame and popularity—including its great success as a fast-selling commodity (textual and otherwise)—Outcault compares himself to Mary Shelley, who "brought forth a Frankenstein" (1898: 7).²⁵ The Yellow Kid, which spread so quickly in New York and elsewhere, "commenced to loom up, in spite of me," Outcault laments. No wonder, then, that he tells his readers (if tongue-in-cheek), "when I die, don't wear yellow crape, don't let them put a Yellow Kid on my tombstone, and don't allow the Yellow Kid himself to come to my funeral. Make him stay over on the east side, where he belongs" (1898: 7).

In brief, the Yellow Kid was omnipresent in the mid-1890s, both as a recurring character in the Sunday comic supplements and as a figure that branched into other areas and medial forms of the time.²⁶ Transmedial proliferation, commercial interest, and consumer demand resulted in the Yellow Kid's leaving his native confines of the newspaper page. He took on three-dimensional form in a variety of specialized objects catering for a diverse audience. Interestingly, this process, too, is addressed in the comic pages themselves. For example, in Outcault/Townsend's second "McFadden's Row" episode for Hearst's *Journal*, a banner reads: "EVERY TING DESE DAYS IS YALLER KID BUY DE YELLOW KID GLOVE YELLOW KID CIGAR YELLOW FELLER WHEEL &c &c &c &c &c &c SAY!" (1896b). Similarly, in Luks's "Bargain Day" episode in Pulitzer's *World* (1897b: 4), a shop window in the background of the page, which is plastered with posters and pictures of the Yellow Kid, serves to convey the kid's status as an advertising tool.²⁷ A crowd of women, men, girls, and boys stands in front of the shop, whose owner offers all kinds of bargains

---

23. Compare also Gordon 1998: 31. On copyright laws, see Munn 1892: 32–33, 93–101; and Putnam 1896: 1–32. On copyrighting of cartoon characters in the first half of the twentieth century, see Harvard Law Review Association 1954. A famous copyright case is *Outcault v. New York Herald*, 146 Fed. 205 (C. C. S. D. N. Y. 1906), referenced in Callmann 1940: 657–59.

24. Compare this volume's first chapter and what Ruth Mayer calls the "very concrete formal, material, and institutional foundations" (2014: 12) of serial figures.

25. In the 1831 introduction to *Frankenstein*, Mary Shelley compares her book to a monster over which she had lost control. Many thanks to Shane Denson for drawing my attention to this fact.

26. I would like to add that Outcault also taught others how to draw the Yellow Kid. In early 1897, together with Townsend and the *Journal*'s artist E. W. Kemble, he went to the New York penitentiary Sing Sing to give a lecture on drawing. The full-page article of this event features sketches of the Yellow Kid produced by the prisoners, attesting to the figure's easy reproducibility ("Our State Art Studio" 17).

27. For a discussion of this particular page, see Gambone 2009: 132–33.

to his consumers. The window presents a Yellow Kid poster sketched by a funny-looking, strangely dressed artist (a caricature-like version of Outcault) and smaller pictures depicting the comic figure. There are also advertisements for "A COLLAR BUTTON" that show a "YELLOW KID," on sale inside, or an "8 CENTS" Yellow Kid doll.

These examples foreground the visual-verbal strategies used by Outcault and Luks to comment self-reflexively on how profitable their creation was and how it had become a mass-marketed commodity. Consequently, the Yellow Kid pages not only reflect on their own status as newspaper supplements but also historicize themselves as products—and producers—of a burgeoning consumer culture. These two aspects in particular—the figure's plurimediality and self-referential comments about its transmedial "existence"—make the Yellow Kid an interesting case study for questions on the significance, the cultural work, and the "generative force" (Mayer 2014: 13) of serial texts in the late nineteenth century.

CONCLUSION

Habitually, comics historians place the ubiquity of the Yellow Kid in the late nineteenth century in the context of the circulation wars between Pulitzer and Hearst. The established argument is that the Yellow Kid rose to fame because there were two competing versions of the comic series in two rivaling newspapers—or, in different words, because Pulitzer and Hearst put the Sunday supplement child center stage in their competition for readers. However, the Yellow Kid was not only to be found within the newspaper pages but also circulated outside his original carrier medium. He inspired merchandise wares, advertisements, and billboard posters and acted as a name-giver for—or protagonist in—plays, musical scores, and songs. Spilling into different areas of public and recreational life, into theaters and music halls, into the streets (in the form of posters) and private households (embodied in purchasable and collectible articles), the Yellow Kid ought to be seen in the light of a whole range of contemporary cultural practices, in the light of new means of production and distribution, and in the light of innovative revenue strategies.

Unfolding the serial logic of the Yellow Kid in this fashion helps us to reconstruct how this figure operated in diverse ways and forms. They include its use as a two-dimensional, penned comic figure in the Sunday newspaper pages, as a (self-)promotional advertising tool (to sell the newspaper and to sell a variety of consumer products), and as a three-dimensional piece of merchandise. Furthermore, the comic figure was adapted to the theater stage in a number of comic plays; and last, there were sports teams and horses that were named after him (a cursory look through the sports sections of the newspapers brings to light the contexts in which the Yellow Kid name appeared). The Yellow Kid's popularity in the mid-1890s prompts questions concerning not only the marketability but also the consumption of cultural products—by this I mean acts and experiences of consumption such as purchasing, reading (and rereading), storing, sharing, and collecting. Analyzing the Yellow Kid's seriality reveals how consumption habits were normalized. Investigating the Yellow Kid's seriality also reveals how it competed with and borrowed from other cultural products and media of its time.[28] A closer look at the serial logic of the Yellow Kid offers, I suggest, a more complete understanding of the reciprocity of medial, institutional, economic, and formal facets of serial figures as well as their mass appeal.

Phenomena such as the popular Yellow Kid offer insights into cultural practices at specific historical times.[29] This is why it is also well worth reconstructing the multiple reading options inscribed in the Yellow Kid comic pages (e.g., in the visual modes—including color and typography—as well as in words, captions, narratives, and the diverse in-between modes of representation). Gardner's argument that newspaper supplement comics are "crowded field[s] where meaning is both *collaborative and competitive*—between images, between frames, and between reader and writer" (2012: xi, emphasis added; see also Frahm 2010: 43) is enlightening in this regard. Carving out these

---

28. Outcault/Townsend's "Studio Party" episode is an interesting case in point: the episode not only alludes to trompe-l'oeil artwork, and to watercolor and landscape paintings of the nineteenth century (together with explicit references to the *Venus of Milo* and Raphael's cherubs) but also references Sir Frank Dicksee's *Romeo and Juliet* (1884) and refers to sculpture art and bust artworks, the genre of self-portraits, as well as to child portraiture oil paintings (1897: 4). On cross-fertilizations of the Yellow Kid newspaper comics and fine arts painting, see Meinrenken 2009, 2010.

29. In 1898, the Yellow Kid disappeared from the Sunday supplements of *The World* and the *Journal* (one of the reasons for this was that both Luks and Outcault started to work on new assignments—in my current book project I will go into this in greater detail). This does not mean, however, that the comic figure was no longer visible. Stage tours continued into the twentieth century (my findings show that the last announcements for "McFadden's Row" theater productions stem from the years 1902 and 1903). In addition to this, the Yellow Kid made sporadic cameo appearances in other newspaper comics in the first decade of the twentieth century. The fact that images of the Yellow Kid began to reappear and spread once more in the newspapers in the second decade of the twentieth century—in advertisements, predominantly for hardware products—prompts further questions about the residual presence of cultural products in the media, the pathos of advertising, and the ways and extent of consumer gratification.

simultaneous collaborations and competitions, that is, their tensions, friction, ambiguities, and playful or strategic inscriptions, demonstrates that the prolific logic of the Yellow Kid already manifests itself in the newspaper pages, which allows for diverse—and continued—engagement with them.[30] This, I believe, necessitates further research into the question of how ideology ties into the serial aesthetics and practices of the Yellow Kid.

I will conclude with a brief remark on what I have come to understand about the period of the Yellow Kid's popularity (the mid 1890s) and about seriality as a praxis and aesthetic principle: the Yellow Kid emerged in an era of the expansion of commercial mass media and during the growth of consumerism. This chapter took the Yellow Kid's appearance and the comic figure's prolific expansion as a paradigmatic (and symptomatic) example of mass cultural productions at the turn of the century. In fact, the Yellow Kid's ubiquity in the last decade of the nineteenth century showcases cultural formations, practices, and processes. To use Richard Ohmann's wording here, the "processes of commercializing [a] 'product,' regularizing its availability, and attracting large audiences to it" (1998: 29) had a lasting impact. To explain such processes and developments "will not," as Ohmann warns us "necessarily tell much about how mass culture attained its present shape, or about how it works in contemporary society. [. . .] Origins do not determine later outcomes. But neither are they inconsequential" (32). For instance, mass-marketing techniques of comic character licensing for corporate products began with such popular figures as Buster Brown (1902), and comics mass-merchandising really took off from the 1920s onwards (Gordon 1998).

This analysis of the Yellow Kid through the prism of seriality has encouraged us to widen the lens of investigation slightly—and, I hope, has provided new insights into the comic figure's emergence. The Yellow Kid may not have been the first popular comic figure in the history of comics, but its popularity is an unprecedented narrative of serial unfoldings across time, space, and media.[31]

---

30. Outcault's "The Great Bull Fight" episode in Pulitzer's *World* visualizes these proliferations: the page does not seem to be able to hold the Hogan's Alley cast; some of the inhabitants leak onto the next page and mingle with the cartoons and text passages on the opposite page (1896: 6–7).

31. This essay is part of a larger project funded by the German Research Foundation (DFG) and associated with the Popular Seriality Research Unit (PSRU). I would like to thank all who read and critiqued earlier versions of this article, especially Frank Kelleter, and the anonymous readers of The Ohio State University Press; thanks also to Darren Paul Foster for his criticism and significant editorial contributions.

BIBLIOGRAPHY

Allen, Robert C. (1980). *Vaudeville and Film, 1895-1915: A Study in Media Interaction* [1977]. New York: Arno.

Ayer, N. W. & Son. (1896). *Ayer & Son's American Newspaper Annual: Containing a Catalog of American Newspapers, a List of All Newspapers of the United States and Canada, 1896*. June 18, 2013. http://digital.library.unt.edu/ark:/67531/metadc9239/.

Bailey, Peter (1983). "Ally Sloper's Half-Holiday: Comic Art in the 1880s." *History Workshop Journal* 16: 4–31.

Baker, Nicholson and Margaret Brentano (2005). *The World on Sunday: Graphic Art in Joseph Pulitzer's Newspaper (1898-1911)*. New York: Bulfinch.

Balzer, Jens and Lambert Wiesing (2010). *Die Erfindung des Comic*. Bochum: Bachmann.

Birnkrant, Mel (n.d.). "A Guided Tour of the Mel Birnkrant Collection: The Yellow Kid." Melbirnkrant.com. August 8, 2013. http://melbirnkrant.com/collection/page7.html.

Blackbeard, Bill (1995). *R. F. Outcault's The Yellow Kid: A Centennial Celebration of the Kid Who Started the Comics*. Northampton: Kitchen Sink.

Brand, Dana (1991). *The Spectator and the City in Nineteenth-Century American Literature*. Cambridge: Cambridge University Press.

Brown, Joshua (2002). *Beyond the Lines: Pictorial Reporting, Everyday Life, and the Crisis of Gilded Age America*. Berkeley: University of California Press.

Callmann, Rudolf (1940). "Copyright and Unfair Competition." *Louisiana Law Review* 2.4: 648–68.

Clark, George Emory (1902). "Art in the Daily Newspapers." *Brush and Pencil* 10.2: 65–77.

De Haven, Tom (1985). *Funny Papers*. New York: Viking.

Denson, Shane and Ruth Mayer (2012). "Grenzgänger. Serielle Figuren im Medienwechsel." *Populäre Serialität: Narration—Evolution—Distinktion. Zum seriellen Erzählen seit dem 19. Jahrhundert*. Ed. Frank Kelleter. Bielefeld: Transcript-Verlag.185–203.

Dillon, Stanley (1898). "Letter." *Omaha World-Herald* (December 22): 8.

Frahm, Ole (2010). "Every Window Tells a Story: Remarks on the Urbanity of Early Comic Strips." *Comics and the City*. Ed. Jörn Ahrens and Arno Meteling. New York: Continuum. 32–44.

Fuller, Wayne Edison (1964). *RFD: The Changing Face of Rural America*. Bloomington: Indiana University Press.

Gambone, Robert L. (2009). *Life on the Press: The Popular Art and Illustrations of George Benjamin Luks*. Jackson: University Press of Mississippi.

Gardner, Jared (2012). *Projections: Comics and the History of Twenty-First-Century Storytelling*. Stanford: Stanford University Press.

Gordon, Ian (1998). *Comic Strips and Consumer Culture, 1890-1945*. Washington: Smithsonian.

Hamilton, Grant (1896). "The '*Yellowest*' Kid in Tammany Alley." *Judge* 31: n.p.

Harvard Law Review Association (1954). "The Protection Afforded Literary and Cartoon Characters through Trademark, Unfair Competition, and Copyright." *Harvard Law Review* 68.2: 349–63.

Harvey, Robert C. (2009). "How Comics Came to Be." *A Comic Studies Reader*. Ed. Jeet Heer and Kent Worcester. Jackson: University Press of Mississippi. 25–45.

Hatfield, Charles (2009). "An Art of Tensions." *A Comic Studies Reader*. Ed. Jeet Heer and Kent Worcester. Jackson: University Press of Mississippi. 132–48.

Hayward, Jennifer (1997). *Consuming Pleasures: Active Audiences and Serial Fictions from Dickens to Soap Opera*. Lexington: University Press of Kentucky.

Henkin, David M. (2006). *The Postal Age: The Emergence of Modern Communications in Nineteenth Century America*. Chicago: University of Chicago Press.

"Here Are the First Pictures Ever Telegraphed." *New York Journal* (October 25, 1896): 31.

Ingersoll Watch (1896). Advertisement. *The World* (December 20), "Comic Weekly" Supplement: 8.

Johanningsmeier, Charles (1997). *Fiction and the American Literary Marketplace: The Role of Newspaper Syndicates, 1860–1900*. Cambridge: Cambridge University Press.

Jones, Gavin (1999). *Strange Talk: The Politics of Dialect in Literature in Gilded Age America*. Berkeley: University of California Press.

Kelleter, Frank (2012). "Populäre Serialität. Eine Einführung." *Populäre Serialität: Narration—Evolution—Distinktion. Zum seriellen Erzählen seit dem 19. Jahrhundert*. Ed. Frank Kelleter. Bielefeld: Transcript-Verlag. 11–46.

Kelleter, Frank and Daniel Stein (2009). "Great, Mad, New: Populärkultur, serielle Ästhetik und der frühe amerikanische Zeitungscomic." *Comics: Zur Geschichte und Theorie eines populärkulturellen Mediums*. Ed. Stephan Ditschke, Katerina Kroucheva, and Daniel Stein. Bielefeld: Transcript-Verlag. 81–117.

Luks, George Benjamin (1896a). "A Snowball Battle in Hogan's Alley." *The World* (December 20), "Comic Weekly" Supplement: 4.

———(1896b). "New Year's Celebration in Hogan's Alley." *The World* (December 27), "Comic Weekly" Supplement: 4.

———(1897a). "Mistletoe Party in Hogan's Alley." *The World* (January 3), "Comic Weekly" Supplement: 5.

———(1897b). "Bargain Day in Hogan's Alley." *The World* (January 10), "Comic Weekly" Supplement: 4.

———(1897c). "A Cuban Filibustering Expedition in Hogan's Alley." *The World* (January 17), "Comic Weekly" Supplement: 4.

Mayer, Ruth (2014). *Serial Fu Manchu: The Chinese Supervillain and the Spread of Yellow Peril Ideology*. Philadelphia: Temple University Press.

McDougall, Walt (1897). "New York's Great Reform Freak Show." *The World* (January 17), "Comic Weekly" Supplement: 1.

Meinrenken, Jens (2009). "Ver-rückte Bilder! Wenn Kunst- und Bildgeschichte sich im Comic begegnen." *kjl&m* 09.3: 46–52.

———(2010). "Künstlermythen im Zeichen der Avantgarde. Zur Bedeutung der Malerei im amerikanischen Zeitungscomic." *Arbeit am Bild. Ein Album für Michael Diers*. Ed. Steffen Haug et al. Köln: Walther König. 122–26.

Meyer, Christina (2012a). "George Benjamin Luks and the Comic Weeklies of the Nineteenth Century." *Journal of Graphic Novels and Comics* 3.1: 69–83.

———(2012b). "Urban America in the Newspaper Comic Strips of the Nineteenth Century: Introducing the Yellow Kid." *ImageText* 6.2. July 25, 2012. http://www.english.ufl.edu/imagetext/archives/v6_2/meyer/.

———(2016). "Medial Transgressions: Sheet Music—Theater—Advertising." *Journal of Graphic Novels and Comics* 7.3: 293–305.

Morgan, Wayne (2003). "'If Your Grocer Does Not Keep the Ivory Soap': Palmer Cox, The Brownies, and 19th Century Marketing." *The Romance of Marketing History: Proceedings of the Eleventh Conference on Historical Analysis and Research Marketing*. Ed. Eric H. Shaw. Boca Raton: Association for Historical Research in Marketing. 22–29.

Munn & Co. (1892). *The Scientific American Reference Book: A Compendium of Useful Information*. New York: Munn & Co., Office of the Scientific American.

Nalbach, Alex (2003). "'Poisoned at the Source?' Telegraphic News Services and Big Business in the Nineteenth Century." *The Business History Review* 77.4: 577–610.

Ohmann, Richard (1998). *Selling Culture: Magazines, Markets, and Class at the Turn of the Century*. 1996. New York and London: Verso.

Olivier, Marc (2011). "Civilization Inoculated: Nostalgia and the Marketing of Emerging Technologies." *The Journal of Popular Culture* 44.1: 134–57.

Olson, Richard D. (n.d.). "The R. F. Outcault Gallery." Neponset.com. November 19, 2012. http://www.neponset.com/yellowkid/gall.htm.

"Our State Art Studio at Sing Sing." *New York Journal* (February 7, 1897), "American Magazine" Supplement: 17.

Outcault, Richard Felton (1896). "The Great Bull Fight in Hogan's Alley." *The World* (August 23), "Comic Weekly" Supplement: 6–7.

———(1898). "How the Yellow Kid Was Born. The Man Who Created It Tells for the First Time." *The World* (May 1), "Comic Weekly" Supplement: 7.

Outcault, Richard Felton and Edward W. Townsend (1896a). "McFadden's Row of Flats." *The Denver Evening Post* (October 23): 9.

———(1896b). "McFadden's Row of Flats." *New York Journal* (October 25), "American Humorist" Supplement: n.p.

———(1896c). "McFadden's Row of Flats—Inauguration of the Football Season in McFadden's Row." *New York Journal* (November 15), "American Humorist" Supplement: 5.

———(1897). "McFadden's Row of Flats—The Studio Party in McFadden's Flats." *New York Journal* (January 3), "American Humorist" Supplement: 4.

Putnam, George Haven (1896). *The Question of Copyright: Comprising the Text of the Copyright Law of the United States, A Summary of the Copyright Laws at Present in Force in the Chief Countries of the World* [1891]. New York: Knickerbocker.

Sabin, Roger. "Ally Sloper: The First Comics Superstar?" *A Comic Studies Reader*. Ed. Jeet Heer and Kent Worcester. Jackson: University Press of Mississippi, 2009. 177–89.

Shultz, A. B. (1897). "The Advantage of Doing Things Yourself." *The World* (January 17), "Comic Weekly" Supplement: 5.

Slocum, John P. (1903). "Is Richard Outcault an Artist?" *Broadway Magazine* 11.6: 491.

Soper, Kerry David (2005). "From Swarthy Ape to Sympathetic Everyman and Subversive Trickster: The Development of Irish Caricature in American Comic Strips between 1890 and 1920." *Journal of American Studies* 39: 257–96.

Townsend, Edward W. and Richard Felton Outcault (1897). *The Yellow Kid in McFadden's Flats*. New York: G. W. Dillingham.

Winchester, Mark D. (1995). "Litigation and Early Comic Strips: The Lawsuits of Outcault, Dirks and Fisher." *Inks: Cartoon and Comic Art Studies* 2.2: 16–25.

Wood, Mary (2004). "The Yellow Kid on the Paper Stage." Xroads.Virginia.edu. May 20, 2008. http://xroads.virginia.edu/~ma04/wood/ykid/yellowkid.htm.

Yaszek, Lisa (1994). "'Them Damn Pictures': Americanization and the Comic Strip in the Progressive Era." *Journal of American Studies* 28.1: 23–38.

PART II

Cinema

CHAPTER 5

Inevitability of Chance
Time in the Sound Serial

SCOTT HIGGINS

THE SOUND SERIAL has curious temporalities.[1] It is a formula of frantic meandering, of a mad rush to nowhere: a format in which the least probable chance always arrives on schedule. These are very long films, lasting over four hours, and prone to directionless repetition, but the whole is divided into tightly defined chapters, each running on an unforgiving fifteen- to twenty-minute timetable. The sound serial's treatment of time goes hand in hand with its peculiar mix of narrative compression and willful inefficiency. This chapter focuses on the issue of time to account for some of the serial's peculiar appeals and to explore the nature of our engagement with cinematic seriality. I will consider how time operates on two levels: the episode and the cliffhanger.

ZORRO AND LARGE-SCALE MEANDERING

By the end of the 1920s, film serials, which were initially produced for an adult, primarily female audience, had become increasingly marginal and targeted to juvenile audiences.[2] This technological and aesthetic transition at the end of the

---

1. Portions of this chapter appear in Higgins 2016.
2. For a discussion of the transition from adult to juvenile serials, see Vela 2000: 132–275.

decade solidified the youth serial into a sustainable formula.³ Columbia, Universal, Republic, and tiny houses like Mascot, Regal, and Principle Pictures produced over two hundred chapter plays (with twelve to fifteen parts) between 1930 and 1956. During the 1940s, the three larger companies each released about four serials a year, enough to supply independent neighborhood and regional theaters with an episode a week (Moak 1940: 21, 23). This was a minor but remarkably sturdy production trend that folded only when its audience of eight- to sixteen-year olds migrated to television and the studio system was finally dismantled.

The whole of a serial is bound together by an overarching enigma, often the mystery of the villain's identity, a long-range goal involving the hunt for a "weenie," the defeat of the villain's plan, or all three.⁴ We might expect that each episode should present a chapter in the ongoing arc, contributing to the large-scale story's forward progress or filling out the world in the manner of an epic, but the relationship between part and whole is not so intuitive. Some chapters, particularly the first and last installments, bind tightly to the arc; they open up enigmas, refine goals, and generate closure. Most others, though packed with incident, do little to bring the grand narrative closer to its end or to embellish the diegesis with texture and detail. Instead, they engage viewers in smaller-scale story structures, navigating from situation to situation and from problem to solution, which are neither entirely independent of nor in service to the whole. That serial chapters are not additive, building brick by brick toward a greater unity, can be clearly gauged by the amount of "wheel-turning" in any given series. *The Golden God*, the first episode of *Zorro's Fighting Legion* (Witney/English 1939), for example, establishes that the mysterious Don del Oro, who appears to the Yaqui Indians as a sort of Aztec robot, is actually a member of the local council of businessmen seeking control of gold from the San Mendolito Mine.⁵ Zorro arrives to organize his legionnaires, unmask Don del Oro, and free the gold for Benito Juarez' new republic. In the final chapter, *Unmasked*, Zorro reveals and defeats Don del Oro, and President Juarez makes Zorro's confidant Ramon the new governor of San Mendolito.

The ten intervening chapters, however, take a circuitous and digressive route to this climax. Don del Oro and the council play an extended game of

---

3. Though youngsters were the prime market for most serials, they by no means made up the entire audience. Guy Barefoot discusses the large contingent of adult viewers in rural and neighborhood theaters (2011: 167–90).

4. The *weenie* was the industry term for an object of power and value pursued by serial heroes and villains. Pearl White, Pathe's preeminent serial queen, reportedly coined the term (Singer 2001: 208).

5. Most sound serials have two directors who shared responsibilities for the final film. I list both directors in parentheses after the first mention of each title.

cat and mouse with Zorro, neither side making much progress. Zorro protects a gold shipment from attack, but this leads Don del Oro's men to blow up the legion's hideout (chapters 1–2). Zorro and the legion discover a secret room in the mine and a traceable gun dropped by a henchman, but neither clue leads any closer to the villain's unmasking (chapters 3–4). The bad guys hijack Juarez' weapons shipment in order to arm the Yaquis, but Zorro recaptures the guns and delivers them to Juarez (chapters 4–6). Don del Oro turns his attention to Ramon and manages to capture him, his sister Volita, and Zorro, who all escape (chapters 6–7). Zorro then contrives to trap a known henchman who begins to confess, "Don del Oro is . . ." before being impaled by a golden arrow shot by a Yaqui assassin (chapters 7–9). Zorro and Ramon pursue the assassin and discover that Don del Oro uses a water wagon with a secret compartment to transport arms. The promise of progress again turns into a dead end (chapters 10–11). Finally, in the last chapters, Zorro rescues and befriends Kala, a Yaqui prince, who promises to help reveal that Don del Oro is a false god. Even this plan fails, and the alliance with Kala comes to naught.

Any viewer seeking the narrative pleasure of a well-crafted mystery or suspenseful adventure yarn from this story would be doomed to frustration and disappointment. It is only in chapter 12 when Don del Oro kills his two remaining comrades and is about to (again) rally a Yaqui insurrection that Zorro confronts and unmasks him, revealing Pablo, Mendolito's chief justice. Precious few of the previous 205 minutes seem essential to reaching this resolution, and viewers' first reaction to the big reveal might be: Who is Pablo? The fact that *Zorro's Fighting Legion* remains one of the most highly regarded of all sound serials suggests we look elsewhere to explain the form's power.

FLASH AND SMALL-SCALE STRUCTURE

Diffuse and wandering large-scale storytelling is matched to episodes that pack incidents into a tightly defined formula. Sound serial chapters tend to alternate action and exposition in a five-part structure: *A b C d E*.

A, C, and E are action sequences spaced at the start, middle, and end of a typical fifteen- to twenty-minute episode. The remaining two parts (b and d) tend to be dialogue sequences in which heroes and villains lay their plans. This structure was really a method of time management. It ensured that various kinds of storytelling would be compressed and neatly parceled out across the fifteen- to twenty-minute chapter.

The exquisitely silly second episode of *Flash Gordon*, titled *The Tunnel of Terror* (Stephani/Taylor 1936), throws the five-part format into sharp relief.

The chapter runs twenty minutes and fifty seconds, including credits, with recognizable action beats at 2:38, 10:00, and 17:50 (A, C, and E). In part A, Ming the Merciless quickly resolves the previous week's cliffhanger by triggering a safety net to stop Flash and Princess Aura's plunge through a trapdoor toward giant "dragons of death" (three iguanas shot in close-up). The expositional sequence b consists of six minutes of cross-cutting between the heroic earthlings Flash, Dr. Zarkoff, and Dale Arden. The watchwords for serial exposition are speed and repetition. Things seem to be moving quickly even as narration restates the same basic information: Flash wonders where Zarkoff and Dale are; Zarkoff asks after Flash and Dale; Dale and Flash demand to know what happened to the other; and Aura swears to keep them apart.

Then, at 8.5 minutes, the episode explodes into its middle action (part C). A fleet of Gyroships piloted by Lionmen attacks the palace as Flash, conveniently locked in an attack ship of his own, blasts into a dogfight. This battle royale of sparklers, kitchen funnels, and fishing line culminates in a spectacular midair collision and crash. Action continues on a more personal scale as Thun of the Lionmen and Flash climb from the debris of their spacecraft and fight hand-to-hand. Flash handily disarms Thun, and within moments the two are sworn allies. Thun explains, "You spared my life, I will help you free the prisoners of who you speak." At the twelve-minute mark Thun and Flash shake hands closing the "middle action" (as serial screenwriters called it) just in time for the next phase of exposition.[6]

Characters usually specify and embark on plans in part d. In *Tunnel of Terror*, Ming prepares Dale for marriage with his dehumanizer ray, while Flash and Thun learn that the ceremony lies at the end of a tunnel "guarded by large beasts." The cliffhanger, part E, begins when a guard informs Zarkoff that "on the 13th stroke of the sacred gong, the wedding ceremony will be completed." The gong is audible in the tunnel outside the chamber, where a horrible lobster-clawed beast crushes Flash on the eleventh stroke. All appears lost as a wipe to black in the shape of monstrous teeth brings on the title card: "See 'Captured by Sharkmen' Chapter Three of 'Flash Gordon' serial to be shown at this theatre next week."

---

6. This is an event from Alex Raymond's comic, but in the original the Gyroships resolve a situation by interrupting Ming's attempt to use the dehumanizer on Dale. Here, the incident is merely an extravagant means for introducing Thun. From a feature-centric perspective, this action sequence is strikingly arbitrary and all too quickly resolved. Without prior mention or anticipatory cross-cutting, the Lionmen appear from nowhere to deliver the requisite spectacle at the appointed time. The fight breaks the pattern of expository cycling through locations and gets things airborne in an otherwise landlocked episode, but it does not significantly alter the story's direction.

The five-part chapter format is action-oriented but supple. Cliffhangers ensure that each episode opens and closes with a physical trap or challenge for the hero, and almost always a chase or a fight occurs in the middle. With action in the first and last three to four minutes, and in the central two to three minutes, viewers are never far from an exciting incident. This temporal structure accounts for the sound serial's peculiar narrative rhythm. Serials appear fast-paced, moving from incident to incident at breakneck speed. Unlike in feature films, turning points follow quickly upon one another as characters race from space to space and challenge to challenge. In only ten minutes of running time, and perhaps an hour of story time, Flash escapes the lizard pit, evades guards, fights a fleet of Gyroships, befriends Thun of the Lionmen, and battles a lobster beast on his way to rescue Dale.

EXPOSITION ON THE RUN

The serial writer's craft depends on filling screen time with visual action. This became a problem for the expositional stretches, which often consisted of villains or good guys talking to one another seated around a table, shot with minimal coverage.[7] Boardroom scenes could be lethally dull, but the episodes' itineraries kept them brief. For example, Columbia's version of Krypton in *Superman* (Bennet/Carr 1948) has a boardroom where Elders debate global warming (and shaking, and melting). Thankfully, the spectacle of destruction arrives at the appointed minute. The format is pushed to near parody in Columbia's *The Spider's Web* (Horne/Taylor 1938), which alternates, for expositional reasons, between boardroom scenes of the good guys in business suits and bad guys in black cloaks.

These stolid, actionless dialogue scenes create visual drag, and so filmmakers struggled to introduce dynamism and novelty into the proceedings. A common tactic involved building up operational and ritual aesthetics around the routine meetings in the villain's camp. This explains why The Wasp in *Mandrake the Magician* (Deming/Nelson 1939) and The Mask in *Spy Smasher* (Witney 1942) appear to their henchmen over giant television screens and why meetings with El Shaitan in *The Three Musketeers* (Clark/Schaefer 1933) and Don del Oro in *Zorro's Fighting Legion* require ritualistic trappings and mysterious appearances by the master villain. In "Tunnel of Terror," our example from *Flash Gordon,* parts b and d contribute their fair share of

---

7. See, for example, the council meetings in *Dick Tracy vs. Crime Incorporated* (English/Witney 1941).

operational gimmickry, including electrical devices in Zarkov's laboratory and the illuminated dehumanizer ray. Ming's Oracle of Teo is the episode's most bizarre spectacle, shoehorned into the plot. The Oracle consists of the master shot of a dance scene from Universal's 1930 film *Just Imagine* (David Butler), which features thirty bare-breasted chorines cavorting before and climbing on a vaguely Asian demon statue with four arms, two of which lift dancers into the air. The film is apparently in permanent rerun on Mongo. Characters view the image on spaceograph screens, but cutting removes this framing device to directly present the exotic dance for our viewing pleasure. The Oracle's function in the plot disappears in the face of its spectacular strangeness, making it emblematic of the sound serial's preference for parts over wholes.

An alternative method for enlivening exposition involved converting time into space with scenes of characters in transit. This tactic has its roots in the chase, one of cinema's oldest narrative forms dating back to 1904 (Keil 2002: 47). Tom Gunning astutely borrows Mikhail Bakhtin's term the *chronotope* to describe the chase's "fusion of spatial and temporal relations" (1991: 131). Repetitive exposition flies by when clothed in a chronotope. The chase is a basic and foundational narrative structure, a virtual machine of causality, but in serials it can be oddly divorced from the logic of pursuit. Instead, we simply follow our heroes' linear movement through contiguous settings. Travel from point to point—by foot, car, horse, elephant, airplane, submarine, or rocket ship—can form the backbone of a chapter. This convention makes practical sense because travel scenes are easily written and make good use of limited production resources. They can be built from reusable footage (as in the horse riding in *Zorro's Fighting Legion* or any Western serial), staged before rear-projection screens (as in the endless auto pursuits in the *Dick Tracy* serials), and create the impression of a large space by repeating contiguous shots of a single set (as in the caverns of Ming's palace). For the serial dramaturge, scenes of travel impart the urgency of the chase by physically depicting the pursuit of a goal, even if the goal is simply to drive to a warehouse or gas plant across town. In the serial, the chronotope did not require interaction between the battling parties, which might force the story toward closure. The five-part formula sets an external clock on all action, and chases or travel fills the schedule by generating movement and space.

If exposition was an unavoidable part of the formula, it was kept short. Serials achieve narrative compression by dispensing with character development, complex motivations, and fleshed-out relationships. Ming succinctly states his desire to conquer the universe, and Aura her desire to conquer Flash. We know that Dale and Flash care for one another because they keep asking where the other is. Where a feature film might linger, the serial zips ahead.

But for all its linear drive, the serial chapter is repetitive rather than complex. Characters have simple goals and plans to achieve them, and these are subject to near-constant articulation. This creates a kind of situational intensity; all roads lead to the next crisis. Middle actions open room for another regrouping of heroes and villains to once again state their goals and make plans. Compression and repetition forge a cinematic world at once clear, direct, and single-minded but also frantic, compulsive, and focused to the point of obsession.

TRENDS AND VARIATIONS

Peril follows a timetable in serial episodes, and the five-part structure could be filled out in varied ways. Abduction and rescue were the most common building blocks. Columbia's superhero serials produced by Sam Katzman exemplify the basic pattern. In the post-cliffhanger expository sequence, the good guys or the villains formulate plans that involve investigation or the laying of a trap. At the midpoint, the investigating party is captured, or the trap sprung, which leads into another expository sequence setting up a rescue attempt. It all ends with the rescuer imperiled by a situation to be resolved next week. The screenwriters of *Batman and Robin* (Bennet 1949) play with the format in chapter 3, "Robin's Wild Ride," when henchmen lock Vicky Vale in a closet while kidnapping an important scientist. A passing janitor swiftly frees her—no need for heroes. Still, Batman's investigation of the scientist's disappearance leads to his apparent electrocution in the cliffhanger. Because their kidnappings fail, the villains rarely make headway, and the heroes just struggle against an immediate threat. Viewers can fixate on local problems of freeing captives and escaping traps and overlook the lack of progress this affords in solving the big puzzle.

The five-part structure was a resilient armature. As chapter lengths dropped in the late 1940s, the format was compacted. Beginning in 1945 with *Federal Operator 99* (Bennet/Canutt/Grissell 1945), Republic Pictures cut running times to just over thirteen minutes where they would remain until the very end (Mathis 1995: 84). The five-part format maintained its sway, pressed down to lean schedule. Episode 3 of *The Crimson Ghost* (Witney/Brannon 1946) and episode 5 of *Radar Men from the Moon* (Brannon 1952) illustrate the convention. In both cases the middle action is motivated by the villain's need for quick cash to complete his secret weapon (a Cyclotrode Ray and a Raygun, respectively). The heavies are dispatched on an armored car robbery (*Ghost*) and a payroll robbery (*Radar Men*). These crimes fail to raise funds in both cases, but they do provide inconsequential action beats. The *Radar Men* robbery is a particularly dodgy affair. The crime itself is elided, and instead we are treated to a stock footage car chase (likely from a *Dick Tracy* serial), featuring anachronistic 1930s vehicles. In both serials the heavies regroup and plan a new action, which leads to the cliffhanger. The five-part format, which had always admitted a good deal of padding, especially through travel sequences, withstood contracted running times quite well.

NO TIME FOR TEARS

The sound serial's treatment of time correlates to its strikingly narrow emotional range. If melodrama, as Linda Williams proposes, depends on the "dialectic of pathos and action" (2001: 30), then sound serials are clearly unbalanced. Suffering, the violation of innocence, and the recognition of loss are, for Williams, inextricably linked with the thrill of action through which heroes struggle to regain and defend virtue (2001: 30–32). Sound serials rehearse the threat of physical suffering defeated by daring action, but they dissociate the thrill from pathos. Put simply, practically no one cries in a sound serial because there is no time to mourn. Sound serials are built on the premise that loss is reversible, that, as Williams puts it, "'in the nick of time' defies 'too late'" (2001: 35). The staging of pathos, of tears brought on by the recognition of powerlessness, is best suited to early chapters where it can guarantee future success and where our attachment to characters has been brief. When loss occurs even slightly later, as with the second episode murders of Frankie and Betsy's (Frankie Darro and Betsy King Ross) father in *The Phantom Empire* (Brower/Eason 1935) or of Tom Wayne's copilot in *The Three Musketeers* (Clark/Schaefer 1933), the moment is passed quickly over so that the adventure might continue.

Spy Smasher (Witney 1942) illustrates the sound serial's methods for dealing with loss. At the start of chapter 4, "Stratosphere Invaders," Captain Pierre Durand, Spy Smasher's French counterpart, condemns himself to a watery grave in a flooded submarine chamber so that he can jettison the hero to safety through a torpedo tube. The film puts all its eggs in the basket of valiant sacrifice, using Durand's death as a cliffhanger and combining it with a heavy dose of operational gimmickry, including the underwater respirator that he fits to the unconscious Spy Smasher, a gauge marking the rising floodwaters, and the torpedo tube itself. In recompense, Durand receives a scant two lines of dialogue as recognition and remembrance in the next scene. Spy Smasher shows his colleague a French flag that Durand pinned to him, and proclaims,

"Some day I'll fasten that on top of the Eiffel Tower in free Paris, in honor of Pierre Durand. I found this official dispatch in the submarine log, I have every reason to believe it's important." Witney's serial elaborates Durand's death for the sake of action but then sweeps him aside to make room for the next clue in the case. Tears of pathos don't fit the schedule.

NYOKA, TIME, AND CLIFFHANGER PROBLEM SPACES

The requirement of churning out episodes of a more or less standardized length over a predetermined run of twelve or fifteen chapters accounts for much of the sound serial's treatment of time. It is in the cliffhanger endings, however, that things get really interesting. Here the management of time ceases to be a necessary evil and becomes a palpable creative tool. The cliffhanger is where filmmakers expended most of their energy. The first step in screenwriting was to specify the cliffhangers that members of the writing team would then build episodes around (Mathis 1975: vii). In a very real way, the story of each chapter was conceived as a way of getting from one cliffhanger to another, and these cliffhangers are by far the most engaging portions of any serial.

Cliffhangers involve viewers in a suspenseful "problem space" in the sense discussed by Richard Gerrig in his book *Experiencing Narrative Worlds*. For Gerrig, a cognitivist, suspense is a participatory structure that cues viewers to seek some piece of withheld knowledge. The "problem space" analogy compares problem solving to searching a space for information that will allow one to achieve a goal (Gerrig 1993: 82). The contours of the trap and the aim of getting away are clear, but the means of liberation, the escape hatch, remains hidden: "To make the reader really feel suspense, the author must sufficiently constrain the space of possible solutions so that the situation appears beyond hope" (1993: 83). Time is essential to the sound serial's construction of a problem space.

For example, consider the cliffhanger that spans chapters 6 and 7 of Republic's 1942 *Perils of Nyoka*, directed by William Witney. Nyoka has been captured by the Taruegs, a cave-dwelling people who guard the coveted Tablets of Hippocrates, which hold both a cure for cancer and a map to untold treasures. Vultura, queen of the jungle and arch villainess, has infiltrated the Taruegs by posing as their sun goddess, and she orders Nyoka killed in a ritual sacrifice. Rube Goldberg has apparently inspired Taureg ritual. Nyoka is bound and hoisted by a rope running through a pulley on the cave ceiling. Beneath her, the Taruegs ignite a crater full of oil. The other end of the rope is anchored to the floor at the far end of the cavern near the "sun idol," a relief-sculpture with a mirrored lens in its center. On Vultura's command, a Taureg uses his key to open a window on the wall above Nyoka. Light streams in across the cavern and strikes the lens at the center of the idol. The lens magnifies and directs the light to slowly burn the rope. In the final moments of the chapter, the rope snaps, plunging Nyoka into the pool of fire.

This is a clockwork mechanism designed for suspense. The first several steps of the ritual (binding, hoisting, igniting the fire pit, and opening the window) progressively reveal the exact fate that awaits Nyoka. Ritual lends the proceedings a kind of mechanical inevitability. Once the infernal machine is set in motion, the only thing to do is wait for the light beam to burn through the rope. Witney and his editors stretch the event out across fifty-five shots and three minutes five seconds of screen time. The editors construct the situation out of repeated details depicting the trap's operation. This cascade of images includes eleven medium shots of Nyoka's struggle, four close-ups of the burning oil, four views of Vultura and the chief surveying the scene, and six shots (from two camera positions) of the smoking rope. Spatial fragmentation is anchored by a regularly returning master shot of the entire cavern, which repeats eight times. Amid this welter of perspectives, shot thirty-four stands out. A high-angle long shot from above Nyoka pointing down into the cavern, the vertiginous composition packs in nearly all the major elements: the victim, the fire, the ceremonial drummers, as well as Vultura and the chief in the background. This strikingly composed shot is also the scene's last image to be held more than two seconds; it launches the episode's final stretch of furious cutting. Decoupage translates time into physical process; each shot reassures the viewer of the sealed problem space and charts the inevitable. Of course the event only *seems* temporally limited; it is very much open to delay and embellishment given the largely indeterminate time span required for the sun's rays to burn rope. There is no way of knowing how long the execution will take, but formal procedure stands in for a literal ticking clock.

Strong deadlines within the diegesis constrain the problem space, while the episode's running time conditions the storyteller's task and the viewer's awareness of the act of narration. The reason is that cliffhangers entail a curious inflection of Hollywood's standard viewing procedures. They manage knowledge in a predictable way, broadcasting the direction of events with utmost clarity. But unlike its feature-film counterpart, the serial disposes spectators to anticipate interruption and delay rather than closure and resolution. From the moment that the perilous situation begins to take shape, we can rest assured that goals will remain blocked and the story's progress halted. The cliffhanger drives awareness to the moment-by-moment passage of time only to interrupt it. No matter how engrossed in the moment we may become, the weeklong break between episodes ejects us from the scene. The cliffhanger's interruption brings with it vivid cataclysm and a loss of narrational control.

And yet, as the cliffhanger situation comes into focus in the last quarter of the episode's running time, so does our faith in its resolution. As Linda Williams observes, "It is as if the more the temporal prolongation of suspense builds, the more sure we can be that the investment of time will have a successful outcome" (2001: 34). There is no surer sign of the hero's survival than the emphasis on her steadily approaching doom. This dynamic pertains to many formula fictions. Serials, though, present an extreme. The compressed running time of each episode, and the sheer repetition of structures from week to week and from title to title, makes conventions ridiculously conspicuous. Viewers' can confidently anticipate interruption and also assume that the apparently inescapable trap will, in some way, fail.

Paradoxically, knowing the formula might enhance engagement for serial fans. In serial narratives, familiarity need not diminish the pleasure of suspense. In a report titled "Spoilers Don't Spoil Stories" published in *Psychological Science,* psychologists Jonathan Leavitt and Nicholas Christenfeld suggest that ignorance of plot twists is irrelevant to the enjoyment of suspense and that foreknowledge might even increase narrative pleasure (2011: 1152). Knowing the outcome of a situation provides something akin to "perceptual fluency" which eases the processing of information and can bolster aesthetic recognition and story engagement (Leavitt/Christenfeld 2011: 1152). The psychologists conclude rather bluntly: "Writers use their artistry to make stories interesting, to engage readers, and to surprise them, but we found that giving away these surprises makes readers like stories better" (1153). In sound serials, the hero's fate is assured, and this might free knowledgeable viewers to better appreciate the trap.

Moreover, the race to interruption allows viewers to indulge in spectacles of catastrophe that would end a continuous narrative. Cliffhangers do not so much forestall climax as they provide a specific kind of climax. Situations play through to their tragic ends. In our episode from *Perils of Nyoka,* as soon as Vultura commands the Tauregs to light the fire pit, we recognize that the episode has reached its final impasse. There will be no further revelation of story information, and the hero will not escape. In lieu of development, the episode delivers vividness. We are caught up in a torrent of details as the rope burns and the drums sound. The camera positions seem to cover the action from every angle, assuring us, against our certainty, that there is no way out. In the scene's fifty-fourth shot the final strand of rope snaps, and in shot fifty-five Nyoka plunges screaming into the fire pit.

INTERRUPTION AND VIRTUES OF DISCONTINUITY

At this moment, the narrator necessarily loses command of the viewer's attentional pulse, releasing him to contemplate various possibilities over the coming week. Serials struggle to make the most of this unconstrained time by posing explicit questions over the end-credits. Columbia's 1940s serials exemplify the practice. *Brenda Starr: Reporter* (Fox 1945) concludes each episode by replaying highlights of the cliffhanger just witnessed with a voice-over that lays out all the questions. For instance, chapter 2, "The Blazing Trap," ends with Brenda apparently crushed beneath a collapsing staircase in a warehouse. The narration, by ubiquitous voice actor Knox Manning, intones:

> How can Brenda survive this terrific crash? How can Chuck help her with two murderous gunmen closing in on her? And what will happen, even if she comes out of the wreckage alive? Don't fail to see *Taken for a Ride*, the third thrill-packed chapter of *Brenda Starr: Reporter* at this theater next week.

This narration seeks to cement the questions that viewers ask at the point of interruption. The big question, that of Brenda's survival, is purely redundant and serves only to underline the cliffhanger convention and repeat a bit of spectacular footage. The second question, though, aims at casting doubt on the most likely solution, the intervention of Chuck, Brenda's partner outside the warehouse. The third question implicitly acknowledges what the viewer well knows and directs attention beyond the current suspense situation: she will live, but what will happen next? The internal recap is one last, desperate, attempt to constrain and guide the viewer's navigation of the episode's problem space. The practice probably helped make the chapter more vivid and memorable on a Saturday matinee program, particularly for a serial like *Brenda Starr* that relies on clichéd cliffhangers.

Under the pressure of time, serial narration leaves the viewer with irreconcilable tension between vividness and the continuation of the story. According to Edward Branigan, a classical narrative normally offers easy engagement by being "generally compatible with whatever we *first* believe" (1992: 97). It does not appear ambiguous or "encourage multiple interpretations, but rather, like the chameleon, it is adaptable, resilient and accommodating" (1992: 98). If so, cliffhangers depart from norms by demanding the viewers to make accommodations, accept contradictory depictions, and revise previous understandings. They are the very opposite of Meir Sternberg's ideal of fair play in which viewers have all important information at hand to solve a mystery (1993: 181). Following any narrative involves a continual recasting of knowledge as narration generates new frames of reference for previous events, but no popular form was as consistently radical in this as the sound serial. In doubling back over action to present an unseen event or simply change those events, cliffhanger "takeouts" or resolutions regularly and overtly mislead the viewer. Here the week of waiting may benefit the form, as the details flee short-term memory.

To borrow Branigan's narratological vocabulary, the narrative deception in *Perils of Nyoka* depends on recasting information in a previously unavailable frame (1992: 96, 113). The cliffhanger recap in episode 7 cleverly revises our understanding of events by reordering them. A four-shot sequence of Larry and his sidekick Red scaling the exterior cliff, inserted early in the proceedings of the cliffhanger so that it can be quickly forgotten, is moved later in the recap.[8] The temporal adjustment is subtle but important because it reminds us of the rescuer's activities even as the Taureg ritual passes the point of no return. The steep, high-angle perspective of Nyoka and the cavern below is repeated, but this time it is presented as an eyeline match from Larry and Red's position on the hill outside the cavern. This revision draws what Branigan calls a new epistemological boundary around the image of Nyoka as it is transformed into a subjective view (1992: 111–12, 138–40). The window, which had been functionally fixed as part of the trap, is reconfigured as a potential solution.

Larry throws his rope to Nyoka and commands her to grab on just before she takes the plunge. Her fall, which was more conclusively fatal in the previous episode, is framed from a new camera position in which a Taureg worshipper stands up and blocks our view, obscuring Nyoka's landing. In the strict sense, this resolution is a "cheat" because it depends on restaging events, effectively changing the evidence. But it also reframes or transforms earlier depictions, catching viewers up in a particular version of film narration's constant regulation and alteration of knowledge. Cliffhangers almost always dissimulate, changing the game to suit conventional ends. *Perils of Nyoka* shows that the cheat need not be cheap and easy. Rather, serial narration could approach the elegance and complexity of a classical feature, but within a decidedly different framework.

Serials wielded discontinuity as a common tool. In fact, they encourage us to unthink discontinuity as narrative weakness. As Shane Denson (2014) points out with reference to the Serial Queen films of the silent era, the advantages of "discontinuous continuity" include the integration of stories into

---

8. Ironically, because of this reordering of events, Larry and Red actually lose ground, as it is now later in the ceremony. Our *awareness of* the parallel line of action is more important than the heroes' literal progress. Once the crosscutting commences, Nyoka's rescue is assured.

daily life (via a week-long interruption) and the training of viewers in the processes of film narration. These qualities endured in the sound era as serials acquainted new generations with the complexities of cinematic storytelling. Temporal compression also plays a role. Any disappointment at being cheated is bought off, in part, by a swift change in topic and our recognition of the formula. At one level, we must let the aberration pass in order to keep up with the story; it helps that no one in the diegesis notices anything strange about witnessing an execution that never happened. At another, simultaneous, level of narration, we see that we have once again been deceived, but we also know that it probably does not matter in the long run: we must grant the narration this leeway if we wish to engage in other serial pleasures.

If the solutions can so rarely live up to expectations fostered by cliffhanger hyperbole, then the screenwriters dispense with them quickly and divert the viewer with new information in the expositional part b. In this case, Nyoka and Larry plan to infiltrate Vultura's camp, and by part E, Nyoka finds herself once again facing certain death dangling from a rope, this time held by Vultura's pet gorilla named Satan. Characters promptly bounce back from trauma, never learning from, and barely registering, their experience. Even when the solution is reasonably well motivated, and not a cheat to be swept under the narrative rug, episodes rarely sacrifice more than five minutes to it, and far less to its repercussions. Having fulfilled its function of bringing viewers back to the theater, the cliffhanger is summarily dropped. The time between cliffhangers constitutes a zero sum game for the players, but a game nonetheless played out on schedule and with urgency.

CONCLUSION

Sound serials managed time to blend wild implausibility and strict conventionality, which embodied a basic and constant appeal: the reassurance of survival and success in the face of staggering improbability. The mad rush to nowhere converted time into space and swept viewers past gaps in causality. Then, in releasing the storyteller's grip, the end of an episode left viewers with a vividly drawn scenario, essentially a set of parameters, roles, and stakes to feed make-believe during intervening weeks. Beyond waiting to buy a ticket, viewers were primed to continue an active and conscious engagement with the story and to take up the mantel of both narrator and participant. Serial temporality was packed with events and then extended past the theater, making time for play.

BIBLIOGRAPHY

Barefoot, Guy (2011). "Who Watched That Masked Man! Hollywood's Serial Audiences in the 1930s." *Historical Journal of Film, Radio, & Television* 1.2: 167–90.

Branigan, Edward (1992). *Narrative Comprehension and Film*. New York: Routledge.

Denson, Shane. "The Logic of the Line Segment: Continuity and Discontinuity in the Serial-Queen Melodrama." *Serialization in Popular Culture*. Ed. Robert Allen and Thijs van den Berg. New York: Routledge, 2014. 65–79.

Gerrig, Richard (1993). *Experiencing Narrative Worlds*. New Haven: Yale University Press.

Gunning, Tom (1991). *D. W. Griffith and the Origins of the American Narrative Film*. Chicago: University of Illinois Press.

Higgins, Scott (2016). *Matinee Melodrama: Playing with Formula in the Sound Serial*. New Brunswick: Rutgers University Press.

Keil, Charlie (2002). *Early American Cinema in Transition*. Madison: University of Wisconsin Press.

Leavitt, Jonathan D. and Nicholas J. S. Christenfeld (2011). "Story Spoilers Don't Spoil Stories." *Psychological Science* 22: 1152–53.

Mathis, Jack (1975). *Valley of the Cliffhangers*. Northbrook, IL: Jack Mathis Advertising.

——(1995). *Valley of the Cliffhangers Supplement*. Barrington, IL: Jack Mathis Advertising.

Moak, Bob (1940). "Hollywood Eyes Serial Cycle." *Weekly Variety* (November 6): 21, 23.

Singer, Ben (2001). *Melodrama and Modernity: Early Sensational Cinema and Its Contexts*. New York: Columbia University Press.

Sternberg, Meir (1993). *Expositional Modes and Temporal Ordering in Fiction*. Bloomington: Indiana University Press.

Vela, Rafael (2000). PhD Diss. "With Parent's Consent: Film Serials, Consumerism, and the Creation of a Youth Audience, 1913-1938." University of Wisconsin Graduate School.

Williams, Linda (2001). *Playing the Race Card*. Princeton: Princeton University Press.

CHAPTER 6

Spectral Seriality

The Sights and Sounds of Count Dracula

SHANE DENSON AND RUTH MAYER

INTRODUCTION

In this chapter we are concerned with the media logics and serial dynamics of iconic popular figures.[1] In particular, we are interested in the way that Dracula embodies and paradigmatically exemplifies a "spectral" logic that enables serial figures to proliferate across media channels, passing from literature to film to radio to TV and to digital media, exhibiting all the while an uncanny sort of resiliency that is the product as much of the figure's flexibility as of its iconicity. By *serial figure,* we mean a type of stock character inhabiting the popular-cultural imagination of modernity—a "flat" and recurring figure, subject to one or more media changes over the course of its career (Denson/Mayer 2012a).[2] We see serial figures as integral and ideologically powerful components of the political and economic order of modernity, part of a system that works expansively to increase commensurability and connectivity. Serial figures operate in this system as mediating instances between the familiar and the unknown, the ordinary and the unusual. It is thus not by accident

---

1. Parts of this chapter are based on an earlier publication investigating different aspects of Dracula's seriality (Mayer 2015).

2. For a delineation of the larger contexts and parameters of popular seriality, see Kelleter 2012 and this volume's first chapter.

that such figures are characteristically liminal, transitional, or border-crossing beings—straddling the divide between nature and technology like Frankenstein's monster (Denson 2012, 2014), between life and death like Dracula, human and animal like Tarzan (Denson 2008), or oscillating between moral and ethnic positions like Sherlock Holmes, Fantômas, or Fu Manchu (Denson/Mayer 2012b; Mayer 2014, 2016). These figures parasitically appropriate the media ensembles of a given period, taking up residence in them and making them their own. In doing so, they function as markers and active agents of the very process of media change. In a certain sense, they *become* media—epitomizing the fact that media are never only transparent means of transportation but that they also imprint their "traces" indelibly onto the "messages" or "contents" they convey (Krämer 1998: 74). If, following Sybille Krämer, we conceive of media as complex *apparatuses* of meaning-making and world-building, rather than mere practical tools to facilitate communication (94), then serial figures may be seen as the embodiments or materializations of a fundamental medial drive to bring about *and* reflect upon change (Engell 2004). Media are always in transition, but some media changes (such as the contestation of the novel as the prime medium of entertainment in the late Victorian era or the transition from silent to sound film) are more consequential and spectacular than others. These large-scale media transformations tend to be read in terms of "innovations" (or, more recently, "updates") and thus suggest that media history is a directed and linear process. But serial figures, with their feedback loops and self-reflective logics of iteration, epitomize the fact that the evolution of media systems is a non-teleological process: overdetermined by competing forces, random, accidental, and consequently always also haunted by a sense that "things could have been otherwise" (Denson 2012). In this respect, not only are serial figures subject to constant narrative revision and adjustment for the sake of "retrospective continuity," but they also invite counter-factual questions ("what if?") about the course of media history itself, thus situating themselves as the ideal conceptual figures for media-archaeological inquiries.[3]

In the following, we will flesh out this picture and explain more precisely what a serial figure is, what it does, and how it operates. Our focus will be on the figure of Count Dracula, who perhaps more than any other serial figure accentuates what we call the *spectral* logic of serial proliferation: that is, a ghostly and flickering relation to presence, or the present, which

---

3. The idea of "retrospective continuity" (or *retcon*) stems from the discourse of comics production and fandom, where it indicates the effort of retroactively aligning different historical manifestations of a comic series or figure in order to ensure overall logical coherence or ideological consistency. On media archaeology, see Huhtamo/Parikka 2011.

characterizes the media historicity of the serial figure and propels its ongoing transformations as it moves between old and new media.[4] We will focus on the early stages of this process, paying particular attention to Dracula's appearance in the medium of print, and to his audiovisual rendering on the cinematic screen, to show that the figure's instability and its liminality are of fundamental importance for its career. In both the original novel of 1897 and the film version of 1931, the figure oscillates between ascriptions of "backwardnesss" and "progress," and in both cases the figure's modernity (or lack thereof) is negotiated through mechanisms of medial self-reflection and temporal deferral, as we intend to demonstrate. It is the figure's simultaneous narrative *and* medial spectrality, that is, the fact that it is never completely present—but rather fleeting, shape-shifting, and amorphous—that keeps the figure alive or, more precisely, *undead*: never quite exhausted by a single, definitive instantiation but always available for yet another serial iteration.

SERIAL FRAMINGS AND THE SPECTRAL INTEGRITY OF THE ICON

A serial figure, generally speaking, is a figure that needs no explanation, no introduction, and no elaborate framing. It is *familiar,* even if one has never dealt explicitly with the figure before. We distinguish here between these perennially familiar serial figures, whose existence transcends any particular instantiation, and series characters, which are developed within (and remain more or less contained in) an ongoing narrative, for example, a serialized novel or a saga. Whereas such characters can potentially grow over time to develop a more or less linear biography, serial figures are inevitably characterized by repetitions, revisions, and even the occasional "reboot" of their entire history. Serial figures, as Umberto Eco wrote of Superman, undergo a "virtual beginning" with each new staging, "ignoring where the preceding event left off" (1979: 117). Of course, both types often blend into one another in the course of their narrative unfolding. Indeed, many of the most successful serial figures (such as Tarzan, Sherlock Holmes, Fu Manchu, or Fantômas) were first introduced in the continuing narratives of magazine productions and then further developed in novel series before eventually mutating into iconic figures as they jumped across various media channels (Denson/Mayer 2012a, Denson/Mayer 2012b).

---

4. On the notion of spectrality, which we extend here for media-theoretical purposes, see Derrida 2006.

Serial figures have an extreme affinity to modern media, and they positively thrive on media changes. Though many such figures were established in literary texts, they all migrated quickly to other media, mutated, fanned out, proliferated, and reproduced without losing their distinctive forms, features, trademark equipment, or gear. As a result, they are particularly good at negotiating the culturally or medially "new," and thus at performing or contesting novelty against the background of a figure's familiarity. They both exoticize *and* familiarize the foreign or unknown by foregrounding it. This marking and familiarization are achieved not only narratively but also formally, by way of serial iteration, recurrence, and looping.

Even before the comics superheroes of the 1930s took up and adapted many of their characteristics, serial figures presented themselves as both long-familiar and strangely new, at once timeless and hypermodern, universal and particular. Nevertheless, the serial figures of the turn of the century were long read almost exclusively in terms of the atavistic, the primitive, or the unconscious—in any case, *not* the modern. In the wake of Northrop Frye's theory of literature as an archive of archetypes (in *Anatomy of Criticism*), this reading of the serial figure or form as the "always already known" became canonical. For Dracula, Frye's impact registers in the assumption that a "majestic immutability" (1995: 130) informed the representation of the vampire through the ages, as Nina Auerbach delineated in her cultural history of the vampire.[5] This assumption then gave way, in the wake of intellectual history and Foucault's "archaeology of knowledge," to a more historical approach, as exemplified by Nina Auerbach's own take on vampires as "personifications of their age" (1995: 3). Instead of transhistorical continuities, scholarship now foregrounded temporal breaks and radical revisions.

But such cultural contextualization alone is not sufficient to get a handle on the plurimedial careers of serial figures. It is imperative that we pay attention *both* to these figures' variability *and* to their iconicity, that is, to the restricted parameters within which a figure is free to move and to mutate while still remaining integral as a particular figure and no other. Toward this end, we have to focus on the serial figure's mediality—or, more generally, its formal framing. However, to understand the constructive force of such framing, one should not stretch the frame too far. If you look not at *Tarzan* but at primate-human hybrids in the history of Western culture, not at *Dracula* but at the vampire from Byron to *True Blood*, not *Frankenstein's monster* but man-machine configurations since the early modern era, you run the risk of overlooking the specific media dynamics of popular seriality, a dynamics of

---

5. As a pertinent example for this approach, see Douglas 1966.

modern media. Connected to the inherent reproducibility of technical mass media, this serial dynamics draws on an awareness of something being *retold*, activating a dialectics of recognition and astonishment, of departures *from* and re-anchorings *of* previously staged narratives and images. The more concrete the anchor points and cross-references are in a serial sequence, the more clearly this logic manifests itself. And it is only in terms of this logic that we can recognize the political-ideological and media-material "work" of the serial figure, its engagement with a specific world-historical *era*.

Dracula himself is very much a product of the late colonial era (Arata 1990: 627; see also Richards 1993 and Gibson 2006), and the threat he poses is accordingly "dynamic, totalizing"; earlier monsters operated "on the margins of society, hidden away in their towers," as Franco Moretti puts it, while modern creatures of horror are figures of expansion and spread. "The modern monsters," writes Moretti regarding Dracula in particular, "threaten to live for ever and to conquer the world. For this reason they must be killed" (1982: 68). Moretti follows up Karl Marx's association of capitalism and vampirism and reads Stoker's novel as both an illustration of this logic and an attempt at alleviating the fears it raises. For Moretti, Dracula embodies the extremes of modern monopoly capitalism *because* he is a "figure of the past" (74). At the end of the novel, both the vampiric Eastern monopolist (who symbolizes the past) and the American financier Quincy Morris (who points toward the future) will be dead, while a pseudo-ethical Victorian capitalism stands victorious and uncontested. But in the long (serial) run, Dracula's method of unfriendly takeovers will get the better of the ostensibly benign Victorian status quo, which the novel is anxious to retain. The monster that is "transformed into a man by mass culture" (Moretti 1982: 82) will use the powerful alliance of capitalism and modern mass media to push ahead into the twentieth century.

To do so, Dracula needs to adjust to the new and upcoming forms of modernity—and at the same time communicate timelessness. The figure's flexibility goes hand in hand with a certain constancy. In our imaginations of him, Dracula always has pointed teeth, he always wears a cape, always sleeps in a coffin, and he concentrates on female victims—and these attributes and habits are true even if, during various stretches of his serial career, he got along without some of these habits and accoutrements. In its iconicity, the figure of Dracula mobilizes a whole army of basic conceptual oppositions, pitting them against one another, but without the prospect of resolution: East meets West, the predator threatens civilized humanity, masculine agency preys on the female victim, and, of course, life and death entwine in the vampire's uncanny body. None of these pairs of terms remains unproblematic or stable in the course of the figure's long career, but all of them reappear again and again in various guises and constellations. In his serial specificity, Dracula thus stands out among vampires: he no longer embodies the sensibility of the early Victorian period, and he has not yet assumed that of our late televisual postmodernity. There is a diffuse, indeed spectral, integrity to the figure across its various media instantiations; its iconic appearance will always be superimposed upon any and all possible concrete manifestations, even if (and perhaps especially if) the figure now appears in a different form.

DRACULA'S MEDIA DIALECTICS

The figure's iconic form has been fixed for us above all by Bela Lugosi's portrayal of the Count in Tod Browning's 1931 film version. Yet Dracula's cinematic iconization did not efface his earlier appearances. Rather, it glossed them over, updating them medially, as it were. To apprehend this serial interrelation of new and old, we need to address the media negotiations of Bram Stoker's 1897 novel from which the figure first sprang to—"life." As we shall see, the novel establishes an unresolved tension between the specificity and generality of mediation that will continue to reverberate in Count Dracula's proliferations across the century's audiovisual channels.

More than perhaps any other serial figure, Dracula reveals the active and creative power of technical media already at his literary point of departure. In Thomas Elsaesser's estimation, which follows Friedrich Kittler's seminal reading in *Discourse Networks*, "[Dracula] may be the only original and authentic myth that the age of mechanical reproduction has produced" (2011: 111). Kittler had read *Dracula* as "that perennially misjudged heroic epic of the final victory of technological media over the blood-sucking despots of old Europe" (1999: 86). And Kittler was not the only critic to see in this novel the document of a media struggle, in which an alliance built on modern technologies of communication is pitted against an ancient and totalitarian power (Wicke 1992, Richards 1993, and Winthrop-Young 1994). We agree that Stoker's *Dracula* should be read as a novel about mediatization and media change, but we are not so sure about its actual position within this battle. More specifically, we are uncertain about the novel's sympathies or tacit alliances. Technical media may prove superior in the battle of forces that the novel both depicts and takes part in. But the opposing camps within this battle are far less clear-cut than one might think. This may have to do with the fact that at the turn of the twentieth century, when Dracula first cringed from the light of day, narrative literature as the favored popular medium of entertainment began to face the competition of other media that laid claim to a more effective and visceral impact than the book. Film was not yet at the forefront of this struggle for clout and attention, but the emerging mass-cultural apparatuses of image production and dissemination with their techniques of condensation and spectacle resound in the novel's take on the effects and effectivity of technologies of communication and transmission (Wicke 1992, Menke 2007, Rubery 2009, and Galvan 2010). Bram Stoker's *Dracula*, we argue, may not openly militate against the media system of the twentieth century, but the novel is by no means as celebratory of its own format's impending replacement as is sometimes assumed.

In line with this reconsideration of alliances and tensions, we contend that Count Dracula serves not so much as an outdated antecedent to the mass-media cultures of modernity but more as an integral element of them, perhaps even their basic principle. He represents, figurally and medially, what Victorian culture has reason to dread. Already at the point of his literary inception, Dracula exhibits a principle of diffusion, of intermedial spectrality, according to which one material form is translatable into another: the humanoid, the wolf, the bat, and fog. This allows him for a time to elude his pursuers, but they too are acquainted with a plurality of media forms: shorthand notation, the telegraph, the phonograph, and the typewriter play instrumental roles in this counterproject. Mina Harker, as Dracula's most important opponent and the driving engine of the international alliance of vampire hunters in the metropolis, is a skilled typist, and she manages to render the fractured records of journals, newspapers, phonograph cylinders, and stenographic notes into the uniform medium of typewritten text, reproduced in triplicate. Mina becomes what Kittler called the "central relay in an immense information network" (1999: 354). This network is a network of the present and of presence, and it works by way of collation and addition: *Dracula*'s "narrative time is always the present, and the narrative order—always paratactic—never establishes causal connections," Franco Moretti contends (84). By compiling it, however, Mina also cleanses the new technological media of communication of their "rawness" and authenticity: "I have copied out the words on my typewriter, and none other need to now hear your heart beat, as I did" (Stoker 1993: 26),[6] she reassures Dr. Seward after reviewing his phonograph cylinders. Simultaneously, and interestingly, she defuses what could be considered the most powerful force field of the late Victorian novel, obliterating the traces of feeling, the trembling and the terror, the horrible events' profound impact on the "soul." At the very end of the novel, her husband, Jonathan Harker, summarizes in frustration that "in all the mass of material of which the record

---

6. Henceforth cited as *D*.

is composed, there is hardly one authentic document; nothing but a mass of type-writing [...]. We could hardly ask anyone, even did we wish to, to accept these as proofs of so wild a story" (*D* 335).

Fortunately, the version of the events that the book ultimately renders is not Mina's purified, streamlined, typewritten collection of data but Bram Stoker's lurid and sprawling "imperial gothic" (Brantlinger 1988). Accordingly, the novel counters the "modern" ideal of totalizing data processing with another, older aesthetics of totality—collating voices, perspectives, and media in order to achieve an impression of synchronicity and homogeneity. *Dracula* thus displays its tacit predilection for the media system of the nineteenth century and its unacknowledged skepticism vis-à-vis the technical media of the coming age. But clearly the novel is fighting a losing battle on behalf of its own format. At the book's end, Dracula will be defeated while Mina has just given birth to a son who shall bear all the first names of the league of vampire hunters. Alas, in the story's longer run, the powers of reproduction are afforded to the vampire rather than the Victorian lady. What distinguishes Mina in the novel—her interiority, her reflection, her robust presence—disqualifies her for a serial career and confines her to the bounds of the book.[7] Dracula, in contrast, who is hardly ever "there" in the novel, transgresses its boundaries and lives on by virtue of his capacity to defer closure and synchronicity.

Dracula taunts his pursuers: "My revenge is just begun! I spread it over centuries, and time is on my side. Your girls that you all love are mine already; and through them you and others shall yet be mine" (*D* 273). In his flickering dispersion he seems to project various options for a future vampiric existence, tentatively envisioning nodes and links to future versions of himself. In that respect, the novel functions—somewhat against its own best interest and almost as if it were being operated by an alien force—as the ideal starting point for the figure's serial proliferation. Ultimately, Dracula's spectral quality resides in his uncanny ability to navigate not only (diegetic) time and space but also to spread diffusely through the very real experiential time-spaces that rub against one another in modernity, in the oppositional trajectories of media particularization and convergent totalization. Transcending the novel, Dracula as a serial figure emerges as a higher-order medium of sorts—a meta-medium

---

7. It is interesting to see, however, that at what looks like the end of Dracula's serial career, in the 1990s, Mina returns to the scene, figuring as a central character (and not only an erotic projection screen) in narratives as diverse as Francis Ford Coppola's film *Bram Stoker's Dracula*, Alan Moore and Kevin O'Neal's popular graphic novel series *League of Extraordinary Gentlemen* (1999–2009), and the 2013 NBC series *Dracula*. All of these versions of the narrative profess to return to the figure's literary and historical origins and to explore its ideological and psychological underpinnings. On the serial logic of *League of Extraordinary Gentlemen*, see Mayer 2014: 101–4, 146–47.

in which the book is contrasted with the emerging audiovisual media into which the Count will successively and temporarily descend in the course of his further career. In the ensuing interplay between first-order and second-order media, the sights and sounds of Dracula will become the sights and sounds of media change itself.

THE ICON AS TRANSITIONAL MEDIUM

The transitional interplay of media figure and media ground is nowhere so tightly focused as in Tod Browning's classic film from 1931, particularly in the iconic image it bequeaths to us of Count Dracula. The film's title card already evidences the plurimedial seriality that the figure had amassed over the previous three decades: "Carl Laemmle presents Dracula by Bram Stoker"—not as a direct adaptation of the novel, but "from the play adapted by Hamilton Deane & John L. Balderston," which in fact refers to two different plays: first a London-based production from 1924 and then a 1927 Broadway play based on it, starring Bela Lugosi. Not mentioned here are Stoker's own theatrical production, performed only once (prior to the novel's publication) for the purpose of securing a copyright; Friedrich Murnau's unauthorized adaptation *Nosferatu* from 1922; or any of the print editions, adaptations, abridgments, and serializations that had appeared since 1897. But what is about to appear on screen will in any case overshadow all of these past interpretations, including the original novel, and it will continue to color our perception of any future instantiation for decades to come.

Significantly, Browning's film kicks off the horror-film cycle of the 1930s, including a series of Universal Studios productions featuring the Count: after *Dracula* (1931) comes *Dracula's Daughter* (1936), then *Son of Dracula* (1943), the monster mash-ups *House of Frankenstein* (1944) and *House of Dracula* (1945), and finally *Abbott and Costello Meet Frankenstein* (1948), in which Lugosi reprises his role one last time. The figure, like the horror-film genre, changes markedly over the course of this series, so it is easy to lose sight of the originary media-historical functionality of Lugosi's icon, which is born in the wake of the transition from silent to sound film. By film historian Donald Crafton's reckoning (1997: 267), this transition was coming to its end by the time *Dracula* appeared in February 1931, but as Robert Spadoni (2007) has argued, the film harnessed a lingering experience of the first sounds that moviegoers had heard emitted from the screen—an uncanny or "ghostly" experience resulting from the incomplete phenomenal coordination of sound and image. The Count gave a body to this recently bygone (but unforgotten, "undead") experience, around which the horror genre itself was initially fashioned.

In this context, Browning's film reenacts the novel's battle between media particularization and generalization, though abstracting it from Mina's and Stoker's divergent efforts to coordinate media fragments into a coherent novelistic narrative and transferring it to a probing of the cinema's recent efforts to coordinate sight and sound into a coherent *audiovisual* whole. Dracula's body is the central site of the struggle, the media stakes of which are made clear in the film's first ten minutes or so, leading up to the Count's appearance and first encounter with his guest. The nondiegetic music with which the film opens will cease after the opening credits, and it will not reappear again until the closing credits. But the opening scene, set inside a noisy horse-drawn coach traveling through Transylvania, locates us more or less unproblematically in the sound era of cinema, as on-screen characters converse and produce audible dialogue. Soon, though, as we move deeper into the wilds of Transylvania, this will stop and give way to an eerie silence. When the sun sets and our traveler Renfield (here playing the role of the novel's Harker) sets out for Borgo Pass, a series of images show the Count's distant castle, first from the outside and then its interior, bringing us swiftly to his coffin. There is no sound at all until the interminable silence is broken by the sound of coffins opening, creaking, bumping, and then rats squeaking, wolves barking and howling, as the camera moves in to reveal Dracula, who has silently appeared. The background of silence contrasts palpably with the use of nondiegetic music during the credits. This might be called a *nondiegetic silence,* as it foregrounds the images *as* silent, setting the stage for an uncanny sound, very different from the normalized sound of dialogue that precedes it. The silence has, of course, a diegetic aspect, but it is also double in the sense that it stands out as the spectral *presence* of a media-material *absence.* (By way of contrast, a "regular," i.e., diegetic, silence might conventionally be marked with the sound of crickets chirping.) Renfield's carriage arriving now at Borgo Pass brings with it—and takes with it again just as quickly—the normalized (i.e., synchronized) sound we heard in the opening sequences, again foregrounding the uncanny silence of Dracula, who awaits Renfield ominously in his own carriage. Renfield's somewhat fearful words to the silent count—"The coach from Count Dracula?"—seem awkwardly obtrusive against the background of silence, and the aural register itself alternates as ground and figure with the image of the tight-lipped Count. Visually, Dracula's bulging eyes accentuate this interplay, as they themselves describe a partially autonomous figure against the ground of the Count's face—thereby singling out vision and visuality to set them in a volatile and oscillating relation with sound and the sonic—before the Count's coach heads off with its passenger toward the castle, where this uncanny give-and-take between sound and silence, aural and visual, continues to intensify.

Along the way, Renfield discovers that a bat has silently replaced his driver, and upon arrival he confirms that the driver is indeed nowhere to be found, while the castle door creaks open, autonomously and ostentatiously. Renfield enters, bats squeak, armadillos rustle. Dracula descends the staircase silently behind the frightened Renfield's back and then pronounces: "I am Dracula." The visibly disturbed Renfield explains hastily that he thought he was in the wrong place. Dracula replies, awkwardly, "I bid you welcome." Wolves begin to howl in the background, and the Count remarks: "Listen to them! Children of the night. What music they make." This self-reflexive foregrounding of sound, captured for the purposes of the uncanny, reimagines *The Jazz Singer*'s famous "You ain't heard nothin' yet!" It will reverberate again in Tarzan's famous yell, and—somewhat paradoxically—in the muteness of Frankenstein's monster, all of which stand in a self-reflexive relation to the sound-film transition (Denson 2007, 2008; Spadoni 2007; and Kelleter 2009).

The interplay of silence/sound, noise/speech, visual/sonic continues in London: there we hear the noisy metropolis, the scream of a first offscreen victim, and the music of the opera house, all of which are contrasted with the silence of the house at night, where a bat waits noiselessly at the window and enters without a sound and where an offscreen transformation allows Dracula to appear just as noiselessly at Lucy's bedside. This is followed by the screams of the madhouse and its raving lunatics, including Renfield, contrasted with the concentrated silence of Seward, the other doctors, and van Helsing before he announces that they are dealing with the undead, Nosferatu. Dracula communicates with Renfield without speech, seemingly with his eyes, which, in the Count's/Lugosi's iconic image, are highlighted with precise rays of light, producing an effect much like the bulging eyes earlier, again making vision/the visual the carrier of (a weird, for us indecipherable, sort of) information, while sound is alienated from the image and rendered as incomprehensible noise—thus "denaturing" the recently naturalized, modern system of communication via synchronized sound and vision. It is significant that sound is produced, if not as dialogue then only by objects and nonhuman animals, never by the Count's body in humanoid form, which is perfectly and uncannily silent both in motion and at rest. Later, the Count's lack of reflection in a cigar-case mirror, first noticed by van Helsing, further problematizes sound/image relations, as Dracula is audible while not (mediately) visible. The fact that he "casts no reflection in the mirror" in fact mirrors or translates the fact that his body also emits no sound. Thus, sound and vision are dissociated from one another, both of them operating as channels of significance *and* its deformation in a joint effort to undo the habitualization of synchronized sound and reveal an experience of disjointedness and material excess at its base. This excess, this spectral materiality, refuses to be contained completely by the new medium of sound film. The latter is shown to be "haunted" by a stubborn spirit of media transitionality, embodied by Dracula, which resists containment in a neat media package just as the Count could not be contained in the novel.

The film reinstates, in this way, the excess that Mina, in the novel, had erased in her transcription of Seward's cylinders. But it does so in a way that sits uneasily with Stoker's own attempt to restore a Gothic "spirit" to the Victorian novel, for the film transfers the mechanism of phonography, and its technical capture of the aurally real, from the level of content to that of the medium, which is self-reflexively foregrounded. Accordingly, the material excess of breath (literally, "spirit") and heartbeat that Mina erased from the cylinders is restored and channeled toward the nervous, embodied reactions of the spectator confronted with the early horror film.

As in the novel, then, but for very different purposes, Dracula again thrives on—and carries forth—an unsettling spirit of media transitionality: whereas Stoker sought to counter the impending changes to the media landscape of the nineteenth century, Browning allows the figure to extend the scope of cinema's sound transition—and with it the vampire's own power. Problematizing the coordination of sound and image, Dracula's uncanny image continually reinstates the distinction between sonic and visual registers, thus thwarting the media coherence of the talkie, obstructing the normalization of a generalized audiovisual mediality. Rather than be contained by the medium of the sound film, Dracula himself becomes the medium in which the particular streams of sound and image can appear, juxtaposed and disjoined, forever at battle. Browning's film thus continues the trajectory of serialization that the Count embarked upon when he escaped and transcended Mina's and Stoker's textualizing efforts in 1897.

The enactment of Dracula as a self-reflexive embodiment of the in-between is not unique to our two case studies, though. Indeed, it manifests itself in most appearances of the familiar figure against ever-shifting medial horizons. In the Hammer horror films that resuscitated Dracula in the 1950s, casting Christopher Lee in his signature role, the Count's interstitial status is marked through the use of color. Hammer Studios were the first to introduce Technicolor to the genre of the horror film, and their use of color contrasts such as the glaring red of the blood on Dracula's colorless face energizes the films' disturbing explorations of the dynamics of sex and desire against the backdrops of propriety and control. Roman Polanski's *The Fearless Vampire*

Killers (1967) and Werner Herzog's *Nosferatu, Phantom der Nacht* (1979) both use the *Dracula* plot to challenge the genre conventions of the cinema of their days and to revisit earlier filmic techniques of narration and visualization, eliciting alternately the appeal of camp and the grotesque. And more recently, the NBC television series *Dracula* (2013) drew heavily on the mise-en-scène of steampunk to transpose the older concerns around the divide between man and beast or life and death onto the dichotomy of biology and technology. In all of these cases, media traditions and innovations are pulled into high relief. The effect, not only on the level of the history of film and moving-image media, is one of defamiliarization and temporal disjunction. The reenactments of the serial figure tend to work against the impression of a regularized temporal *flow* and highlight modes of deferral or disassociation. Dracula tends to be behind or ahead of his time, but he is never in sync, never entirely there.

CODA

The careers of serial figures unravel through stages of acceleration and abeyance, and although the Count experienced a serialized revival in NBC's *Dracula* (2013–14), which received moderate critical and audience acclaim, it remains to be seen whether the figure will make it in the twenty-first century. (The series was canceled after one season.) The figure's aesthetic and narrative logic certainly differs significantly from the many popular vampires that haunt the filmic, televisual, and computer screens of our time. As the NBC series exemplifies once more, whenever Dracula has been revisited in recent decades, he has been staged as a markedly historical figure in markedly historical settings. This was already the case in Francis Ford Coppola's *Bram Stoker's Dracula* (1992), a film that seemed to inaugurate the figure's demise: "It may be that Coppola has killed Dracula at last and that he will fade out with the twentieth century" (1995: 209), writes Auerbach in her seminal study, which devotes only a footnote to Coppola's adaptation (1995: 16). The film professed to return to the original script of the novel, and it reveled, indeed, in a lavish display of late Victorian ornamentality and decadence, adopting techniques of early cinema such as multiple exposure or rear projection in lieu of computer-generated effects to pay homage to the aesthetic (and media-technical) "spirit" of the period depicted.

In one of the film's many scenes that are not in fact based on the novel, we witness the first encounter between Count Dracula and Mina Harker in the streets of London. Dracula accosts Mina and asks her, in heavily accented English, about the location of the cinematograph: "I understand it is a wonder of the civilized world." Mina, in keeping with a Victorian code of conduct, rebukes his advances primly: "If you seek culture, then visit a museum. London is filled with them. Excuse me." With this, the filmic Mina stands in sharp contrast to her literary predecessor who welcomed technical innovations wholeheartedly. But the Count's appeal wins her over, and she finally accompanies him to a public screening of early erotic trickfilms and actualities like the Lumières' *L'arrivée d'un train* (1895), which forms the backdrop of their erotic encounter. Those critics who reflected in some detail on the film's adaptation of Stoker's novel came almost invariably to the conclusion that, in spite of its deviation from Stoker's original plot, this particular scene proved "paradoxically in keeping with the novel" (Foster 2009: 78; see also Winthrop-Young 1994: 108, 125). Yet the authenticity effect of this scene would seem to have less to do with Stoker's novel than with Coppola's determination to create an atmosphere of periodicity that rigorously adheres to, or even feeds on, the familiar visual archive of turn-of-the-century London. Thus, instead of following the cues laid out by the film and its ponderous title and judging it in terms of its faithfulness to the original (or lack thereof), it may be more rewarding to approach *Bram Stoker's Dracula* as another episode in a larger serial process. To view it in this manner requires that we explicitly set it in relation to those many other "derivative" works that have defined Dracula's serial career, including, in particular, the many Dracula films that have gone before it—*despite* Coppola's reluctance to reference their audiovisual repertory in his heavy-handed quest for the authenticity of origins.

Tod Browning's *Dracula* is an obvious point of reference because it was so eager, as we have seen, to "map" the serial figure in terms of its media transitionality (in keeping with what may well have been a dominant association with the novel in the 1930s). Browning's Dracula is a figure on the brink, marking the novelty and mutability of the media environment in which it nests provisionally while readying itself to move on. Coppola's Dracula also bears witness to the media changes of its day, but in a very different manner. The film appeared in a period of thoroughgoing media change: *Jurassic Park*, which with its use of CGI "heralded a revolution in movies as profound as the coming of sound in 1927" (Shone 2004: 213), was released in 1993. One year prior, Coppola's postmodern film showed itself acutely aware of cinema's impending digital transformation but opted for an acknowledgment of media change in reverse, so to speak, signaling back in history rather than projecting forward into the future. While Coppola's Dracula, like Stoker's and Browning's, is a liminal figure, this film's self-reflection in terms of mediality is thus more a plot device than a formal feature. The figure's uncanny force and intangibility indicate the power of the past instead of the possibilities of the future, precisely because the film interlinks these qualities with the accomplishments of a technomodernity that is nostalgically revisited *as an irretrievably bygone era*. At worst, *Bram Stoker's Dracula* indulges in a romantic view of history (and of film and media history in particular). At best, however, the film draws attention to its performance of a loop in the figure's serial trajectory, thus attesting to the fact that seriality need not take a sequential, unidirectional, or teleological course, and that the type of seriality embodied by iconic serial figures in fact hardly ever does. Seen from this angle, the actual trajectory of the figure's development could have been otherwise—will paradoxically always already *have been* otherwise. It is in this respect that the figure exhibits its spectral logic, and it is by virtue of this logic that it can repeatedly elude attempts to contain it; against the advances of Mina and van Helsing, of Stoker, or of Coppola, Dracula absconds into an alternate media history, which the figure delineates as an ongoing revisionary process in the face of whatever media transformations are occurring at the moment. The flipside of this is that the figure's continued serial existence is highly contingent upon material processes that are outside its control, so that the future it imagines for itself remains perennially precarious. We simply cannot predict the future fate of a serial figure like Dracula. The only thing we can say with certainty is that it will travel wherever media changes will take it, and that if it persists in its spectral state of undeath, it will continue to reflect these changes and to act upon them, serving both as the object of medialization and as a medium in its own right.

BIBLIOGRAPHY

Arata, Stephen D. (1990). "The Occidental Tourist: Dracula and the Anxiety of Reverse Colonization." *Victorian Studies* 4: 621–45.

Auerbach, Nina (1995). *Our Vampires, Ourselves*. Chicago: University of Chicago Press.

Brantlinger, Patrick (1988). "Imperial Gothic: Atavism and the Occult in the British Adventure Novel, 1880–1940." *Rule of Darkness: British Literature and Imperialism, 1830–1914*. Ithaca: Cornell University Press. 227–54.

Crafton, Donald (1997). *The Talkies: American Cinema's Transition to Sound, 1926–1931*. New York: Charles Scribner's Sons.

Denson, Shane (2007). "Incorporations: Melodrama and Monstrosity in James Whale's *Frankenstein* and *Bride of Frankenstein*." *Melodrama! The Mode of Excess from Early America to Hollywood*. Ed. Frank Kelleter, Barbara Krah, and Ruth Mayer. Heidelberg: Winter. 209–28.

———(2008). "Tarzan und der Tonfilm: Verhandlungen zwischen 'science' und 'fiction.'" *"Ich Tarzan": Affenmenschen und Menschenaffen zwischen Science und Fiction*. Ed. Gesine Krüger, Ruth Mayer, and Marianne Sommer. Bielefeld: Transcript-Verlag. 113–30.

———(2012). "Marvel Comics' Frankenstein: A Case Study in the Media of Serial Figures." *Amerikastudien* 4: 531–53.

———(2014). *Postnaturalism: Frankenstein, Film, and the Anthropotechnical Interface.* Bielefeld: Transcript-Verlag.

Denson, Shane and Ruth Mayer (2012a). "Grenzgänger: Serielle Figuren im Medienwechsel." *Populäre Serialität: Narration—Evolution—Distinktion. Zum seriellen Erzählen seit dem 19. Jahrhundert.* Ed. Frank Kelleter. Bielefeld: Transcript-Verlag. 185-203.

———(2012b). "Bildstörung: Serielle Figuren und der Fernseher." *Zeitschrift für Medienwissenschaft* 7: 90-102.

Derrida, Jacques (2006). *Specters of Marx: The State of the Debt, the Work of Mourning, and the New International* [1993]. London: Routledge.

Douglas, Drake (1966). *Horror!* New York: Macmillan.

Eco, Umberto (1979). "The Myth of Superman." *The Role of the Reader: Explorations in the Semiotics of Texts* [1972]. Bloomington: Indiana University Press. 107-24.

Elsaesser, Thomas (2011). "Freud and the Technical Media: The Enduring Magic of the Wunderblock." *Media Archaeology: Approaches, Applications, and Implications.* Ed. Erkki Huhtamo and Jussi Parikka. Berkeley: University of California Press. 95-188.

Engell, Lorenz (2004). "Historizität als Serialität im Zeitalter des Fernsehens." *Die Medien der Geschichte: Historizität und Medialität in interdisziplinärer Perspektive.* Ed. Fabio Crivellari et al. Konstanz: UVK. 181-94.

Foster, Paul (2009). "'The Amazing Cinematograph': Cinema and Illusion in Francis Ford Coppola's Bram Stoker's Dracula." *Textual Revisions: Reading Literature and Film.* Ed. Brian Baker. Chester: Chester University Press. 58-82.

Galvan, Jill Nicole (2010). *The Sympathetic Medium: Feminine Channeling, The Occult, and Communication Technologies, 1859-1919.* Ithaca: Cornell University Press.

Gibson, Matthew (2006). *Dracula and the Eastern Question: British and French Vampire Narratives of the Nineteenth Century East.* New York: Macmillan.

Huhtamo, Erkki and Jussi Parikka (2011). "An Archaeology of Media Archaeology." *Media Archaeology: Approaches, Applications, and Implications.* Ed. Erkki Huhtamo and Jussi Parikka. Berkeley: University of California Press. 1-26.

Kelleter, Frank (2009). "Schallmauern im Lichtspielhaus: Populärkultur, 'Trans-National America' und *The Jazz Singer*." *Film Transnational und Transkulturell: Europäische und amerikanische Perspektiven.* Ed. Ricarda Strobel and Andreas Jahn-Sudmann. München: Fink. 107-20.

———(2012). "Populäre Serialität: Eine Einführung." *Populäre Serialität: Narration—Evolution—Distinktion. Zum seriellen Erzählen seit dem 19. Jahrhundert.* Ed. Frank Kelleter. Bielefeld: Transcript-Verlag. 11-46.

Kittler, Friedrich (1999). *Discourse Networks 1800/1900.* Stanford: Stanford University Press.

Krämer, Sybille (1998). *Medien, Computer, Realität.* Frankfurt/Main: Suhrkamp.

Mayer, Ruth (2014). *Serial Fu Manchu: The Chinese Supervillain and the Spread of Yellow Peril Ideology.* Philadelphia: Temple University Press.

———(2015). "Dracula: Die serielle Figur als Medium und Grenzgänger." *Total: Universalismus und Partikularismus in postkolonialer Medientheorie.* Ed. Ulrike Bergermann and Nanna Heidenreich. Bielefeld: Transcript-Verlag. 117-33.

———(2016). "'Never twice the same': Fantômas' Early Seriality." *Modernism / Modernity* 23: 341-64.

Menke, Richard (2007). *Telegraphic Realism: Victorian Fiction and Other Information Systems.* Stanford: Stanford University Press.

Moretti, Franco (1982). "The Dialectic of Fear." *New Left Review* 136: 67-85.

Richards, Thomas (1993). *The Imperial Archive: Knowledge and the Fantasy of Empire.* London: Verso.

Rubery, Matthew (2009). *Novelty of Newspaper: Victorian Fiction after the Invention of the News.* Oxford: Oxford University Press.

Shone, Tom (2004). *Blockbuster: How Hollywood Learned to Stop Worrying and Love the Summer.* New York: Free Press.

Spadoni, Robert (2007). *Uncanny Bodies: The Coming of Sound Film and the Origins of the Horror Genre.* Berkeley: University of California Press.

Stoker, Bram (1993). *Dracula* [1897]. Ware: Wordsworth.

Wicke, Jennifer (1992). "Vampiric Typewriting: Dracula and Its Media." *ELH* 2: 467–93.

Winthrop-Young, Geoffrey (1994). "Undead Networks: Information Processing and Media Boundary Conflicts in *Dracula*." *Literature and Science*. Ed. Donald Bruce and Anthony George Purdy. Amsterdam: Rodopi. 107–25.

CHAPTER 7

Hollywood Remaking as Second-Order Serialization

FRANK KELLETER AND KATHLEEN LOOCK

INTRODUCTION: SERIALITY AND FILM REMAKING

If one of the most basic challenges of serial storytelling consists in telling a familiar story as a new story, to what extent can we think of film remakes as examples of popular seriality? After all, remakes do not pretend to be episodes of a series; they do not claim to continue an ongoing story; they do not try to expand a given storyworld. Or do they? As a number of film scholars have pointed out, the distinction between a genuine film remake and a sequel, a prequel, or any other type of filmic iteration is more uncertain than these straightforward terms would seem to suggest (e.g., Verevis 1997, 2006). What counts as a "remake" and what counts as a "sequel" changes throughout the medium's history. In fact, such fluctuations in the designation of iterative formats are dependent on what is going on in the serial practices of other popular media at a given time, not just cinema alone.

Still, all of these formats—film remakes, sequels, prequels, and so on—are primarily concerned with translating repetition into variation (Eco 1990). This observation involves more than simply a matter of narrative technique. Iterative modes of cinematic storytelling are propelled by the same project that animates the capitalist production of culture at large: they aim at an endless innovation of reproduction (Kelleter 2014b). This helps explain why research on remakes often feels that it has to touch on sequels or film series as well (Horton/McDougal 1998b, Forrest 2008, Loock/Verevis 2012, and Klein/Palmer 2016). In this chapter, we argue that remakes, sequels, prequels, and so forth, are best understood as historical varieties of a serial practice that is distinct to Hollywood's commercial film culture (though not exclusive to it).[1] We call this media-specific practice cinematic *remaking*; our focus is on the self-reflexive historicity of its formats in Hollywood cinema.

Since the early days of cinema, films have recycled familiar stories, including other films. Commonly, this recourse to tried and tested story repertoires—the use of prefabricated material—is economically motivated. As a result, remakings have long been scorned by film critics who, until recently, tended to discuss them as unimaginative financial schemes.[2] But if the study of popular seriality shows anything, it is that the commercial foundation of popular series is inextricably interwoven with their aesthetic activities. The challenge of innovative reproduction is both commercial and creative; one aspect cannot be separated from the other. Serial stories are not commodities "on the one hand" and sites of aesthetic experience "on the other," but they do what they do—in terms of both production and reception—*as* creative commodities.

Thus, if we want to move beyond a "hermeneutics of suspicion" (Felski 2011) without falling back on art-philosophical disclosures of transcendence, it is useful to view the commercial nature of popular storytelling cultures not as an underlying conspiracy that should be either unveiled (in the service of critique) or outsourced to other disciplines (in the service of aesthetic appreciation), but as their particular mode of existence which comes with specific affordances, constraints, and self-descriptions.[3] This means complicating

---

1. In the main, this chapter presents an outline of the larger project "Retrospective Serialization: Remaking as a Method of Cinematic Self-Historicizing," conducted within the Popular Seriality Research Unit at Freie Universität Berlin. See Kelleter 2012b, 2015a; Loock/Verevis 2012; and Loock 2012, 2014a/b, 2015, 2016a/b.

2. On this unfavorable discourse, see Horton/McDougal 1998b, Mazdon 2000, Forrest/Koos 2002, Verevis 2006, Oltmann 2008, Loock/Verevis 2012, and Loock 2015. As a contemporary example, see the subtitle *Why Don't They Do It Like They Used To* for an academic study on horror film remakes (Roche 2014).

3. On the commercial dimension of popular seriality, compare Hagedorn 1988, 1995; Kelleter 2012a; and this volume's first chapter. As an example of a more "symptomatic" interpretive model centered on the industrial aspect of literary adaptations, see Murray 2011. We borrow the term *mode of existence*, with some hesitation, from Latour 2013. What we mean is a mode of doing things that gains self-knowledge and reproductive motivation through self-descriptions (in the systems-theoretical sense of the term; see Luhmann 1999)—in other words, a mode of improbable practical reproduction. However, we also believe that the ontological glamour of Latour's term risks defeating ANT's nonphilosophical promise. Perhaps this explains, *ex negativo*, the enthusiasm with which it has been greeted in Latour's Anglo-American philosophical reception (a scholastic realm that has yet to absorb Luhmann).

high-cultural philosophies of cinematic art and certain culturalist approaches that depict popular reception as essentially a "scene" of reading/viewing in which a single recipient is confronted with a distinct work that reaches him or her from some outside realm of authority: culture as an eventlike encounter. This scenario of Subject versus Object, "describing the 'self' as if it were an island surrounded by sharks" (Latour 2013: 190)—or, alternatively, as if it were surrounded by inspirational beings and transcendent mediators—has prompted many a narrative theory to cast popular reception as a confrontation between textual action and personal reaction, objective offer and subjective contribution, and sometimes even interpellation and resistance. Almost all critical models derived from nineteenth-century romantic philosophy, including a number of Marxist, phenomenological and vitalist approaches, are organized by some variation of this constellation. Not coincidentally, it is also a favorite scenario of Western popular storytelling itself.

It is noteworthy in this context that hostile attitudes to film remakes or sequels are, almost as a rule, strongly invested in the idea of the feature film as a self-contained work of art that has transcended its commodity status. From this perspective, with all its emphasis on media closure and authorial unity (habitually condensed in the figure of the cinematic auteur), remakes and sequels are likely to appear as profit-oriented copies of some valuable original. This is an intriguing argument, not only because it has been made so often—at least until recently—but also because the very distinction between original and copy, on which this argument rests, tends to erase the commercial mode of existence of the supposed source text. As a matter of fact, in virtually all cases of cinematic remaking the so-called original was itself designed as a commodity, meaning that its aesthetic accomplishments, including its susceptibility to be recognized or rebranded as a work of unique vision, were rooted in (rather than opposed to) the culture of commercial filmmaking. Even more important, many "originals" turn out, on closer inspection, to have been remakes themselves. MGM's 1939 version of *The Wizard of Oz,* for instance, was not only an adaptation of a piece of literature (which kicked off a literary series in turn) but also a remake of previous film and musical versions.[4] In other words, the rhetoric of the cinematic artwork has often served to distract from the way in which "originals" and "classics" are actually produced—how they come into "being"—in popular cinema, namely, through practices of repetition and variation that are structurally akin to the more explicitly serialized aesthetics of other popular media.

---

4. For a more detailed discussion of the Oz narratives, see Kelleter 2012b and chapter 12 in this volume.

To discuss these serialities of Hollywood cinema, we will, in the following, briefly clarify three frameworks of analysis (the feature film's media-specificity, remaking as a practice, and the concept of "second-order observation") before focusing on two exemplary phenomena in greater detail (remaking in the DVD era; and the *Planet of the Apes* franchise). In this manner, the present chapter proceeds from the general and theoretical to the specific and analytical. Its overall argument concerns the historical self-reflexivity of cinematic remaking, understood as a media-specific practice of serial self-observation.

SERIALITY AND THE HOLLYWOOD FEATURE FILM

The Hollywood feature film has developed media-distinct varieties of popular seriality that differ from the serial processes of dime novels, radio soaps, television series, or (nonfeature) film serials of the silent and early sound era.[5] As always, the evolutionary trajectory of serial storytelling in a particular medium is dependent on the technological possibilities and limitations of that medium, as well as on the medium's strategies of positioning itself toward other media of serial storytelling, in terms of both commercial competition and cultural legitimacy (Denson 2011 and Denson/Mayer 2012). It is telling in this regard that the first defining forms of popular seriality were developed in media characterized by relatively fast rhythms of production and reception, such as newspapers and radio. These "quick" media, with their short-cycled but regular consumption frequencies, encourage the explicit serialization of narrative material, typically in the form of recurring episodes or ongoing installments. They also invite continuations adjusted to the quotidian routines of their audiences.[6] The greater the time pressures of commercial production (e.g., a new comic strip every day), the more we can expect efficient standardizations to emerge, such as an industrial division of labor, program-based types of reception, or episodic structures (even in the case of ongoing narratives).

---

5. Of course, film serials were a defining element of silent cinema. After the consolidation of the Hollywood studio system and with the advent of sound, they survived as deliberately short formats with fast-paced patterns of production and reception, mostly presented as highly standardized chapter plays in conjunction with, but clearly distinguished from, stand-alone feature films that were billed as the main event of a cinema show (Lahue 1964, 1968; Stedman 1971; and Cline 1984). The separation of film serials and feature films into distinct cinematic formats in the late 1910s and throughout the 1920s illustrates the media-ecological basis of popular culture at large. On the cross-fertilization of film serials and feature films, see Canjels 2011 and Henderson 2014. On the specific seriality of nonfeature film serials, see Higgins 2016 and chapter 5 in the present volume. On serialized feature films, see below.

6. On this point, see chapter 13 below.

Popular seriality thrives on speed—hence its early affinity to daily or weekly media. Even when they produce epic effects, as "vast" narratives (Harrigan/Wardrip-Fruin 2009), commercial series remain recognizable as "fast" and shifting narratives, enacting a regime of storytelling predicated on the quick succession of smaller interacting elements for the purpose of durable audience reengagement (Kelleter 2015b). By contrast, the Hollywood studio system, with its elaborate structures of production, its oligopolistic market, and its various efforts to establish the medium's cultural legitimacy against its vaudeville roots, has advanced a storytelling culture that is not naturally favorable to the creation of series and serials. American feature films of the studio era had to employ strategies of repetitive variation that were slower, more laborious, less rhythmical, and altogether more mediate—though no less organized—than the ones we find in the seriality practices of newspapers, radio, or (later) television. And while there are examples of feature film series in the studio era—Andy Hardy, Charlie Chan, Blondie, Pa and Ma Kettle, and so on—these productions commonly relied on serialization strategies developed in other media (especially radio and comics) and were often marketed as contributions to transmedia franchises. Overall, however, innovative reproduction in Hollywood feature films did not and does not *typically* culminate in *explicitly* serialized stories. Instead, innovative reproduction is frequently pursued through a more implicit practice of serialization: the practice of cinematic remaking, in which a source text that was initially identified as a stand-alone story is reactivated, repeated, changed, and indeed continued in the act of remaking.

REMAKING CONSIDERED AS A PRACTICE RATHER THAN A FORM

To study remaking as a cinematic practice (Dusi 2011) rather than as a distinct cinematic form that can be defined in a typology of structural features means to investigate how different designations of filmic iteration came into existence in the first place and how they served to make and unmake such recognizable industry "formats" as the film remake, the sequel, the prequel, the trilogy, the reboot, and so forth. There have been numerous attempts to classify such iterative modes typologically, with each new undertaking refueling the debates about the formal properties of distinct types (e.g., Leitch 1990, Eberwein 1998, and Junklewitz/Weber 2011). Definitions that emerge from such endeavors provide useful signposts, but their competition is often characterized by a normative insistence that we use the right words, as if cinematic formats existed as ideal forms that are then articulated more or less precisely by this or that film. This is obviously not the case—not only because formal boundaries are always fluid but because cinematic remaking is a reflexive, multi-agential, and temporally shifting process, ultimately competition-based and spanning the fields of production and reception. Consequently, not only are these formats not ideal, but they do not even exist (for long) in historically canonized shapes. What is understood and active as a "remake" in 1965 is different from what is understood and active as a "remake" in 2017.

We therefore propose to examine cinematic remaking as an evolving cinematic *formatting practice*—that is, a practice that generates media-specific modes of variation and organizes them in historically variable categories, such as, currently, the "remake" (in the more limited sense of a feature film that repeats the narrative of another feature film), the "sequel" (which continues the story of one or more protagonists), the "spin-off" (which diversifies an existing narrative universe without having to focus on an established character constellation), the "revision" (which tells a familiar story from a markedly new perspective), the "spoof" (which does so in a parodist or satirical mode), the "re-imagining" (a revision usually attributed to a director's artistic vision), the "prequel" (which constructs a backstory for popular character constellations or storyworlds), the "franchise" (which, as an explicitly legal entity, engages in transmedia storytelling and is not necessarily structured in continuing story arcs but can also renew itself episodically or at the level of storyworld), and—most recently—the "reboot" (which seeks to remake an entire series or franchise rather than a single narrative, usually with revisionary ambitions). And then, of course, there are the more expansive remaking practices of "genres" and "cycles." The catalogue of these terms is not systematic because it cannot be systematic. The formats named and differentiated in this fashion exist as the result of what they are doing, which is another way of saying that we are dealing with auto-adaptive, evolutionary structures.

The key question, then, is: how does it become possible—perhaps even necessary—at a particular moment in the history of popular seriality to distinguish between a variation that is called a *remake* and a variation that is called a *reboot*? Phrasing the problem like this has interesting methodological consequences. Perhaps most importantly, any investigation of remaking as a formatting practice, while not being required to participate in typological controversies, needs to study them as part of the research field itself. If that is done, scholastic distinctions and debates become visible as lively forces within a larger network of actors that sustains this particular storytelling culture.[7]

---

7. For a more detailed exposition and illustration of this research program, using the example of HBO's *The Wire*, see Kelleter 2014a.

Consequently, we suggest analyzing how public discourses, media scholarship, industry operations, audience engagements, packaging practices, and the aesthetic activities of "remade" films themselves all enact cinematic seriality. Which categories, evaluations, procedures, and so on, of filmic iteration are invented, identified, or performed by whom (or what) at which point? What effects are coming to pass?

RETROSPECTIVE SERIALIZATION, CINEMATIC SELF-HISTORICIZATION, AND SECOND-ORDER OBSERVATION

Periodical series tend to produce highly committed audiences (Hills 2002), such as the "forensic fandoms" identified by Jason Mittell (2006, 2015) in the context of digital-age television (where formerly academic modes of interpretation migrate in large numbers to the realm of consumer practices). Compared with these more typical series, cinematic remaking formats operate at a more abstract level of imagined collectivization (to invoke Benedict Anderson).[8] A change has set in only recently, with remaking formats beginning to borrow serial structures from television and other media rather than vice versa (Elsaesser 1998 and Loock 2016a). For the longest time, however, cinematic audience engagement differed in important ways from the reception cultures of more explicitly serialized media. As so often is the case, *Star Wars*—with its extremely dedicated and active fandom—can be named as an exception. But then, the first *Star Wars* films were almost unique in using sequels in an openly prospective manner and across media. The success of this strategy certainly paved the way for developments in the convergence era, where we find cinematic remaking formats fully attuned to the logic of the digital (and arguably becoming more televisual in the process).

For the most part of their history, however, cinematic remaking formats have enacted less direct types of serial communality. Unlike daily cartoons or telenovelas, feature film iterations cannot structure rhythms of everyday life. Instead, they often structure seasonal, generational, and media-historical sequences. Summer blockbusters, for example, usually exhibit features of generic remaking. Or, on a larger temporal scale, while there may be no ongoing fandom for *Invasion of the Body Snatchers*, a media generation can recognize itself *as* a media generation in the way its version of *Invasion of the*

---

8. On the relationship between popular seriality and what Anderson calls "imagined community" (1991), see Chatterjee 1999; Denson/Mayer 2012; Kelleter 2012a, 2014b; Mayer 2015; and chapters 1 and 14 in this volume.

Body Snatchers varies from those that precede it. In a similar fashion, a cinematic period can define itself against a previous one in the way it produces *King Kong*. It should be noted, for example, that remakes and sequels are frequently produced *because* of the advent of new technologies, such as sound, color, or 3-D. More succinctly put, remakes, sequels, and similar formats can act as markers of shifting media affordances. Following Harold Innis (1950), one can perhaps say that cinematic remaking, as a communication practice, is more "time-biased" than it is "space-biased": while radio soaps or television series bind together disparate localities through synchronized procedures, film remakes and sequels provide temporal continuity markers, sometimes for entire cultures that can recognize themselves in the films they keep remaking. Thus, cinematic seriality encourages communities of knowledge and belonging that tend to be more far-ranging than the concentrated fan cultures of fast-paced television series. Cinephile culture, for instance, the seedbed of various institutions of professional attachment and expertise (such as film studies departments or the New Hollywood), can indeed be thought of as a popular fan culture—a fan culture, however, whose object is not this or that particular narrative or storyworld but the medium of cinema itself. Calling this a "culture" implies that its reproduction takes place beyond any idealized "scenography of Subject and Object" (Latour 2013: 201) because it always co-involves audiences, producers, conferences, theories, cinema journals, and numerous other agents of continuation.

Against this backdrop, one serial operation in particular stands out as a signature practice of iterative filmmaking: retrospective serialization. It has often been remarked that remakes and sequels tend to canonize their source texts (Corrigan 2002, Quaresima 2002, Oltmann 2008, and Loock 2012). Frequently, it is only after a remake has been produced and after its success or failure has reactivated interest in the material that the initial film version becomes established as a "classic" or "original." A similar dynamic is active at the level of formatting (though not always with canonizing effects, as we shall see in the next section) when a stand-alone film is reinterpreted *by* its sequel as the launching pad *for* a sequel. Sometimes even the title of the first film is changed to place it in serial succession. As we know, there was no film called *Episode IV: A New Hope* in 1977. Similarly, many a trilogy recognizes and addresses itself as a trilogy only after a third film has come out (and even then it will typically provide connecting options for further extensions). This kind of retrospective serialization can be understood as a special case of the dynamics of recursive progression that defines popular seriality at large.[9]

---

9. See chapter 1 in this volume; for *Episode IV,* see footnote 14 there.

FIGURE 7.1. *Body Snatchers* poster (Warner Bros., 1993) featuring the tagline "The Invasion Continues."

Thus, any remake will almost automatically reflect on the praxeological conditions under which it reactivates old material, even when it adds nothing new to an already familiar plot. This is why all remakes contain progressive elements, even (and especially) in their acts of retrospection. They invariably explore possibilities of variation and continuation. Consider the poster of Abel Ferrara's 1993 *Body Snatchers*, the third remake of Don Siegel's 1956 *Invasion of the Body Snatchers* (figure 7.1).[10] "The Invasion *Continues*," the poster con-

---

10. For a more detailed discussion of *Invasion of the Body Snatchers*, see Loock 2012.

fidently announces, even though in terms of its plot, this film is not a sequel. The obvious question is: At which level of popular storytelling is something being continued here? Evidently, recursive progression in this case takes place in a sphere of storytelling at one remove from (though enacted through) the film's plot: initially unconnected versions of one and the same narrative are retrospectively serialized at a higher level of cinematic self-observation. In this manner, even the most faithful repetition, such as Gus Van Sant's *Psycho*, inevitably adds something to the story reproduced (Kelleter 2015a). Moreover, new versions usually herald these additions as innovations, that is, as progressive elements in the history of the medium itself. In other words, remaking operates as a method of *cinematic self-historicization*: cinema writes its own history with remakes, sequels, or prequels—and it does so within the evolving network of expectations, recognitions, allusions, variations, and reinterpretations that makes these iterations possible and keeps them in circulation.[11] Tracing this network and its acts of self-historicization—and doing so within a media-ecological framework (i.e., within the framework of cinema's changing relationship to other media of serial narrative)—means watching remade films with an eye toward the technological, institutional, and personal actors and actions that make them watchable in the first place. Two exemplary cases shall illustrate this point in the following analytical sections, which will focus on specific historical and praxeological moments within the larger theoretical argument sketched out so far: the material (storage) conditions of remaking in the DVD era and iterations of *Planet of the Apes* as examples of pop-generational self-awareness.

REMAKING IN THE DVD ERA: STORAGE, INTERTEXTUALITY, AND SERIAL CONSUMPTION

Until the rise of stay-at-home television entertainment in the 1950s which would eventually supply audiences with regular reruns of old Hollywood movies, the opportunity to rewatch a film depended entirely on prolonged first runs and re-releases.[12] "Repeat viewing was [. . .] a practice not favored by a distribution system almost fully geared to novelty," notes Vinzenz Hediger:

---

11. Our concept of self-historicization builds on various theories of (popular) media's temporal reflexivity, for example, Haverkamp/Lachmann 1993, Engell 2010, and Denson/Mayer 2012. Wloszczynska also talks about "the 'thinking remake'" (2012).

12. Hediger points out that runs of up to sixty-two weeks (e.g., for Cecil B. DeMille's *The Ten Commandments*, 1923) were not uncommon during the silent era, when film screenings

> Up until the early 1940s, film production ran from 500 to 800 films annually, and films were distributed through a system of runs, zones and clearances that favored rapid turnovers. Accordingly, films hardly ever stayed on the bill for more than one week or even a few days. An average film took two years to descend the ladder of the distribution system, from urban first run in prestigious palaces to lower-run and rural theaters. After their two-year distribution period most films were withdrawn and disappeared into the vaults of the studio. (2004: 26)

During the early years of what is commonly called the Golden Age of Hollywood, films were essentially treated as ephemeral commodities—quickly outdated and forgotten, unless they were remade. In 1938, Hollywood's leading fan magazine, *Photoplay*, explained to its readers that a remake was, in fact, the best chance a film narrative had for an afterlife: "In addition to the 'flash in the pan' film, which is seen by many audiences and then consigned to oblivion," *Photoplay* remarked, "there are those perennial classics that live forever in the form of 'remakes'—new versions of old films that are often remade two or three times" ("Match Them" 42). This statement provides an insight into how the memory of motion pictures was kept alive—predominantly via the survival of narratives—before television reruns and the emergence of new information-storage technologies like VHS and DVD. It also suggests that remaking helped to construct and to communicate a cinematic past—understood as an imagined story archive—through processes of repetition and variation (Loock 2016b).

Today, the mnemonic and archival functions of remaking have changed dramatically. Instead of *replacing* earlier film narratives with updated versions, remakes now interrelate with their precursors in more explicitly material and entangled ways. Television reruns have extended the life span of old Hollywood movies and transformed them into new "classics" that coexist alongside the latest release. Since the 1980s, with the swift rise of VHS and, later, DVD, private viewers can become collectors and cultural archaeologists of the cinematic past; individualized possibilities to repeatedly view (and personally engage with) films have in turn influenced Hollywood's current remaking practices.

As Constantine Verevis observes, "A remake and its original [circulating] in the same video marketplace [. . .] radically [extend] the kind of film literacy—the ability to recognize and cross-reference multiple versions of the same property—that was inaugurated by the age of television" (2006: 18). Remakes in the DVD era generally build on this new film literacy and seek

---

were still accompanied by "lavish stage shows" (2004: 27). In the sound era, first-run engagements were reduced to only a few weeks.

to address a double audience consisting of those who are familiar with an earlier version and those who are not. As Leonardo Quaresima puts it, the film remake ideally "assumes that its viewer is an intertextual viewer [who finds pleasure] in juxtaposing and comparing" (2002: 80). As such, it offers an array of references for viewers in the know, for example, the repetition of famous lines, in-jokes, and cameo appearances from actors who starred in an earlier film (Leitch 1990 and Loock 2012). Tim Burton's 2001 *Planet of the Apes*, for example, contains several intertextual moments that are designed to mirror the 1968 original. Astronaut George Taylor's iconic lines "Get your stinkin' paws off me, you damn dirty ape!" and "Damn you, damn you, damn you all to hell!" are slightly altered and spoken by the apes this time ("Get your stinkin' hands off me, you damn dirty human!"; "Damn them, damn them, damn them all to hell!"), whereas Charlton Heston, who played Taylor in the original, returns as an ape himself. Coproducer Ralph Winter said about Heston's uncredited role: "It's like an Easter egg for aficionados to find out who is he playing and how that resonates in the story. [. . .] I think the fans will appreciate it" (quoted in Landau 2001: 68).

In the same context, DVD marketing strategies invite the serial consumption of films in the form of "Original & Remake" or "Double Take" special editions, which sell two films in the same production package, and "Complete Collections," which include all sequels to date and often come in elaborately designed boxes. By the early 1990s, studios had already noticed that the theatrical success of remakes and sequels stirred VHS sales and rentals of the original films, and they reacted by repackaging older titles to coincide with the release of a new remake or sequel (Natale 1991). Such "piggybacking" strategies soon became more sophisticated and were no longer restricted to cinema. In his analysis of TV-to-DVD publishing and the rise of the season box set, Derek Kompare (2006) suggests that the introduction of DVD technology produced new home video practices. Improved audiovisual quality and larger storage capacity (allowing for the inclusion of numerous extra features) "raised the cultural status of video releases" and favored a shift in domestic media consumption from rental to acquisition (Kompare 2006: 346). Not surprisingly, a new focus on video sales also "prompted [. . .] a greater emphasis on packaging and overall design, enhancing the perceived value of an object meant for permanent ownership and display rather than temporary use" (348).[13] The developments outlined by Kompare for television series (before

---

13. Gray (2010) and Mittell (2010) have expanded on Kompare's analysis, stressing that DVD publishing, though a transitional phenomenon, has transformed television series from events to be experienced into more authoritative, sometimes obliquely oeuvre-like cultural objects.

the rise of online streaming) can also be traced, with some qualifications, in the production of cinematic "Original & Remake" editions and "Complete Collections." Assembling a film and its remake or sequel in one and the same production package to be consumed alongside each other bestows previously maligned remaking formats with a new temporal specificity and, in connection with this, a new kind of pop-cultural (at times campy) value.

Films such as *The Day the Earth Stood Still* (1951/2008), *Planet of the Apes* (1968/2001), *The Fly* (1958/1986), *The Omen* (1976/2006), *Amityville Horror* (1979/2005), *The Flight of the Phoenix* (1965/2004), *Anna and the King* (1946/1999), *The Thomas Crown Affair* (1968/1999), and *Cape Fear* (1962/1991) have been released in this fashion on DVD. All of these packages, which are often produced for an international (non-U.S.) market, share certain design patterns. First, the words "Original & Remake" are featured prominently on the front or in such sentences as "The classic original and smash hit remake." Second, the title is sometimes quoted twice and sometimes shared by both films, either establishing the artistic autonomy of the remake or stressing its indebtedness to the original. Third, and most strikingly, all DVD covers consist of halves representing an image of the original on the left side and of the remake on the right; central characters are either shown back-to-back (looking in opposite directions), positioned to face each other, or spliced together to form one image, as if existing in the same storyworld. The new film's most prominent innovation is generally highlighted by this juxtaposition.

The DVD cover for a German release of *The Day the Earth Stood Still*, for example, features a picture of the humanoid robot Gort composed of different halves joined together to form a whole. The left half is taken from the 1951 version, in which Gort was made of smooth, shiny metal—an armor of seamless perfection. The right half depicts the robot as he appears in the 2008 remake: CGI-redesigned and composed of a dark, shimmering material that is supposed to be a vast swarm of "nano bugs." This arrangement draws attention to the remake's state-of-the-art special effects, while suggesting that the "Original & Remake" should be watched in sequential order to fully experience the development of this cinematic narrative within the technological trajectory of sci-fi storytelling.

Similar marketing strategies are applied to sequels when they are sold as "Complete Collections" after the release of a (presumably) final installment. Box sets of *Star Wars*, *Back to the Future*, and *The Godfather* are obvious examples, because they retrospectively create and promote trilogies (i.e., almost classical, self-contained structures) or—in the case of *The Godfather*—a comprehensive family "saga" that has finally reached its conclusion. Yet (non-U.S.) viewers can also watch the *Jaws Quadrilogy*, including "Jaws 1–3" and the fourth sequel, *Jaws: The Revenge*; or the *Psycho Collection*, containing "Psycho I–IV." In each case, a once discrete, critically acclaimed, and by now classic film—Steven Spielberg's 1975 blockbuster *Jaws* and Alfred Hitchcock's 1960 *Psycho*—is converted into the first part of a series that is advertised with and by the box set. Thus, rather than canonizing an (already canonical) source text, these cinematic iterations highlight its status as an elastic piece of popular storytelling. Apparently, many viewers welcome such collections *as* series. Comments in Amazon's review section reveal that numerous customers who bought the *Psycho Collection* had already watched Alfred Hitchcock's film and were interested in the sequels or had seen Gus Van Sant's 1998 remake (not usually considered part of "the canon"). Some even wondered why the remake and the new A&E television series *Bates Motel* (since 2013) were not part of the set, feeling that these latest additions to the "film series" should have been included for the sake of completeness (Robin 2006 and Schlüter 2014). Seriality apparently is understood by these digital-age viewers more in terms of an expansive storyworld than in terms of linear narrative progression.[14]

Other DVD editions have responded to this desire and are specifically designed for fan cultures obsessed with storing and archiving. These collections contain all of the films to date—regardless of whether they are sequels, remakes, or sequels of remakes—in one single box. Thus, the Dutch *The Fly Chamber Collection* includes Kurt Neumann's 1958 horror classic *The Fly* and its two sequels, *Return of the Fly* (1959, Edward Bernds) and *Curse of the Fly* (1965, Don Sharp), as well as David Cronenberg's 1986 remake and its sequel *The Fly II* (1989, Chris Walas). The ostentatious box, which is protected by a transparent plastic package with small flies printed on it, comes in the shape of a miniature version of the "telepod" featured in Cronenberg's film. The door of this telepod shows a lenticular flicker picture of Seth Brundle (Jeff Goldblum) morphing into the fly creature. Clearly, this DVD box is meant to be more "than [a] container for the discs"; rather, it resembles a "collectable media object" that "demands to be displayed, dismantled, used, and discussed" (Mittell 2010).[15]

The effect of gathering such dissimilar versions of the same popular material and making them watchable as interdependent parts within a joint storytelling universe—a universe no longer defined (merely) by the continuation

---

14. On the question of remake and (serial) storyworld in the case of *Psycho*—and Gus Van Sant's version in particular—see Kelleter 2015a. On serial storytelling from Hitchcock's film to *Bates Motel*, see Loock 2014b.

15. Mittell's article addresses box sets of television series, which, though often indebted to the same gimmicky aesthetic that has characterized secondary-distribution media at least since VHS, tend to be less overt than film DVDs in their pop-cultural self-performance.

of plotlines or even a shared fictional storyworld—points toward what Shane Denson has called "a non-linear form of 'concrescent' (compounding or cumulative) seriality" (2011: 532, with a nod to Whitehead and, more specifically, to Newcomb's 1985 interpretation of some episodic TV series as "cumulative narratives"). Interestingly, however, the design of *The Fly* box devotes its chief attention to the most highly acclaimed movie, establishing a framework of viewer expectations that runs contrary to the chronological order of the films (also represented on the package), but that nevertheless defines a point of orientation from which audiences will look backward and forward. By singling out Cronenberg's remake, *The Fly Chamber Collection* functions as what Jonathan Gray has called an "entryway paratext," in the sense that it tries to "control and determine [the viewers'] entrance to a text" (2010: 35). Thus, while the box somehow promises that the 1986 film will be "the best" of the five iterations, it simultaneously suggests that the others are necessary viewing if one wants to properly appreciate Cronenberg's masterpiece. In this fashion, DVD publishing of remakes and sequels not only facilitates access to different versions but also enables a mode of reception that foregrounds viewers' second-order engagement with a narrative's media-historical aspects. What used to be an implicit function of cinematic variations becomes both an increasingly explicit part of their reception and an important influence on their production practices.

Similarly, the UK *Planet of the Apes: Evolution Collection* (figure 7.2) includes all seven *Planet of the Apes* movies released between 1968 and 2011. While the collection can no longer claim to be complete (one more sequel came out in 2014; another one is scheduled for release in 2017), it still provides a meaningful record of the *Apes* films that bears testimony to how cinematic techniques, sociohistorical concerns, and cultural self-descriptions have indeed "evolved" over four decades. Moreover, the set invites a mode of consumption that generates and accumulates knowledge about changing possibilities and limitations of cinematic variation—a mode of consumption, in other words, that reveals how remakes, sequels, and prequels function as markers of media-generational change.

PLANET OF THE APES AND MEDIA-GENERATIONAL CHANGE

Like *King Kong, Invasion of the Body Snatchers, Psycho, Rocky,* and others, *Planet of the Apes* belongs to those stories that have been continually retold and updated in Hollywood films. Each new installment has helped to preserve a rich

FIGURE 7.2. DVD cover of *Planet of the Apes: Evolution Collection* (20th Century Fox, 2011).

and reliable repertoire of popular narratives for future generations by placing familiar characters and plots in new cultural, political, or technological contexts. Franklin J. Schaffner's *Planet of the Apes* (1968), based on Pierre Boulle's novel *La planète des singes* (1963), tells the story of four astronauts who crash-land on a planet ruled by apes. The only female astronaut has died in hibernation, but the surviving crew members set out to explore their unknown surroundings. Shortly after encountering a group of mute humans, they are attacked by apes on horseback. One astronaut is killed, another is captured and lobotomized, and the third—Charlton Heston's character George Taylor—is taken prisoner. Chimpanzee scientists Zira and Cornelius, who feel compassion for the enslaved humans, recognize Taylor's intelligence and help him and a woman named Nova to escape. In the end, when Taylor finally reaches what the apes call the "Forbidden Zone," he sees the half-buried Statue of Liberty, realizing that he has landed not on an alien planet but on a future Earth.

The film was a commercial and critical success—"so much so," writes Eric Greene, "that the studio requested a sequel. And another. And another. And another" (1996: 1–2). All in all, four more feature films were released between 1970 and 1973: *Beneath the Planet of the Apes* (1970), *Escape from the Planet of the Apes* (1971), *Conquest of the Planet of the Apes* (1972), and *Battle for the Planet of the Apes* (1973). By the mid-1970s "the market was flooded with Apes juvenilia and toys, including model kits and [. . .] action figures" (Paul Woods quoted in Verevis 2006: 93). "Go Ape!" marathons lured fans back into the cinemas to watch all of the *Ape* movies rereleased as a quintuple bill, and a short-lived live-action series (CBS, 1974) and an animated series (NBC, 1975–76) based on *Planet of the Apes* and its sequels were broadcast on television. Over the following decades, interest in the *Apes* franchise was maintained by what Verevis has described as an "exhaustive cultural production" that eventually "generat[ed] interest in, and speculation about, a remake" (2006: 93). This included "the reprint of Boulle's novel, the rerun of the television series on the cable Sci-Fi channel, and the recycling of Apes iconography by visual and performance artists. In its most popular reincarnation, *Planet of the Apes* was (closely) remade in an episode of *The Simpsons* ('A Fish Called Selma') as an all-singing, all-dancing Broadway musical titled 'Stop the Planet of the Apes[,] I want to get off!'" (93).

Twentieth Century Fox, aware of the *Ape*'s pop-cultural capital, tried to revive the franchise in the late 1980s. The project went through various stages and had several well-known names attached to it—among them James Cameron, Chris Columbus, Michael Bay, Arnold Schwarzenegger, and Oliver Stone (Pendreigh 2001). In 2001, Tim Burton's big budget remake—or, "reimagining," as it was called—earned mostly negative reviews and ultimately failed to reboot the franchise (despite its open ending and built-in options for sequelization). Film critic David Edelstein saw the film as "proof of Hollywood's simian instincts: Monkey see old hit, monkey do remake" (2001). However, a decade later, in 2011, Rupert Wyatt's *Rise of the Planet of the Apes* eventually proved the "rise-ability" of the franchise. This much acclaimed prequel in turn spawned sequels, starting with *Dawn of the Planet of the Apes* in 2014, and *War for the Planet of the Apes* scheduled for release in 2017.

In their entirety, the *Apes* films produce seriality effects that manifest themselves, among other things, as reflexive expressions of media-generational change. To begin with, many of their self-references draw attention to technological advances in cinematic storytelling, providing opportunities for viewers to identify, however nostalgically, with a specific standard of commodity production that has come to define their age group's experience of popular culture. In 1969, John Chambers, who had designed the ape makeup for the first film, was awarded an Honorary Oscar for his "outstanding achievement" (Booker 2006: 97). Thirty-three years later, the makeup in Tim Burton's remake was seen as "far more sophisticated, realistic, and expensive" (97), showcasing progress in special-effects techniques that many critics at the time described as "a quantum leap." Yet most of the same critics agreed that the new makeup was "not one bit more effective" (97) than the earlier films' look, which still managed to evoke an entire landscape of cultural production now gone and yet present as archived memory.[16]

Just ten years later, *Rise of the Planet of the Apes* set new standards once more, with Weta-Digital's groundbreaking mixture of performance capture and digital animation. This technology communicated the film's relationship to its own media environment in more self-evident and successful ways than the makeup artistry of the 2001 remake. It had already been employed in the latest *King Kong, The Lord of the Rings,* and *Avatar.* Andy Serkis, who played King Kong and Gollum, now starred as Caesar, the movie's genetically altered chimpanzee protagonist. Critics claimed this film was "his best computer-captured work" (Valero 2013), and Serkis's performance fueled the debate about whether motion-capture actors should be eligible for the Academy Award (Stevens 2011). Advances in technology also made it possible to film performance capture in real outdoor environments (instead of blank soundstages) for the first time, eliminating the barrier between visual effects and live action. These qualities were significantly enhanced during the production of the sequel, *Dawn of the Planet of the Apes* (which also added 3-D technology): more than 85 percent of *Dawn* was shot outside in the rainy forests of British Columbia.

In short, the early films, the 2001 remake, and the 2011 prequel/reboot—made so many years apart—all lay claim to being state-of-the-art, thereby reflecting, with varying degrees of success, distinct media-specific moments of an expansive narrative consumer aesthetics. In this manner, popular culture's increased availability for re-performance and comparison invites deeply autobiographical engagements with commercial material, to the point of

---

16. On the serial dialectics of simultaneous presence and absence, spectacularly dramatized as "spectral" seriality in horror films and some of their philosophical extrapolations, see chapter 6 in the present volume.

structuring individual personalities and their life stories in terms of progressing brand (dis)attachments. But media generations can also recognize themselves in the cultural concerns of remade films, which are usually accentuated more sharply there than in nonserialized formats (Kelleter 2012b). As Greene has argued, the first *Planet of the Apes* and its sequels "allegorized racial conflict and the Vietnam War": "Apocalyptic images of cataclysmic race wars, nuclear destruction, struggles for dominance, ecological and biological devastation [. . .] resonate throughout the Ape saga" and comment on the "tumultuous public contestations of the character and meaning of United States society" in the late 1960s and early 1970s (1996: xii, 7–8). By contrast, some critics disliked Tim Burton's remake exactly because they considered it "devoid of [. . .] contemporary resonance [. . .], chiefly an occasion for special effects, endless chases, chaotic combat sequences, Rick Baker's intricate makeup, and the witty production design of Rick Heinrichs" (Atkinson 2001). However, Verevis also points out that "[the] decision to assign a wide range of behaviours to both humans and apes transforms the earnest attempts at racial allegory of (especially) the latter films of the Apes series into a concern of 'species guilt'" (2006: 94). Similarly, Andrew O'Hehir identified "a jittery catalogue of millennial anxieties" in Burton's work (quoted ibid.).

Equally alert to its own timeliness, *Rise of the Planet of the Apes* in 2011 dramatizes contemporary fears of genetic engineering and—in the postcredits scene that paves the way for *Dawn of the Planet of the Apes*—the possibility of a viral pandemic spreading across the globe. *Dawn*, in fact, is deeply involved in a cultural climate that keeps envisioning impossible escapes from the factuality of the Anthropocene by way of "post-anthropocentric" transcendence. As if sublimating its own dependence on global revenue streams and marketable proliferation, this sequel of a prequel of a remake—the second installment of a rebooted franchise in conglomerate-era Hollywood—delineates ecological change as a reassuringly sequential catastrophe. We are shown biopolitical warfare with reversed roles but with a straightforward trajectory: always ahead.

CONCLUSION

These are just a few examples of the peculiar seriality of film remakes, sequels, prequels, franchises, and so forth. They serve to underline how studying Hollywood remaking as a practice of cinematic and pop-cultural self-historicization requires us to do more than we can do in this chapter; it requires us to trace in high descriptive detail the industrial, public, quotidian, economic, and academic practices and discourses that animate specific remakings and their storytelling ensembles, because together with the aesthetic activities of the films in question, these networked acts and actors produce something that can be called *second-order seriality*: ongoing narratives about (and through) ongoing narratives.

BIBLIOGRAPHY

Anderson, Benedict (1991). *Imagined Communities: Reflections on the Origin and Spread of Nationalism* [1983]. London: Verso.

Atkinson, Michael (2001). "Devolution of the Species." *Village Voice* (July 31). June 3, 2013. http://www.villagevoice.com/2001-07-31/film/devolution-of-the-species/1/.

Booker, Marvin Keith (2006). *Alternate Americas: Science Fiction Film and American Culture*. Westport, CO: Praeger.

Canjels, Rudmer (2011). *Distributing Silent Film Serials: Local Practices, Changing Forms, Cultural Transformation*. New York: Routledge.

Chatterjee, Partha (1999). "Anderson's Utopia." *Diacritics* 29.4: 129–34.

Cline, William C. (1984). *In the Nick of Time: Motion Picture Sound Serials*. Jefferson, NC: McFarland.

Corrigan, Timothy (2002). "Which Shakespeare to Love? Film, Fidelity, and the Performance of Literature." *High-Pop: Making Culture into Popular Entertainment*. Ed. Jim Collins. Oxford: Blackwell. 155–81.

Denson, Shane (2011). "Marvel Comics' Frankenstein: A Case Study in the Media of Serial Figures." *American Studies/Amerikastudien* 56.4: 531–53.

Denson, Shane and Ruth Mayer (2012). "Grenzgänger: Serielle Figuren im Medienwechsel." *Populäre Serialität: Narration—Evolution—Distinktion. Zum seriellen Erzählen seit dem 19. Jahrhundert*. Ed. Frank Kelleter. Bielefeld: Transcript-Verlag. 185–203.

Dusi, Nicola (2011). "Remaking als Praxis: Zu einigen Problemen der Transmedialität." *Serielle Formen: Von den frühen Film-Serials zu aktuellen Quality-TV- und Online-Serien*. Ed. Robert Blanchet et al. Marburg: Schüren. 357–76.

Eberwein, Robert (1998). "Remakes and Cultural Studies." *Play It Again, Sam: Retakes on Remakes*. Ed. Andrew Horton and Stuart Y. McDougal. Berkeley: University of California Press. 15–33.

Eco, Umberto (1990). "Interpreting Serials." *The Limits of Interpretation*. Bloomington: Indiana University Press. 83–100.

Edelstein, David (2001). "Beneath the Planet of the Apes: Tim Burton's Remake Doesn't Measure Up." *Slate* (July 27). June 3, 2013. http://www.slate.com/articles/arts/movies/2001/07/beneath_the_planet_of_the_apes.html.

Elsaesser, Thomas (1998). "Cinema Futures: Convergence, Divergence, Difference." *Cinema Futures: Cain, Abel or Cable?* Ed. Thomas Elsaesser and Kay Hoffmann. Amsterdam: Amsterdam University Press. 9–26.

Engell, Lorenz (2010). "Erinnern/Vergessen: Serien als operatives Gedächtnis des Fernsehens." *Serielle Formen: Von den frühen Film-Serials zu aktuellen Quality-TV- und Online-Serien*. Ed. Robert Blanchet et al. Marburg: Schüren. 115–33.

Felski, Rita (2011). "Suspicious Minds." *Poetics Today* 32.2: 215–34.

Forrest, Jennifer, ed. (2008). *The Legend Returns and Dies Harder Another Day: Essays on Film Series*. Jefferson, NC: McFarland.

Forrest, Jennifer and Leonard R. Koos, eds. (2002). *Dead Ringers: The Remake in Theory and Practice*. Albany: State University of New York Press.

Gray, Jonathan (2010). *Show Sold Separately: Promos, Spoilers, and Other Media Paratexts*. New York: New York University Press.

Greene, Eric (1996). *Planet of the Apes as American Myth: Race and Politics in the Films and Television Series*. Jefferson, NC: McFarland.

Hagedorn, Roger (1988). "Technology and Economic Exploitation: The Serial as a Form of Narrative Presentation." *Wide Angle* 10.4: 4–12.

——— (1995). "Doubtless to Be Continued: A Brief History of Serial Narrative." *Speaking of Soap Operas*. Ed. Robert C. Allen. Chapel Hill: University of North Carolina Press. 27–48.

Harrigan, Pat and Noah Wardrip-Fruin (2009). *Third Person: Authoring and Exploring Vast Narratives*. Cambridge, MA: MIT Press.

Haverkamp, Anselm and Renate Lachmann, eds. (1993). *Memoria: Vergessen und Erinnern*. München: Fink.

Hediger, Vinzenz (2004). "'You Haven't Seen It until You Have Seen It at Least Twice': Film Spectatorship and the Discipline of Repeat Viewing." *Cinéma & Cie* 5: 24–42.

Henderson, Stuart (2014). *The Hollywood Film Sequel: History & Form, 1911–2010*. London: BFI.

Higgins, Scott (2016). *Matinee Melodrama: Playing with Formula in the Sound Serial*. New Brunswick: Rutgers University Press.

Hills, Matt (2002). *Fan Cultures*. London: Routledge.

Horton, Andrew and Stuart Y. McDougal, eds. (1998a). *Play It Again, Sam: Retakes on Remakes*. Berkeley: University of California Press.

——— (1998b). "Introduction." *Play It Again, Sam: Retakes on Remakes*. Ed. Andrew Horton and Stuart Y. McDougal. Berkeley: University of California Press. 1–11.

Innis, Harold (1950). *Empire and Communications*. Oxford: Clarendon.

Junklewitz, Christian and Tanja Weber (2011). "Die Cineserie: Geschichte und Erfolg von Filmserien im postklassischen Kino." *Serielle Formen: Von den frühen Film-Serials zu aktuellen Quality-TV- und Online-Serien*. Ed. Robert Blanchet et al. Marburg: Schüren. 337–56.

Kelleter, Frank (2012a). "Populäre Serialität: Eine Einführung." *Populäre Serialität: Narration—Evolution—Distinktion. Zum seriellen Erzählen seit dem 19. Jahrhundert*. Ed. Frank Kelleter. Bielefeld: Transcript-Verlag. 11–46.

——— (2012b). "Toto, I Think We're in Kansas Again (and Again and Again): Remakes and Popular Seriality." *Film Remakes, Adaptations and Fan Productions: Remake/Remodel*. Ed. Kathleen Loock and Constantine Verevis. Basingstoke: Palgrave Macmillan. 19–44.

——— (2014a). *Serial Agencies: "The Wire" and Its Readers*. Washington: Zero Books.

——— (2014b). "Trust and Sprawl: Seriality, Radio, and the First Fireside Chat." *Media Economies: Perspectives on American Cultural Practices*. Ed. Marcel Hartwig, Evelyne Keitel, and Gunter Süß. Trier: wvt. 47–66.

——— (2015a). "Das Remake als Fetischkunst: Gus Van Sants *Psycho* und die absonderlichen Serialitäten des Hollywood Kinos." *Pop. Kultur und Kritik* 7: 152–73.

——— (2015b). "'Whatever Happened, Happened': Serial Character Constellation as Problem and Solution in *Lost*." *Amerikanische Fernsehserien der Gegenwart*. Ed. Heike Paul and Christoph Ernst. Bielefeld: Transcript-Verlag. 57–87.

Klein, Amanda Ann and R. Barton Palmer, eds. (2016). *Cycles, Sequels, Spin-Offs, Remakes, and Reboots: Multiplicities in Film and Television*. Austin: University of Texas Press.

Kompare, Derek (2006). "Publishing Flow: DVD Box Sets and the Reconception of Television." *Television and New Media* 7.4: 335–60.

Lahue, Kalton C. (1964). *Continued Next Week: A History of the Moving Picture Serial*. Norman: Oklahoma University Press.

——— (1968). *Bound and Gagged: The Story of the Silent Serials*. New York: Castle Books.

Landau, Diana (2001). *Planet of the Apes: Re-imagined by Tim Burton*. New York: Newmarket.
Latour, Bruno (2013). *An Inquiry into Modes of Existence: An Anthropology of the Moderns*. Cambridge, MA: Harvard University Press.
Leitch, Thomas (1990). "Twice-Told Tales: The Rhetoric of the Remake." *Literature/Film Quarterly* 18.3: 138–49.
Loock, Kathleen (2012). "The Return of the Pod People: Remaking Cultural Anxieties in *Invasion of the Body Snatchers*." *Film Remakes, Adaptations and Fan Productions: Remake/Remodel*. Ed. Kathleen Loock and Constantine Verevis. Basingstoke: Palgrave Macmillan. 122–44.
———(2014a). "Das Comeback der 80er: Zum Remake-Zyklus im aktuellen Hollywood-Kino." *montage AV* 23.1: 177–93.
———(2014b). "'The past is never really past': Serial Storytelling from *Psycho* to *Bates Motel*." *Serial Narratives*. Ed. Kathleen Loock. Special issue of *LWU: Literatur in Wissenschaft und Unterricht* 47.1–2: 81–95.
———(2015). "Die Fortsetzungen von *Jaws*." *Der weiße Hai Revisited: Steven Spielbergs* Jaws *und die Geburt eines amerikanischen Albtraums*. Ed. Wieland Schwanebeck. Berlin: Bertz+Fischer. 231–44.
———(2016a). "Retro-Remaking: The 1980s Film Cycle in Contemporary Hollywood Cinema." *Cycles, Sequels, Spin-Offs, Remakes, and Reboots: Multiplicities in Film and Television*. Ed. Amanda Ann Klein and R. Barton Palmer. Austin: University of Texas Press. 277–98.
———(2016b). "Sound Memories: 'Talker Remakes,' Paratexts, and the Cinematic Past." *The Politics of Ephemeral Digital Media: Permanence and Obsolescence in Paratexts*. Ed. Sara Pesce and Paolo Noto. New York: Routledge. 123–37.
Loock, Kathleen and Constantine Verevis (2012). "Remake/Remodel: Introduction." *Film Remakes, Adaptations and Fan Productions: Remake/Remodel*. Ed. Kathleen Loock and Constantine Verevis. Basingstoke: Palgrave Macmillan. 1–15.
Luhmann, Niklas (1999). *Die Gesellschaft der Gesellschaft*. Frankfurt: Suhrkamp.
"Match Them If You Can." *Photoplay* (November 1938): 42–43, 83.
Mayer, Ruth (2015). "Die Geburt der Nation als Migrationspraxis: Benedict Andersons *Imagined Communities*." *Schlüsselwerke der Migrationsforschung: Pionierstudien und Referenztheorien*. Ed. Julia Reuter and Paul Mecheril. Berlin: Springer VS, 2015. 263–74.
Mazdon, Lucy (2000). *Encore Hollywood: Remaking French Cinema*. London: BFI.
Mittell, Jason (2006). "Narrative Complexity in Contemporary American Television." *The Velvet Light Trap* 58: 29–40.
———(2010). "Serial Boxes." *Just TV* (January 20). September 7, 2014. http://justtv.wordpress.com/2010/01/20/serial-boxes/.
———(2015). *Complex TV: The Poetics of Contemporary Television Storytelling*. New York: New York University Press.
Murray, Simone (2011). *The Adaptation Industry: The Cultural Economy of Contemporary Literary Adaptation*. London: Routledge.
Natale, Richard (1991). "Classics on Video Get Jolt from Hot Remakes." *Variety* (December 9): 3, 8.
Newcomb, Horace (1985). "*Magnum*: The Champagne of TV?" *Channels of Communication* (May/June): 23–26.
Oltmann, Katrin (2008). *Remake | Premake: Hollywoods romantische Komödien und ihre Gender-Diskurse, 1930–1960*. Bielefeld: Transcript-Verlag.
Pendreigh, Brian (2001). *Planet of the Apes: or How Hollywood Turned Darwin Upside Down*. London: Boxtree.
Quaresima, Leonardo (2002). "Loving Texts Two at a Time: The Film Remake." *Cinémas* 12.3: 73–84.

Robin (2006). "Das hätte man besser machen können." Amazon.de (June 7). September 7, 2014. http://www.amazon.de/review/R1PDHO8ELCO5TI/ref=cm_cr_pr_perm?ie=UTF8&ASIN= B000F2CA10.

Roche, David (2014). *Making and Remaking Horror in the 1970s and 2000s: Why Don't They Do It like They Used To?* Jackson: University Press of Mississippi.

Schlüter, Christoph (2014). "Psycho-Quadrilogie—immer noch sehenswert!" Amazon.de (April 6). September 7, 2014. http://www.amazon.de/review/RBXP8S2R9C7DU/ref=cm_cr _pr_perm?ie=UTF8&ASIN=B0000E5SJD.

Stedman, Raymond William (1971). *The Serials: Suspense and Drama by Installment.* Norman: University of Oklahoma Press.

Stevens, Dana (2011). "Rise of the Planet of the Apes: An Animal-Rights Manifesto Disguised as a Prison-Break Movie." *Slate* (August 4). June 3, 2013. http://www.slate.com/articles/arts /movies/2011/08/rise_of_the_planet_of_the_apes.html.

Valero, Gerardo (2013). "Rise of the Planet of the Apes." RogerEbert.com (January 12). June 3, 2013. http://www.rogerebert.com/far-flung-correspondents/rise-of-the-planet-of-the-apes.

Verevis, Constantine (1997). "Re-Viewing Remakes." *Film Criticism* 21.3: 1–19.

——(2006). *Film Remakes*. Edinburgh: Edinburgh University Press.

Wloszczynska, Katharina (2012). "Das 'denkende' Remake." *Revisionen—Relektüren—Perspektiven*. Ed. Simon Frisch and Tim Raupach. Marburg: Schüren. 315–29.

CHAPTER 8

New Millennial Remakes

CONSTANTINE VEREVIS

WHEN ASKED in a recent interview what appealed to him about "rebooting a series that had already been interpreted," Christopher Nolan replied that when he undertook *Batman Begins* (2005), the first installment in Warner Bros.' *The Dark Knight Trilogy*, "there was no such thing conceptually as a 'reboot.' That idea didn't exist" (Foundas 2012/13: 7).

This chapter takes Nolan's comment as a starting point for a preliminary investigation of the state of cinematic remaking in the first decades of the new millennium. In an earlier period, the 1980s and 1990s, filmmakers and their production companies had been forced to defend serial filmmaking—specifically, film remakes and sequels—against accusations that aesthetically inferior remakes (and commercially timid sequels) were evidence that Hollywood had exhausted its creative potential.[1] By the beginning of the new millennium, however, there was evidence of a discursive shift, with subsequent industry discourses framing publicity more positively around a new film's "remake" status by ascribing value to an earlier version and then identifying various filters—technological, cultural, authorial—through which it had been transformed ("value-added"). In the first instance, this move can be seen as

---

1. Lütticken, for example, opens "Planet of the Remakes" with an account of the "widespread critical and popular aversion to remakes of classic—and even not-so-classic—films" (2004).

a commercial strategy (a way to sell a back catalogue), but it also identifies a serial practice in which the remake does not simply follow an original but recognizes new versions as free adaptations or variations that actualize an implicit potentiality at the source. This trend, which has increasingly led to authorized remakes that bear only a generic resemblance to their precursors, seems to have found its apotheosis in the "reboot": a legally sanctioned version that attempts to disassociate itself textually from previous iterations while at the same time having to concede that it does not replace—but adds new associations to—an existing serial property.[2] In other words, it marks out not merely a critical-historical moment in which remakes no longer linearly follow and supersede their originals but also a digitized, globalized one in which multiple versions proliferate and coexist.

NEW MILLENNIAL REMAKES ARE INTERMEDIAL

Recent accounts of Hollywood cinema (notably, Schatz 2009, Elsaesser 2012, and Balio 2013) tell a similar story, namely, that since the turn of the century a combination of forces—conglomeration, globalization, and digitization—has contributed to a new historical period of "postproduction."[3] For these writers, postproduction signals the way in which production *practices* have changed significantly over the past two decades (with an increased emphasis on editing, sound design, and special effects; compare Elsaesser 2012), but it also signals a *transformed media culture,* one characterized by a proliferation of viewing screens and new communicative technologies (iPhones, Twitter, Instagram), a rapid increase in digital distribution (downloading, streaming), and intensification of interest in moving-image content (iTunes, Netflix, YouTube) (Corrigan 2012).[4] As Nicolas Bourriaud describes it, post-production, and the *art* of post-production—that is, the proclivity of filmmakers to interpret, reproduce, remake, and make use of available cultural products—is a response to the "proliferating chaos of global culture in the information age [. . .] characterized by an increase in the supply of works [and an associated] eradication of the traditional distinction between production and consumption, creation and copy, readymade and original work" (2002: 13).

---

2. On this point, see the category of *non-remake*: a film that goes under the same title as a familiar property but has an entirely different plot (Verevis 2006: 7).

3. This term is taken, in the first instance, from Bourriaud 2002.

4. For a recent discussion of the impact of new media technologies, see Stenport/Traylor's (2015) claim that contemporary remakes/adaptations exemplify conceptual frameworks for digital information organization.

Costas Constandinides' recent work on *adaptation* (a term that he uses to describe practices of cinematic remaking) accords with this account of post-production, specifically his argument that the shift of all culture to digitized forms of production, distribution, and communication—along with the capacity of digital modes to remake and remodel existing material and media—at once undermines oppositions between original and copy and demands a theory of "post-celluloid adaptation" (2010: 19–26). In such an account, the remake is not (as in earlier definitions) described as a film based upon another film (or films) but defined from an intermedial perspective as the *translation* of narrative units and popular characters from a preexisting (celluloid) medium to a new, digital one:

> Post-celluloid adaptation can be [...] defined as the transition of familiar media content from a traditional medium—print, film, and television—to a new media object or a set of new media objects that embrace the concept of the main end-product. [Furthermore, post-celluloid adaptation] does not simply describe the transition of familiar images from an older medium to a new [one], but a process that is a symptom of the cultural logic of convergence culture. (Constandinides 2010: 24)

The suggestion that cinematic remakes are bound up in questions of translation and intermediality is not an exclusive one (e.g., Dusi 2012 and Evans 2014) and is evident enough in, for instance, the Todd Haynes–directed television miniseries remake of *Mildred Pierce* (HBO 2011), a version (of a novel, a film, and a textbook melodramatic film noir) that Pam Cook describes as a "multidimensional cultural event that has no single [point of] origin":

> The [*Mildred Pierce*] miniseries is decidedly *transmedia*—announced as a film on the credits, made for television, based on a book—signalling the *convergence* characteristic of contemporary media and the variety of [ways it opens up to] potential consumer experiences. (Cook 2013: 379; emphasis added)

Haynes had already explored the domestic drama in his 2002 film *Far from Heaven*, a revision of the narrative economy and moral structures of the melodramas of Douglas Sirk (in particular, *All That Heaven Allows* 1955) and other filmmakers, such as Rainer Werner Fassbinder, Max Ophüls, and John Stahl (Willis 2003). Haynes's miniseries version of *Mildred Pierce* similarly invokes multiple intertextual structures, not only the melodramatic urgency at the center of Cain's 1941 novel, which the miniseries "sticks [to] as close as the most clinging mother" (Smith 2011: 19), but also Michael Curtiz' 1945 film version, referenced in the remake's visual approach through its employment of reflected surfaces, frames within frames, and shots through windows and doorways (Stevens 2011). Moreover, like *Far from Heaven*—which not only remakes film history but also recuperates some thirty years of feminist film theory—Haynes's version of *Mildred Pierce* invites comparison with classic Hollywood film and recalls "the foundational debates that preoccupied film studies during the highly significant phase of its development as an academic discipline in the 1970s and 1980s" (Bergfelder/Street 2013: 371).

This intermedial (or "transmedial") relationship between old and new (millennial) media is perhaps more immediately focused around an example such as Peter Jackson's 2005 blockbuster remake of *King Kong* (Merian C. Cooper and Ernest B. Schoedsack 1933). The original story's mythic dimension, its inherent spectacularity, and open interpretability had made it a site of ongoing cultural and industrial remaking, with theatrical reissues (1938, 1942, 1946, 1952, 1956), sequels (*Son of Kong* 1933), spin-offs (*Mighty Joe Young* 1949), cross-cultural adaptations (*King Kong vs. Godzilla* 1962), and—following the massive commercial success of Steven Spielberg's *Jaws* (1975)—Dino De Laurentiis's epic remake, *King Kong* (1976), an overt parable of Third World exploitation that ends, in hubristic swagger, with Kong ascending the (then recently completed) twin towers of the World Trade Center. Riding the crest of a wave of fan enthusiasm for his *Lord of the Rings* trilogy, Jackson revisited the story of *King Kong* with solemn respect and an estimated $200 million budget, treating his remake to impressive, state-of-the-art digital effects. More significantly, Jackson employed new media strategies to engage fans, and render the film's official "website a powerful paratext of the main text, or created a 'database as non-linear narrative'" (Constandinides 2010: 24; also see Gray 2010). As Cynthia Erb (2009) points out in her extended reception study of the multiple versions of *King Kong*, Jackson established a relationship between the 1933 film and the 2005 remake by way of a collection of video-blog entries, initially shown on a Jackson-approved independent fan website, before the remake was released on DVD, as *King Kong: Peter Jackson's Production Diaries* (2005). The diaries not only demonstrate Jackson's personal investment in, and creative transformation of, a pioneering (special effects) classic but also underline the significance of establishing an approach to new millennial remakes that attends to the transformation of popular serial forms in and through new media platforms.

The *remediation* that characterizes the example of *King Kong*—and the way this extends into the immersion of the viewer through the interactive pleasures of game play and IMAX 3-D technologies—is evident in the more recent example of *RoboCop* (2014), a remake, or "reboot" as it has typically been labeled, in which the film, or "main end-product," clearly draws upon previous versions of the phenomenon and its global reputation as film series and video game.[5] The example of *RoboCop* demonstrates how a digitally networked culture organizes and manages information, with Sony Pictures setting up the film's official website—as the homepage for (the fictional) OmniCorp, creator of the RC2000 (or RoboCop) project—to embrace the potential of the web and so engage a "multiplicity of textual relationships that function across collaborative media [. . .] for [textual and] commercial purposes" (Constandinides 2010: 24). Online features, such as OmniCorp's Keynote announcement of the RC2000 Project at CES 2027, resist any simple reduction of the site to its promotional function and of the remake to any direct or singular relationship between itself and Paul Verhoeven's *RoboCop* (1987). Instead, the 2014 *RoboCop* adopts a nonlinear and nonhierarchical database logic, inserting the new millennial version into a collection of artifacts—*RoboCop* (1987), *RoboCop 2* (1990), *RoboCop 3* (1993), *RoboCop* television series (1994), *RoboCop: Prime Directive* miniseries (2000), *RoboCop vs. Terminator* video game (2006)—and extending its content across new aesthetic and media forms (most evidently the website's hyperlinks to social media and online game platforms). Despite some withering review comments—for instance, the perceived anomaly of a "PG-rated reboot" of Verhoeven's vicious, R-rated critique of Reaganomics (Nayman 2014)—*RoboCop*, like *King Kong* before it, demonstrates that in the new millennium it becomes increasingly difficult to lay claim to a clear-cut distinction between feature film and other media forms (James 2010). In a contemporary context, networks of interdependence across media require that new millennial remakes be understood as part of a more generalized condition of intermediality.

NEW MILLENNIAL REMAKES ARE TRANSNATIONAL

A digitally networked communications context transforms the way in which films are made, distributed, and consumed, generating new commercial and textual configurations of adaptations and remakes (Hutcheon 2013). Participatory and social-media cultures precipitate new (unauthorized) versions of recognizable properties and proprietary characters for immediate dissemination on the Internet: consider, for example, noncommercial fan productions such as fanvids, mash-ups, and recut trailers (described in Loock/Verevis 2012). These appropriations have become part of a remix culture (e.g., in the

---

5. For the term *remediation*, see Bolter/Grusin 1999.

Our RoboCop Remake online spoof), but official adaptations and remakes just as clearly support and maintain commercial conglomerate interests, including the negotiation of intellectual property rights and payments. Such authorized forms of cultural transfer are not restricted to Hollywood remakes of foreign, or non-English-language, films (Graser 2009) or to the relentless pursuit of synergy and brand extension characteristic of so-called total film (Elsaesser 2012). Trade journals such as *Variety* cast a wider net, reporting that "remakes are ringing up box office gold in Europe, prompting a proliferation of local hits being redone for neighboring markets and causing some curious cases of cross-pollination" (Vivarelli 2011: 6). European investment in remake rights is consistent with the logic behind the selling of formats for television—in a prominent example, the Danish/Swedish crime series *Broen/Bron* (2011), remade on the United States–Mexico border as *The Bridge* (USA 2013), and again as the Sky Atlantic and CANAL-PLUS TV series *The Tunnel* (UK/France 2013)—and coproduction deals where even large companies seek to limit their budgets and cover a broader audience right from the outset. Once stigmatized as "an American cheap trick," remakes of film (and television) properties that have been substantial commercial successes in single European markets increasingly provide universal themes and subject matter for cross-border translation or transliteration. *Variety* cites, among others, the example of France's *Bienvenue chez les Ch'tis/Welcome to the Sticks* (2008) remade as a German-Italian coproduction, *Benvenuti al sud/Welcome to the South* (2010), earning $50 million in Italy alone (Vivarelli 2011).

In the case of a high-profile European export, *The Girl with the Dragon Tattoo* (novels and films), Yellow Bird, the production company behind the Swedish-Danish film version (*Män som hatar kvinnor* 2009), bought the rights to Stieg Larsson's 2005 novel (the first of the so-called *Millennium Trilogy*) shortly after its release and consequently earned a main production credit in the Hollywood version, *The Girl with the Dragon Tattoo* (2011). As Neil Archer points out, citing a 2011 production report, for Yellow Bird "'cross border thinking and higher budgets' are key to the company's success, which in itself underlines the already transnational, genre [oriented] and property-conscious nature of the company and its output" (2012/13: 5). The transatlantic collaboration yielded a much-anticipated remake, directed by David Fincher and starring Daniel Craig and (in the title role) Rooney Mara. Although the remake performed financially "below expectation" (Gant 2012), Fincher's "cutting edge Hollywood narrative skills" and "authorial interests," established in psychothrillers such as *Se7en* (1995) and *Zodiac* (2007), transformed the dull mise-en-scène and clumsy exposition of Oplev's first adaptation into "thumping pumping cinema" (Newman 2012a: 18). This type of example resists and complicates earlier suggestions that cross-cultural remakes are simply evidence of American "cultural imperialism" (Vincendeau 1993). Indeed, concerns around moves to lift exemptions (originating in the 1990s General Agreement on Tariffs and Trade talks) that treat European films differently than they do other products under international free-trade rules in the European Union were recently reversed by Wim Wenders, who argued that abandoning the EU cultural exemption would in fact hurt Hollywood just as badly as it would Europe because EU films would not be there as counterpart to enrich and inform American cinema, specifically, through the U.S. practice of remaking European feature films and television formats (Macnab 2013).

The cross-pollination described by Wenders can be found in a recent example such as *Prince Avalanche,* David Gordon Green's 2013 remake of the little-known Icelandic film *Either Way/Á Annan Veg,* directed by Hafsteinn Gunnar Sigurðsson (2011). Green's reputation as U.S. independent filmmaker was principally forged across his first two features: *George Washington* (2000), a coming-of-age drama, described at the time of its release as a "poetic, tender, utterly individual and richly atmospheric" film (Kemp 2001: 49), and the indie romance of *All the Real Girls* (2003) which perfectly aligned "poetic rapture [and] gauche self-consciousness" with the antics of its star-crossed lovers (Brooks 2003: 37). Green's indie star had faded with his later involvement in studio comedies, such as the Judd Apatow–produced stoner film *Pineapple Express* (2008), but *Prince Avalanche*—insofar as it borrowed from the earlier indie dramas its unhurried pace and naturalistic aesthetic, and took from the later work its more comic characterizations—brought together the two contradictory impulses. Less evident (from the press kit and reviews that described *Prince Avalanche* as a "loose adaptation" of *Either Way*) was just how closely, not only in terms of plot and dialogue but also mise-en-scène, Green's film followed Sigurðsson's version. With *Either Way* producer and cinematographer Árni Filippusson acting as executive producer, and with the input of long-time collaborators—Tim Orr (cinematography), Richard A. Wright (production design), and David Wingo (music, with the Austin-based band Explosions in the Sky)—Green maintained the original film's 1980s period setting but transposed the Icelandic location to a section of landscape in central Texas, scorched and rendered ghostly by wildfire, to vividly evoke a sense of place. More tellingly, Green "personalized" the work, opening it up by way of a series of visual and musical interludes that, similar to *George Washington,* served to loosely hold the film together, as if by some "tenuous poetic connective tissue" (Jones 2004: 39).

The cross-border thinking of new millennial remakes is not limited to such examples from European and U.S. film but extends beyond, to instances of global or "world" cinema. Indeed, a significant development in recent accounts of cinematic remaking has been the recognition of intensive cross-cultural interactions, foregrounded through such notions as a mediascape of globalization and its uptake in descriptions of *transnational* film remakes. These discussions work to reverse the unidirectional routes of influence identified by critics of globalization and emphasize more-dynamic transactions and avenues of cultural exchange. In one example, Iain Robert Smith (2008) embraces a framework of "critical transculturalism" to engage with debates on the "transnational flows of media [and] intersecting nature of cultural production" in and through an exploration of Turkish appropriations of American popular culture, specifically the case of *Turist Ömer Uzay Yolunda/Tourist Ömer in Star Trek* (1974). In another instance, Hilary Hongjin He (2010) examines the "intercultural dialogue" established between Hollywood and China in "localized versions" of films such as the action-thriller *Connected/ Bao chi tong hua* (2008), remade in Hong Kong from the 2004 U.S. film *Cellular* and regarded as the first official Chinese remake of a Hollywood film. In a more recent example, Zhang Yimou's *A Woman, A Gun, and A Noodle Shop* (2009) transposes Joel and Ethan Coen's debut neo-noir thriller *Blood Simple* (1984)—itself a rewriting of the hard-boiled fiction of James M. Cain—to rural Northern China in the guise of a slapstick period comedy. These accounts capture the multidirectional nature of cinematic remaking: simultaneously looking "outwards (transnationalism, globalization), inwards (cultural traditions and aesthetic conventions), backwards (history and memory), and sideways (crossmedial practices and interdisciplinary research)" (Wang 2008: 10). These (and other) descriptions of worldwide media traffic insist that new millennial remakes be understood as part of more general migratory movements and practices of global translation.[6]

NEW MILLENNIAL REMAKES EMBRACE THE POSTAUTEUR

In Elsaesser's account of new millennial Hollywood, the forces of conglomeration, globalization, and digitization require that (blockbuster) films perform well not only locally (U.S. domestic) and internationally but also on multiple platforms, including "the film's internet site, the movie trailer, the video game and the DVD as both textual and promotional entities" (2012: 284). If one

---

6. For other "world cinema" examples, see Phu (2010) on *Ringu/The Ring*, Richards (2011) on *Kuch Kuch Hota Hai*, and Shin (2012) on *The Happiness of the Katakuris/The Quiet Family*.

accepts Elsaesser's suggestion that global Hollywood has entered a digital or franchise era of post-production, a blockbuster like Steven Spielberg's 2005 version of *War of the Worlds* (previously adapted as *The War of the Worlds* 1953) can be understood as a "signature product," an instance in which a pre-existing film or property no longer provides a (closed) narrative model but rather functions as a blueprint for remediation. Ideally, the blockbuster remake becomes a prototype and basis for generating serial forms (sequels, series, and cycles), producing tangible objects (DVDs, soundtracks, and books), and providing commodity experiences (games, rides, and theme park attractions) (Elsaesser 2012: 283–85). Extending this line of argument, one can describe the way in which new millennial filmmakers, for example, postauteurs such as Christopher Nolan, David Fincher, and Steven Soderbergh (in examples such as *Batman Begins*, *The Girl with the Dragon Tattoo*, and *Ocean's Eleven* 2001), seek to insert themselves into the innumerable flows of global film and media production, not by setting out to create something that is new (original) but rather by remaking what already exists: revising it, inhabiting it, and putting it to use (Bourriaud 2002). In a global marketplace, available forms are remade and remodeled, and then "serialized" and "multiplied" in sequels, series, and cycles across expanding territories and media platforms (Lewis 2001 and Elsaesser 1998).

The paucity (until quite recently) of critical approaches to the film remake has been attributed to the concept's "anti-authorship quality" (Quaresima 2002: 75), but with the new millennial remake, the authorial agency and "brand-name vision" of the postauteur becomes a key element of promotion and reception (Corrigan 1998). Thus, Steven Soderbergh can create a version of *Solaris* that directly invokes earlier properties—Andrei Tarkovsky's 1972 film and Stanisław Lem's 1961 novel—but upon the film's release reviewers noted that Soderbergh had transformed the source material even more than Tarkovsky, abandoning its broad philosophical questions to focus primarily on the love story: the relationship between Kris (Chris in the remake) and his wife Rheya, and—in a reprise of Alfred Hitchcock's *Vertigo* (1958)—their opportunity for a "second chance." Although Soderbergh claimed that his interest in *Solaris* was driven by the ideas at the center of the book—"[the novel] just seemed to be about everything I [was] interested in personally"—reviewers drew attention to the thematic and stylistic similarities between *Solaris* and Soderbergh's other film work, describing the remake as an authorial revision: a property transformed according to auteur predilections into "an intimate two-hander between a man and a woman" (Romney 2003: 14). In a further comment, one that underlines how cinematic remaking can be understood in terms of a filmmaker's desire to repeatedly express and modify a particular aesthetic sensibility and worldview, Amy Taubin calls *Solaris* "the most personal, interiorized narrative of [Soderbergh's] career, [a film that] could be his *Pierrot le fou* or *Vertigo*" (2002: 78).

In a more recent example, the press kit for *Passion*, Brian De Palma's 2012 French-German (English-language) remake of Alain Corneau's psychodrama *Crime d'amour/Love Crime* (2010), announces: "Brian De Palma returns to the sleek, sly, seductive territory of *Dressed To Kill* [1980] with an erotic corporate thriller fueled by sex, ambition, image, envy and the dark, murderous side of PASSION," before going on to note that "the screenplay is written by De Palma with additional dialogue by Nathalie Carter [and is] based on the French film *Crime d'amour*." Separated by only a few years from Corneau's original, De Palma's *Passion*—a film initiated by the same Paris-based production company and characterized by its use of hi-tech, glass, and polished-steel interiors—"presents [itself as] a model of production and distribution strongly influenced by [the] contemporary audiovisual landscape": the principal characters, Christine (Rachel McAdams) and Isabelle (Noomi Rapace), "shoot on their mobile, edit on their laptop, project it at the staff meeting, and stick it on YouTube" (Álvarez/Martin 2013). In and through this distinctive mise-en-scène, De Palma not only engages his signature preoccupations (doubling and artifice, including an elegant, extended split-screen sequence that ends with a violent murder) but also offers a crucial innovation: a "knotty, triangular construction [that] rotates through Christine, Isabelle and Dani [Karoline Herfurth]," transforming the two-sided conflict of the original players (Kristin Scott Thomas as Christine and Ludivine Sagnier as Isabelle) into a "disturbing, *serial chain* [in which] the competitiveness never ends, but [in an eloquent metaphor for the remake itself] only ever perpetuates itself, *expanding and renewing* with each new turn of the screw" (Álvarez/Martin 2013; emphasis added).

In a perhaps less evident example, Nathan Lee mounts an inspired postauteur defense of Rob Zombie's 2007 remake of John Carpenter's 1978 *Halloween*, one of a cycle of contemporary treatments of an entire era of American low-budget horror films bracketed by George A. Romero's *Night of the Living Dead* (1968) and the Romero-backed *Night of the Living Dead* remake by Tom Savini (1990). As described by Kim Newman, the tone for the new cycle was set by films such as Marcus Nispel's *The Texas Chainsaw Massacre* (2003; Tobe Hooper 1974) and Zack Snyder's 2004 remake of Romero's 1978 *Dawn of the Dead,* but ten years on "the cycle has yielded too many unmemorable redos of the likes of *When a Stranger Calls* and *Prom Night* plus genuinely disastrous takes on *Halloween* and *It's Alive*" (2013: 91). Contra Newman, Lee's assessment recognizes not only how the *Halloween* remake is repurposed within a new discursive field but also how it is re-envisioned in/as a genuine authorial innovation:

> Given the hallowed status of the original, [and] the prejudice and blind spots of critical orthodoxy [...] *Halloween* (07) has not been seen for what it is: *the remake as legitimate parallel creation*. An independent feat of imagination that extends, amplifies, and in certain regards improves on the source material, this most original and morally complex of the current [horror] remake cycle properly belongs to a discussion of the distinctly remade: Schrader's *Cat People* [1982], Carpenter's *The Thing* [1982], *Invasion of the Body Snatchers* per Kaufman [1978] and Ferrara [*Body Snatchers*, 1993]. (2008: 26; emphasis added)

Elsewhere, Lee writes that Zombie's *Halloween* is a film that "demands to be taken on its own terms," a work that is "[close] in spirit to Soderbergh's rethinking of Tarkovsky in his *Solaris*" (2013: 50). In a contemporary context, postauthorship describes a shift in emphasis from a regime of rights based on authorship and originality toward one centered on trademark and reproducibility (Grainge 2008: 11), but the new millennial remake also provides unique possibilities for the means of expression.

NEW MILLENNIAL REMAKES ARE CHARACTERIZED BY PROLIFERATION AND SIMULTANEITY

The new millennium is characterized by an exponential increase in content and availability, not only through films on DVD but through films (and fragments of films) via VOD streaming and on the Internet. If the new millennium is distinguished by unprecedented access, then selection becomes a major concern: not how to see films but how to choose between them (Cousins 2010). Just one expression of this is found in Paul Schrader's comments around his film *The Canyons* (2013), a work that he describes as an example of "post-Empire" independent filmmaking. Schrader borrows the term from *The Canyons*' cowriter, Bret Easton Ellis, who says that American film has come into a late, or postimperial, period: the U.S. film empire was of the twentieth century, but U.S. culture has now entered a period in which it is making films out of the remains of the empire, "the junk that's left over" (Gross 2013: 26). For Schrader, the number-one fact of digital cinema is that it has become easier to get a (low-budget) film financed, but—because of the sheer volume of work that gets made—it is increasingly difficult to get anyone to see it. In the case of *The Canyons,* Schrader says that he "got lucky" with the "noise factor" surrounding the film. He says that he and Ellis, along with *The Canyons'* lead actors, Lindsay Lohan and porn-star James Deen, had "some cachet" with interest groups:

> We were in with four different sub-groups of interested people. [. . .] Lindsay has four million (Twitter) followers, and James has half a million. Bret has 250,000. [. . .] When you're pitching a movie, that's the question they ask: Is it going to make noise? Are you going to hear this above the din of the avalanche of film productions? And if the idea has noise, then they are interested in it. [. . .] And this idea [*The Canyons*] had noise. Some of it by design, some of it by luck. (Gross 2013: 27)

As the volume of films and versions of films increases and accelerates across media and delivery platforms, not only do presold titles and characters contribute to the noise factor (especially for genre films), but the same confluence of factors—conglomeration, globalization, and digitization—also feeds a fascination among audiences and practitioners with recycled properties, or what Simon Reynolds (2011) calls a "retromania" for revivals, reissues, and remakes. Moreover, where remakes were once understood to compete economically and culturally with their previous versions, contemporary remakes typically enjoy a more complementary relationship with their originals, with publicity and reviews often drawing attention to earlier versions (which are increasingly available and so appear closer in time). For instance, as recently as 2011, *Video Ezy* magazine ran a promotion ("Not Lost in Translation") which not only used the line "laughter is an international language, something proven by the fact that this month's hilarious comedy *Dinner for Schmucks* actually comes from a hugely successful French film titled *The Dinner Game*" to advertise a new release, but also drew attention to a whole back catalogue of double (or doubled) features: *The Departed* (2006) and *Infernal Affairs* (2002), *Let Me In* (2010) and *Let the Right One In* (2008), *The Ring* (2002) and *Ringu* (1998), *Vanilla Sky* (2001) and *Open Your Eyes/Abre los Ojos* (1997), and several others.

The significance of the noise factor is plainly evident in authorized (non-)remakes such as *Ocean's Eleven* and *The Italian Job* (2003)—films that retain little more than the title from a previous version in order to invest the new production with a narrative image and added aesthetic and commercial value. Thus, the 2003 version of *The Italian Job* might be seen as just another generic heist movie and star vehicle for Mark Wahlberg and Charlize Theron, but its presold title and iconic Mini Cooper tunnel chase sequence functions both as a marker of distinction and as an opportunity for remodeling (literally in the case of film's tie-in with the 2001 new generation Mini Cooper S series). To this end, the film's Paramount Pictures website included comments by director F. Gary Gray: "I liked a lot of things about the original. It had great style and unforgettable performances. But the film that we've made is for modern audiences, with updated technology." Executive producer James Dyer similarly noted that the 1969 version was a point of departure, not replication: "[Our] movie is a little different. It's not a remake [. . .] but it does use similar tools to tell the story: heist, armored truck, gold, Mini-Coopers." Following the 2003 theatrical run of *The Italian Job*, both versions were simultaneously released to DVD, with extras on the remake DVD not only drawing attention to the original but featuring scenes from it. The subsequent release of Paramount Home Video's "*The Italian Job* Gift Set" DVD edition, which included both 1969 and 2003 versions, demonstrates that just as adaptations of literary properties often lead viewers back to source novels for a first reading, remakes encourage viewers to seek out original—or *parallel*—film properties (Corrigan 2002).

A remake title, proprietary character, or signature tune may contribute to audience interest around a new release and mark it out in a digitized culture distinguished by accelerated proliferation, but it also plays a part in the identification of a body of work for commemoration and canonization. It is clear that the popularity and reputation of some titles—such as *The Evil Dead* (2013/1981) and *Fright Night* (2011/1985), *Fame* (2009/1980), and *Footloose* (2011/1984)—is present in advance of their remaking, and it is equally evident that U.S. remakes of relatively little known properties do not draw much attention to their European originals. But in other cases remakes *reintegrate* previous versions into a new present, just as cover versions of popular music so often do for original recordings. For instance, Kim Chapiron's *Dog Pound* (2010) occasioned another look at the institutional reformism of Alan Clarke's social-realist *Scum* (1979), with the latter subsequently remastered for release on DVD/Blu-ray (2013). Similarly, Breck Eisner's 2010 remake of George A. Romero's 1973 *The Crazies*, following remakes of all three films in Romero's *Dead* franchise, is said to be "among the best of the recent run of do-it-over-again movies" for the fact that it gives "a feeling that *Romero really lives in this story*" (Newman 2010: 51; emphasis added). Or, in an example which demonstrates that originals are never pure or singular, Len Wiseman's "80s style blockbuster reboot" or "uber-digi remake" of *Total Recall* (2012) not only revisits key scenes from Paul Verhoeven's 1990 version but "lazily rips off entire images and scenes from *Blade Runner* [1982], inciting in us the desire to leave this irritation behind and go and see *that* movie again" (Atkinson 2012b: 104). In a contemporary media landscape—one characterized by self-referencing and interconnection—the new millennial remake becomes (in this case, quite literally) an archive of and for the future.

NEW MILLENNIAL REMAKES DO NOT ERASE OR OVERWRITE BUT COEXIST

Film remakes provide an illustration of new millennial film culture, perhaps most clearly in the concept of the "reboot," borrowed from computer technology to describe the process of "beginning again" to recommercialize a film property or franchise by denying or nullifying earlier iterations. Citing examples such as Zack Snyder's *Man of Steel* (2013); Marc Webb's *The Amazing Spider-Man* (2012); J. J. Abrams's *Star Trek* (2009); and "the quintessential reboot," Christopher Nolan's *Batman Begins,* William Proctor argues that the reboot differs conceptually from the remake insofar as it is a franchise-specific concept:

> A remake is a singular text bound within a self-contained narrative schema; whereas a reboot attempts to forge a series of films, to begin a franchise anew from the ashes of an old or [critically or commercially] failed property. In other words, a remake is a reinterpretation of one film, a reboot "re-starts" a series of films that seek to disavow and render inert its predecessors' validity. (2012a)

In making this distinction, part of Proctor's aim is to shore up the concept of the reboot in face of opportunistic advertising that seeks to promote (mere) sequels—*Tron Legacy* (2010), *Terminator Salvation* (2009), or *The Mummy: Tomb of the Dragon Emperor* (2008)—by assigning them a reboot label and thus aligning the films with the critical and commercial success of the Dark Knight trilogy.

The term *reboot,* along with a string of (remake) euphemisms (e.g., *encore, reworking, refitting, retooling, retread, redo, makeover*) has gained cultural currency in recent years. For example, *Sight and Sound* magazine reports, "Most of the industry's recent reboots have been expensive disasters [. . .] as with this reconstitution of John Carpenter's *The Thing*" (Atkinson 2012a: 76); "Danny Cannon's *Judge Dredd* (1995) is likely to be remembered as the version that got it wrong. [. . .] However, a generation on, the flop has got its reboot" (Newman 2012b: 34); and "there is a memorable scene in the 1982 film of *Conan* [*the Barbarian,* in which Conan is harnessed to a massive millstone that he must turn in perpetuity] but there is no equivalent scene in Marcus Nispel's relaunched or remade or rebooted *Conan*" (Pinkerton 2011: 57). Perhaps the most inspired employment of the term is found in Tim Lucas's account of the serial saga of

Edgar Rice Burroughs's *Tarzan the Ape Man*, specifically the films made after Johnny Weissmuller's departure from the series. Describing a set of eleven post-Weissmuller film titles (five films starring Lex Barker and another six Gordon Scott), Lucas writes: "*Tarzan's Greatest Adventure* (1959) reboots the franchise in the same way that *Casino Royale* did with the Bond films. [...] Scott rises admirably to the occasion [...] and carries the film to the most exciting climax of the entire series" (2010: 88). Each of these examples, even the retrospective designation of the Tarzan films, supports the notion of (franchise) rebooting, but the idea that a new version somehow erases (or overwrites) previous iterations is at odds with a digitally networked culture in which new media do not replace the old but add layers and associations to it. As Proctor says, "a reboot is a brand-new product, yet it is already old. [...] There is no blank slate" (2012b).

The fact of multiple, parallel versions that coexist rather than erase or overwrite is evident in Tim Burton's 2001 remake—or failed reboot—of Twentieth-Century Fox's *Planet of the Apes* (1968).[7] Poised at the beginning of the new millennium, Burton's version was backed with an estimated budget of $110 million. It was seen by some as a "jittery catalogue of millennial anxieties" (O'Hehir 2012: 12) but more typically as a film that had transformed the B-movie aesthetic of the *Planet of the Apes* film and television series into a B-movie blockbuster: "a wild concept coated in incongruous corporate gloss" (Brooks 2001: 56). Despite its differences, the re-imagined *Planet of the Apes* owed much to Schaffner's version: its reputation, its progeny, and especially its well-remembered ending in which astronaut Taylor (Charlton Heston) realizes in his discovery of a bomb-blasted Statue of Liberty that the ape planet is actually a postapocalyptic Earth. Indeed, reviews of *Planet of the Apes* consistently focused on Burton's transformed ending, in which astronaut Davidson (Mark Wahlberg) crash lands on the steps of the Lincoln Memorial, only to find that the chiseled features of Abraham Lincoln have been replaced by those of gorilla General Thade, describing it as "spectacularly befuddling" and a "monkey-puzzle of an ending" (Brooks 2001: 56). As disingenuous as the Burton ending might be, these reviews miss a more obvious point, namely, that the *Planet of the Apes* remake has a twist ending because the original does. Thus, it may well be the case that the "crazed final coda [...] makes little in the way of logical sense, and clashes conspicuously against the pedestrian narrative that precedes it" (Brooks 2001: 56), but the ending makes perfect *remake sense,* displaying a narrative logic that builds upon—rather than cancels—the memory of the cult original.

---

7. For more on the *Apes* franchise, see the preceding chapter in this volume.

Vivian Sobchack finds something similar in Ridley Scott's *Prometheus* (2012), a reboot of the *Alien* franchise, impressively extended through its fictional Weyland Industries website. As described by Sobchack, the estimated $130 million film is a work that gets caught (literally) between a rock (the planet LV-233) and a hard place (the spaceship *Prometheus*). More precisely, the difficulty some viewers found with *Prometheus* was that it presented itself as a type of remake—a prequel to Scott's *Alien* (1979)—and a completely original film—a reboot of the *Alien* franchise—only to fall apart because, like Burton's *Planet of the Apes,* it obeys a remake logic that is not matched to the narrative logic of the discreet (rebooted) episode. The result was confusing, illogical, and disjointed plotting. In Sobchack's metaphor, the bedrock in this case is the industry franchise and mythic universe initiated by Scott's sci-fi horror hybrid *Alien*—afterwards sequelized in James Cameron's *Aliens* (1986), David Fincher's *Alien 3* (1992), and Jean-Pierre Jeunet's *Alien Resurrection* (1997)—and the tension between remake and reboot logic is evident in Twentieth Century Fox's own promotional material which presents *Prometheus* as a film that "started out as a prequel" but wants to function as a "stand-alone film [. . .] that tips its hat to elements of the original *Alien*" (2012: 33). Ultimately, the film leads back to the future, with the planet's various xenomorphic life forms transmuting at the end into "the old alien we've come to love—a kind of annunciation of a hoped-for sequel to the prequel" (2012: 33). However, the key question for Sobchack, as for the reboot, remains: "how to get out of this double bind between origins and originality?" (34). As she puts it:

> While [*Prometheus* has been] rightly criticized for its unforthcoming and ultimately incoherent narrative, and its often arbitrary character motivation and editorial (il)logic, *Prometheus* is indeed coherent as an allegory of its own struggle with and resistance to its origins. [. . .] That is, not able to escape that old mythology completely and unable to integrate it with a new one, the film instead signifies the resistance brought to bear against both. (34)

As much a discursive formation as an industrial or textual one, the category of the reboot thus reimagines not simply a specific film (or films) but the concept of the remake for the new millennium.

CONCLUSION

The five interrelated "theses" put forward in this chapter—new millennial remakes are intermedial, new millennial remakes are transnational, new millennial remakes embrace the postauteur, new millennial remakes are characterized by proliferation and simultanity, and new millennial remakes do not erase or overwrite but coexist—begin to sketch out a provisional map, or at least some significant lines and contours, for a "media-historic profile" of new millennial remakes (Kelleter/Loock 2014). The remake has never been a static thing but a concept that is always evolving. And while it may be too early to draw conclusions as to the nature of a distinct historical period, these notes should demonstrate that the present and future of cinema is a re-vision of its past, *especially* in the new millennium, and that aesthetic and economic evaluations of film remakes (good or bad, success or failure) are less interesting than the cultural and historical significance of new millennial remaking practice.

BIBLIOGRAPHY

Álvarez López, Cristina and Adrian Martin (2013). "To the Passion." *Lola* 4. April 6, 2014. http://www.lolajournal.com/.

Archer, Neil (2012/13). "*The Girl with the Dragon Tattoo* (2009/2011) and the New 'European Cinema.'" *Film Criticism* 37.2: 2–21.

Atkinson, Michael (2012a). "The Thing." *Sight and Sound* 22.1: 76–78.

———(2012b). "Total Recall." *Sight and Sound* 22.10: 104–5.

Balio, Tino (2013). *Hollywood in the New Millennium*. Basingstoke: Palgrave Macmillan.

Bergfelder, Tim and Sarah Street (2013). "Introduction: *Mildred Pierce*, Pedagogy and the Canon." *Screen* 54.3: 371–77.

Bolter, Jay David and Richard Grusin (1999). *Remediation: Understanding New Media*. Cambridge: MIT Press.

Bourriaud, Nicolas (2002). *Postproduction: Culture as Screenplay: How Art Reprograms the World*. New York: Lukas & Sternberg.

Brooks, Xan (2001). "*Planet of the Apes*." *Sight and Sound* 11.10: 54–56.

———(2003). "*All the Real Girls*." *Sight and Sound* 13.9: 37.

Constandinides, Costas (2010). *From Film Adaptation to Post-Celluloid Adaptation: Rethinking the Transition of Popular Narratives and Characters across Old and New Media*. New York: Continuum.

Cook, Pam (2013). "Beyond Adaptation: Memory, Mirrors, and Melodrama in Todd Haynes's *Mildred Pierce*." *Screen* 54.3: 378–87.

Corrigan, Timothy (1998). "Auteurs and the New Hollywood." *The New American Cinema*. Ed. Jon Lewis. Durham: Duke University Press: 38–63.

———(2002). "Which Shakespeare to Love? Film, Fidelity, and the Performance of Literature." *High-Pop: Making Culture into Popular Entertainment*. Ed. Jim Collins. Oxford: Blackwell. 155–81.

———(2012). "Introduction: Movies and the 2000s." *American Cinema of the 2000s*. Ed. Timothy Corrigan. New Brunswick: Rutgers University Press. 1–18.

Cousins, Mark (2010). "Overwhelmed by Options." *Sight and Sound* 20.2: 41.

Dusi, Nicola (2012). "Remaking as Practice: Some Problems of Transmediality." *Cinéma & Cie* 12.18: 115–27.

Elsaesser, Thomas (1998). "Fantasy Island: Dream Logic as Production Logic." *Cinema Futures: Cain, Abel or Cable?* Ed. Thomas Elsaesser and Kay Hoffmann. Amsterdam: Amsterdam University Press. 143–58.
——— (2012). *The Persistence of Hollywood*. London: Routledge.
Erb, Cynthia (2009). *Tracking King Kong: A Hollywood Icon in World Culture*. Detroit: Wayne State University Press.
Evans, Jonathan (2014). "Film Remakes, The Black Sheep of Translation." *Translation Studies* (January 30). April 6, 2014. http://www.tandfonline.com/.
Foundas, Scott (2012/13). "Cinematic Faith. Interview with Christopher Nolan." *Film Comment*, Special Supplement (Winter): 7–11.
Gant, Charles (2012). "Is the Hollywood Remake Dead?" *The Guardian* (March 30). April 6, 2014. http://www.theguardian.com/film/2012/mar/29/is-the-hollywood-remake-dead.
Grainge, Paul (2008). *Brand Hollywood: Selling Entertainment in a Global Media Age*. London: Routledge.
Graser, Marc (2009). "H'wood Mines Europe's New Wave for Remakes." *Variety* (March 16–22): 6–7.
Gray, Jonathan (2010). *Show Sold Separately: Promos, Spoilers, and Other Media Paratexts*. New York: New York University Press.
Gross, Larry (2013). "*The Canyons*." *Film Comment* 49.4: 22–29.
He, Hilary Hongjin (2010). "Connected through Remakes: Intercultural Dialogue between Hollywood and Chinese Cinema Industries." *Asian Cinema* (Spring/Summer): 179–92.
Hutcheon, Linda with Siobhan O'Flynn (2013). *A Theory of Adaptation*. London: Routledge.
The Italian Job. Official Website. May 28, 2004. http://www.italianjobmovie.com/flash/index.html.
James, Nick. (2010). "Syndromes of a New Century." *Sight and Sound* 20.2: 34–38.
Jones, Kent (2004). "A Niche of One's Own." *Film Comment* 40.5: 39–41.
Kelleter, Frank and Kathleen Loock (2014). "Retrospective Serialization: Remaking as a Method of Cinematic Self-Historicizing." popularseriality.de (March 13). April 6, 2014. http://www.popularseriality.de/en/projekte/aktuelle_projekte/retrospektive-serialisierung/index.html.
Kemp, Philip (2001). "*George Washington.*" *Sight and Sound* 11.10: 49.
Lee, Nathan (2008). "Horror Remakes." *Film Comment* 44.2: 24–28.
——— (2013). "True Believer." *Film Comment* 49.3: 48–50.
Lewis, Jon (2001). "Following the Money in America's Sunniest Company Town: Some Notes on the Political Economy of the Hollywood Blockbuster." *Movie Blockbusters*. Ed. Julian Stringer. London: Routledge. 61–71.
Loock, Kathleen and Constantine Verevis (2012). *Film Remakes, Adaptations and Fan Productions: Remake/Remodel*. Basingstoke: Palgrave Macmillan.
Lucas, Tim (2010). "Them Tarzan." *Sight and Sound* 20.2: 88.
Lütticken, Sven (2004). "Planet of the Remakes." *New Left Review* 25. April 6, 2014. http://newleftreview.org/II/25/sven-lutticken-planet-of-the-remakes.
Macnab, Geoffrey (2013). "Protect and Survive." *Sight and Sound* 23.7: 19.
Nayman, Adam (2014). "*Robocop.*" *Sight and Sound* 24.4: 82.
Newman, Kim (2010). "*The Crazies.*" *Sight and Sound* 20.4: 51.
——— (2012a). "The Icegirl Cometh." *Sight and Sound* 22.2: 16–18.
——— (2012b). "A Sense of Dredd." *Sight and Sound* 22.10: 32–34.
———. (2013) "*Evil Dead.*" *Sight and Sound* 23.5: 91.
O'Hehir, Andrew (2001). "Gorilla Warfare." *Sight and Sound* 11.9: 12–15.
Passion. Official Website. April 6, 2014. www.passionthemovie.com.
Phu, Thy (2010). "Horrifying Adaptations: *Ringu, The Ring*, and the Cultural Contexts of Copying." *Journal of Adaptation in Film and Performance* 3.2: 43–58.

Pinkerton, Nick (2011). "*Conan the Barbarian.*" *Sight and Sound* 21.10: 57.
Proctor, William (2012a). "Regeneration and Rebirth: Anatomy of the Franchise Reboot." *Scope* 22 (February). April 6, 2014. http://www.academia.edu/3099488/Regeneration_and_Rebirth_Anatomy_of_the_Franchise_Reboot.
———(2012b). "Beginning Again: The Reboot Phenomenon in Comic Books and Film." *Scan* 9.1 (June). April 6, 2014. http://scan.net.au/scn/journal/vol9number1/William-Proctor.html.
Prometheus. Official Website. April 6, 2014. http://www.weylandindustries.com/.
Quaresima, Leonardo (2002). "Loving Texts Two at a Time: The Film Remake." *CiNéMAS* 12.3: 73–84.
Reynolds, Simon (2011). *Retromania: Pop Culture's Addiction to Its Own Past.* London: Faber and Faber.
Richards, Rashna Wadja (2011). "(Not) Kramer vs. Kumar: The Contemporary Bollywood Remake as Glocal Masala Film." *Quarterly Review of Film and Video* 28: 342–52.
RoboCop. Official Website. April 6, 2014. http://www.robocop.com/site/.
Romney, Jonathan (2003). "Future Soul." *Sight and Sound* 13.2: 14–17.
Schatz, Thomas (2009). "New Hollywood, New Millennium." *Film Theory and Contemporary Hollywood Movies.* Ed. Warren Buckland. London: Routledge. 19–46.
Shin, Chi-Yun (2012). "'Excessive' Remake: From *The Quiet Family* to *The Happiness of the Katakuris.*" *Transnational Cinemas* 3.1: 67–79.
Smith, Iain Robert (2008). "'Beam Me Up, Ömer': Transnational Media Flow and the Cultural Politics of the Turkish *Star Trek* Remake." *The Velvet Light Trap* 61: 3–13.
Smith, Paul Julian (2011). "All She Desires." *Sight and Sound* 21.8: 19–22.
Sobchack, Vivian (2012). "*Prometheus.*" *Film Comment* 48.4: 30–34.
Stenport, Anna Westerdahl and Garrett Traylor (2015). "The Eradication of Memory: Film Adaptations and Algorithms of the Digital." *Cinema Journal* 55.1: 74–94.
Stevens, Isabel (2011). "All That the Miniseries Allows." *Sight and Sound* 21.8: 21–23.
Taubin, Amy (2002). "Back to the Future." *Filmmaker* 10.4: 78–85.
Verevis, Constantine (2006). *Film Remakes.* Edinburgh: Edinburgh University Press.
Vincendeau, Ginette (1993). "Hijacked." *Sight and Sound* 3.7: 23–25.
Vivarelli, Nick (2011). "Remake Mania Strikes Europe." *Variety* (February 21–27): 6.
Wang, Yiman (2008). "The Transnational as Methodology: Transnationalizing Chinese Film Studies through the Example of *The Love Parade* and Its Chinese Remakes." *Journal of Chinese Cinemas* 2.1: 9–21.
Willis, Sharon (2003). "The Politics of Disappointment: Todd Haynes Rewrites Douglas Sirk." *Camera Obscura* 18.2: 130–75.

PART III

Television

CHAPTER 9

The Ends of Serial Criticism

JASON MITTELL

WHY DO WE study serial narratives?[1] Our goals in this volume are wide-ranging, spanning the intrinsic value of understanding aesthetic objects to situating serial narratives within broader contexts of culture and society. For my own explorations of contemporary serial television, I have considered both the poetics of how storytelling works within the bounds of its medium and the cultural question of how television matters in the lives of its viewers (Mittell 2015). In this chapter, I focus on a question that, though common to most media scholarship, has not been a core issue in my own work so far: what do television narratives mean? Or, more accurately, how might we talk about the meanings of serialized television and their relation to issues of cultural power and representation? And, in an additional layer, how does seriality (in a range of practices) impact our understandings and criticisms of such meanings?

For most scholars analyzing a media text, typical research questions are: What does it mean? Why does it matter? Such questions explore the political meanings of a text in terms of representations, ideologies, and competing positions on issues of cultural importance. Textual meanings of this sort can then be contextualized within the larger cultural field of contemporary capitalism, class struggle, identity categories, and political power to highlight why

---

1. This chapter was adapted from a previously published version in Mittell 2015.

such moments matter beyond the mere fact of being represented within a television series. These are important issues and they deserve a central place in the field of media studies. However, they are not the questions that have motivated my own serial criticism. Instead, I have focused on two related but different questions: How does it mean? How does it matter? To answer the first question, I use historical poetics to analyze the formal storytelling techniques employed by television series, placing those choices in the contexts of the industry and its creative personnel to understand why meaning-making happens the way it does.[2] The second question focuses on the cultural circulation of television programs, considering how critics, viewers, and fans continue serial television's signification beyond the texts themselves. At times, such circulation makes series "matter" in the explicitly material sense, creating paratexts that further the processes of meaning-making.[3] Fusing historical poetics and cultural studies aims at offering a better understanding of how serial television programs work as both aesthetic texts and cultural practices.

For some critics these questions are sufficient, providing ample room to explore issues of form and function that matter for television seriality. However, other scholars conceive of the field as primarily dedicated to uncovering meaning and analyzing cultural politics. From this perspective, a project that focuses on the "how" of television storytelling seems insufficient unless used as a means toward answering other questions. I find myself at a middle ground in this debate: I am sufficiently interested in the "how" to focus on poetics and practices, but I also believe that questions of meaning and power are important and should be part of my scholarly equation. Thus, a contextualized historical-poetic approach appears to me both an end in itself and a means to get toward different ends.

Regarding these different ends, we might shuffle the two questions I posed above into two new ones: What does it mean through how it means? Why does it matter through how it matters? In other words, how can we use historical poetics and the study of cultural circulation to explore questions of political meaning and social significance? And how might our own critical practices be embedded in such serial systems? Uncontroversially, I believe that having a more robust account of how television storytelling works should give us a deeper understanding of its meanings and cultural power, but as I will demonstrate, accounting for the formal mechanics and cultural practices of seriality makes politicized textual analysis much more complex.

---

2. For more on historical poetics as it has been developed within film studies, see Bordwell 1989, 2007; and Jenkins 1995.

3. For examples of cultural studies of the discursive circulation of television textuality, see Brooker 2001, Mittell 2004, Jenkins 2006, and Gray 2006.

SERIAL REITERATION AND *HOMELAND'S* VIDEO CONFESSION

To explore the challenges of political interpretation, consider the opening segment of *Homeland*'s first season finale, "Marine One," which first aired on the premium cable channel Showtime on December 18, 2011. The episode begins with a single-take video testimonial that Sgt. Nicholas Brody is making to explain why he plans to die a suicide bomber, killing numerous American politicians and military personnel as part of a conspiracy led by a radical Middle Eastern terrorist. Staring directly into the camera, he says the following:

> My name is Nicholas Brody and I'm a sergeant in the United States Marine Corps. I have a wife and two kids, who I love. By the time you watch this, you'll have read a lot of things about me, about what I've done, and so I wanted to explain myself. So that you'll know the truth. On May 19, 2003, as part of a two-man sniper team serving in Operation Iraqi Freedom, I was taken prisoner by forces loyal to Saddam Hussein. Those forces then sold me to an al-Qaeda commander, Abu Nazir, who was operating a terrorist cell from across the Syrian border, where I was held captive for more than eight years. I was beaten, I was tortured, and I was subjected to long periods of total isolation. People will say I was broken, I was brainwashed. People will say that I was turned into a terrorist, taught to hate my country. I love my country. What I am is a Marine, like my father before me and his father before him, and as a Marine, I swore an oath to defend the United States of America against enemies both foreign and domestic. My action this day is against such domestic enemies: the vice president and members of his national security team, who I know to be liars and war criminals responsible for atrocities they were never held accountable for. This is about justice for 82 children whose deaths were never acknowledged and whose murder is a stain on the soul of this nation.

The video then cuts off as the episode continues onto a conventionally shot and edited scene. To make sense of this sequence, we need to consider it in multiple contexts, as that is certainly how it might be variably consumed. For a few viewers, this may have been the first episode of *Homeland* they had seen, making for quite a confusing viewing experience. Assuming that such a novice viewer recognizes it as belonging to a fictional program, the clip is still marked as "authentic" via excessive mediation—visible viewfinder symbols, red "Record" indicator, black-and-white image, and direct address to the camera all connote that this is actual footage being made within the storyworld.

Brody's tone and emotional intensity convey that he is telling the truth, or at least what he believes to be true. And if true, it is quite a radical political statement: accusing the vice president of being a war criminal, responsible for mass killings of children and covering up their deaths, and claiming that the patriotic duty of a U.S. Marine is to commit an act of violent retribution.

Of course, most viewers saw (or will see) this footage in a broader context following eleven hours of storytelling, stretched out over two months of screen time (or less if consumed after its initial airing). Throughout the season leading up to this moment, we questioned whether Brody had been turned to work for his captors, witnessed his conversion to and faithful practice of Islam, saw via flashback the brutality inflicted upon Brody during his captivity, and eventually discovered his plot to become a suicide bomber against Vice President Walden. Most important for this sequence, we witnessed (again via flashback) the event that turned him firmly against his government: a U.S. drone bombing that destroys a school in Syria and kills eighty-two children, including terrorist leader Abu Nazir's son Issa, whom Brody had lived with as teacher and friend. After the attack, Nazir shows Brody the vice president's news conference where he denies that any children have been wounded in the bombing, thus inspiring Brody's act of vengeance. For viewers like me, this serial context validates Brody's statements and beliefs so that his video declaration of patriotism through terrorism rings emotionally true in a fashion that seems utterly out of place on commercial American television.

In the context of its original airing in fall 2011, *Homeland*'s first season marked the first time that many of its viewers had seen the issue of drone strikes debated on American television—press coverage of the issue was quite marginal within U.S. media, growing somewhat in frequency and depth of coverage in late 2011 after one high-profile strike, but even then it would remain a specialized "fringe" topic reaching only dedicated news consumers (until it became more openly debated in 2013; see McKelvey 2013). By dramatizing a drone strike, visualizing the deaths of innocent children, and having a sympathetic, white American character empathize with the Arab victims, *Homeland* offered dramatic outlet for a dissenting view of American military action, found at the time only in pronouncements of the extreme antiwar left but never, so far, on mainstream television.

Given this context, what is the political meaning of this clip? As it begins the episode, it is a shocking moment of emotionally motivated outrage, giving legitimacy to the perspectives of terrorists who see themselves as victims of terrorism carried out by the American military. We have come to care about Brody as a character, seeing him as deeply flawed and (despite his denial in the video) broken, but also justified to take extreme action against a corrupt and arguably criminal administration—all of which marks this video as a radical statement that viewers are invited to endorse or at least consider as valid. However, the episode continues: Brody hides the memory card on which he recorded his confession (so that his terrorist allies can find it) and then continues with his plan to kill the vice president, secretary of defense, CIA leaders, and numerous other politicians, military personnel, and civil servants within a military bunker. He does attempt to trigger the bomb, but it fails; after repairing the bomb in the bathroom, he gets a phone call from his teenage daughter Dana who inspires him to abandon his plan, as he realizes what his suicide attack would do to his wife and children. The episode ends with Brody shifting plans to become an agent of Nazir from within the government, rather than violently disrupting it. This development serves the dramatic needs of seriality, as it allows Brody to continue to the next season, and it sustains the dual espionage and romance plots between Brody and Carrie Mathison, the CIA agent who is convinced that he is a traitor. But this course of events also shifts the terms of Brody's dissent away from the political and toward the personal, where his familial connection to Dana eclipses his ties to surrogate son Issa. If in the beginning of the episode, the video frames an act of anti-American violence as the duty of a patriotic Marine, the episode's conclusion counters such radicalism by reframing Brody's dissent as a simpler act of revenge for a loved one's death—a move that is likely to shift our allegiance back to Carrie and her unquestionably patriotic pursuit of Brody and Nazir.

But season one is not the only context for this video. It reappears nine months later (as originally aired) in *Homeland*'s second season, where the video is shown in five of the season's twelve episodes, creating a serialized ripple effect for everyone who watches it. In the second episode, CIA Division Chief Saul Berenson discovers the video hidden among the belongings of a suspect in Beirut; he shows it to Carrie (in the next episode), who reacts with flooding emotion as she realizes that her discredited accusations against Brody were correct. The fourth episode begins with Saul showing the video to his boss at the CIA, David Estes, to confirm that Brody, now a Congressman and likely vice-presidential candidate, is a traitor. In these reiterations, the meaning of the video transforms from a statement of political dissent into a piece of evidence for American agents fighting terrorism. The sentiments that Brody expresses become irrelevant and are not repeated on-screen; all that matters for the CIA is that Brody is a traitor. The video's radical politics are thus erased as it becomes an object within the investigation, and the drama focuses on how the CIA will catch Brody and what the consequences of his betrayal might be. In Robert Allen's terms (1985), the video switches from a syntagmatic element that moves the plot forward to a paradigmatic element that triggers character reactions and emotions—and notably these reactions never consider Brody's argument that resisting American military hegemony might be viewed as a form of patriotism. This serial succession of characters viewing the video invokes *Homeland*'s reflexive impulse as established in early episodes, where viewers saw themselves mirrored in Carrie's video surveillance of Brody. Such scenes emphasized the central role that the act of watching characters watch other characters on a screen in their most intimate and unguarded moments plays in *Homeland*; regular viewers learned that these reflexive moments matter.

The fourth appearance of Brody's video in the second season is when Brody himself sees it in episode five, "Q & A." Captured by the CIA and interrogated to learn what he knows, he is forced to watch his own confession after denying any involvement with Abu Nazir or knowledge of Issa; the scene is appropriately visualized here via the meta-representation of surveillance cameras as we watch Carrie in the observation room watch Brody watch himself. Viewing the video serves both as a paradigmatic trigger for Brody's emotional reaction to his own past actions and as a plot device that creates a procedural game for the rest of the episode in which Brody and Carrie attempt to out-manipulate each other. "Q & A" completes the video's depoliticization, as Carrie frames Brody's betrayal firmly within the realm of the personal—his love for Issa and Walden's individual monstrosity in ordering and covering up the drone strike—but it avoids the political debate of whether the United States itself is culpable for such military action and whether it is noble to resist such dominance. By the end of the dramatically compelling episode, it is clear that Carrie and her CIA colleagues are the good guys, that Brody wants to redeem himself by helping them, and that the violence at the center of the plot is the act of individual "monsters" like Vice President Walden and Abu Nazir, disconnected from the broader military issue of drone strikes that forged the content of the original video.

The video's final appearance in the second season finale restores its political function but reinscribes it into hegemonic meanings: after the CIA headquarters is bombed, al-Qaeda releases the video to U.S. media in order to frame Brody for the attack. This repurposing of the video marks its radical sentiments as clearly villainous and foreign, disassociating them from the sympathetic character of Brody himself. This effect is reinforced as we watch Brody's family viewing the clip on television, where his daughter Dana's shock and denial underscore the sense that this is not who Brody is now, if he ever really had been this person. Brody himself, on the run with Carrie, sees the video on television—a scene reminding viewers of Brody's current innocence and ultimate refusal to pursue his original plan, while reinforcing our understanding that the "real" terrorists are the "Arab" foreigners who released the video, not the white Marine voicing dissent in it. After this, the video does not appear in the third season, which concludes Brody's story arc by making him a secret martyr in the service of American intelligence, though publicly known as the terrorist responsible for destroying the CIA building.

Within these broader serial contexts, what is the political meaning of Brody's video? Is it a radical critique of American military policy, an irrational statement by a grieving and broken man that might later be retracted, or the ventriloquized voice of Middle Eastern terrorists speaking through a brainwashed soldier? Each of these interpretations could be correct, depending on when you ask: *Homeland*'s serial timeframe changes the video's meaning, even though the video itself remains intact. And this is the challenge of trying to analyze meaning in a serial text: it changes as you watch it—or rather: *how* it means shapes *what* it means. Significantly, in this process, a serial text's past is not "undone," for despite later reframings, the initial airing of Brody's video still conveyed a radical critique that does not fully disappear, either within the storyworld or from the minds of viewers.

We can understand these serial instances of political reframing through the lens of *articulation,* as defined by Stuart Hall (Grossberg 1986): dominant forms of political ideology are forged by the contingent linking of social practices to cultural meanings, which frequently shift and transform within new contexts. In this fashion, Brody first articulates a terrorist bombing, linking it to American patriotism; then *Homeland* rearticulates the video, linking it to antiterrorist pursuits; and eventually the series frames Brody as wrongly accused, solidifying the dominant notion that terrorists are dark-skinned foreigners, not white Marines. Serial articulation depends on the practice of reiteration, where repeating and reframing help define which linkages are maintained and which are discarded over the course of a series, highlighting how the political interpretations of serial narratives are always subject to revision and recontextualization. Seriality itself is wrapped up within this notion of articulation, as the connections between the already-seen and the new installment are the chemical reactions that create resonances of meanings, emotional engagements, and layers of cultural politics that encourage viewers to keep watching for new linkages and recontextualizations.

Any attempt to account for *Homeland*'s political meanings must remain open and unfinished until the series concludes, for it has demonstrated a willingness to revisit and revise, sometimes drastically so, its politics. This is not true for all series. It seems pretty clear after the first season of *The Wire* or *24* on which side of the political fence these narratives will be pitching their tent, although both do shift over time concerning particular issues, such as gender representation or the role of ethnicity. But for a series like *Homeland*, whose politics are more ambiguous and thus more in need of interpretation, any analysis must be contingently grounded within a particular moment of storytelling, not an overall perspective. The reason is not that a conclusion will necessarily provide ideological closure and thus resolution, but that finality here means that there is no more time to revise and resubmit narrative positions—no more opportunity for the narrative to provide further articulations of its politics or to enter into dialogue with its serialized past.[4]

This consideration of deferred closure evokes a classic concept in the political analysis of television storytelling: the "cultural forum." As argued by Horace Newcomb and Paul Hirsch (1994, analyzing conventional episodic forms), the power of television narratives to raise cultural *questions* is at least as important as their power to provide ideological *answers*. Television's ability to act as a cultural forum is even more vital for long-form serialized narratives whose potential answers providing closure are deferred for weeks, months, or even years. Such temporal gaps highlight how much political meaning-making occurs within the broader temporal frame of serial consumption, as the politically explosive questions that *Homeland* raises remain ambiguously unanswered for months, creating a temporal gap for viewers and critics to fill with their own shared practices of interpretation and debate.

SKYLER'S STORIES: *BREAKING BAD* AND CHARACTER CHEMISTRY

The *Homeland* example focuses on the question of "How does it mean?" as a factor in shaping a program's politics, where serial poetics impact interpretation. To explore "How does it matter?"—or the ways in which a program's cultural circulation shapes its political significance over the course of time—consider the gender politics of *Breaking Bad* in light of its serialized reception. *Breaking Bad* is Walter White's story. There is no question that he is the center of the narrative, arguably more so than any other individual figure in a multiseason American television series, where narratives typically focus more on ensembles and relationships than on an individual character study. But despite this singular focus, the series does tell other stories, too, and one of the most interesting and compelling is Skyler White's. In fact, I argue that the series tells at least three versions of Skyler's story over the course of its run, each

---

4. For more on the role of serial narrative and ideological closure, see Mumford 1995.

adding a different layer to her characterization.[5] When viewed together, these three layers help us understand the series' narrative strategies, genre norms, approaches to gender, and cultural reverberations and reception practices.

The first layer places Skyler at the narrative center, imagining the storytelling as focused on her experiences and perspectives. If we focus primarily on Skyler's character's arc, *Breaking Bad* becomes a very different type of tale, offering a melodramatic account of deception, adultery, and ultimately an abusive, dangerous marriage that she repeatedly tries to escape from but always gets drawn back into. It is the story of a woman who finds herself married to a loser, a cypher, and finally a monster. To understand this level of Skyler's story, consider the program's narrative from her perspective. Skyler starts the series in a fairly content and comfortable place: pregnant with a second child, married to a stable if boring schoolteacher, and closely bonded to her son and sister. Walt starts acting erratically around his fiftieth birthday, revealing that he has terminal lung cancer. Skyler goes back to work to help pay for their medical bills, even though her boss Ted's affections disturb her. When Walt undergoes cancer surgery, he accidentally confirms Skyler's suspicions of a web of deceptions worse than she had imagined, and thus she leaves him as soon as he has recovered.

Soon after their separation, Walt tells Skyler his secret: that he has been cooking crystal meth. This leads to a power struggle over a potential divorce, with Skyler lashing out by having an affair with Ted, who has his own corrupt business practices that she finds herself involved in. As Skyler learns more about Walt's business, she uses her bookkeeping skills to help launder money and purchase a car wash as a front, rationalizing her decision that helping Walt is better for the family than breaking the law for Ted. In the face of Walt's angry response, she decides to remain to "protect this family from the man who protects the family." Skyler clearly feels that she can manage Walt and his growing hostility, until she learns that he murdered his drug-dealing boss, Gus Fring. While viewers have witnessed Walt's procession of increasingly amoral killings for years of screen time, in Skyler's mind he has quite suddenly transformed from a meek criminal chemist who is in over his head to a scheming murderer willing to blow up a nursing home to take out an enemy. In fear of what else he might do and how she too has made moral compromises, Skyler retreats into catatonic fear and defensiveness, placing her in a state of passive paralysis as a battered spouse. Eventually Skyler convinces Walt that they have too much money to ever spend, and he quits the business and tries to return to a mild-mannered suburban life.

---

5. I explore these variations of Skyler's stories in more depth in Mittell 2015.

However, just as they adjust to a cash-infused state of semi-normalcy, brother-in-law Hank discovers Walt's secret, and Skyler finds herself forced to collaborate with Walt to protect the family. Skyler's story climaxes when Walt returns home, apparently having killed Hank, as their marriage explodes when she cuts him with a kitchen knife, and Walt runs off into exile with baby Holly. The relationship culminates with one of the most harrowing and meaningfully layered telephone calls ever put onto film, when Walt bullies Skyler in an over-the-top rant that is both a performance designed to absolve her from culpability in the eyes of the police and an expression of his deep-seated masculinist rage and resentments. This phone call has multiple meanings that mimic the layers of Skyler's stories. At its most explicit, Walt's blustering attack resonates with the serial melodrama of Skyler's tale of spousal betrayal and abuse, with a tone of hectoring rage evoking soap opera villainy.[6] As a culmination of Walt's abusive relationship with Skyler, this call marks their separation and leads to her final downfall: broke and broken, paying for Walt's crimes by losing everything financially and familially, and embodying the tale of a wronged wife destroyed by her husband's criminal ambitions and emotional abuse.

Of course, *Breaking Bad* is not Skyler's story. Walt is the protagonist, so we are invited to see his perspective on their marriage and share his singular knowledge. Thus the phone call is framed as part of Walt's plan, a performance of hypermasculine bullying designed to exonerate Skyler—this summarizes Walt's attitude toward his family throughout the series, as he convinces himself that he must endanger and deceive them in order to save and protect them. Throughout *Breaking Bad,* Skyler is positioned as the object of Walt's story, with the narrative events of betrayal, infidelity, and failed reconciliations presented to us through the lens of his actions and attitudes. If the first layer is Skyler's Story as melodramatic tragic heroine, then the second is Walt's Story of Skyler, with his perspective as well-intentioned patriarch given narrative authority and predominance. We view Skyler through Walt's eyes, sharing the secrets that he keeps from her. And the secret of the phone call is his intent to perform the role of abusive crime lord to save her, a meaning she slowly realizes. However, he is also articulating his lingering resentment of how her interference disrupted his master plans. On this level, Walt—as the Machiavellian gangster quick to knock down anyone who stands in his way—believes every word he says. Even though he pronounces half-truths that strip out the nuance of his feelings for Skyler, they are still truths. These multiple meanings

---

6. For this observation, I would like to thank Kristen Warner, who, in a personal conversation with me, compared Walt's telephone call to a rage-call made by *Days of Our Lives* über-villain Stefano.

highlight how difficult it is to separate Skyler's story from Walt's version of her story, as we ultimately experience both stories as serially articulated together and linked to numerous threads from years of narrative unfolding.

Murray Smith's (1995) conceptual framework for understanding characterization in film offers a vocabulary for understanding this effect. Throughout *Breaking Bad,* Walt provides our primary character alignment, as we are closely attached to his experiences and can access his perspective on events more than any other character's point of view. However, our moral allegiance to him is variable—we begin the series feeling allied to this sad and desperate man making a chain of poor choices, but our allegiance is challenged with each amoral act, and eventually most of us will find him morally repugnant and detestable. By contrast, we perceive Skyler mostly from Walt's perspective, moving from loving commitment to growing frustration as she impedes his transformation into a "real man" (via his criminal alter ego Heisenberg). Thus we regard Skyler as both the object of his affection and as an obstacle for his self-realization. This conflict drives the ambivalent feelings viewers have toward Skyler. Even though he rationalizes that he turns to crime for her and his kids, we know long before he admits in the finale that he is doing it for himself, because he likes it and it makes him feel alive. We like it too, as it drives the narrative pyrotechnics and makes the story feel alive. Thus, while we might rationally understand that Skyler is morally superior to Walt, emotionally we are invited to regard her as a problem to be overcome on the path to narrative fulfillment.

The phone call reveals and links these two stories of Skyler, the abused spouse, and Walt, the scheming mastermind. But the third story zooms out to the meta-level of *Breaking Bad* as a popular-serial text, focusing on viewer receptions of Skyler and her story. While we might debate how much of what Walt said to Skyler was an articulation of the character's underlying hostility toward his wife, there is no question that most of his rant resonated with much of what some fans had already been saying. In one of the most notorious and well-publicized examples of fan antagonism toward a character, a significant portion of *Breaking Bad*'s fans actively disliked and even hated Skyler, treating her as the series' true villain. To name but one of many instances: the Facebook page "Fuck Skyler White" had more than 31,000 fans at its peak, with posts and comments dripping with aggressive misogyny. Hatred of Skyler among such viewers is unwavering, prompting vitriolic comments that root for Walt to abuse or kill Skyler and even extending such violent fantasies to actress Anna Gunn.

Series creator Vince Gilligan denounced the Internet's den of Skyler-haters as "misogynists, plain and simple," as he saw no other way to justify such antipathy toward a character who is often a voice of reason against Walt's amoral selfishness (quoted in Brown 2013). Anna Gunn took her defense a step further via the unprecedented step of writing a *New York Times* editorial that decried the anti-Skyler vitriol and called out its misogyny as deeply rooted in contemporary American society. As Gunn suggests, "Because Skyler didn't conform to a comfortable ideal of the archetypical female, she had become a kind of Rorschach test for society, a measure of our attitudes toward gender" (2013). The series itself critiqued Skyler-hate by putting the misogynistic words of these viewers in Walt's mouth, having him perform them semi-disingenuously at the character's peak of evil and hatred. But this mirror found its own reflection on anti-Skyler Facebook pages, with comments like "I climaxed when Heisenberg called Skyler a stupid bitch. I've been waiting five seasons for that." Needless to say, not all fans perceived the phone call as multileveled.

However, we cannot simply dismiss anti-Skyler sentiments as misreadings, whether driven by misogyny or more rational perspectives. We must acknowledge that the ways people make meaning around an ongoing serial do matter, even if they seem to be "wrong" by standards of textual design, authorial intent, moral judgment, or even basic human decency. Hating Skyler is a significant part of *Breaking Bad*'s cultural circulation, and thus an aspect of its gender politics as serially articulated, if not textually intended or justified. Whatever intents we might attribute to the series, it is a text that has prompted misogyny, both by attracting such viewers to its audience and by triggering hateful reactions among a significant subset of them. Such practices cannot be simply overridden or invalidated by a nuanced textual analysis. Although I find them both deplorable and unjustified by the text, they still matter.

Indeed, I would highlight such Skyler-hate as "matter" in a literal sense, its discursive materiality being a toxic by-product of *Breaking Bad*'s experimental character chemistry. The series attempts to create a risky genre fusion, embedding a character grappling with a broken, abusive marriage more common to a serial melodrama within a high-octane gangster drama. Since we experience Skyler via our alignment with Walt, whose allegiance transforms over the course of the series, *Breaking Bad* functions in part as a "women's film" narrated in reverse, told through the rationalizing perspective of the abusive spouse whom we only slowly grow to recognize as the villain. In Walt's abusive phone call, we can see melodrama and gangster story coexist uncomfortably alongside the unstable vector of character transformation, but we also detect the seeping ooze of misogynistic toxic waste produced by this chemical reaction. While *Breaking Bad* is rightly hailed for its groundbreaking innovations in charting character change and moral transformation, Skyler's multiple stories reveal what is catalyzed by Walt's metamorphosis, including the venomous reactions to being bonded to such an unstable figure, as they leak out beyond the confines of the storyworld itself.

Analyzing the cultural politics of a complex serial text is tricky business. The challenges of being able to nail down the meaning of *Homeland*'s vision of patriotism and terrorism, and *Breaking Bad*'s gender politics, underline how such interpretive analysis, despite its centrality to the field at large, is both too easy and too hard. It is fairly straightforward business to interpret a television program using the field's well-established critical tools, isolating the particular episodes and moments that best support an argument or focusing on opinions that will help label a text ideological and/or progressive. But once you account for how serial television works over time and across various cultural sites, it becomes hard to say anything about a program's politics with any conviction that is not draped in contingency, partiality, and competing perspectives. That might also be true for a stand-alone cultural work like a novel or film, as a text's multiple layers of meaning contradict itself and create enough interpretive varieties to sustain decades of competing scholarly interpretations. But a serial text talks back to its critics by rearticulating the meaningful moments through reiterations and recontextualizations, as with *Homeland*'s video, or by putting the words of its most rabidly misogynist viewers into its protagonist's mouth, as with *Breaking Bad*'s climactic phone call. Interpretive criticism of a moving target that both serially rearticulates itself and directly incorporates its own cultural reception is of a distinctly different order than the stable polysemy of a novel or film, or even the postserialized finality of a television series that has completed its run.[7]

Trying to answer the question of what it all means to interpret and critique a serial text's cultural politics leaves me with that most shameful conclusion for an academic: I don't know. That is not to suggest that we ignore issues like *Homeland*'s presentation of patriotism or *Breaking Bad*'s perspective on patriarchy, but such questions require us to reframe what we mean by *interpretation* itself as a serial endeavor—always in flux, replete with gaps and ellipses, inclusive of endless contexts and paratexts, and always frustrating in its incompleteness. Writing serial criticism requires the critic to accept such potential shifts and open-ended contingency as part of the terrain of both text and context, giving up the certainty that is often asserted in academic arguments.

---

7. For serial narratives as "moving targets," see this volume's introduction.

BIBLIOGRAPHY

Allen, Robert C. (1985). *Speaking of Soap Operas*. Chapel Hill: University of North Carolina Press.

Bordwell, David (1989). "Historical Poetics of Cinema." *The Cinematic Text: Methods and Approaches*. Ed. R. B. Palmer. New York: AMS. 369–98.

——(2007). *Poetics of Cinema*. New York: Routledge.

Brooker, Will (2001). "Living on *Dawson's Creek*: Teen Viewers, Cultural Convergence, and Television Overflow." *International Journal of Cultural Studies* 4.4: 456–72.

Brown, Lance (2013). "In Conversation: Vince Gilligan on the End of *Breaking Bad*." *Vulture* (May 12). April 1, 2013. http://www.vulture.com/2013/05/vince-gilligan-on-breaking-bad.html.

Gray, Jonathan (2010). *Show Sold Separately: Promos, Spoilers, and Other Media Paratexts*. New York: New York University Press.

Grossberg, Lawrence (1986). "On Postmodernism and Articulation: An Interview with Stuart Hall." *Journal of Communication Inquiry* 10.2: 45–60.

Gunn, Anna (2013) "I Have a Character Issue." *The New York Times* (August 23). November 9, 2013. http://www.nytimes.com/2013/08/24/opinion/i-have-a-character-issue.html.

Jenkins, Henry (1995). "Historical Poetics and the Popular Cinema." *Approaches to the Popular Film*. Ed. Joanne Hollows and Mark Jancovich. Manchester: Manchester University Press. 99–122.

——(2006). *Convergence Culture: Where Old and New Media Collide*. New York: New York University Press.

McKelvey, Tara (2013). "Media Coverage of the Drone Program." Joan Shorenstein Center on the Press, Politics and Public Policy. February 28, 2013. http://shorensteincenter.org/2013/02/media-coverage-of-the-drone-program/.

Mittell, Jason (2004). *Genre and Television: From Cop Shows to Cartoons in American Culture*. New York: Routledge.

——(2015). *Complex TV: The Poetics of Contemporary Television Storytelling*. New York: New York University Press.

Mumford, Laura Stempel (1995). *Love and Ideology in the Afternoon: Soap Opera, Women, and Television Genre*. Bloomington: Indiana University Press.

Newcomb, Horace and Paul M. Hirsch (1994). "Television as Cultural Forum." *Television: The Critical View*. Ed. Horace Newcomb. New York: Oxford University Press. 503–15.

Smith, Murray (1995). *Engaging Characters: Fiction, Emotion, and the Cinema*. New York: Oxford University Press.

CHAPTER 10

Sensing the Opaque
Seriality and the Aesthetics of Televisual Form

SUDEEP DASGUPTA

FROM DRILLABLE TEXT TO TEXTUAL BLOCKAGE

The history of the serial form in television narrative foregrounds the centrality of three features: the construction of meaning, the viewing experience, and the intended audience. The inability of television studies to stabilize this triple relationship of meaning, experience, and audience displays the complex transformations of the medium itself, and recent work has begun to mark another moment in this dynamic. In "Forensic Fandom and the Drillable Text," Jason Mittell (2009) argues that contemporary media technologies and fan practices transform television serials into sites of investigation. The fan's investment in the text takes the form of detective work. The essay on the drillable text extends Mittell's (2006) argument about the rise of narrative complexity in long-form television: the long-form narrative constructs the text as a *site for investigation* and the fan's engagement as a *mode of tracking meaning-production*. Mittell argues for seeing "such programs as drillable rather than spreadable [. . .], encouraging forensic fandom that invites viewers to dig deeper, probing beneath the surface to understand the complexity of a story and its telling. [. . .] Such programs create magnets for engagement, drawing viewers into story worlds and urging them to drill down to discover more" (2009). Mittell's argument is based on the idea that "the television text is always constructed as continuously there *for someone*" (Brunsdon 1990: 62). The audience emerges as the invited, pulled-in, urged-on, magnetized element of a dialogic encounter between text and viewer.

In this chapter, I will focus on and develop an understanding of the presence of opacity in televisual seriality. *Nonresolvable opacities*, which punctuate and stretch out across the serial form, produce moments of rupture in the televisual text that absorb viewers into the sensory power of the presence of images while pulling them out of the narrative's investigatory dynamic. In a complex dialectic of narrative absorption and opaque presentation, television seriality invites investigation while also presenting opaque moments that assert their own nonsignifying presence. These moments do not represent anything—or worse, they could not even represent anything—because their presence throughout the long-term form refuses to be fully subjugated to the logic of communication, meaning-making, or narrative closure, however complex and spread out. The image exceeds narrative by both contributing to and overshooting meaning through sheer presence. I do not claim that televisual opacity appears only now, with shows like *Mad Men*. Rather, I argue for acknowledging this hitherto neglected dimension of TV seriality and analyze three specific forms of its presence in *Mad Men*. This type of analysis, I argue, also implies developing a more complex understanding of the serial viewing experience and the need to expand our understanding of TV spectatorship generally.

Opacities in the extended textuality of the serial form accompany rather than overturn the relationship of drillable text and forensic fandom. This raises the question of what kinds of audience, and what forms of audience experience, are precipitated by such simultaneous experiences of meaning-making and textual blockage. What if the text is not just an occasion "to be savored and dissected on both online and offline fora" (Mittell 2009)? If we factor opacities into the text, transformations in experience need addressing. Mittell's "forensic fandom" questions the assumption that television viewers are passive—an assumption whose dubiousness has long been underlined by television scholars and received fresh impetus with the rise of interactive digital media and fan practices. But the passive/active couplet is only one of many forms in which experience can be analyzed. Absorption/theatricality is another mode of characterizing viewing experience. The notion of absorption (Fried 1998) bears interesting parallels with Mittell's magnetizing pull of the drillable text. And indeed, the dialectic between the theatrical tendency of presentation and frontal confrontation on the one hand and narrative absorption and visual involvement on the other is one way in which I will approach the question of audience experience.

The dialectic of absorption and expulsion (the drillable text and the opaque text) complicates audience experience to suggest a hybrid experiential encounter with the television serial. This hybridity of the audience experience produces an oscillation between deciphering meaning and registering presence. Thus, the second way in which "experience" functions in my argument is explicitly linked to the term *aesthetics*. Understood less as an analytic category limited to the study of art, aesthetics is understood here as a sensory experience produced in an encounter (Kant 1988, Adorno 1991, Hansen 2012, and Rancière 2012)—in this case, the encounter between the viewer and a temporally extended and spatially spread-out, long-form television text: the serial. The aesthetics of seriality involves the sensorial dimensions of experiencing a specific, constructed form of textuality.

The opacity of the text I identify has both a long history in the different arts and its own particular inflection in television history. Moments of nonsignifying opacity in serial narration, I argue, block the hunt for meaning and produce a composite text and aesthetic experience. This indeterminacy of meaning destabilizes the aesthetic experience of the text: even if the serial can ultimately be summed up at the end of its run as a completed narrative, the blockages to meaning distributed throughout the text perforate it by sinking into non-meaning. This perforated seriality makes it impossible to describe the experience of the text as solely one of decipherment. By inserting into audience experience not just meaning-production through the interpretation of clues but also the sensory registration of images, objects, sounds, and colors in their nonsignifying opacity, the aesthetic experience of some forms of contemporary televisual seriality produces a wavering and mobile spectator. Emancipated from simply the role of the investigator, this type of viewer is both the inwardly propelled and the outwardly expelled spectator. The drillable *and* perforated opaque text sets his or her aesthetic experience in motion.

TELEVISION AS THEORY

An extract from AMC's *Mad Men* shall explain my argument. This reading is *not* an example of nonsignifying opacity. Rather, it captures hybrid spectatorship precisely as a cognitive and nonsignifying experience. The extract functions as a meta-commentary on the mixed modes of spectatorship and textual blockage that I propose to include in scholarship on serial television.

The scene is from season two, episode seven: news has spread through the offices of the Sterling Cooper advertising agency that Cooper has purchased a new painting. Some employees walk into Cooper's office, shoes in hand (Cooper is something of an aesthete enamored of Oriental art and will not permit shoes in his office):

> CRANE: Shh, don't touch anything.
> SAL (knowingly): It's a Rothko! Why the hell didn't Dale say that?
> (A shot of them from behind, staring silently at the painting in the center of the frame.)
> CRANE: Ten thousand dollars.
> JANE: So, it's smudgy squares, eh? That's interesting.
> (She walks away.)
> CRANE: Two possibilities. Either Cooper loves it, and you have to love it— or he thinks it's a joke and you look like a fool when you pretend to dig it.
> SAL: Like you can pretend to understand this.
> CRANE: Maybe he has a brochure here or something that explains it.
> COSGROVE: I don't think it's to be explained.
> SAL: He's an artist okay? It must mean something.
> COSGROVE: Maybe it doesn't. Maybe you're just supposed to experience it. 'Cause when you look at it, you feel something, right? It's like . . . looking into something . . . very . . . deep.
> (Camera moves closer and closer to the painting. Silence.)
> COSGROVE: You could fall in.
> SAL: That's true. Did someone tell you that?
> COSGROVE: How could someone tell you that?
> CRANE: This is pointless, let's go!
> (They walk out. The camera turns 180 degrees and stays on the painting.)
> (Beep. Crane walks in, Cooper at desk.)
> COOPER (disinterestedly): So . . . media purchases. Starting in March, I'm looking at column five.
> (Shot of Crane staring sideways, worriedly, at the Rothko.)
> COOPER: . . . under regional affiliates.
> (Cooper notices that Crane disregards him, staring at painting instead.)
> COOPER: Mr. Crane! Focus! We didn't make you head of television to shorten your attention span!
> CRANE: Sorry, sir (glances to his left) . . . I was admiring your painting.
> (Cooper turns his head to the Rothko.)
> COOPER (sighing appreciatively): Oh! The eye is drawn to it.
> (Full-length shot of the Rothko.)
> CRANE: It's very modern. Mark Rothko. I've read about him.

COOPER (warily): And?
CRANE (nervously): What do *you* think about it?
COOPER (condescendingly): Nobody's ever asked me that.
(Shot of an awkward Crane.)
COOPER (aggressively): Probably because it's none . . . of . . . their business.
CRANE: Right.
(Shot of Cooper, who glances at painting then at Crane.)
COOPER (calculatingly, as if setting a trap): How does it strike you?
CRANE (sighs): Sir, I know nothing about art.
COOPER: Mister Crane, you are here because of numbers. Stick to that. Don't concern yourself with aesthetics. You'll get a headache.
CRANE: Of course.
(Shot of them together in frame, silently reading.)
COOPER: People buy things to realize their aspirations. It's the foundation of our business.
(Shot of Crane listening, eyebrows raised inquiringly.)
COOPER: But between you and me and the lamp-post, that thing should double in value by next Christmas.
CRANE (laughing in relief)
COOPER (suddenly serious): Where were we?
CRANE: Column five here . . .

The characters in front of the painting—which stares back at them without revealing any meaning or, rather, revealing too many meanings—can be seen as replicating us watching the serial. Sal's assertion that an artwork must have meaning mimics a forensic fan's relation to the drillable text. But the drillability of the text is given a twist by Ken Cosgrove. He "digs" the text, appreciating its power to sensually affect him, to let him "fall in." Obviously, digging and drilling are not the same thing. The propulsion dramatized here is not the magnetic pull to start a forensic search for the painting's meaning but a sensorial acknowledgment of the painting's power to move spectators, to impel them to come "inside" a sensorially intense experience.

The serial, however, produces not *only* a nonsignifying viewing encounter. Cooper's guarded, often aggressive switching of modes in his interaction with Crane illustrates the pull-push dynamic of *Mad Men* itself. By thwarting Crane's desire to know what he thinks of the painting, Cooper throws back the question at Crane, who must nervously admit that he knows nothing about art. However, rather than coming out as the aesthete whose appreciation of art is "no one's business" to inquire into, Cooper then pulls Crane back in by proposing a theory. People buy art to realize their aspirations, he offers, suggesting his own reason for buying the painting. This is the classic fetishistic reading of the art object as commodity, which the ad agency also employs to sell the products of its clients. The initial doubt ("What exactly *is* Cooper's reason for buying the painting?") is seemingly set to rest at the end of the exchange. The painting is simply an investment whose value is expected to double by next Christmas. However, the audience has also seen how appreciatively, almost wistfully, Cooper gazes at the painting. Is this simply the gaze of aspirational pleasure, in Bourdieu's (1987) sense? Cooper's motivations are multiplied without a definitive answer.

Which of these three responses of Cooper are we to believe? Is he an aesthete with an appreciation of art that Crane, head of the television department, can never understand, his position in the firm a function of the degraded medium he has been assigned to, the proverbial medium of short attention spans? Or, paradoxically, is it television that now gives us an opportunity to appreciate Rothko's art—only to reduce it to two forms of functionality: a sign of distinction by which an insecure consumer might realize his "aspirations" or, alternatively, a mercenary motivation to buy art as a simple investment? The sequence refuses to offer us one stable conclusion qua meaning. Most importantly, Cooper's motivations are complemented by Cosgrove's sensorial appreciation of the power of color and form. The drillable text supplies three meanings (Cooper's), while the appreciated, "diggable" text provides one aesthetic experience with no regard for meaning (Cosgrove's). An attention to aesthetics here does not provide a headache, but perhaps it provides disorientation. The painting is an investment, a sign, an art object, a thing ("smudgy squares"), and the instigator of a captivating sensory experience.

OPACITY AND THE SERIAL FORM IN TELEVISION

Charlotte Brunsdon has argued that the experience of viewing TV—supposedly distracted, episodic, extended, and domestic—almost militates against describing this experience as "aesthetic." Given today's proliferation of high-definition TV, DVD extras, and frenetic fan activity, TV's "anti-aesthetic" (Brunsdon 1990: 63) needs to be rethought. Such a rethinking would need to interrogate the place of popular seriality within the high/low culture divide. Creeber's (2004) defense of serial television's power to address and interrogate the complexities of lived experience clearly undercuts a quality discourse that would separate popular seriality from aesthetic and political value.

All of these transformations at the aesthetic level necessitate a new understanding of the role played by "meaning" in popular seriality, particularly in term of its changing relations to formal structure. Feuer (1984) suggests a counterintuitive relationship between the formal features of the TV text and its politics. In the midst of sharply divergent readings of the politics of primetime serials, she asks: "How can the same programmes yield up such diametrically opposed readings?" Feuer suggests that

> serial form and multiple plot structure appear to give TV melodrama a greater potential for multiple and aberrant readings than do other forms of popular narrative. [. . .] Every ideological position may be countered by its opposite. Thus the family dynasty sagas may be read either as critical of the dominant ideology of capitalism or as belonging to it, depending upon the position from which the reader comes at it. (1984: 15)

Well aware of the *production* content of television, Feuer reminds us that the polysemic and multiple plot structures of serials—that is, the formal features of these texts—are designed to appeal to as wide an audience as possible, or to put it another way, "to avoid offending any segment of that audience" (15).

Analysis of the meaning of the text is linked to the formal structure of the text's open-ended temporality and its intrinsic complexity through multiple plots. Meaning in itself does not guarantee the politics of a text—the relationship between the form of the text and its content is crucial, and this relationship precisely undercuts the form/content distinction. As Feuer argues:

> Although the sitcoms contained overtly liberal "messages," their strong drive toward narrative closure tended to mask contradictions and force a false sense of social integration by the end of each episode. For example, the problems raised by *All in the Family* had to have easy solutions within the family so that a new "topical" issue could be introduced in the next episode. (15)

The *form* of the serial thus opposes its meaning—or the politics of its content—canceling out the politics based on meaning by structurally resolving contradictions within the time span of an episode.

Given this sometimes supportive, sometimes contradictory relation between form, content, and politics, transformations in form across categories are crucial. As Creeber argues, "Unlike the single play the episodic nature of the serial form means that it also shares important characteristics with the series. This means that the serial can frequently break free of the narrative limitations of single drama and exploit some of the most seductive elements of serialisation" (2004: 9). Referring to Horace Newcomb's 1974 argument about intimacy and continuity in soap operas, Creeber rightly argues that

> the combination of a continuous narrative structure contained within a clearly defined narrative arc [. . .] allows television [seriality] to exploit its tendency towards "intimacy" and "continuity" yet without dispensing with the powers and possibilities offered by its gradual movement [. . .] towards narrative closure and conclusion. (9)

Thus, the formal blending—rather than genre blending—of televisual textuality fuses different modes of *experience,* from the intimacy fostered by soap operas to the cognitive frenzy of Lostpedians drilling into *Lost* to decipher clues *before* narrative closure has been achieved (Mittell 2009). Significantly, what is at stake is *meaning.* Aberrant readings, multiple readings—whatever the end result, it is important to note that the activity in question is a reading process.

Feuer's argument, and to some extent Creeber's, is that the extended temporality of the TV serial makes *meaning-attribution* dependent on the temporal extension of the meaning of events, plotlines, character development, and the like. Whether episodic, intra-episodic (with commercial breaks), or across the narrative arc of the season and the serial as a whole, the viewing experience is marked by interruptions that produce suspense and expectations. Interruptions are understood in terms of plot and the unfolding of meaning. As "a [temporal] system that is highly predictable and thus dependable and reassuring," these "prerogatives" of "dependability and reassurance" have "strong cognitive and emotive implications" (Buonnano 2008: 120). There is a rhythm to the experience and appearance of opacity-qua-meaning, and its temporal structure is assured by the form of the text (the episodic series and the episode-exceeding serial).

Meaning-making as a process that counters opacity by drilling into the text is predicated on the distribution of *temporarily* opaque moments within a decided structure. The logic of "the strategic interruption" (Buonnano 2008: 123) is to produce intervals where meaning-making takes place in the absence of an unfolding plot. According to Buonnano, these intervals "are not pauses or rests: they are spaces in the working of the imagination. In these liminal spaces, trapped between what we have already learned from a story and what we are still to learn, the imagination overloads itself with expectations and reaches out toward the new discoveries that will follow with the resumption of narrative flow" (123). This suggestive argument, designed around the cognitive imagination, resonates powerfully with the opposite of meaning-making and story production, helping to bring out what is specific about nonsignifying opacity and noncognitive experience in the serial form.

If we follow the first point above about the blurring of forms across series, serials, and the like, we could say that the practice of attributing meanings and coming to conclusions (the final forensic report) is a *combination* of punctuated (often episodic) moments and a long drawn-out process either concluding in the end of a serial or abruptly ending sans closure (cancellation).[1] Either way, analyses of television seriality must factor in both experiences of temporality: the drive to finalize meaning at the end of a complex, temporally extended viewing experience and moments of sensorial intensity, that is, the proliferation of perceptions whose opacity is not driven primarily by meaning construction.

How would an understanding of this parallel mode of experience alter the form-audience-experience relationship, acknowledging the registration of sensory presence as integral to the viewing experience? Meaning of whatever kind (dominant, multiple, delayed, aberrant) comes to us only through the concrete, sensuous particularity of the images and sounds we register. The historico-conceptual perspective sketched above has, like Sal in Cooper's office, asked about television's audiovisual text: "What does it mean?" Fans and critics have hunted for brochures, or written their own, to explain the meanings of the texts. But what if we pause to consider the materiality of sound and image in its own right, *prior* to any hunt for meaning? What if, like Cosgrove, we momentarily disregard meaning and give in to the sensory experience? And what if this priority of material presence does not vanish once meaning is established, but subsists throughout the experience of the serial form?

The popularity of TV seriality has so far prevented TV criticism from seriously engaging with the presence of opacity. Acknowledging serial opacities would put into doubt the meaning of the "popular" in seriality and expand the significance of this particular media form beyond the high/low culture divide. The peculiar temporal dimensions of seriality, in particular its extended character and planned interruptions, are the formal parameters within which different forms of opacity circulate. The review above shows that opacity within this temporal structure was primarily understood as a *temporary delay* in the fixing of meaning. Opacity and temporality were related primarily in terms of how this temporal delay is exploited across an extended text to intensify

---

1. Newman (2006) provides a useful typology of the multiple temporalities of television narrative. My argument extends the interruptive moments in the search for meaning by calling attention to moments of opacity across these temporalities.

imagination and curiosity—the "What will happen next?" or "Is this why this happened?" sorts of questions. As we will see below, the three forms of opacity identified in my reading of *Mad Men* bear *some* proximity to these questions, but they extend beyond a plot-driven identification of meaning. The forms of opacity identified below are less clues, catalysts, or instigators for the tracking of plot development; rather, they are moments that intensify the experience of blankness: opacities that do not promise an eventual explanation which will reveal their meaning.

OPACITY AND THE EXCESSIVE IMAGE

The perforated text (coexisting with the drillable text) is characterized by moments where the narrative drive of the plot is accompanied by the sensory registration of opacities. These opacities counter the transparency of meaning and turn textual considerations toward its experiential dimensions, as opposed to its communicative functions. This argument is not new, however muted it seems in studies of television. The history of forms across the arts, from painting, literature, film, poetry, as well as popular media from the vaudeville theater to the fairground, understands experience as a shifting relationship between the registration of the power of sheer presence on the one hand and the absorption into narrative meaning on the other. In art history, Clement Greenberg's (1965) campaign for modernist art was based precisely on a rejection of the narrowly communicative function of the artwork and a turn inward toward the specificities of the medium.[2] Importantly, this inward turn was characterized as a political strategy aimed at withdrawing from the commodity-communicative function of the art object under capitalism. Similarly, Tom Gunning's (2004) reading of early cinema's frontal address to the spectator and its theatrical presentational style was less about narrative constructions of meaning than about a knowing audience that he described as "(in)credulous." This audience was hardly naïve but sought out sensational and thrilling experiences in film, as in the fairground, even though it knew that these experiences of disorientation, fear, and disgust did not really threaten its bodily integrity or safety. It was an audience credulous and incredulous at the same time, fully aware of the constructed character of the illusion. These are just two art-theoretical examples that have marked aesthetic experience as mixed: cognitive and physical,

---

2. For a substantial extension of Greenberg's argument from modernist painting to cinema, see Kovács 2007. Kovács convincingly shows that modernist painting's withdrawal from purely communicative and "realist" narrative form is carried on and transformed by cinema.

intellectual and sensory, material and mental. The transparency of communication, in these accounts, is accompanied by, interrupted through, or refused wholesale by strategies in art, film, and literature.

How might this tradition of aesthetic theory be relevant for understanding opacity in televisual seriality? In particular, how does the text that is drillable for meaning relate to the perforated text punctured by moments of opacity? In film melodrama, the enigmatic and the opaque have often manifested themselves in stylistic excess. This overwrought visual style has been seen as a symptom of the inability of the text to openly avow the human price of social normativity.[3] Social contradictions, particularly gender and racial oppression, were *figured* rather than represented "realistically" by drawing attention to the visual construction of the image. Willemen (1971) argued that this visual excess, which blocked any "seeing through" the text at its meaning, required a depth hermeneutic to construct a second text below the first, theatrically constructed one.[4] In fact, this is an early version of what Mittell calls the "drillable" text. Opacity is encountered through visual excess but analytically resolved by constructing a second text below it. In a TV soap opera, however, "character relationships of an 'hysterical' nature are expressed, but the *mise-en-scène represents* this hysteria rather than being itself hysterical and thus calling into question that which is represented" (Feuer 1984: 9; emphasis added). The peculiar pleasures of TV melodrama consist not in any depth hermeneutic but in turning up the volume on emotional excess, the moral simplicity of right and wrong. In TV melodrama, the materiality of sound and image accentuates and amplifies meaning rather than obstructing it, as in film. Many TV series, including *ER, CSI, West Wing, Scandal,* and others, do employ fast-moving shots and rapid-fire editing, but this visual excess speeds up action and furthers the plot rather than blocking meaning.[5]

Opacity-as-excess functions differently at specific historical moments in different media forms. In contemporary television serials and visual culture generally, I argue, the excessive nature of opacity returns, but this excess is not just symptomatic (as in film melodrama) or just emotional and "hysterical"

---

3. See Dasgupta/Staat (2008) for an argument that style here functions *as* meaning rather than *for* meaning.

4. The technique of calling attention to the act of observation is described in Luhmann (2000) and also developed within a phenomenology of film by Sobchack (1999). In different ways, both Luhmann's and Sobchack's arguments build on a materialist phenomenology of visual experience that oscillates between absorption and theatricality (Fried 1998).

5. See Caldwell 1995 on "televisuality": the visual excess of television advertises technological capacities rather than undermining the meaning of the plot through opacity. The use-value of the overwrought television image was primarily to promote the coming-of-age of the medium itself in the hi-tech age.

(as in 1980s television). Rather, opacity becomes the sheer presence of non-meaning figured within the text.

Attempting to transcend the mere deciphering of objects as bearers of meaning, Bill Brown reviews a spate of writing on objects and things, noticing that these texts "ask why and how we use objects to make meaning, to make or re-make ourselves, to organize our anxieties and affections, to sublimate our fears and shape our fantasies" (2003: 4). The *use-value* of objects is that of bearing meaning for a range of purposes, whether aspirational, as Cooper in *Mad Men* notes, or compensatory, or concerning their potential for stabilizing or shaping identities. Conjoining opacity to Brown's consideration of objects, one could say that objects function here as redolent of meaning, however transparent and visible or hidden and symptomatic. Brown's readings of late nineteenth-century American literature (when consumerism and capitalism made a dramatic entry onto the social stage) eschews the temptation of immediately reading objects as meaning-laden. As Brown argues: "Even as the prose fiction of the nineteenth century represents [. . .] the way commodity relations came to saturate everyday life [. . .], this fiction demonstrates that the human investment in the physical object world, and the mutual constitution of human subject and inanimate object, can hardly be reduced to these relations" (2003: 5). This has particular relevance for the readings of *Mad Men* below, since the show is suffused in a world of objects for consumption and the attribution of meaning to them through advertising.

What other forms of investment could humans have with objects besides the commodifying imperative and its attendant dimensions of specular possession, meaning-fixation, and industrial production? In order to answer this question, Brown suggests,

> the doubleness of the commodity (its use value and exchange value) might be said to conceal a more fundamental difference, between the object and itself, or the object and the thing, on which the success of the commodity, the success of capitalism, depends [. . .]. Value derives from the appropriation of a pre-existing surplus, *the material object's own excessiveness*. (2003: 13–14; emphasis added)

Brown captures crucial features of what I call *nonsignifying opacity*. First, the object is divided within itself, or is both an object and a thing. It is a presence, simply object matter before it is made amenable to consumption, including consumption and processing by meaning-making. This is what is meant by the "priority" of nonsignifying presence mentioned in the first section. For something to mean, it must be embodied, be object matter, whether as surface, color, volume, or sound wave. This is the "preexisting" surplus of the object. The televisual image is indeed an effect of capitalist production practices and the culture industry—its every detail is designed and produced—yet for all that, the end product is delivered to the spectator as "matter," as a combination of image and sound in movement. This prior surplus is its excess. It is excessive in that it exceeds the possibility of being tied down to meaning, which arrives *après-coup* as simply one mode of encountering the image. Second, reducing this excessive surplus to "commodity relations" threatens to disturb the experience of viewing. The spectator position here should be understood not just as the human subject reading the inanimate object/image for meaning. Miriam Hansen marks another approach to understanding the world of images, indebted to Kracauer, Benjamin, and Adorno, who were "interested in what cinema *does*, the kind of sensory-perceptual, mimetic experience it enabled" to construct an "evolving phenomenology of modernity" (2012: xvii). The excessive, nonsignifying materiality of the image is crucially linked to experience and to how sensory perception provides a phenomenology of a historical period. Still, the reduction of objects and images to meaning-construction is more frequent in scholarship than are discussions of sensory perception and "object matter." For example, *Mad Men* has spawned a great deal of literature about advertising, consumerism, and capitalist visualization. And rightly so—the topic of the serial and the stylized construction of its images invite such analyses.

But the "object matter" of *Mad Men,* in the double sense of proliferating objects *in* the serial and the deployment of sound and image *by* the serial, constitute its excessiveness, precisely in Brown's sense. The experiential dimensions of viewing the serial, its phenomenological density, offers a materialist encounter with objects and images whose very opacity prior to meaning is a resource deployed throughout the extended narrative. The powerful sensory presence of the object-world of *Mad Men* cannot be separated from the period it portrays and the attendant nostalgia and exoticism triggered when viewed from the present. This excessiveness of images as objects, and objects in images, produces an experience of mobility and disorientation.

OPACITY IN *MAD MEN*

The temporality of the excessive object's opacity can no longer be calculated by a systemic logic of interruption.[6] The objects within the frame, as well as the

---

6. In other words, when analyzed regarding opacity, the complex temporality of the plot exceeds the meaning-bound understanding of the "flexi-narrative" (Nelson 2004).

images on-screen, continually *accompany* their use-value as elements in the plot. In this sense, the liminal space of the temporal interruption is replaced by a liminal space for continually registering presences and forms. Furthermore, the registration of these forms—the colors of dresses and rooms, the gleam of car bonnets, and the glow of wall hangings—is a sensorial rather than a cognitive exercise. Instead of a coupling of imagination with cognition ("How will the story unfold in the break between episodes?"), the sheer opacity of the show accompanies its entire duration as an experience parallel to cognitive calculation. Thus, the object-suffused world of the advertising agency and the glamorous lives of its employees, as well as the images that represent them for us, are presentations of presences of things, or of "the object divided within itself," in Brown's words. This presentations of things—the "sense of things" rather than the meaning of things—is a continual component of our experience of the serial. Liminality is not a gap in-between the plot's unfolding: it is the excessive space just beyond and before the border that marks the practice of meaning-making. In addition to this continual opacity of the sense of things as presence, opacity appears within single episodes, in the shape of moments or sequences of sounds and images.

It is in the first category, I argue, that opacity comes closest to meaning-making, by provoking the question: What exactly is going on here? yet withdrawing from the possibility of providing definitive answers. In season one, episode six, when Don Draper meets Rachel Menken, a Jewish department-store owner, knowledge—but of what exactly?—is precisely the issue. A possible ad campaign to market Israel as a tourist destination leads Don to approach Rachel as a potential source of information for the agency. The erotic attraction between them dominates Draper's seemingly straightforward demand for information. The ludicrous stereotyping (a Jew should know how to market Israel) is exactly one of the nonchalant ways in which *Mad Men* presents the violence of racism, sexism, and anti-Semitism. Yet Rachel parries with Don rather than simply acquiescing or refusing his desire for information. Talking of Israel, she says, "A country . . . for those people, as you call us, seems very important." (This statement is visually accompanied by the sensory apprehension of her smoldering cigarette, her painted face, her dress.) "Then why aren't you there?" asks Don—to which she replies that her life is here, in New York. Her first statement suggests a statement of fact by a person in the know (she is one of "those people"), yet her answer dismissively brushes off any implication that *she* would find it important to live in Israel. Raising her eyebrows curtly, she emphatically stresses, "I will visit, but I don't have to *live there.*" At this point, their hands caress and she remarks that the Greeks had two meanings for the word *utopia*: "eutopos meaning the good place, and utopos meaning the place that cannot be." The desire between Rachel and Don becomes palpable at this point, even as it seems mediated by their discussion of Israel. The two meanings of *utopia* suggest the impossibility of their being a couple (Don is married); union would be a good place but at the same time that which cannot be. Weaving together these two topics—the "Jew" explaining Israel as eutopic homeland, Rachel and Don's impossible utopic future as a couple—the conversation is both absorbing-qua-meaning and opaque since one is not able to identify when they are speaking in code and when they are not. What Israel means to her ("an idea") is not much help to him if he wants to market Israel to American "Jews." Her statement (a homeland is "very important") suggests that there is more to know, but what follows refuses and evades any further probing. This opacity—he is not going to get much on Israel—is intertwined with the acknowledgment of impossible desire, further complicating the meaning of what exactly is going on, but refusing any resolution. The "good place" to be would be a place of knowing more, about her, about what Israel means for a "Jew," about their possible future. Instead he gets *something*, which is her evasiveness about Israel, while at the same time ending up in a place "that cannot be," where no amount of interrogation will neatly line her up as a "Jew" with either "Israel" or him. Her movement in and out of his desire to know is a shifting play between opacity and meaning, evasion and information, a good future and its impossibility.

All of this is communicated to us through the mediation of objects and images: her exquisitely made-up face and her jewelry, the smoke of the cigarettes and the click of the cigarette lighter, Draper's suit, the luxurious setting of the restaurant, its clientele, the flowers, and the drapery. This universe of things is not just a setting but a presence in its own right through which and with which the meandering and coded conversation between Draper and Mencken winds its way. Like Crane confronting the Rothko, Don went looking for the brochure that would explain Israel (Rachel) and found a source of information that talks but does not explain. *Mad Men* multiplies events and conversations such as these, while also providing clear plotlines and meaning-making. At the cognitive and sensorial levels, any analysis of the experience of the serial must attend to this mixed, hybrid experience. Its liminality resides precisely in the imagination conjuring up narrative closure *and* the sheer presence of images, objects, and words without providing resolution between such opacity and the transparency of meaning seemingly secured at the end.

The second type of opacity takes the form of moments rather than dialogues, fragments of events that have the character of stand-alones that are not embedded in sequences of meaningful actions such as conversations. The camera directs us to observe something without offering us any reason why we should do so. What is observed is an unexplained fragment, something like a snapshot unmotivated by preceding and succeeding images and sounds. The opacity of these scenes, distributed throughout the series, turns them into moments of perforation rather than drilling sites, where all we are asked to register is the presence of things and actions rather than any follow-up causality. Such forms of opacity can be distributed along a spectrum of relationships between sequentiality and causality (in the Aristotelian sense, where sequentiality—however stretched-out and complex—helps establish causality through a sense of anticipation and its resolution). As extreme examples, we can name events whose minor status is marked by the fact that there is no question of a follow-up. In season four, episode eight ("The Summer Man"), Draper writes in his diary. This act has an explanatory function in the diegesis, explicitly presenting Draper's thoughts through voice-over. However, later in the New York Athletic Club where he is swimming laps, the visual construction shifts registers. It could be seen simply as representing an event, and a particularly seasonal one, swimming. However, framing makes us aware of another swimmer in the lane next to Draper. And through a shot of Draper's face we are made aware of Draper's awareness of the swimmer. As he finishes his laps, the camera focuses on Draper's face as he turns and stares, almost glares at the other swimmer. What happened there? The camera lingers uncomfortably long on Draper's gaze, uncomfortably that is, because this shot is met by no returning gaze, no sequence of explanatory shots, no voice-over. The sequence, by ending in the too-long shot of Draper's stare, functions almost independently of any cause-and-effect sequence. It simply shows a stare, but no reciprocity, no meaningful visual construction to explain it. Such moments of opacity are the archetypal units of a series, in the industrial sense, since they are not meant to form a meaningful unit. There is no causal sequence, only a sequence of nonsignifying moments.[7]

The third form of opacity exploits the temporal structure of the serial form but deliberately subverts any link between sequentiality and causality. The opacity of events in this form is simply unexplainable if the question asked is: Why *now* does this take place? Complex deployments of temporality, such as the explanatory flashback or the retrospectively grasped flashforward, are common. They all tie down a significant event to a causal nexus that fixes meaning. In the case of the marital breakdown of Betty and Don

---

7. For one example of theorizing the seemingly non-narrative presence of such shots in cinema, see Bordwell/Thompson 1972. Rancière (2007) provides the most conceptually sophisticated analysis of this enigmatic presence of the image (his focus is on photography). For an extended discussion of the philosophical relationship of sense and sense-making in Rancière's aesthetic theory, see Dasgupta 2009, 2013.

Draper, however, while the sequentiality of events progresses toward closure, the *form* in which sequences of events relate to a causal link is deliberately obfuscatory. The sequence of plot events provides no answer as to why one specific moment in the narrative leads to Betty breaking with Don. In season two, episode eight, Betty suspects that Don has cheated on her. She confronts him, while searching for clues of his infidelity and finding none. Strangely, the absence of clues does not diminish her belief in his infidelity, and he does not push this fact but almost passively acquiesces to her judgment. Causally, this event could be seen to precipitate marital breakdown (even as Don's peculiarly passive response to Betty is hard to explain). Instead, the tension between the two is dissipated somewhat when Don caringly nurtures Betty in the midst of her father's death, thus delaying the inevitable. In episode ten of the next season, Betty discovers Don's lie about his identity (he is actually Dick Whitman and has stolen another's identity). Oddly, this discovery—he has deceived Betty from the beginning—does not hasten the end of their marriage. Most tellingly, when Betty finally asks Don for a divorce, this decision is punctuated by two climactic televisual events—the assassinations of John F. Kennedy and Lee Harvey Oswald. Betty watches live on television as Harvey is shot, and she breaks down dramatically. Shortly after, in the same episode, she asks for a divorce. If sequentiality is understood through a cause-and-effect relationship, the demand for a divorce can be seen as caused by witnessing political assassinations. Logically, this makes no sense.

Only experiencing the extended temporality of the gradual breakdown (infidelity in season two, discovery of deception in season three) makes the event (demanding a divorce) understandable. But it does not explain how and why the first two events were reconciled with Betty and Don continuing their marriage. The assassinations function perfectly as significant, historically explosive events, but the event that follows them (the demand for a divorce) makes no causal sense—the textual construction of the sequence poses the question: why *now*? (Her ongoing secret affair with Henry Francis could have been reason enough.) This why-question is the result of delinking the sequence of narrative events from narrative causality. As Dana Polan argues, "This general lack of an overall narrative drive to the series means that it is hard also to read any determining logic in the movement from episode to episode" (2014: n.p.).[8] In terms of *meaning*, opacity is here produced precisely because the construction of meaning through causality is refused.

---

8. Polan's detailed discussion argues that *Mad Men*'s open-ended structure is characterized not so much by plot complexity than by producing a viewing experience that breaks the link between sequentiality and meaning-making. Compare also Ames's collection (2012)

According to Buonnano (2008), the liminal space of imaginative experience continues throughout the viewing experience. We are drawn into the plot and its narrative construction of meaning, but we are also increasingly aware that the narration of events does not necessarily explain their sequence or the significance of certain events. The image exceeds its potential for meaning. The overall profusion of opacity as object matter (the "sense of things" in objects and images) and the punctuated liminal moments, sequences, and shots produce a hybrid cognitive/sensorial mode of experience.

CONCLUSION

What does the temporality of experiencing meaningless opacity in serial television tell us about (media) history? Fredric Jameson argues that the coherence ascribed by Lukács (1974) to literary realism broke down in modernity. Like social reality, the wholeness of the text was fractured by autonomous segments, which figured "the situation of contingency, or meaninglessness, or alienation" (Jameson 2009: 160). This period, analyzed by Simmel, Benjamin, and Kracauer, has been superseded in postmodernity, Jameson argues, where the fracturing of the whole has produced another kind of fragmentation.[9] He claims that "the broken pieces of the image world" have "been superseded by [. . .] cultural renarrativization"; thus, the fragments that break up the narrative speak again, that is, are renarrativized. And this speaking is by "the vanishing away of affect in the postmodern" (160). Opacities in the narrative serial form are indeed interruptive; they fragment coherency, producing liminal moments of incomprehension within the regulated and dependable system of the serial (as Buonnano calls it). Yet precisely because these images and the objects in the images are excessive prior to their use-value as ciphers, symbols, or symptoms, they affect the sensory experience of the serial. Their excessive nonsignifying character refuses "cultural renarrativization" and develops a further historical transformation in the image beyond Jameson's specific argument about the postmodern image. Rather than representing stereotypes in an affectively impoverished world of images, they

---

on temporality in television narratives, though most essays focus on meaning, textual construction, and fan (inter-)actions.

9. An incisive early analysis of the transformation in form and the presence of objectivity in literature, with particular attention to Lukács's work, can be found in Jameson 1974. The precise relationship between formal transformations and the politics of historical experience, which Jameson analyzes, is important for my argument but cannot be developed here. It is simply touched on in this conclusion.

confront the viewer with presences; they orchestrate the senses rather than finalizing sense-making and heighten the affective intensity of the viewing experience. Jacques Rancière's discussion of this double presence of sense and sense-making, an effect of what he calls the "aesthetic regime" (2013), finds a particular permutation in the distribution of opacities in seriality. The different forms of opacity analyzed above concretize the play between the intensification of sensorial experience and the drive toward making sense and identifying the meaning of a text. In this fashion, nonsignifying opacities in seriality are one side of a divided image world, the sensory presence that accompanies sense-making.

The cultural critique of the image world, undertaken so persuasively by Jameson with regard to postmodernity, needs to include this moment when opacity arises once more, specifically in television seriality. As the continual presence of things as objects/images, as the interruptive moments in which enigmatic events offer yet refuse meaning, and as excisable fragmentary segments (shots and sequences without causality)—in these three forms, opacities reemerge as presences without narrative potential. The political implications of this contemporary politics of form cannot be undertaken here—they present a concern that critics such as Adorno (1991), Foster (2002, 2011), Jameson (2009, 2014), Rancière (2013), and others have considered elsewhere. However, the mutation or transformation of forms of opacity is a significant dimension of serial television and hence an important topic for television scholarship.

The experience of being pulled into the text by its magnetic power, which Mittell identifies in practices of forensic fandom, must be understood in connection with the experience of sensorial apperception. Absorption—canonically identified by Michael Fried as one mode of experience of the artwork—has always been closely identified with the narrative insertion of the spectator into a diegetic world. In this sense, what Fried describes as the viewer's absorption in painting is similar to Mittell's forensic fan digging into the text through magnetic invitation. Moments of opacity, distributed in serial narratives, disorient the spectator, leading him or her away from the serial's narrative unfolding. I use the word *disorientation* here because, as Richard Rushton (2004) shows, one can be as absorbed by a narrative as by a spectacle. Similarly, Hansen exploits the German word *Erfahrung*'s etymological association with traveling and cruising (*fahren*) to argue that such destabilizing visual experience "stresses the subject's precarious mobility rather than a stable position of perception vis-à-vis an object" (2012: xiv). The experience of distributed opacities of the serial text heightens a persistent sense of the sheer presence of objects that destabilize the viewing subject's drive to continually ascribe everything seen to identifiable meanings and plot development. The spectacular involves absorption, too (special effects, theatricality in musicals, Gunning's "cinema of attractions," etc.). In the case of opacities, disorientation is caused precisely because the forensic spectator on the hunt for meaning is *also* the registering body of sensations of excessive things, objects, and images. The spectator is thrown out of the cognitive practice but drawn in by the opaque power of nonsignifying images.[10] *This* is the push-pull disorientation of the subject experiencing both opacities and meanings. Pulled into the narrative by clues only to be absorbed by the inscrutable presence of opacities, and moving along a narrative landscape that is pursuing closure through meaning while producing holes in the text that thwart signification with nonsignifying presences—here lies the experiential hybridity of the mobilized spectator of television seriality.

BIBLIOGRAPHY

Adorno, Theodor W. (1991). *Aesthetic Theory* [1970]. Minneapolis: University of Minnesota Press.

Ames, Melissa, ed. (2012). *Time in Television Narrative: Exploring Temporality in Twenty-First-Century Programming*. Jackson: University of Mississippi Press.

Bordwell, David and Kristin Thompson (1976). "Space and Narrative in the films of Ozu." *Screen* 17.2: 41–73.

Bourdieu, Pierre (1987). *Distinction: A Social Critique of the Judgment of Taste* [1979]. Cambridge, MA: Harvard University Press.

Brown, Bill (2003). *A Sense of Things: The Object Matter in American Literature*. Chicago: University of Chicago Press.

Brunsdon, Charlotte (1990). "Television: Aesthetics and Audiences." *Logics of Television: Essays in Cultural Criticism*. Ed. Patricia Mellencamp. Bloomington: Indiana University Press. 59–72.

Buonnano, Milly (2008). *The Age of Television: Experiences and Theories*. Bristol: Intellect.

Caldwell, John Thornton (1995). *Televisuality: Style, Crisis, and Authority in American Television*. New Brunswick: Rutgers University Press.

Creeber, Glen (2004). *Serial Television: Big Drama on the Small Screen*. London: BFI.

Dasgupta, Sudeep (2009). "Jacques Rancière." *Film, Theory and Philosophy: Key Thinkers*. Ed. Felicity Colman. London: Acumen. 339–48.

——(2013). "The Spiral of Thought in the Work of Jacques Rancière." *Theory and Event* 16.1: n.p.

Dasgupta, Sudeep and Wim Staat (2008). "Of Surfaces and Depths: The Afterlives of 'Tales of Sound and Fury.'" *Mind the Screen: Media Concepts according to Thomas Elsaesser*. Ed. Jaap Kooijman et al. Amsterdam: Amsterdam University Press. 43–59.

Feuer, Jane (1984). "Melodrama, Serial Form and Television Today." *Screen* 25.1: 4–17.

Foster, Hal (2002). *Design and Crime (And Other Diatribes)*. London: Verso.

——(2011). *The Art-Architecture Complex*. London: Verso.

---

10. My argument here extends Rushton's analysis of the shifting relationship between absorption and theatricality. For Rushton (as for Mittell and Willemen), opacity is important only from the perspective of meaning-making. The object's excessive character, as Brown (2003) describes it, is not factored into his reading of film narrative.

Fried, Michael (1998). *Art and Objecthood: Essays and Reviews*. Chicago: University of Chicago Press.
Greenberg, Clement (1965). "Modernist Painting." *Art and Literature* 4: 193–201.
Gunning, Tom (2004). "An Aesthetic of Astonishment: Early Film and the (In)Credulous Spectator." *Film Theory: Critical Concepts in Media and Cultural Studies: Vol. 3*. Ed. Philip Simpson et al. London: Routledge. 114–33.
Hansen, Miriam (2012). *Cinema and Experience: Siegfried Kracauer, Walter Benjamin, and Theodor W. Adorno*. Chicago: University of Chicago Press.
Jameson, Fredric (1974). *Marxism and Form: Twentieth-Century Dialectical Theories of Literature*. Princeton: Princeton University Press.
——(2009). *The Cultural Turn: Selected Writings on the Postmodern, 1983–1998* [1998]. London: Verso.
Kant, Immanuel (1988). *Critique of Judgment* [1790]. Oxford: Clarendon.
Kovács, András Bálint (2007). *Screening Modernism: European Art Cinema, 1950–1980*. Chicago: University of Chicago Press.
Lukács, Georg (1974). *The Theory of the Novel: A Historico-Philosophical Essay on the Forms of Great Epic Literature* [1963]. Cambridge: MIT.
Luhmann, Niklas (2000). *Art as Social System* [1995]. Stanford: Stanford University Press.
Mittell, Jason (2006). "Narrative Complexity in Contemporary American Television." *Velvet Light Trap* 58: 29–40.
——(2009). "Forensic Fandom and the Drillable Text." *Spreadablemedia*. May 3, 2014. http://spreadablemedia.org/essays/mittell/#.U2UJQ_mSySo.
Nelson, Robin (2004). "Hill Street Blues." *Fifty Key Television Programmes*. Ed. Glen Creeber. London: Arnold.
Newman, Michael, Z. (2006). "From Beats to Arcs: Towards a Poetics of Television Narrative." *Velvet Light Trap* 58: 16–28.
Polan, Dana (2014). "What's Next? Part 1." *Unitcrit* (May 3). May 7, 2014. http://unitcrit.blogspot.nl/2014/05/mad-world-on-kritik-prelude-to-mad-men.html.
Rancière, Jacques (2007). *The Future of the Image*. London: Verso.
——(2012). *La méthode de l'égalité: Entretien avec Laurent Jeanpierre et Dork Zabunyan*. Montrouge: Bayard.
——(2013). *Aisthesis: Scenes from the Aesthetic Regime of Art*. London: Verso.
Rushton, Richard (2004). "Early, Classical and Modern Cinema: Theatricality and Absorption." *Screen* 45.3: 226–44.
Sobchack, Vivian (1999). "Towards a Phenomenology of Nonfictional Film Experience." *Collecting Visible Evidence*. Ed. Jane Gaines and Michael M. Renov. Minneapolis: University of Minnesota Press. 241–54.
Willemen, Paul (1971). "Distanciation and Douglas Sirk." *Screen* 12.2: 63–67.

CHAPTER 11

The Inevitable, the Surprise, and Serial Television

SEAN O'SULLIVAN

> The one quality that every great scripted show has in common is surprise.
> —MATT ZOLLER SEITZ (2014)

> It was a way for me [...] to set up an ending that felt both unpredictable and inevitable.
> —NOAH HAWLEY, QTD. IN SEPINWALL 2014

WHEN CONSIDERING the matter of surprise in the narrative arts, it seems appropriate to begin with the thoughts of Alfred Hitchcock. The director famously defined *surprise,* for the benefit of François Truffaut, in contradistinction to suspense. "We are now having a very innocent little chat," he began, helpfully advertising the uneventful as an ideal starting point for the unexpected. "Let us suppose that there is a bomb underneath this table between us. Nothing happens, and then all of a sudden, 'Boom!' There is an explosion." Hitchcock termed this sudden development—the sequel to "nothing" happening—"surprise," because until this point the "scene" has been "absolutely ordinary, of no special consequence" (Truffaut 1985: 73). For Hitchcock, surprise is a maneuver that exists almost beyond temporal marking, a shift perhaps analogous to the cut in cinema, the instantaneous transition from one state of affairs to another.

Suspense, however, depends on both time and knowledge. In this storytelling choice, Hitchcock explains, "the bomb is underneath the table and the public *knows* it [...]. The public is *aware* that the bomb is going to explode at one o'clock and there is a clock in the décor" (emphases original). The narrative elongation of temporal parameters—familiar to any moviegoer who has seen a bomb's countdown clock take considerably more than a quarter hour of screen time to advance from fifteen minutes to zero—makes suspense the realm of anxiety about a promised destination, about a threat that lingers over the storyworld, whether that storyworld's characters are privy to it or not. In the realm of suspense, the Hitchcock public should be "made perfectly aware of all of the facts involved" (72). We might call suspense the territory of epistemological masochism on the part of the public or audience and of epistemological sadism on the part of the storyteller. For Hitchcock, the grand gourmand of emotional pain, there was no question about which was the greater technique. In the first version of the bomb explosion, we get "fifteen seconds of surprise"; in the second version, we get "fifteen minutes of suspense." The conclusion, he informs Truffaut, is that "whenever possible the public must be informed."

I would like to adapt Hitchcock's formulas to consider two adjacent narrative questions of serial television. First, I will translate the central opposition from one between surprise and suspense to one between surprise and the *inevitable*. Hitchcock's key elements of surprise will work well enough: the sudden, unexpected transition from the ordinary to the special; the viewer's state of ignorance; and the brevity of the effect. I will say more about the inevitable as we proceed; for now, I would characterize the inevitable as a particular adaptation of the characteristics of suspense, across variables of both time and knowledge. Suspense contains the seeds of the inevitable, in the expectation that a bomb will go off at a certain moment. Of course, the bomb may not go off, due to external factors; but our narrative engagement depends on the certainty that something will happen, at some definable moment, and that this future happening will have significant consequences for the story that we are watching. Hitchcock described this as the public "participating in the scene" (73), although we might more accurately call this vicarious surveillance, since of course we can do nothing to stop this something from happening—even as we are cued to want to stop this something, or at least to feel both our epistemological power and our participatory powerlessness.[1] The inevitable

---

1. The critical discussion of suspense is extensive, and my goal here is to use Hitchcock's scenario as a launching pad for my own project, rather than a full engagement with the meanings of that term. Perhaps the most circulated analysis is Noël Carroll's, which defines the condition of suspense as an emotional state of uncertainty. The closest intersection between our approaches concerns what Carroll calls "recidivist suspense," or the sensation of suspense that a viewer/reader paradoxically experiences upon revisiting a text, even though the suspenseful outcome is already known (Carroll 1996: 89). I see the paradox of the inevitable as the reverse of recidivist suspense: we sense that there is really no structural doubt to the outcome, even though we don't know what that outcome will be. Caroline Levine offers another version of Carroll's paradox in claiming that suspense is always about rereading, even the first time

amplifies both the power and the absence of power and stretches those fifteen minutes of storyworld time to something potentially much, much longer. When the inevitable holds sway, the storyworld itself is a kind of bomb, one that does not so much detonate as create a mood of perpetual predetonation; and the detonation itself is not a bright, loud flash but a disaster of extreme slow motion, decelerated and distressing in the dilation of the event. Knowledge, in the realm of the inevitable, is not so much a specific data point (such as "the bomb will go off in fifteen minutes"). Rather, it is an array of information nodes, the combination of which requires a particular perspective on the storyworld with which we are engaged. The inevitable is systemic; it is a lien on a story's range of narrative possibilities.

My second translation has to do with how Hitchcock's terms function in the environment of serial narrative. The interplay between surprise and suspense, or between surprise and the inevitable, could certainly hold for any single moment within a serial: so we know about the bomb, or we don't know about the bomb. But, unlike a single feature film, serials create trails for themselves. What is "ordinary" and what is "special" are defined not by some presumed convention of the ordinary—such as an "innocent little chat" around a table—but increasingly by the conventions that a serial sets out for itself. So, if it happens that on more than one occasion an innocent chat around a table has turned suddenly into a scene of bloody chaos, we are much less likely to see that specific narrative circumstance as inherently "innocent." The serial practices of routine and disruption gradually acquire meanings and connections particular to the experience of that serial. "Nothing," the central precondition for surprise in Hitchcock's description, could represent any state that precedes change or disruption within the patterns that a serial has chosen to create for itself. No serial operates in a vacuum, of course; existing genre conventions, to name just one element, may critically shape the circumstances for surprise. But it is worth underlining the degree to which surprise may become locally contingent within a serial's unfolding. Surprise can be a defining aspect of the narrative apparatus, the recognition of which marks the difference between an adept and a newcomer, in the experience of that serial.

How the inevitable might operate differently in a serial from a standalone narrative is a question I will explore below. One might suggest, as Matt Zoller Seitz does in the first epigraph for this chapter, that surprise is the primary ingredient for "every great scripted show" (by which he means serial

---

we experience a text—since we have to keep returning to our "hunches and suspicions" until the unknown becomes "intelligible" (Levine 2003: 80). Again, my approach flips this process around, emphasizing the vaguely known (the inevitable) rather than the unknown as the condition of narrative elongation.

television). The implication may be that the inevitable, or what we cannot be surprised by, is either unnecessary or possibly deleterious. If surprise exists as the mark of excellence, does the inevitable denote the mark of failure—of disappointment, since what we know will happen triumphs over what we cannot foresee? The validation of surprise appears to be the recent strategy of channels such as FX, whose slogan—"Fearless"—implied a willingness to go places where no other programmer might, in effect to surprise its audience over and over again. Or Showtime, whose warning to the viewer—"Brace Yourself"—fetishized sudden bumps and shifts, perhaps with the result that surprise becomes scheduled rather than unpredictable. Surprise may be in the ascendancy as a storytelling value, despite its déclassé roots in soap opera. My goal here is not to validate the surprise over the inevitable, or vice versa. Rather, I want to consider the struggle between the inevitable and the surprise as a key part of how U.S. serial television's ambitions have defined themselves over the last fifteen years. It is precisely the investigation of both of these terms, and of the interplay between them, that has served as a vital instrument of these serials' self-definition. What follows is a preliminary sketch of one way we might consider the dialogue between restriction and freedom, between what must be and what might be, in contemporary television.

•

George Hearst, the villain of the third season of HBO's *Deadwood*, takes control of the Dakota mining town by choking off its range of narrative possibilities. "My instructions," he tells Cy Tolliver, "would have to do with bringing the inevitable about." As the embodiment of unrestrained capital, Hearst serves not simply as an emissary of history but as a person who actually did bend the narrative of this place in the 1870s by taking control of the Homestake Mine. He also operates to instruct the viewers that the apparent wealth of storytelling options in which the other characters lived are in fact a sharply limited trust, one in which their space for developmental maneuver is tightly circumscribed. Hearst's identification with the inevitable represents the industrialization of a seemingly milder claim made by saloonkeeper Al Swearengen a season and a half earlier. In that precorporate context, as Swearengen and hotelier E. B. Farnum are parceling out bribes for Yankton politicians, Farnum complains that the ad hoc government that the camp's fathers have created may have to pay for projects other than the administration of graft, such as an infirmary and a garbage dump. Swearengen responds by recognizing that the development of communal living brings certain requirements: "That type shit's inevitable." The language of inevitability is inscribed in the logic of the series, a relentless machinery visible not just to the audience but to the inhabitants of the storyworld itself (O'Sullivan 2009: 324).

A differently phrased, but very much parallel, depiction of the inevitable operates in a show that ran contemporaneously with *Deadwood* on HBO, namely, *The Wire*. That series' emphasis on the unrelentingly cyclical, and on the circumscription of narrative directions, is omnipresent. As an illustration, I offer three characters underlining this state of affairs, at the hinge between the end of the fourth season and the beginning of the fifth. In the late stages of the final episode of season four, Bunny Colvin, frustrated by the limitations on the possibility of educational transformation imposed by forces both personal and impersonal in Baltimore, asks rhetorically, "When do this shit change?" As if hearing this question, to which everyone already knows the answer, detective Bunk Moreland, in the cold open (or teaser) of season five, takes the occasion of the familiar police trick of the prisoner's dilemma, played on two neophyte criminals, to comment to one of his colleagues, "How many years you figure we've been doing this same shit?" A few minutes later in the episode, Jimmy McNulty complains to his associates in a bar about the promise that a new administration had offered him, a promise of a "new day" in Baltimore, a promise that quickly disappears: "Shit never fucking changes," he laments. (It is worth noting that in each of these three moments from *The Wire*, as with Al Swearengen's observation to E. B. Farnum, the language of inevitability is expressed through the vocabulary of excrement. The apparent simplicity and iterative familiarity of the workings of the alimentary canal are seen as analogous to the apparent simplicity and iterative familiarity of the workings of these narrative environments. Shit, I am sure Alfred Hitchcock would agree, is no surprise.)

These regular announcements about the inevitable make it seem as if *Deadwood* and *The Wire* are constantly pumping the brakes, rather than flooring the accelerator, of their narratives. On many occasions, David Simon, the creator and showrunner of *The Wire*, claimed that the spiritual ancestor of his series, both rhetorically and procedurally, was Greek tragedy; in one such interview, he said, "When you go see those plays performed, if they're done well, you know the ending with absolute certainty" (Sepinwall 2008). That may be well and good for a two- or three-hour experience in a fixed space, where a theatergoer is strapped in her seat, prepared for the enactment of a known tale rather than the unforeseen developments of a new one. But absolute certainty, or the rule of the inevitable, would seem to be a disastrous selling point for serial storytelling. Serials operate by enforced hiatus, by interruption and deferral; if those regular interruptions turn into dead zones, into spaces through which viewers or readers have little impetus to move, without a central promise of the serial contract, a promise of "a new day" in Baltimore—even in the most basic serial sense of a new day, that is, one sequence of narratable time that may look a lot like the sequence of narratable time that preceded it but that will differ at least slightly in some respect—then the financial and absorptive conditions of serial storytelling are deeply imperiled. Whatever the utility of the inevitable in, say, a first-person short story by Edgar Allan Poe, the commercial parameters of serial publication make what cannot be changed appear to be a regular, and increasingly problematic, hindrance.

We might contrast *Deadwood* and *The Wire* with a third show, *Breaking Bad*. Two central elements of this series—one a defining premise, the other an oft-stated paratextual declaration—would seem to make inevitability part of its modus operandi as well. The defining premise is that its protagonist, Walter White, receives a diagnosis of terminal lung cancer in the pilot—an apparently strict bracketing of the range of eventual destinations. The paratextual declaration, even more familiar than David Simon's invocation of Greek tragedy, was creator and showrunner Vince Gilligan's tagline—used, supposedly, to pitch the series to AMC—that the show would trace Walter White's transformation "from Mr. Chips to Scarface." This enunciated not only an arc but an arc with a particular kind of terminus—presuming a common awareness that *Scarface* ends in a self-martyring hail of bullets. Indeed, we have the apparently indisputable evidence of the DVD case for the last half-season: the case informs us that "the final episodes bring the unforgettable story of Walter White to its *inevitable* close" (*Breaking Bad* 2013; emphasis added). But I would argue that *inevitable* is precisely the wrong word for the serial operations of *Breaking Bad*. Instead, the initial premise and Vince Gilligan's pitch line represent very different kinds of narrative mappings from the domain of inevitability in *Deadwood* and *The Wire*. In fact, *Breaking Bad* serves as an apotheosis of an opposite storytelling mode, one with which serial narrative (correctly or not) has long been most closely associated—namely, surprise. If the dominant momentum of *Deadwood* is magnetic dread, the dominant momentum of *Breaking Bad* is the thrill of the unpredictable. More broadly, we should think about a number of recent American dramatic series within a continuum, a continuum that distinguishes roughly between narratives of surprise and narratives of the inevitable. Among the potential uses of this continuum is the way it suggests affinities between series that are in many ways sharply different as storytelling structures—not least *Deadwood* and *The Wire*, which, for all the connections I discern in terms of their commitment to the inevitable, in fact have relatively little in common in terms of narrative design. The inevitable and the surprise represent registers of serial experimentation, discrete ways of thinking about order and accident in televisual storytelling.

The key distinction I am making between surprise and the inevitable is between *narrative design* on the one hand, and *storyworld conditions,* or what we might call the storyworld's *environment,* on the other. The weight in the first case is on manifest strategies of story construction; the weight in the second is on preconditions of the diegesis in which stories are told. The issue of design is central because I am intent on separating the surprise/inevitable bifurcation from mere genre codes or stylistic conventions. So, if we watch a procedural, it may seem inevitable that by the end of the hour the police, or the forensic scientists, doctors, or lawyers will have painstakingly solved something, bringing order to chaos—or at least gone most of the way toward that transformation. But there is nothing inherent in the storyworld to make order inevitable; rather, it takes the specific abilities of experts to negotiate the sequence of surprises that they encounter. This leads us back to one of *Breaking Bad*'s two apparent inevitable conditions—namely, Walter White's transformation from Mr. Chips to Scarface. There is nothing inevitable in the environmental conditions of the show, from its inception, in either the high school where Walter teaches or in the Whites' home, or in Albuquerque, New Mexico, to motivate this metamorphosis. Rather, it is the triumph of design over storyworld that actuates the show. These triumphs of design are everywhere, and they manifest themselves as moments of surprise, as junctures where we don't get what we might expect—to the degree that getting the unexpected becomes a regular feature of watching the show, something that may eventually seem inevitable to the viewer (as when, in a procedural, an investigative genius brings light to darkness) but that in fact is always an operation of working against the grain of routine.

Among the most prominent gestures of surprise are the show's time shifts, including the recurring and temporally opaque images of a pink teddy bear in a pool in season two; flashbacks such as Jane Margolis and Jesse Pinkman's visit to the Georgia O'Keeffe museum in season three, and Skyler and Walter White's first appearance in their house in the final episode of that same season; or the flash-forwards at the start of both halves of season five, featuring Walter at breakfast on his fifty-second birthday and the abandoned White home as a skateboarders' domain. The fact that so many of these temporal surprises occur in the space of the teaser or cold open—as all the examples I just cited do—made that specific narrative room a kind of gift to be opened each week, where the surprise often came from a basic question of what we were doing in a particular time frame or physical space, as with the array of dipping sauces that inaugurated the fifth-season episode "Madrigal." If the cold opens offered surprise as narrative delight, then the storytelling corners into which the show often wrote itself at the ends of episodes, or the ends of seasons, represented surprise in its most traditional mode—the shocking event as episode closure.

Arguably, *Breaking Bad* aimed to redeem this maneuver for a certain kind of television show—the kind of show that, to avoid the loathsome terminology of "prestige" or "quality," typically ends up on critics' ten-best lists at the end of the year or in volumes such as this one. The shocking event would leave us wondering how the show's world would consequently proceed—that is, wondering about the solutions the writers would devise for the problems they had chosen to create. So persistent was the sense of how-the-hell-are-they-going-to-imagine-their-way-out-of-this, as a narrative closing trope for *Breaking Bad*, that we could consider "Granite State," the series' penultimate episode, as, in fact, the last episode of the series. As a narrative enterprise, *Breaking Bad* flourished in the gaps between episodes, in the speculation about how the final shot of each installment would play out and lead on to the beginning of the next; the viewers' interest, like that of any meth junkie, was always fixed on the next score, the even better thing just around the corner (O'Sullivan 2013). The show's recurrent twists, and most importantly their astonishing successes, were to a large degree a victory of the writers (or, if one prefers, showrunner Vince Gilligan) over the world they and he had created. The prestidigitations of Gilligan and company went hand in hand with Walter White's—his miraculous escapes and re-inventions mirroring the show's own capacity for discovering another way to illustrate and engineer its universe.

As to the defining premise, Walter's fatal condition: we know from the long history of serials, whether soap opera or nineteenth-century British fiction, that medical diagnoses are the most elastic of storytelling circumstances. In the case of *Breaking Bad*, we have obvious moments such as the end of the second-season episode, "Four Days Out," when Walter learns that his cancer seems to be on the wane and that his tumor has shrunk considerably—a surprise (of a kind) that appears to sabotage his plan to go out in a blaze of meth-making glory, after having amassed a nice pile of cash for his family. This is one of several instances of what we might call *narrative* remission in the series, when the supposed inevitability, or at least omnipresence, of the diagnosis is severely compromised. Sometimes we get moments of triumph or simply recalibration, when the conditions of the narrative seem to have been altered by fiat. So, Walter's victory over Gus Fring at the end of season four, punctuated with the revelation of the protagonist's lily-of-the-valley infamy, works to celebrate design over accident, the ability to shape the world to one's desires, with no shadow of looming coughs or IV drips. On the flip side, the end of the midpoint of season five, which concludes with Walter's not-brilliant decision to place *Leaves of Grass* on top of the toilet for brother-in-law Hank Schrader to discover, suggests something other than an inevitable consequence. Rather, we get a storytelling choice designed to put two men on a collision course.

Consider how differently these three series begin. *Deadwood* shows Seth Bullock about to leave Montana for a new mining camp, aiming to leave behind his responsibilities as sheriff and re-invent himself as a businessman. But someone named Clell Watson has made the unfortunate choice of stealing a horse and landing himself in a jail cell—causing a lynch mob in turn to appear, demanding summary justice. Seth is thus required to perform yet another act as sheriff, hanging Watson "under color of law"—a signal that the Western's supposed scope for allowing people to become something other than who they already are will be radically curtailed in this series. Bullock will spend the entire first season avoiding the "badge," the external symbol of his internal compass, until he finally cannot hold off the inevitable any more—agreeing to assume the office of sheriff in the season's final episode. Retrospectively, we can see that prologue in Montana—an anterior event granted to no other character in the series—as serving the primary purpose of inscribing the inevitability of social codes, even in a camp such as Deadwood, where, as Clell Watson informs the audience, there is "no law at all." Whatever the illusion of freedom, constraint will operate inevitably on the inhabitants.

The pilot of *The Wire* offers a different parable of inevitability, staging an instructive dialogue between detective Jimmy McNulty and an unknown citizen. The two sit on a curb, at a nighttime crime scene, discussing the recently killed Snot Boogie and the problem of why he was allowed to gamble with associates, given his propensity to steal the pot of money. "Got to," says the citizen. "This America, man." If the prologue of *Deadwood* skirts narrative necessity, giving us a moment that could be delayed until later, the first cold open of *The Wire* flouts serial sequencing completely. We will never hear from this citizen, or about Snot Boogie, ever again. Rather, this set piece exists to make *conditions*—rules simultaneously inexplicable and unbreakable—the causal agents of the series; human individuals may simply function as bystanders to narrative machinery. "Got to" illustrates in blue and red flashing lights the logic of inevitability, of compulsion, of the things that operate whether we want to or not, that will drive *The Wire*'s five seasons of storytelling.

Breaking Bad does not begin with a parable or a potentially disposable scene, and it does not begin by minimizing the free will of individual agents. *Breaking Bad* begins with a pair of pants flying through the air, and a guy driving a RV in his tighty whities and a gas mask. This is as far away from the "got to" of *The Wire*, or the "got to" of *Deadwood*, as we can imagine; there is no "got to" here. Rather, there is the terrifying, and humorous, spectacle of what happens when characters decide to believe there are in fact "no laws at all" that they must continue to abide. The mismatched characters at the center of the first episode—Walter White and Jesse Pinkman—offer two versions of lawlessness, one deliberately choosing to make surprise an ethos, the other cluelessly opting for improvisation over planning. The rules that Walter White respects are the rules of chemistry, but those laws of science, within the diegesis, are the only "got to" that *Breaking Bad* obeys. The narrative itself spins in irregular, elliptical orbit around its point of origin. Even the production contexts in which the first season was made—the writers' strike, which forced an abbreviation of the episode count by two, giving Vince Gilligan the opportunity to "throw out those two episodes completely and start somewhere else" (McFarland 2013)—underscore the contingent, the circumstances around which plans must be suddenly altered, rather than the regularity (one might almost say the inevitability) of traditional TV production. Another chance, in other words, for design to rewrite storyworld conditions.

The terms and consequences of inevitability and surprise allow us to divide six of the most-discussed series of the last fifteen years of U.S. television evenly into two camps.[2] *Deadwood* and *The Wire* are two representatives of the inevitable. The third series that I would assign to that category is *Six Feet Under*. Just as inevitability in *Deadwood* resides in a controlling *tension* (between promise and restriction), and inevitability in *The Wire* resides in a social *circumstance* (cycles of personal and institutional behavior), so the inevitability of *Six Feet Under* resides, or at least begins, in a narrative *premise*. *Six Feet Under*, set in a Los Angeles funeral home, is the first show in the history of American television to make the iterated presence of death not a puzzle to be solved (as with a procedural), not an outrage or a spectacle, but rather a commonplace. Death here, to return to Hitchcock's terms, is the ordinary, and not the surprise. The series uses the problem of mortality as a quotidian, governing anxiety, examining the persistence of narrative desire and characterological subjectivity in the face of the inevitable. To some degree,

---

2. If space permitted, we could discuss many other recent shows. We might deem *Homeland* an example of a "hyper-surprisey" series, one genetically committed to the twist even more than its predecessor in the vein of conspiracy thriller, *24*. The end of the fourth episode of the third season of *Homeland*, for example, provided surprise as reverse suspense—suddenly revealing vital information that seemed a deliberate refusal of audience "participation," in Hitchcock's sense. Or we might reword the perpetual agon in *Lost* between Locke and Jack as a struggle between the inevitable and the surprise, couched in the show's vocabulary of fate and free will. It is perhaps the difficulty of reconciling inevitable and surprise that produced the possibly problematic situation of that show's final episode, or indeed its entire final season. The radical unpredictability of a show like *Louie* makes surprise even more conceptual (and less about shock) than in *The Sopranos*. There is also *The Newsroom*, a show often accused of using the retrospective inevitability of recent historical events to unfairly critique some characters and celebrate others—in effect to misrepresent surprise as the inevitable. And we have the infamous promise of apparent inevitability offered by the title of *How I Met Your Mother*, one resolved in a narrative act of bait and switch.

the series' anxiety mirrors that of Nate Fisher, the thanatophobe who might loosely be termed the central character. It is his return from Seattle to help run the family business, after the death of the father in a car accident, that inaugurates the show—a fate he has been trying to avoid since childhood. In the pilot, facing his father's corpse in the morgue, Nate ideates a vision of his father articulating that very problem: "This is what you've been running away from your whole life," Nathaniel Sr. says. "And you thought you'd escape? Well, guess what? Nobody escapes." "Nobody escapes" hardly seems the most promising catchphrase for a serial; certainly the fantasy of escape, indeed the act of series-long escape, is what drives Walter White in *Breaking Bad*. Nate Fisher's crippling resistance to both the permanent (relationships, jobs) and the unavoidable shows him as the most passive or reactive hero of this recent generation of American television—making him something closer to the protagonists of European art cinema or the New Hollywood. His crises are primarily internal and spiritual; even when external calamities arise, they seem symptomatic of his defining fear and reluctance. His own mortal calamity, the medical condition that will eventually doom him, is the internal and invisible brain condition of AVM, an abnormality of the arteries and veins that bears no outward signs. Consider, by contrast, the many *external* registers of Walter White's lung cancer, whose corporal debilitations are frequently apparent and the treatment for which—aggressive chemotherapy—produces the hair loss that will be the signature evidence of Walter's alter ego, Heisenberg.

If *Six Feet Under* traffics in the serial narrative of passivity rather than activity, we might also say that its key storytelling markers are *events* rather than *incidents*. By *incidents* I mean happenings within a storyworld (often unexpected happenings) that trigger direct narrative consequences. Death is the most prominent available incident in a serial, and in a procedural it is the source for action from start to end of each episode, or for an entire season in series like *True Detective* and *Top of the Lake*. In *Breaking Bad*, deaths either promote action or indicate the relative position of power of central characters. But the ubiquity of death in *Six Feet Under* makes the catalytic status of any single demise ambiguous. I am using "event" to signal a vaguer instance of happening than an incident; death in this series provides differing degrees of *tellability* (to use a conventional barometer of narratology), of the possibly significant. Death here can be narratively neutral; its presence does not necessarily warrant the mark of the unusual. Perhaps the clearest example of the territory between incident and event in *Six Feet Under* is the second-season episode "The Invisible Woman," which begins with a woman named Emily Previn choking to death alone in her apartment. The Fisher family can find no immediate family or friends to contact, and Ruth, the matriarch, chooses to treat this as an incident—that is, she goes to the apartment in a quasi-detective capacity, to try to learn more about the broader circumstances of Emily Previn's life. But she learns nothing; she is unable, in other words, to turn this event into an incident, into something marbled with narrativity. Ruth's motive lies in the fear that she herself will be abandoned at some point, and the episode ends with her crying before pictures of her children when they were young. That image of passivity—or, more accurately, passivity as emotional or psychological activity—serves as a synecdoche for the series' contemplation of the inevitability of the long term, alongside the rewards and sensations of the immediate.

In the category of the surprise, I would propose *The Sopranos* and *Mad Men*, along with *Breaking Bad*. Given their range of subject, personnel, and methodology, the three series I have discussed under the inevitable are in fact rather strange bedfellows (more on which later). But surely there are no stranger bedfellows than *Breaking Bad* and *The Sopranos*—two shows that are as fundamentally different as any in the recent pantheon. If *Breaking Bad* was an innovative, transformative show because it embraced television—reveling in the medium's relentless drive, its tropes and maneuvers, its addiction to genre, even its potential cheesiness—*The Sopranos* was an innovative, transformative show because it resisted television—happy to frustrate expectations and leave stories dangling, preferring to understand itself as a collection of short stories, or maybe songs on an album, or a cluster of somewhat-related movies. It was a show just as interested, if not more interested, in retarding plot as in advancing it—in stark contrast with *Breaking Bad*'s nose for what's next (O'Sullivan 2013). But *The Sopranos*, like *Breaking Bad*, chose to operate in a space of storytelling freedom, and not the storytelling obligation of *Deadwood* and *The Wire*; it wanted the persistent opportunity to change course. *Mad Men* followed a similar methodology, as expressed in the words of Matthew Weiner, its showrunner and a *Sopranos* alumnus: "I don't want people to know what to expect ever when they turn the show on" (Sepinwall 2009). *Mad Men* does have one aspect in common with *Deadwood*: they are both historical dramas. But I would argue that history is not deeply relevant to the balance between surprise and the inevitable. The fact that some of the incidents we see may actually have happened is not the controlling question; rather, it is the matter of how a series chooses to design those incidents or, more precisely, how it chooses to design the parallel serial world in which those incidents may or may not impinge. Don Draper, the center of *Mad Men*, is in many ways the obverse of Nate Fisher. But in the pilot, Draper delivers a line of dialogue that could have come from the mouth of that troubled funeral director: "You're born alone, and you die alone, and this world just drops a bunch of rules on top of you to make you forget those facts." In the context of *Mad Men*, death, like history, will become a vehicle for generating variety and surprise—for changes of tone and reversals of fortune, rather than the slowly ticking bomb of the inevitable. *Mad Men* fervently avoids the limits of expectations in ways that *Deadwood*, *The Wire*, and *Six Feet Under* did not.

The most explicit illustration of the difference between *Breaking Bad*'s and *The Sopranos*' deployment of surprise lies in their diametrically opposed decisions about how to end themselves. Whatever the assumptions about Walter White's arc, the final two episodes operated as a thesis and antithesis: a penultimate vision of storytelling extinction—the specter of White forever adrift in a New Hampshire cabin, removed from the zone of surprise—followed by a finale that allowed Walter to stage a series of surprises, taking revenge upon or paying unexpected visits to the most prominent people affected by his transgressions. The closing gestures of *Breaking Bad* were as much about style—the series' style and the protagonist's style—as about a specific sequence of occurrences. White and the series deployed surprise as a pleasure point for viewers all the way to the bittersweet end, from the stealthy administration of poison in the tea of an enemy to the rococo rigging of a machine gun to mow down a clan of skinheads. The "operational aesthetic"—the term Jason Mittell (2006: 35) has popularized to describe such meta-narrative engagement—here taps into viewers' interest in *how* things are done in the designs of story. The governing "how" of *Breaking Bad* lies in the territory of clever, unforeseen gestures that turned tables and confounded expectations.

In *The Sopranos*, surprise worked less as an aesthetic, or a "narrative special effect"—another term Mittell uses to consider storytelling as spellbinding magic (2006: 35). This was a series with a much quieter motor, allowing for moments of disruption but just as happy with dilation and ennui. Surprise in *The Sopranos* emerged primarily in the relation of episodes to each other—in such infamous deviations from the central storytelling artery as the third-season episode "Pine Barrens"—and in transformations of tone and mood, in hard cuts from noisy Mafia environments to the stillness of Jennifer Melfi's psychiatric office: hence the particular significance of the series' final and infamous gesture of surprise, its cut to black. The primary effect of surprise in *Breaking Bad* resulted from what lay on the other side of the surprise—the reaction both inside and outside the diegesis to the surprise's consequences. *The Sopranos* instead brought us, quite literally, to the "ordinary" table that Alfred Hitchcock claimed as the exemplary location for surprise. In the final moments, we get a "very innocent little chat" in a diner: Tony Soprano, his wife Carmela, and his son A. J. discuss menial jobs and onion rings while daughter Meadow tries to parallel-park outside. There is a bomb here, but it is not a diegetic one—not the one Hitchcock describes, and not the kind of explosion that *Breaking Bad* would be happy to construct. What is bombed here is the very existence of the diegesis, and it is the narrative design that detonates that bomb. The sudden and unprepared-for blowing up of this table, and these people, removes us instantly from the scene; there is no "after" against which the precise power of the surprise can be measured.

That manner of serial surprise proves difficult to reconcile with some traditional narratological arguments about values of plotting. This issue requires a much fuller airing than I can provide here—but it is worth considering one such narratological argument, namely, Marie-Laure Ryan's essay "Cheap Plot Tricks, Plot Holes, and Narrative Design." Ryan's delineation of implausible coincidences, inconvenient misunderstandings, and other techniques to create tension or resolve intertwined stories offers a helpful taxonomy of storytelling fissures, those places where narrative-as-construct intersects with narrative-as-representation. The one blind spot in the argument—which otherwise focuses almost exclusively on novelistic or dramatic fiction—occurs when Ryan addresses the ending of *The Sopranos,* a termination that she judges an example of "interrupted action," and in many ways "the ultimate CPT [cheap plot trick]" because the series' refusal demonstrates "the author's inability to tie the strands of the plot in a satisfactory way" (Ryan 2009: 65). Ryan's approach, as she acknowledges from the start, favors an Aristotelian prescriptivism, where anagnorisis and "the inner disposition of characters" lead to ideal endings as opposed to "*ad hoc* external circumstances which bear the stamp of the author's fabrication" (Ryan 2009: 57). In effect, her argument privileges the inevitable over the surprise—where the inevitable stands for a logic borne out by the moral consequences of characterological behavior. Hence for Ryan the peripeteia of Oedipus is the golden example, since the surprises of that tragedy are really the consequences of inevitable circumstances, both external and internal. Within this logic, we would say that Nate Fisher of *Six Feet Under* and Omar Little of *The Wire* reach approved conclusions, because they are generated by some "satisfactory" combination of circumstantial plausibility and ethical justification.

But, as I have argued elsewhere, the preference for satisfaction or the satisfactory represents the imposition of a certain kind of contained narrative on the messy sprawl of serials (O'Sullivan 2014). If the logic of the inevitable works against serial tendencies toward shocks and sleights of hand, the logic of surprise works against more conventional narratological values of progression and shape. One term for that shape is "narrative arc," used by Ryan to propose that we can forgive CPTs when/if their uses are mitigated by a "satisfactory resolution" (2009: 72). I would suggest that *arc*—a termed explicitly lampooned in *The Sopranos* as early as the middle of the first season, when Christopher Moltisanti worries that he is himself a character without a satisfying narrative trajectory—privileges containment and teleology as values. Those values are contrary to the broken, recursive processes of serials; arcs, if they exist, are always contingent, always vulnerable to deviation. If we want serials to be "satisfactory," we will have to reject the form's very processes, forcing conventions of the whole onto the actual pieces of serial narrative. *The Sopranos*' commitment to surprise, which may seem more muted than that of *Breaking Bad* on the level of incident or narrative special effect, reached its climax in the cut to black that denied the delivery of both momentary and long-term pleasures, both the fizz of *Breaking Bad* and the muckraking exposition of *The Wire*. Interpretive attempts to "fix" the ending of *The Sopranos*, by telling us what "actually" happened, represent the desire to graft inevitability (such as the death of the leading man in a tragedy) or satisfaction on a narrative that spent eighty-six episodes running away from those criteria; the imported values of tragedy and closure attempt to suppress fractures rather than emphasize them. So, while the inevitable—as figured by *The Wire, Deadwood,* and *Six Feet Under*—may seem to suggest a more ambitious, because more contrary, program than the surprise in serial terms, *The Sopranos* demonstrates how disruptive a radical commitment to an agenda of surprise can be to our expectations of how narrative should and does work.

As a coda, and as a parallel to the very different practices of surprise embodied by *Breaking Bad* and *The Sopranos,* I will return to the two series with which I began this televisual consideration—*Deadwood* and *The Wire*—to provide a sketch of the potential strangeness and possible usefulness of the dynamic of inevitable/surprise. These two shows would seem to have a great deal in common: chiefly, they are both representations of a community and of how societies function. In *Deadwood*, that society is incipient; in *The Wire*, it is calcified. But that shared narrative mission masks the fact that in many ways these shows are drastically different. Broadly speaking, we could characterize *The Wire*'s inevitability as embedded in a tradition of naturalism (a connection I am far from the first to make).[3] Naturalism typically begins with the presumption of a force field, a fixed system of laws around which characters and events operate. That force field may go by the name of "Baltimore," or the drug war, or the de facto segregation of major American cities, or the decline

---

3. See, for example, Kecia Driver Thompson's efforts to align *The Wire* with the likes of Theodore Dreiser and Frank Norris. Thompson (quoting Donna Campbell) points out that "characters in naturalism" "engage in accidental gestures that prove to be their undoing or in endless loops of pointless activity" (2012: 107). Such a description surely resonates across the five seasons of the series.

of the shipping industry. Naturalism makes the gravitational pull of structures the central element for all the moving parts of the narrative. By contrast, *Deadwood*'s inevitability stages the intersection of a high Romantic approach to character with an analytical attention to the obligations of the social contract. The fantasy of the Western is the fantasy of re-invention, of the attempt to make the self (rather than the structure) the primary locus of identity. But the ineluctable—a word that David Milch has used to describe the dissolution of the series itself—impinges on that vision of the individual as free agent, most explicitly in the necessities of belonging and in the integrative work of communicative technologies (like the telegraph, figured in the show as an allegory of television).

Here are four other significant divergences between these series among the many we might identify. One, the use of the title sequence, where *The Wire* allows us to watch a version of an entire season before it is aired, while *Deadwood* more modestly makes the initial physical surroundings, stripped of characterological specificity, its port of entry. Two, the use of language or dialogue, which in *The Wire* connects characters through iterations of vocabulary (particularly the terminology of "the game"), while *Deadwood* connects them through recondite patterns of syntax. Three, the extremely different attention to serial storytelling, or publishing by installment, especially in the context of individual seasons, with *The Wire* (and its showrunner) valorizing the rhetoric of payoff and of an arrival as a clarification and culmination of all that has come before it, and *Deadwood* (and its showrunner) making each individual day and each individual episode an equally vital and viable destination. And four, the radically separate ways in which they narrate the individual's relationship to the system. The unsentimental world of *The Wire* is one in which people are replaceable—underscored through the closing montage of the finale, through such substitutions as Sydnor for McNulty—and where organizations operate in parallel modes of dysfunction. In *Deadwood*, no one is replaceable; it is the inability to find a new Wild Bill Hickok, after the fourth episode, that organizes this place and this story. *Deadwood* concludes with the dead body of one character standing in for the live body of another; the tragedy of this event is not that fundamental forces made it inevitable but that individuals decided to make an awful bargain, because of those fundamental forces.

The inevitable, like the surprise, is a very big tent. At times, artists may want to bring those two tents together—as suggested by the second epigraph to this essay. Showrunner Noah Hawley tried to combine them at the end of the first season of the FX series *Fargo*, bridging the particular, personal story of police officer Molly Solverson with the scattered elements of several networks of crime. A series that often followed *Breaking Bad* in its sudden shifts of scene and juxtapositions of tone also provided a focused identity for its central figure of an officer of the law, who, like Seth Bullock in *Deadwood*, had borders of behavior that could not be escaped. The challenge of conclusion lay in bringing together, in Hawley's words, "the unpredictable and the inevitable" (Sepinwall 2014), that is, the surprise and the inevitable. Each of these terms brings the other into conversation; reliance on one often entails, but does not have to entail, rejection of the other. By considering further how what we cannot expect and what we cannot ignore intersect, we can continue to explore the territories both old and new carved out by the most ambitious serials of our moment.

BIBLIOGRAPHY

Breaking Bad (2013). "The Final Season." Sony Pictures Entertainment.
Carroll, Noël (1996). "The Paradox of Suspense." *Suspense: Conceptualizations, Theoretical Analyses, and Empirical Explorations*. Ed. Peter Vorderer, Hans J. Wulff, and Mike Friedrichsen. Mahwah, NJ: Lawrence Erlbaum Asssociates. 71–91.
Levine, Caroline (2003). *The Serious Pleasures of Suspense: Victorian Realism and Narrative Doubt*. Charlottesville: University of Virginia Press.
McFarland, Kevin (2013). "The Writer's Strike of 2007–08 Changed *Breaking Bad* for the Better." *The A. V. Club* (August 6). July 22, 2014. http://www.avclub.com/article/the-writers-strike-of-2007-08-changed-ibreaking-ba-101217.
Mittell, Jason (2006). "Narrative Complexity in Contemporary American Television." *The Velvet Light Trap* 58: 29–40.
O'Sullivan, Sean (2009). "Reconnoitering the Rim: Thoughts on *Deadwood* and Third Seasons." *Third Person: Authoring and Exploring Vast Narratives*. Ed. Pat Harrigan and Noah Wardrip-Fruin. Cambridge: MIT. 323–32.
——— (2013). "Story Land: *Breaking Bad* 5:15." *Kritik* (September 23). July 22, 2014. http://unitcrit.blogspot.com/2013/09/breaking-bad-season-515-story-land.html.
——— (2014). "Serials and Satisfaction." *Romanticism and Victorianism on the Net* 63. July 22, 2014. http://www.erudit.org/revue/ravon/2013/v/n63/1025614ar.html?lang=en.
Ryan, Marie-Laure (2009). "Cheap Plot Tricks, Plot Holes, and Narrative Design." *Narrative* 17.1: 56–75.
Seitz, Matt Zoller (2014). "*Mad Men* Mid-Season Recap: The Moon." *Vulture* (May 26). July 22, 2014. http://www.vulture.com/2014/05/mad-men-recap-season-7-finale-moon-landing-bert-cooper-dies.html.
Sepinwall, Alan (2008). "*The Wire* Ends." NJ.com (March 10). July 22, 2014. http://blog.nj.com/alltv/2008/03/sepinwall_on_tv_the_wire_ends.html.
——— (2009). "*Mad Men*: Creator Matthew Weiner's Thoughts on the Season Premiere." NJ.com (August 16). July 22, 2014. http://www.nj.com/entertainment/tv/index.ssf/2009/08/mad_men_creator_matthew_weiner.html.
——— (2014). "*Fargo* Creator Noah Hawley Talks Season 1, and the Possibility of Season 2." Hitfix.com (June 18). July 22, 2014. http://www.hitfix.com/whats-alan-watching/fargo-creator-noah-hawley-talks-season-1-and-the-possibility-of-season-2/.

Thompson, Kecia Driver (2012). "'Deserve Got Nothing to Do with It': Black Urban Experience and the Naturalist Tradition in *The Wire.*" *Studies in American Naturalism* 7.1: 80–120.
Truffaut, François (1985). *Hitchcock* [1984]. New York: Touchstone.
The Wire (2002). Episode 1:1. "The Target." DVD commentary. HBO.

PART IV

Transmedia and Digitality

CHAPTER 12

"All Over the Map"
Building (and Rebuilding) Oz

HENRY JENKINS

> The story is in the world; not the other way around. That is to say, a world is big and hopelessly uncontrollable. It spills messily outside the edges of any one story. [. . .] The challenge of genres like science fiction and fantasy is to not only spin a good tale, but to invent for that tale an imagined backdrop that seems to stretch clear into the horizon.
>
> —TRAVIS BEACHAM (2013)

DISNEY OFFERED *Oz the Great and Powerful* (2013) to viewers as a spectacular world to map and explore far more than as a story to be experienced.[1] One teaser ad showed the yellow brick road, heading past rambling green hills. Another showed a tornado carrying the hot air balloon to Emerald City. A final ad (figure 12.1) revealed an expansive vista showing an enchanted landscape, a haunted forest, two different castles implying rival kingdoms, a town made of china cups, and other film locations. The advertisements echoed the highly iconic campaign for Tim Burton's *Alice in Wonderland* (2010), a commercial hit Disney was eager to associate with its upcoming release. Both had been based on classic children's books, involving journeys into magical realms and promising to show the traditional characters as we had never seen them before.

Critics objected to Tim Burton's radical rewriting of *Alice in Wonderland*, overlooking more than a hundred of years of "alternative Alices" (Sigler 1997), starting within months of the book's first publication. When *Oz the Great and*

---

1. Alternative versions of this essay have appeared in *The Scientific Journal of Sapientia University* 9 (2014): 7–30; and Wolf 2017 (forthcoming).

FIGURE 12.1. Advertisement for *Oz the Great and Powerful* (Disney, 2013) displays key elements from its fictional world.

Powerful was first announced, some protective fans decried what were perceived as plans to develop a "prequel" to the beloved MGM musical. For many, *The Wizard of Oz* is a story, more or less what is depicted in the Judy Garland version, a distilled version of L. Frank Baum's first Oz novel. Dorothy is swept away from Kansas by a cyclone, lands among the Munchkins, and kills the Wicked Witch of the East; she travels down the Yellow Brick Road, meets her three companions (Scarecrow, Tin Man, Cowardly Lion), and gets dispatched by the Wizard (really, a humbug) to kill the Wicked Witch of the West and returns home—there's no place like it! Let us call this the canonical story.

One of my students described *Great and Powerful* as "all over the map," unconsciously evoking Frank Kelleter's (2012) reference to the Oz Universe's "narrative sprawl." Precisely! By showing so much of Oz, the film inspires the collective activity of a global community of Oz fans who, as Kelleter notes, have worked continuously across the twentieth century to construct "entire networked orders of knowledge about Oz" (2012: 34), stimulating pleasurable debates about what elements are canonical and which do not "belong." Let us call that network of information *Ozness*. Disney's film thus falls into the gap between narrow conceptions of the canonical story and the *Ozness* claimed by its more hard-core fans.

Over the past few decades, Hollywood and the games industry have developed more sophisticated tools for modeling and rendering synthetic worlds.

Art directors and production designers are playing a more central role in the development of screen stories. DVD extras, coffee-table books, and web-based encyclopedias and concordances document the particulars of these imagined worlds. Many contemporary filmmakers—Tim Burton and Zack Snyder come to mind—are more compelling world builders than storytellers. We need a better critical vocabulary for discussing their work, and I will be building up some basic concepts that might inform such an aesthetic across this essay. Yet, at the same time, many viewers and critics remain rooted in a classical aesthetic, which tends to view these detailed renderings as an excess ("eye candy") distracting from the hero's journey, and we need to recognize why this shift toward world-building over storytelling may be disruptive for those who come to contemporary media with such expectations.

In *Film Art*, David Bordwell and Kristin Thompson use the MGM Oz film to explain the concept of "function": "Even an element as apparently minor as the dog Toto serves many functions. The dispute over Toto causes Dorothy to run away from home and to get back too late to take shelter from the cyclone; and later Toto's chasing a cat makes Dorothy jump out of the ascending balloon and miss her chance to get back to Kansas. Even Toto's gray color, set off against the brightness of Oz, creates a link to the black and white of the Kansas sequences at the film's beginning" (1990: 46). In Bordwell and Thompson's hands, *The Wizard of Oz* becomes *the* textbook example of how tightly integrated each element is into the storytelling process. Every element has one or more functions to play, or it does not exist at all.

Yet competing logics also shape the film's design and the spectator's experience. Hollywood's growing focus on immersive screen experiences creates a context where world-building exists alongside, sometimes serving and sometimes privileged over, storytelling as a source of meaning and pleasure. In discussing contemporary entertainment franchises, Derek Johnson (2013) suggests that these world-building practices might be understood as a form of "overdesign." Game designers incorporate affordances that any given player may never encounter and that may support emergent practices. Similarly, contemporary films and television series incorporate more details than any given viewer may notice, more than any given narrative will use, since a successful film may spawn sequels (or may extend into other media) and since this practice enables the continuation of a long-form television series. Just as Bordwell and Thompson have shown how each detail might serve multiple story functions, each detail also contributes in multiple ways (some unanticipated at the time of their creation) to the storyworld.

For both readers and writers, the experience of Oz is shaped by prior expectations that determine what kinds of stories they might tell and what kinds of characters they might encounter. The world of Oz emerged gradually, over several decades, as Baum himself kept returning to and adding onto its territory, and as subsequent authors took over and further extended Oz. Ultimately, the texts of Oz accumulated a vast set of characters and locations described in the printed books, visualized through their illustrations, and performed on screen, on stage, or in other media. Once we have a deeper understanding of how Oz functions as a world, we will consider two different strategies by which later authors attach themselves to that world—one focused on notions of nostalgic return (where the plots center on efforts to restore Oz to its former glory) and the other focused on the process by which Oz became the place we know in the canonical story. Both approaches work only if subsequent authors link their efforts to expand the Oz universe back to elements from the canonical story, while respecting the network of associations over which the most hard-core fans steward.

WORLD-MAKING AND WORLD-SHARING

> Imaginary worlds may depend relatively little on narrative, and even when they do, they often rely on other kinds of structures for their form and organization. [...] A compelling story and a compelling world are very different things, and one need not require the other.
> —MARK J. P. WOLF (2013: 3)

In a discussion of what film theorists might draw from the work of Nelson Goodman (1978), Dudley Andrew explains, "Worlds are comprehensive systems which comprise all elements that fit together within the same horizon. [...] These elements consist of objects, feelings, associations, and ideas in a grand mix so rich that only the term 'world' seems large enough to encompass it" (1984: 38). Andrew stresses the underlying logic determining which elements belong in a particular world: "The plot may surprise us with its happenings, but every happening must seem possible in that world because all the actions, characters, thoughts and feelings come from the same overall source" (39). While much contemporary writing about world-building focuses on fantasy or science fiction, Andrew's prime example, Charles Dickens's London, suggests that the same concept might apply to realist or historical fictions. London is a real place with an actual geography and history, but Dickens's London is an imagined space, a particular set of choices about what to include, a set of interpretive norms about what to pay attention to as we read a story. Dickens's London is not the same as Arthur Conan Doyle's London, with those differences only partially explained in terms of the different genres within which their stories operate. Andrew, following Goodman, sees worlds as intertextual structures, which persist across works: "The world of Dickens is obviously larger than the particular rendition of it which we call *Oliver Twist*. [. . .] In fact, it is larger than the sum of novels Dickens wrote, existing as a set of paradigms, a global source from which he could draw" (39)—and, as we will see, from which subsequent authors (Sam Raimi in the case of Oz) may also draw.

From a similar starting point in aesthetic philosophy and narrative theory, Marie-Laure Ryan stresses what the expansiveness of imaginary worlds means for the reader, who must assemble bits of description (in a prose work) or visual details (in an audiovisual text) to form a mental construct of the storyworld. She suggests that the viewer is "guided" by "textual declarations" but builds "this always-incomplete image into a more vivid representation through the import of information provided by internalized cognitive models, inferential mechanisms, real-life experience, and cultural knowledge, including knowledge derived from other texts" (2001: 91). This process of speculation, inference, and elaboration may continue beyond the borders of the original text. Umberto Eco stresses how fans transform a fragmentary and contradictory text, such as *Casablanca*, into a cult object: "The work must be loved, obviously, but this is not enough. It must provide a completely furnished world, so that its fans can quote characters and episodes as if they were aspects of the fan's private sectarian world, a world about which one can make up quizzes and play trivia games so that the adepts of the cult recognize through each other a shared expertise" (1990: 198). Such details, for example, the name of Rick's doorman, may evoke the original story but may also inspire personal and collective speculations about what other kinds of events might occur in this cherished space. And, as Mimi Ito (2011) says of more recent examples from Japanese "media mix" culture, these details may facilitate social exchanges, as fans talk together and pool knowledge.

Also writing about production and consumption practices in Japan, Otsuka Eiji describes how a series of collectible cards, each depicting individual characters and their backstory, each sold with chocolate candies, can evolve into a larger mythological system as small bits of information accrue over time. Otsuka, then, draws a parallel between this form of serialized consumption and the ways that details assemble within a television serial: "There are countless detailed 'settings' prepared yet not directly represented within this episode, including, in the case of *Gundam*, the era in which the main characters live, the place, the relations between countries, their history, their manners of living, the personal histories of the respective characters, the nature of their interpersonal relations, and even, in the case of the robots, the concordance between the functions matching their design and the science of the era. [. . .] Each one of these individual settings will as a totality form a greater order, a united whole" (2010: 107). Just as the child collects cards or stickers as tokens of a fictional world, the fan watching a television series forms mental links between a range of details that constitute a fictional world.

If Andrew turns to Goodman, Mark J. P. Wolf (2013) starts with J. R. R. Tolkien and his conception of *sub-creation*. In this account, worlds are invented by authors, often as a way of stepping outside and looking at the primary world of our lived experience from an alternative perspective. For Tolkien, this kind of imaginative world-building is seen as sub-creation, because it builds upon what he sees as the primary act of creation—the divine creation of the physical universe. Wolf proposes that we might evaluate the strengths of these imagined worlds based on three core criteria—inventiveness, completeness, and consistency: "Without enough invention, you will have something set in the Primary World [. . .], not a world unique, different and set apart from our own. Without an attempt at completeness, you have the beginnings of expansion beyond the narrative, but not enough to suggest an independent world; too many unanswered (and unanswerable) questions will remain which together destroy the illusion of one. And without consistency, all the disparate and conflicting pieces, ideas, and designs will contradict each other, and never successfully come together to collectively create the illusion of another world" (2013: 34). What may strike more casual viewers as insignificant details matter because they are part of a larger system: a well-constructed world operates according to multiple logics (say, historical, anthropological, ecological, political, economic, etc.) which often intersect each other in complex ways and which fans learn to read from the depicted details as openings for new speculation.

If Andrew's account focuses on the works of a single author, more recent accounts discuss worlds as structures that scaffold collaboration. Writing about the expansive worlds created for *Star Trek* and *Battlestar Galactica*, Derek Johnson explains, "What emerges from the professionalized social networks sharing franchise worlds [. . .] is meaningful, ongoing creative elaboration of shared production resources. [. . .] By establishing a systematic set of principles to govern the look, sound and behavior of narrative characters, events, and setting—and introducing increasing complexity over time—these science fiction series constructed their worlds as creative contexts that could support the emergent production and elaboration of further content" (2013: 109). Here, the world acts both as a set of enabling conditions for various franchise extensions and as a set of constraints that determine what any given author cannot change without higher-up approval. Just as Johnson describes world-sharing in the professional sphere, Otsuka describes how understanding the underlying principles of worlds paves the way for grassroots forms of production, such as the Japanese Otaku community's wide-scale generation of amateur manga: "if, at the end of the accumulated consumption of small narratives, consumers get their hands on the grand narrative (i.e. the totality of the program), they will then be able to freely produce their own small narratives with their own hands" (2010: 109). For Otaku, new contributions to this textual system are best understood not in terms of their originality but in terms of what each variant contributes to our understanding of the whole.

To paint in somewhat broad strokes, traditional storytelling often works through exposition, sharing backstory, while world-building more frequently works through description, accumulating meaningful details, though of course, in both cases, the situation is more complicated in practice. These details are not plot devices; rather, the plot often exists as a means through which to explore different aspects of a given world. These constructs work at multiple levels: as a set of meaningful elements, as spatial and social systems that help us to understand those elements in relation to each other, and as a larger logic that can be used by authors (professional and amateur) to expand the original storyworld in new directions. These worlds get deployed by authors (singular or multiple) in the process of generating stories and by readers in the process of "going beyond the information given." Having provided this overview of contemporary critical perspectives on world-building in popular fiction, I now want to sharpen my focus upon the particulars of Oz and the way that its world has been built up and deployed over time. We will return in the conclusion to the issue of how one might assess a work that relies on world-building more than storytelling.

THE PARTICULARITY OF OZ

> All of this is Oz as a piece of modern American popular culture: a wide and constantly expanding realm of interlocking, transmedially active, mass-addressed commercial stories. With their narrative sprawl and their openness to ever new uses, these serial products complicate traditional narratological notions of beginning, middle, and end, source and adaptation, original and copy.
>
> —FRANK KELLETER (2012: 26)

The Wizard of Oz was the first of fourteen books L. Frank Baum wrote about Oz between 1900 and 1919. Baum did not initially imagine Oz as a franchise or even as a book series, since he invented many such lands for children, yet he felt trapped by its growing popularity alongside less than spectacular sales for his other works. He sought to escape Oz many times, but in the prefaces to the subsequent books, he depicted himself as being dragged back by eager young readers who wanted to know more about Oz. Baum wrote in his introduction to *Dorothy and the Wizard in Oz* (1908):

> It's no use; no use at all. The children won't let me stop telling stories of the Land of Oz. I know lots of other stories, and I hope to tell them, some time or another; but just now my loving tyrants won't allow me. [. . .] This is Our book—mine and the children's. For they have flooded me with thousands of suggestions in regard to it, and I have honestly tried to incorporate as many of these suggestions as could be fitted into one story. [. . .] There were many requests from my little correspondents for "more about the wizard." It seems the jolly old fellow made hosts of friends in the first Oz book, in spite of the fact that he frankly acknowledged himself "a humbug." The children had heard how he mounted into the sky in a balloon and they were all waiting for him to come down again. So what could I do but tell "what happened to the Wizard afterward"? You will find him in these pages, just the same humbug Wizard as before. (1990: 9)

Each book begins in a similar way, describing his latest story as filling in particular narrative gaps ("what happened to the Wizard afterward?") or mapping a particular corner of the fictional world.

Michael O. Riley has offered the richest account of how Baum's conception of Oz evolved: "Oz did not grow organically from a central idea. Rather, it developed in successive versions, each enlarging while superseding the one before and each reflecting Baum's current idea of what constituted the most magnificent and alluring fairyland in the world" (1997: 133). We can get some sense of this elaboration process by looking at the maps of Oz: a relatively simple rendering in early titles becomes ever more detailed as the series continues. As Riley notes, Baum would increasingly locate his other storyworlds on the borderlands around Oz, seeking to create a larger framework for his total creative output: "In the *Road to Oz*, Baum had drawn all his imaginary countries together into the same Other-world, but he had given no information about their geographical relationships. Now [in *Tik-Tok of Oz*] he actually shows the reader how they are connected. The fact that their positions on the map do not always agree with the textual descriptions is overridden by the centrality of Oz and the interconnectedness of Baum's entire Other-World" (186–87). Writing about the centrality of world-building to

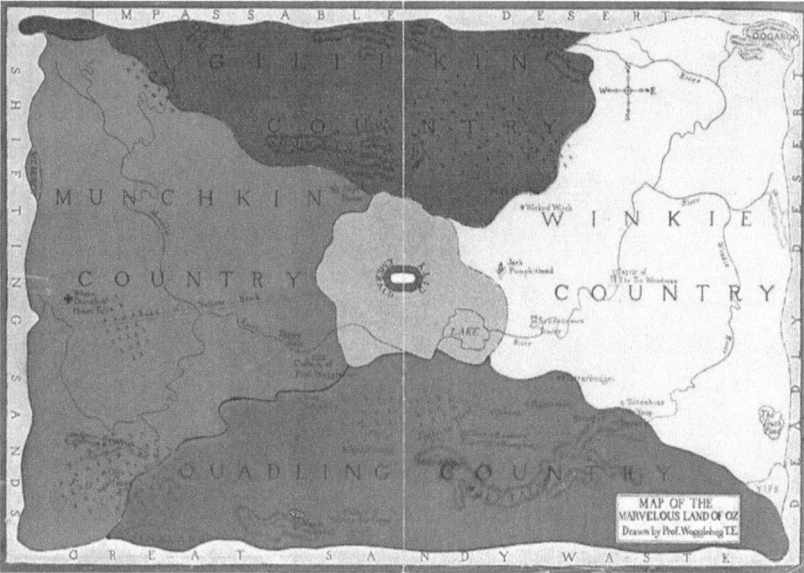

FIGURE 12.2. Map from *Tik-Tok of Oz* (1914) details spaces mentioned in earlier stories.

early twentieth-century popular fiction, Michael Saler notes the way authors tapped "the indexical idioms of scientific objectivity" in order to enable readers to play around with fantasy realms: "Maps in particular were important for establishing the imaginary world as a virtual space consistent in all its details" (2012: 67). Saler describes the ways that H. Rider Haggard fabricated weathered maps, pottery shards, and other artifacts of imagined races, all to encourage the reader's belief in *She* and *King Solomon's Mines*. Baum described himself often as the "Royal Historian of Oz," suggesting his role in "documenting" and "recounting" a world rather than inventing one (figures 12.2 and 12.3).

In today's terminology, we might describe these "New Romances" as multimodal: they mobilized the affordances of multiple forms of representation. Our understanding of Oz was partially a consequence of Baum's own narrative prose and partially a reflection of the vivid illustrations contributed by William Wallace Denslow (for the first book) and John R. Neill for the subsequent titles. Those who know only the MGM film may think of the shift from sepia in the Kansas scenes to full Technicolor in the Oz sequences as Hollywood's invention, but the books were already color-coded, with Kansas described in monochromatic terms. Here is a scene from the first chapter of *The Wonderful Wizard of Oz* (1900):

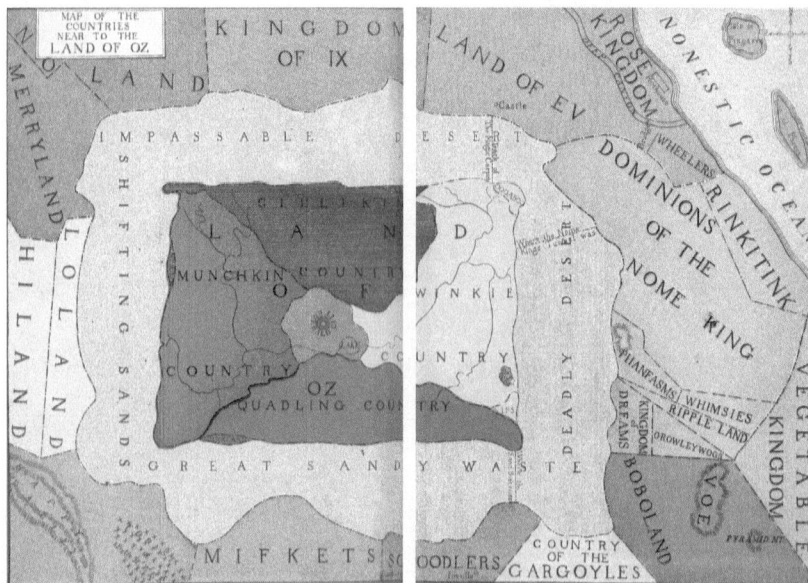

FIGURE 12.3. A more elaborate map of Oz also from *Tik-Tok of Oz* (1914) includes lands from other L. Frank Baum stories.

When Dorothy stood in the doorway and looked around, she could see nothing but the great gray prairie on every side. [...] The sun had baked the plowed land into a gray mass, with little cracks running through it. Even the grass was not green, for the sun had burned the tops of the long blades until they were the same gray color to be seen everywhere. Once the house had been painted, but the sun blistered the paint, and the rains washed it away, and now the house was as dull and gray as everything else. [...] The sun and the wind [...] had taken the sparkle from [Aunt Em's] eyes and left them sober gray; they had taken the red from her cheeks and lips, and they were gray also. (Baum 1987: 12)

Denslow's illustrations for this opening chapter were similarly monochromatic, a grayish tan color. Each of the imagined lands had its own associated color—Munchkin Country (blue), Gillikin Country (purple), Winkie Country (yellow), Quadling Country (red), and the Emerald City (green). But, beyond this, Denslow's illustrations helped to shape how subsequent generations imagined Oz; the illustrations were often more vivid than Baum's sometimes sparse descriptions.

Baum's Oz might also be seen as an important predecessor of transmedia storytelling. As Mark Evan Swartz (2000) documents, Baum personally wrote and oversaw a lavish Broadway musical based on the canonical story in 1902, adding many key details to the Oz world, including, for example, Dorothy's last name. The musical's cast also modeled performance practices—such as the Scarecrow's rubber-legged dance moves—which informed the MGM movie. This first musical was followed by several more stage productions, with some subsequent books being more or less novelizations of plots Baum developed for other media. Baum ran his own motion picture production company to further expand upon his storyworld, introducing new peoples and lands that exploited the affordances of the trick film genre. At one point, there were competing Oz comic strips: one written by Baum, the other developed by Denslow, who was seeking to assert some legal rights over his contributions as an illustrator. Matthew Freeman (2014) demonstrates how Baum used his comic strip pages as a bridge, connecting events depicted in the second Oz book, *The Marvelous Land of Oz*, back to the characters and situations depicted in the original novel and foreshadowing Dorothy's return in subsequent books. Baum further extended his storyworld through the publication of *The Ozmapolitan*, a "faux newspaper" that featured an interview with the Scarecrow about his desire to be reunited with Dorothy, an event actually depicted in Baum's comic strip (Freeman 2014). Finally, Baum went on a lecture tour where he acted as an authorial interface between these various media. In this performance, *The Fairylogue and Radio Play*, Baum played a tour guide to his realm, his lecture illustrated with scenes staged by live actors, 114 glass magic lantern slides, and 23 motion picture clips, each hand-colored, and produced by Chicago's Selig Polyscope studios.

Following his death in 1919, Baum's role as the architect, author, promoter, historian, and geographer of this wonderful land was passed along to a series of authorized successors. Denslow's replacement, John R. Neill, illustrated thirty-six Oz books and wrote three of his own between 1904 and 1942. Ruth Plumly Thompson added another nineteen books, ending in 1939, and the official series only concluded in 1963. For a good part of the twentieth century, an Oz book was released each year during the Christmas season, a kind of beloved holiday ritual for many American families. Across that time, the Oz narrative was updated to reflect the tastes and concerns of each era, yet these various collaborators drew on a shared blueprint of the world (not always without contradictions) to create a series (not always without continuity errors) that could, in theory, though less and less in practice, be read from beginning to end. And from there, we might add a range of other unauthorized contributors.

As more of the Oz books revert into the public domain, there are at least four Oz-themed television series currently in development for U.S. television. And beyond the realm of commercial production, there is a vast array of fan-generated material. *The Baum Bugle*, for example, has been published since 1957 as a vehicle through which fans and scholars alike might explore Oz.

On the one hand, Oz presents enormous difficulty in terms of cognitive mapping. It can be hard to hold all these details in our minds at once, so subsequent artists working across a range of media have tended to focus on some elements to the exclusion of others. On the other hand, popular memory of Oz has been reduced to a single book, a single film, a single plot, which needs to be respected if any subsequent work is to be accepted by a broader audience. This gradual narrowing of popular memory acts as a conservative force, making it less likely that future writers will draw from the subsequent books or extensions into other media. From the start, screen adaptations have depended on our prior knowledge of Oz, some of which gets evoked explicitly, and some implicitly through the details mobilized in a particular text. We can see this process at play in the *Great and Powerful* ads discussed earlier. Most readers will recognize the Yellow Brick Road, the hot air balloon, and the cyclone as referring to the core story, some may recognize the multiple variations of the Flying Monkeys as redesigns and expansions of a canonical race, while a relatively few may recognize that the Dainty China Country (found in Quadling Country) was a subplot in the original novel.

I will now consider two different narrative strategies—one focused on restoring Oz to its lapsed glory, the other focused on providing backstory—that have been deployed in recent Oz films; both approaches build upon—and provide space for the further expansion of—the Oz world as it has been handed down to us from its earlier incarnations across diverse media.

RESTORING OZ

> Literature has time and again demonstrated its ability to promote a haunting sense of the presence of a spatial setting and a clear vision of its topography. [...] These mental geographies become home to the reader, and they may for some of us steal the show from the narrative action.
>
> —MARIE-LAURE RYAN (2001: 121)

In her analysis of world-building, Ryan explores how a deeper sense of spatial immersion may contribute to "emotional immersion." Ryan talks about the "madeleine effect" (2001: 121), referring to a moment in Marcel Proust's *In Remembrance of Things Past,* when the taste of a cookie dipped into tea brings back intense memories of the village where the narrator grew up. A film that builds on a preexisting world may have a similar emotional impact, a sense of nostalgic loss or homecoming. Our desire to return to an imaginary homeland may satisfy our desires to hear a familiar story retold, to return to a familiar place, and to reengage the memories we associate with it. Given how formative our childhood experiences of Oz have been for many generations of Americans, Oz-extensions tap both memories of pleasurable elements in the storyworld and of real-life rituals around its consumption. My pleasure in Oz is connected with memories of anticipating the annual Thanksgiving broadcasts of the MGM film, a collective experience shared by many of my elementary school classmates and by the ways we playacted the characters in our backyards. The fictional characters are complexly overlaid with memories of childhood friends. For any new text to evoke this nostalgic return, it has to provide at least some of what made Oz feel like home: the world needs to be recognizable; the right details need to be chosen and rendered acceptably.

Let us consider how this sense of nostalgic return and the expansion of the storyworld coexist in Disney's *Return to Oz* (1985). The film merged plots from Baum's subsequent Oz books, especially *The Marvelous Land of Oz* and *Ozma of Oz,* but altered them to allow for a stronger continuity with the canonical story. Dorothy, for example, here displaces Tip, a Gillikin lad, who was *Marvelous Land*'s original protagonist. (In the book series, Dorothy did not return from Kansas until *Ozma,* the third book.) As the film starts, Dorothy and her family are still experiencing aftershocks from the events of the first book/film. Uncle Henry has started to rebuild the family cottage, swept away by the cyclone, but the house remains half-constructed, as he has lacked the motivation to complete his task. Dorothy is struggling with uncertainty about the status of her Oz memories: no one else believes her story. And in what may be the darkest moment in any Disney movie, Aunt Em leaves her with a sinister psychologist, who wants to use electroshock to erase Oz from her memory.

As Dorothy escapes from the asylum in the middle of a thunderstorm, a flash flood sweeps her and her pet chicken, Billina, back to Oz, but she discovers that Oz has lost much of its magic. Dorothy wanders down piles of scattered bricks, all that remains of the yellow brick road. The Emerald City is bleached of color, its walls are covered with graffiti, the locks on the gates have rusted, and the streets are ruled by gangs of "Wheelers" who harass her. Along the way, she also sees plaster figures we fear may be her former companions' bodily remains. This nightmarish landscape is all the more poignant because we recognize these places from other versions: we have a deep sense of what has been lost. What happens next satisfies our desire to see things set right again.

From this starting point, the film introduces new characters to assist Dorothy through her journey. Her companions—Tik-Tok, Jack Pumpkinhead, and the Gump—all come from Baum's books: the same is true of the story's villains—Mombi the Witch and the Nome King. However, the film must court the audience's acceptance by situating these new figures in relation to elements from the canonical story. And the film ends with a further expansion of the Oz universe—a grand parade celebrating Dorothy's success incorporates diverse characters, some fairly obscure (including Father Christmas whom Baum transplanted to Oz from his other children's books). This sequence provides a sense of Oz's expansiveness, rewarding fan mastery while servicing the needs of more casual viewers whose knowledge need not extend beyond those familiar characters in the foreground.

Another key moment comes when Dorothy is locked into an old attic, where she stumbles onto a dust-covered portrait of the Scarecrow and company, a painful reminder of her loss, and where she and Pumpkinhead cobble together the Gump from old furniture and a taxidermied moose head. In the first instance, the attic functions as a space where we store old artifacts and associated memories. The portrait reminds us of a lack that must be filled by reuniting Dorothy with her missing friends, the ones with whom she shares her adventures in the canonical story. In the second incident, the attic suggests the ways that these materials can be remixed and reconceived in order to generate new life. This is world-sharing in a nutshell, and I would argue that the scene provides readers with a way of reconciling the canonical story with a more expansive notion of *Ozness*.

BECOMING OZ

> [Screenwriter Mitchell Kapner] started talking about how he was reading L. Frank Baum's books to his children at night. And he said, "Did you ever think about doing a story on how the Wizard became the Wizard?" I knew he was onto something with that question. Baum had created such a magnificent world with dozens and dozens of characters and fantastical set pieces.
>
> —JOE ROTH (QTD. IN CURTIS 2013: 32–33)

Paradoxically, a prequel comes both *after* (in the production history) and *before* (in the storyworld), although in the case of *Oz the Great and Powerful,* it also exists *alongside* a range of other Oz texts (in this case, *Wicked,* a text to which this contemporary Oz film is very much indebted). Much of the film's plot is designed to move the pieces on the board toward the place where *The Wizard of Oz* begins. We can appreciate the effort only because we have been to this place before, while the characters are undergoing these experiences for the first time. So, to cite a few examples, this film shows us how the Scarecrow was made and recounts the incident that left the Cowardly Lion afraid of his own shadow. We see how the Wizard's hot air balloon got to Oz. We see the Wicked Witch of the West accept her wickedness and retreat from Oz toward the wilds of the Winkie Country, and in the process we see the conflict between Glinda the Good and the other witches intensify. More importantly, we witness the Wizard's transition from a humbug sideshow magician—a man without roots or convictions—into the ruler of the Emerald City. In fact, the film shows us how he became the "man behind the curtain," including several sequences where the curtain is pulled aside to show him manipulating the controls of his various contraptions. Critics have described James Franco's performance as Oscar, the Wizard, as flat and uninspired, overlooking the fact that Oscar is not intended to be the protagonist of his own narrative, that he is consistently shown to lack the qualities of a hero, and that the film shows us how he comes to be able to pass himself off as bigger than he is. If we are going to get him to the place he must occupy in the canonical story, we must show how he gained power while lacking many of the qualities we associate with great leaders. And in that sense, the most significant actions in the film center on the processes of conceiving, planning, and staging illusions, often involving the behind-the-scene labor of a group of Tinkerers (stand-ins for the Disney Imagineers). Oscar is not much of a man, not much of a wizard, but a very gifted illusionist.

Mark J. P. Wolf tells us, "Backstories are often told in the compressed form associated with low narrative resolution, and the histories of different locations in a world are often told to the story's main characters as they travel from one place to the next" (2013: 202). In the case of *Great and Powerful,* these priorities are reversed—the entire film can be understood as primarily preoccupied with the pleasures of backstory and with the mapping of meaningful locations, and it was this shift in emphasis that confused viewers less familiar with the source material; they often experienced only a series of digressions and diversions. Some have characterized this quest for backstory as the kind of tragic flaw of our transmedia culture, with every detail needing to be traced back to its origins, yet it is hard to deny the fascination many fans have in backstory, whether it is used to explain character motivations or to add greater coherence and completeness to the storyworld. In many ways, what happened before the story is as compelling a question as what happens next.

Consider one compelling use of backstory. While in Kansas, Oscar is visited by a woman in a blue gingham dress (Dorothy's iconic outfit in both the books and the MGM film), who may be the one great love of his life—Dorothy's (future) mother. We never meet Dorothy's mother in any of Baum's books. Here, she is given both a face and a name: Anna. Oscar and Anna have been childhood playmates and sweethearts, perhaps lovers; he sees her "every few months" as the show rolls into town. Anna holds out hope that they might get married, but Oscar lacks the commitment to lay down roots, refusing to join the ranks of "men like my father who spent his whole life tilling the dirt only to die face down in it." This poignant scene offers fertile ground for speculation: How might it change our understanding of the events of the canonical story if we read the Wizard as Dorothy's biological father? Michelle Williams plays both Anna (in the Kansas scenes) and Glinda (in the Oz sequences), paving the way for a romantic entanglement between Glinda and Oscar, which might explain why Glinda, knowing what she does, nevertheless sends Dorothy to meet the Wizard in the canonical story.

For the most part, the dispersed bits of backstory revealed here are not terribly surprising: most often, these stories locate the Wizard as the catalyst, whose entry into Oz sets so many other things into motion. Just as Dorothy must restore Oz in *Return*, Oscar must arrive in order to prepare Oz for the events of the canonical story. Despite this lack of narrative drive, what makes the film immersive is that longtime Oz fans are able to explore this vast and wonderful world, seeing parts of it for the first time, through Oscar's eyes. And we can also see things and know things the character himself does not know, a process best illustrated by one throw-away detail. As Oscar and his companions move on down the Yellow Brick Road, we can see rainbow-colored horses (the "horses of a different color" from the MGM film) in a neighboring pasture: the camera does not emphasize the horses, and the characters do nothing to call attention to them, allowing them to function much like an "Easter egg" in a video game—a reward for observant and knowing fans.

Oz the Great and Powerful adopts a journey structure, using the characters' movement through space to motivate its fascination with the world. The film's restlessness is already hinted at by the movie's opening—a long tracking shot through the heart of the carnival. From there, we see Oscar escape from the angry husband of one of his casual lovers, ascend in the hot air balloon, and get carried away via cyclone to the Land of Oz. From his hot air balloon, we see sweeping vistas of Oz's otherworldly landscape, as Oscar floats over the Impassable Desert and crash lands in the midst of a lush garden. Once he has landed, his travels take him down the Yellow Brick Road, through the Emerald City, and through many other key spaces, including some familiar from the MGM film (the haunted forest, the Munchkin lands) and some not (the Dainty China Country). Each space plays some narrative role but also rewards our desire to see, with our own eyes, in as much detail as possible, the landscapes Baum imagined.

Having built such a beautifully rendered world, mostly through digital effects, why waste it on a single narrative experience when we can imagine the prospects of a digital version of Oz, where fans can explore at their own pace? While such a digital game world does not yet exist, we can satisfy some of these same urges by looking closely at the coffee table book *The Art of Oz the Great and Powerful* (Curtis 2013), which shows many spaces designed for the film, including some we never see on screen. Such books do not simply provide visual spectacle: the more we scrutinize these renderings, the more insights we may gain about the fictional world. Such books also share the thinking (and contributions) of diverse production contributors, including screenwriters, producers, directors, actors, production designers, costumers, makeup artists, special effects designers, and many others. Reading closely, we can see how sharing core design principles allowed them to make independent decisions that contribute to the creation of an immersive storyworld.

Here, for example, the production designers discuss how they grounded their conceptions of different Oz locations in relation to alternative art movements (which they felt shed light on the characters' personalities). Robert Stromberg, the film's production designer, explains, "I decided early on that I wanted Emerald City to be very masculine with strong, hard lines. As a result, Art Deco became the driving inspiration. On the other hand, in Glinda's world, I wanted a much more feminine quality, more curves. So I chose Art Nouveau to inform the classic Disney castle motif we chose for her kingdom" (Curtis 2013: 96). These two styles are already heavily coded within Oz's iconography: the MGM film's Emerald City relied on the then-contemporary Art Deco style to suggest its modernity, while *Return to Oz* harkened back to the Art Nouveau style popular at the time Baum wrote the original novel. These design choices are grounded in the long history of attempts to illustrate, stage, and film Oz, themselves part of the intertextual process of world-sharing we have been discussing across this chapter.

Through this world-sharing process, each new Oz text announces its arrival, making a bid as either remaining true to the spirit and detail of the original or as representing a different interpretation of the familiar realm. *Oz the Great and Powerful* must not simply produce a world; it must also reproduce it, and part of what allows us to accept this new version is the presence of many different details linking it back to prior Oz texts. Of course, intellectual property constraints make this a particularly complex dance,

FIGURE 12.4. The Yellow Brick Road in *The Wizard of Oz* (MGM, 1939).

FIGURE 12.5. The Yellow Brick Road in *Oz the Great and Powerful* (Disney, 2013).

since Disney is laying claim to what is found in the Baum books, but the rights to the visual elements we most associate with Oz (those in the MGM film) belong to another studio. Disney has to evoke the earlier film without duplicating it so closely that it constitutes plagiarism. Consider, for example, the film's end title, which is set against a blue sky and a rainbow (a homage, clearly, to "Somewhere over the Rainbow"). Or consider another sequence

FIGURE 12.6. Ozma's headdress in *His Majesty, the Scarecrow of Oz* (Oz Film Manufacturing Co., 1914).

FIGURE 12.7. Ozma's headdress in *Return to Oz* (Disney, 1985).

where Oscar and his companion enter Munchkinland inside giant bubbles, a scene meant to evoke Billie Burke's memorable entrance as Glinda. The film's depiction of Winkie Country and Munchkin Country still draws on the color coding introduced in the Baum books and builds on iconography created by Denslow and Neill, yet it also depends on architectural details that evoke the MGM musical, as might be suggested by the two images in figures 12.4 and 12.5 showing the starting point for the Yellow Brick Road.

We can note similar borrowings in *Return to Oz*, for example, the use of the Ruby Slippers—another MGM invention (Baum's Dorothy wore silver shoes instead)—or the design of Ozma's headdress (figures 12.6 and 12.7), which comes directly from the original illustrations in Baum's books and from the costume designs for his stage productions and films.

All of this is to say that world-building involves a process of intertextual citation and the performance of authorship. Yet our current legal culture makes it hard to acknowledge such direct lines of influence, even when they are essential for maintaining audience credibility and emotional immersion. Given this legal conundrum, the "making of" materials mask any connection to the MGM movie, which is not directly mentioned at all in the *Art* book and which is acknowledged only briefly in the DVD's "Making of" video. There, *Great and Powerful* is depicted as the fulfillment of a lifelong dream of Walt Disney to produce his own Oz movie. We are told that Disney had planned to create an animated Oz as a follow-up to *Snow White and the Seven Dwarves*' box office success but was preempted by MGM's decision to produce its own version. The DVD extras share production designs and test footage for a live-action musical version Disney announced in the 1950s which would have used the young cast members from *The Mickey Mouse Club*. The video authenticates the new film as the fulfillment of a key aspiration of the corporation's

FIGURE 12.8. *Oz the Great and Powerful* (2013) evokes Disney's *Snow White and the Seven Dwarves* (1937).

founder. And, as if to further authenticate *Great and Powerful* as a true Disney movie, as shown in figure 12.8, the film provides us with scenes of the Wicked Witch pondering her appearance in a mirror and clasping a magic apple, both evoking iconography associated with Disney's *Snow White*. The *Art* book also cites *Snow White* as a key reference for the design of the Dark Forest (Curtis 2013: 89). We might also note that Stromberg's team fit Glinda's castle within a larger tradition of Disney castles from animated features and theme park attractions.

CONCLUSION

What have we learned about worlds in our journey through the lands of Oz? Worlds are comprehensive systems that operate at multiple levels. Worlds include clusters of details that make a story feel as if it is operating within a real place, potentially supporting many other stories. Such worlds may exist across longer periods of time, beyond a single medium, and can be experienced from the perspectives of various characters. Such details also contribute to a larger system, a set of assumptions about the nature of the world, which might draw upon multiple disciplines of knowledge, might enable different fans to bring their expertise to bear, and might allow the work to be read again with new insight. A well-designed world opens up—rather than closes off—the creative and interpretive process. Many such worlds have, from their origins, been collaborative: Oz emerged from the shared contributions of both authors and illustrators and absorbed new life as the series was continued by multiple subsequent writers, some authorized as part of the story canon, some offering radical reworkings, but all working from some shared understanding of what constitutes *Ozness*.

This shared conceptual model explains the continuity of details across different versions—the reduction of Oz's "narrative sprawl" (Kelleter 2012: 26) into a much smaller number of elements that constitute the canonical story, as the MGM musical has restricted the amount of aspects from Baum's original texts that survive in popular memory. Yet the most committed Oz fans dedicate themselves to exploring its less-traveled paths and uncharted corners. This shared conceptual model also allows for coordination and collaboration within large-scale productions—whether Baum's own Broadway spectacles or today's blockbuster movies and AAA video games. More and more thought goes into the planning of these franchise worlds, and their screen representations become more richly detailed to reflect contemporary trends toward "overdesign."

In an era of immersive entertainment, audiences are demanding worlds that engulf us, worlds that sustain exploration, even if a small part of their potential is going to be realized within any given work. Yet audiences also often hold on to the idea that they should be paying attention to the story and that excessive details may be seductive, pulling us off the path the protagonist is pursuing. We do not know what to do with a film in which the world-making may be more compelling than the narrative. Much as we have come to value the role of performance sequences across a range of popular genres, we may need to rethink the ways that worlds offer "other structures" that reward audience attention. We need to think more deeply about how the aesthetic criteria by which we evaluate worlds—according to Wolf (2013): their inventiveness, their completeness, and their coherence—relate to the much more fully articulated criteria by which we evaluate stories.

Much of the current writing on world-building (especially Wolf 2013) has stressed the act of "sub-creation." Often, there is a tendency to dismiss worlds that are not sufficiently "original," because they borrow too heavily on genre conventions or specific earlier works. Instead, this chapter has emphasized the intertextual nature of worlds. In an essay dealing with fan fiction, Abigail Derecho introduces the concept of "archontic literature": "A literature that is archontic is a literature composed of texts that are archival in nature and that are impelled by the same archontic principle: that tendency toward enlargement and accretion that all archives possess. Archontic texts are not delimited properties with definite borders that can be transgressed. [...] An archontic text allows, or even invites, writers to enter it, select specific items they find useful, make new artifacts using those found objects, and deposit the newly made work back into the source text's archive" (2006: 64–65). This approach values not invention per se, but generativity, that is, the degree to which any given work helps to sustain the larger process of cultural production. We have considered a few of the strategies by which storytellers might justify their return to a familiar fictional world. On the one hand, as in *Return to Oz*, the story may seek to link the reader's nostalgic desire to revisit a world that feels like home with a story that returns the protagonist to that same space and, through her, brings that world back to life. On the other hand, the text might start with an unanswered question—most often, in this model, as in *Oz the Great and Powerful*, a question of backstory—and then use that question to motivate a new narrative that fills gaps in our understanding. Baum himself often justified the extensions of the Oz storyworld in this same way, as responding to questions from his readers. Accompanying such extensions, there is a desire to "authenticate" the new text as legitimately fitting within the shared world, and so there is a performative aspect of world-sharing, where certain elements that seem essential to the reader's experience are deployed to pave the way for further expansion and exploration. As a storyworld moves across media, as it gets renewed for a new generation, it has to respond to audience expectations about what this world looks like and what kinds of things we expect to see there.

BIBLIOGRAPHY

Andrew, Dudley (1984). *Concepts in Film Theory*. Oxford: Oxford University Press.
Baum, L. Frank (1987). *The Wonderful Wizard of Oz* [1900]. New York: HarperCollins/Books of Wonder.
——(1990). *Dorothy and the Wizard in Oz* [1908]. New York: HarperCollins/Books of Wonder.
——(1996). *Tik-Tok of Oz* [1914]. New York: HarperCollins/Books of Wonder.
Beachem, Travis (2013). *Pacific Rim: Tales for Year Zero*. New York: Marvel.
Bordwell, David and Kristin Thompson (1990). *Film Art: An Introduction*. New York: McGraw-Hill.
Curtis, Grant (2013). *The Art of Oz the Great and Powerful*. New York: Disney.
Derecho, Abigail (2006). "Archontic Literature: A Definition, a History, and Several Theories of Fan Fiction." *Fan Fiction and Fan Communities in the Age of the Internet*. Ed. Kristina Busse and Karen Helleckson. Jefferson, NC: McFarland. 61–78.
Eco, Umberto (1990). "Casablanca: Cult Movies and Intertextual Collage." *Travels in Hyperreality*. New York: Harvest. 197–211.
Freeman, Matthew (2014). "Advertising the Yellow Brick Road: Historicizing the Industrial Emergence of Transmedia Storytelling." *International Journal of Communication* 8: 2362–81.
Goodman, Nelson (1978). *Ways of Worldmaking*. Indianapolis: Hackett.
Ito, Mimi (2008). "Gender Dynamics of the Japanese Media Mix." *Beyond Barbie and Mortal Kombat: New Perspectives on Gender and Gaming*. Ed. Yasmin B. Kafai et al. Cambridge: MIT. 97–110.
Johnson, Derek (2013). *Media Franchising: Creative License and Collaboration in the Culture Industries*. New York: New York University Press.

Kelleter, Frank (2012). "'Toto, I Think We Are in Kansas Again (and Again and Again)': Remakes and Popular Seriality." *Film Remakes, Adaptations and Fan Productions: Remake/Remodel.* Ed. Kathleen Loock and Constantine Verevis. New York: Palgrave McMillan. 19–44.

Otsuka Eijii (2010). "World and Variation: The Reproduction and Consumption of Narrative." *Mechademia* 5: 99–116.

Riley, Michael O. (1997). *Oz and Beyond: The Fantasy World of L. Frank Baum.* Lawrence: University Press of Kansas.

Ryan, Marie-Laurie (2001). *Narrative as Virtual Reality: Immersion and Interactivity in Literature and Electronic Media.* Baltimore: Johns Hopkins University Press.

Saler, Michael (2012). *As If: Modern Enchantments and the Literary Prehistory of Virtual Reality.* Oxford: Oxford University Press.

Sigler, Carolyn (1997). *Alternative Alices: Visions and Revisions of Lewis Carroll's Alice Books.* Lexington: University Press of Kentucky.

Swartz, Mark Evan (2000). *Oz before the Rainbow: L. Frank Baum's The Wonderful Wizard of Oz on Stage and Screen to 1939.* Baltimore: Johns Hopkins University Press.

Wolf, Mark J. P. (2013). *Building Imaginary Worlds: The Theory and History of Subcreation.* New York: Routledge.

——ed. (2017). *Revisiting Imaginary Worlds: A Subcreation Studies Anthology.* New York: Routledge (forthcoming).

CHAPTER 13

Popular Seriality in Everyday Practice
Perry Rhodan and *Tatort*

CHRISTINE HÄMMERLING AND MIRJAM NAST

INTRODUCTION

What does being a fan mean in everyday life? How do individuals craft continuous attachments to particular serialized stories in the midst of complex familial, professional, and leisure commitments that constitute everyday routine? What kinds of practices are introduced into the quotidian so as to make room for such attachments (Röser/Thomas/Peil 2010)? To understand the process of what we have termed *quotidian integration,* we undertook two case studies—one with readers and one with viewers—of two German examples of serial narrative. Working with an ethnographic approach, we accompanied devoted readers and viewers and conducted extensive interviews covering the intertwining of their biographies and lifestyles with mass-mediated fictional storytelling. With such empirical methods, focused on practice, it is possible to document the rhythms of consumption as well as preparatory and follow-up activities surrounding favored series which we will present in this chapter.

Our study focused on the German sci-fi pulp novel series *Perry Rhodan* and the German TV police procedural *Tatort*. These two examples were chosen for two likenesses—an exceptionally long running time and weekly installments—and their difference in genre and medium. *Perry Rhodan* has been published in weekly, novella-length publications since 1961 and unfolds in a parallel universe—called the *Perryversum* by fans—of ever greater complexity, with new narrative strands taking up additional time-and-space adventures. *Tatort* has been airing on German, Austrian, and Swiss TV on Sunday evenings, during prime time, since 1970. Prefiguring a format familiar to American viewers of CSI, *Tatort* features investigative teams in different German cities. While the criminal case is solved during the ninety-minute running time of each episode, narrative strands within a given investigative team and its characters continue, with at present twenty-two irregularly alternating cities and teams.

Studying how recipients integrate these serial narratives into their lives, we rely on the (German) concept of "Alltagsintegration" (Bausinger 1983: 24–37, Röser 2007, and Röser/Thomas/Peil 2010), which translates into English as *quotidian integration*. Thus, we focus on the habitual dimension of media reception, that is, on symbolic and social follow-up practices at the level of everyday life. But unlike earlier works on quotidian integration, we have taken into consideration the diversification of serialized media practices and technologies in the digital age. This diversification impacts *Tatort* and *Perry Rhodan* alike: it shapes reception in such a way that similarities between both serial narratives and their integration in daily lives become visible.

We begin with a description of the dominant mode of reception for each series: watching *Tatort* as a weekly television broadcast and reading *Perry Rhodan* weekly on pulp novel paper. From there, we broaden our view to encompass alternative modes and techniques of consuming these narratives. On this backdrop, we compare how recipients integrate the series into their quotidian rhythms and their daily routines, and we offer a categorization of aspects that are pertinent for both series. In the final section, we look at our findings through the lens of media-theoretical questions concerning the diversification of modes of reception in the convergence era. Based on empirical evidence, we argue that even with ongoing changes in the delivery systems of serial narrative, reception practices remain surprisingly stable.

CLASSIC MODES OF SERIAL RECEPTION

(a) *Perry Rhodan.* Every week, Paul Schilling buys a *Perry Rhodan* booklet.[1] He goes to a vendor where he is known and greeted as a *Perry Rhodan* reader.

---

1. Our comparative study builds on qualitative fieldwork carried out between October 2010 and February 2013, supported by a grant from the German Research Foundation (DFG) in the context of the Popular Seriality Research Unit (PSRU). Our analysis is based on fifty-nine qualitative, semistructured interviews with recipients of *Perry Rhodan* and *Tatort*. Our

Generally, he buys the newest issue on Friday, the day on which it appears, and reads it over the weekend; he wants to finish reading before the next installment is published, as it is important to him to be up-to-date. Rarely, more than three or four issues will accumulate, and if this happens, he reads them "chop-chop, chop-chop, one after the other." He usually enjoys the new installment at home, in a comfortable setting, drinking cappuccino. Initially, he shared the booklets with his brother but now no longer passes them on to other people. *Perry Rhodan*, he says, is "actually totally private, is my hobby." Paul collects the booklets and owns the complete series. For issues 1–1500, he kept a list, accounting for what he has read and which editions he owns. Today, this kind of bookkeeping is less important to him.

Most fans read *Perry Rhodan* in similar ways. The pulp novels—published in weekly editions of 80.000[2]—are sold at kiosks and bookstores in train stations; additionally, readers can also subscribe. First-edition booklets are the most relevant medium. One has to read them to partake in further fan practices, such as story competitions, online discussions, and live fan gatherings.

(b) *Tatort.* Luise Richard works a lot during the week; on Sundays, however, all she does is take walks or go to church with her husband, who commutes to another city where he works. When he reaches his second home on Sunday, they watch *Tatort* simultaneously and later talk about it on the phone. This is their weekly routine and an important part of their conjugal life. Up until a year ago, Luise would be joined by her mother watching the police procedural, but now her mother is ill, and it has gotten harder for her to follow the storyline, which makes both of them feel uncomfortable. That is why Luise mostly watches *Tatort* alone now. While doing so, she sometimes knits or drinks a glass of wine. She is quite absorbed by the show and hates to be disturbed by her otherwise beloved son. The phone is placed right next to her, but no one would call at this time of the week, as all of her friends know that this is her *Tatort* time. Even though she is working as a computer scientist and uses the Internet for all sorts of things, she always watches *Tatort* when it is first aired on TV. Only that way can she talk about it directly afterwards

---

interviewees represent a diverse sample concerning age, gender, and formal level of education, but also regarding modes of reception. Due to structural differences in the two series, more participants in our research called themselves *fans* of *Perry Rhodan*, whereas *Tatort* viewers often expressed further distinctions concerning which investigators they liked or disliked. Interviews were tape-recorded and transcribed; they have been archived by the authors as well as their universities. We have used pseudonyms for all interviewees except for individuals who were interviewed as experts of a certain field; they agreed to be cited under their own names.

2. According to an oral statement of chief editor Klaus N. Frick at the *Perry Rhodan*-WeltCon (World Convention) 2012. See also Lovelybooks 2016.

with her husband. When he can manage to be there with her on a Sunday, they watch *Tatort* together, holding hands.

This is how one of our informants watches the most popular German police procedural, and it serves as an example of how viewers integrate the series into their weekly and daily routines, their relationships, and their lives.[3] New episodes of *Tatort* regularly reach seven to thirteen million viewers as broadcasts (Schröder 2015). Although reruns of older *Tatort* episodes are aired nearly every evening, most people watch only the latest episode on Sunday nights. In Germany, *Tatort* represents one of the most visible and long-lived examples of what Henry Jenkins (2011) calls *appointment-based* television, as opposed to *engagement-based* television.

Based on the biographical interviews carried out, a preference for—or at the very least a persistence of—these classic modes of reception can be noticed, which we attribute to the anchoring of reception in minor and major everyday practices discussed later on. First we will examine emerging alternative modes of reception and their relevance to our two cases.

ALTERNATIVE MODES OF RECEPTION

Digital communication continually generates new devices to access media content, and hence to generate new possibilities of quotidian integration. We use the term *device* here in a Foucauldian sense, building on Knut Hickethier's (2003) utilization of Foucault's concept of the *dispositif* for media studies. For Hickethier, the "television dispositif" encompasses technology, institutions, programs, reception modes, and an understanding of subjectivity as a network of relationships (1995: 63). Thus, new technomedial conditions always allow viewers to add further content to a serial and its narrative strands, thereby enlarging existing serial universes.

(a) **Some notes on media, technologies, and their impact on culture.** According to Henry Jenkins, "History teaches us that old media never die, they don't even necessarily fade away. What dies are simply the tools we use to access media content—the 8-track, the Beta tape. [. . .] Delivery technologies become obsolete and get replaced; media, on the other hand, evolve. Recorded sound is the medium. CDs, MP3 files, and 8-track cassettes are delivery technologies" (2006: 13).

---

3. For a content-based analysis of *Tatort*, the longest-running television crime series in Germany (since 1970), whose production culture reflects the federal structure of the German nation, with different states producing their own subseries within the larger *Tatort* franchise, see Hißnauer/Scherer/Stockinger 2014a/b.

Still, shifts in delivery systems might bring differences in content—extras are included or omitted. Following media historian Lisa Gitelman, Henry Jenkins differentiates: "Delivery systems are simply and only technologies; media are also cultural systems." This explains why Jenkins talks about media "convergence" rather than media revolutions (2006: 14). Building on Ithiel de Sola Pool (1983: 23), he writes:

> A service that was provided in the past by any one medium—be it broadcasting, the press, or telephony—can now be provided in several different physical ways. So the one-to-one relationship that used to exist between a medium and its use is eroding. (2006: 10)

Although it can be questioned if media were ever restricted to unified uses, Jenkins's distinction is highly useful in analytical terms. It calls attention to the fact that media change should not be reduced to technological change; cultural practices must be taken into account, enlarging the focus from access to participation (2006: 15). But change in delivery systems also leads to change in quotidian integration. Not only practices of diegetic participation but also cultural patterns of how recipients make serial narratives socially meaningful are influenced by new technological possibilities, even though some practices show surprising stability. Jenkins relies mostly on U.S.-American data and observes that "media convergence impacts the way we consume media. [. . .] Fans of a popular television series may sample dialogue, summarize episodes, debate texts, create original fan fiction, record their own soundtracks, make their own movies—and distribute all of this worldwide via the Internet" (2006: 16).

Yet, while all these opportunities exist for fans of *Tatort* or *Perry Rhodan* as well, most recipients do not make use of them. Fandom is not always shared, not everything is considered worth sampling, and some texts rarely evoke coproductions. To gather *Tatort* and *Perry* fans under the roof of early adopters of new media technologies would miscast these fan communities. Thus, when theorizing popular seriality, one must take into account the specifics of cultural background, which often differ strongly from those U.S. practices that serve as the material base for many media theories offered today. For example, regarding our two German case studies, it can be said that their online communities do not operate analogously to U.S. online communities. Also, class distinctions based on media consumption seem to play a greater role in Germany than they do in North America. Nevertheless, some convergence practices are present and will be sketched in the following.

(b) Alternative delivery technologies, media devices, and content. Aside from the weekly new booklet, *Perry Rhodan* fans can also purchase an e-book and an audiobook every week. The same novel may thus be acquired through three different delivery systems. According to chief editor Klaus N. Frick (one of our interviewees), *Perry Rhodan* represents a substantial component (three to five percent) of the German-language e-book market. Apart from that, alternative, shortened, or enlarged content is also available in other print-based editions, such as hardcovers or paperbacks (which also exist in digitized versions).

Additional media such as audio plays, comics, and computer games are equally relevant for fan collectors. Many *Perry Rhodan* readers show great interest in such products, sometimes with explicit regard to the franchise's history. Thus, although a *Perry Rhodan* feature film from 1966 is generally considered poor or at best a curiosity, many readers have seen it. By contrast, *Tatort* reception is mainly bound to its Sunday night broadcast. Although DVRs or the Internet would allow most viewers to do without the broadcasting model, *Tatort* as a series is culturally bound to the end of the weekend and to a living-room atmosphere. Still, new episodes are also watched outside one's home by a sizable number of recipients—at a friend's place or in bars, in what Germans call "public viewing" (Dieterich 2009: 273).

Furthermore, there are more and more viewers who watch the Sunday episodes at a slightly later time, on another station some hours later, or on digital programming-devices. We also found increased interest in viewing the latest episode on the web platform ARD-Mediathek or on YouTube. In addition, since December 2009, Disney has been selling *Tatort* episodes in DVD format (T-Online News 2009). There are audiobook versions and—as the latest innovation—there is the interactive online game *Tatort Plus*.

Keeping these options and innovations in mind, we will now present evidence of how fans of the two series consume weekly installments and what continuities and contrasts are manifest.

PARALLELS AND DIFFERENCES

What are the prevailing reception practices of *Perry Rhodan* and *Tatort* fans? What are the prevailing ways of experiencing these serial narratives, and what impact do they have on the overall habits of everyday life? We are interested in the nature of different modes of reception, in their accessibility, and in the similarities and differences between the reception cultures of both series.

(a) Choosing from a wide selection of media devices, delivery technologies, and contents. The opportunity to follow "your" series (and its spin-offs) in different media formats alters modes of reception and their relationship

Diversity of delivery technologies not only enables recipients to communicate about narrative content via Internet platforms, Twitter, and other digital devices, but it also forces them to make decisions. For *Perry Rhodan* and *Tatort*, we found that most viewers *do not* change their mode of reception once they get used to it. They stick to their favorite or handiest practice. For many, it is hard to imagine another routine, bound to different delivery technologies. Thus, *Perry Rhodan* fans point out that they have become used to the pulp novel format. They appreciate its handy, light weight, along with the smell of paper—a key characteristic of print for these readers—and they enjoy thumbing through it and making themselves comfortable with it, for example in a bathtub. They also appreciate booklet inserts such as posters; they like the cover and illustrations, both of which e-books do not offer. Most regular *Tatort* viewers, too, cannot imagine suddenly not watching the show at home and going to a bar instead, or to watch it at another time of day. Not surprisingly, it is the youngest segment of the *Tatort* audience that shows a somewhat greater flexibility regarding the place and time of consumption.

What is more, reception in both cases is often accompanied by the use of a number of other communication systems, such as telephone or the Internet. Hasebrink and Popp speak of a "repertoire of media" (2006) within which reception patterns unfold. Individual likes, dislikes, and formative experiences contribute to the privileging of some devices and the avoidance of others. In *Tatort* reception, for instance, there is ample use being made of second screens, such as tablets or smartphones, mostly in order to communicate with other viewers (dpa 2013). Similarly, some *Perry Rhodan* readers like to share their thoughts about the newest installment on the series' official online platforms.[4]

Technological diversification can also lead to a decline of the readers' or viewers' sense of obligation toward the narrative—or to a shift in what is regarded as obligation. While readers might no longer feel obliged to follow the series in routinized rhythms, they still try to stay up-to-date. Beyond that, *Perry Rhodan* readers feel little obligation to make use of all the surplus options created by diversified delivery systems. While *Tatort* viewers, knowing that the online version will be available for a week, express a certain sense of freedom to shift from the strict Sunday evening time slot (even if they stick with it), *Perry Rhodan* readers are more selective in their utilization of alternative reception modes. Thus, reading the newest installment is widely

---

4. Our informants mentioned especially the platform Forum Perry Rhodan. Newcomers to the series tend to use the online wiki Perrypedia, in combination with the hardcover collections, to catch up on the history of the serial universe.

considered obligatory; the regular, weekly "dose" is anticipated with excitement, and if one has fallen behind, one makes an effort to read up quickly. Of course, this also reflects the difference between ongoing and episodic storytelling: as *Tatort* offers finished stories, its viewers are rarely upset when they miss an episode.

(b) **The setting.** The immediate physical conditions of serial reception—its "where" and "how"—shape what Kaspar Maase (2008a) has described as the specific "aesthetic experience" of popular culture. Whereas canonized or professional aesthetic experience stresses concentration and close attention to the artifact, Maase sees quotidian aesthetic experience characterized by bundles of divided and shifting attention in search of (physical) pleasure. Complex multisensory perception and intense body involvement are hallmarks of popular aesthetics (Maase 2008b). Thus, spatial configurations and physical activities are essential factors of serial reception, especially in the sense of habitualizing pleasure(s). For our informants, coziness is an important component of their interaction with *Tatort* and *Perry Rhodan*. The act of reading or viewing the latest episode is regularly prepared with various routines, such as arranging blankets and cushions—interestingly, in strong contrast to the series' content, which focuses on strange and uncomfortable challenges, dangers, and adventures. For *Perry Rhodan*, "mobile settings" are also important and much appreciated among fans. Reading the booklet on the commuter train is considered a classic mode (and setting) of reception. The transportability of the booklet format is one of the reasons for its staying power. Transportability is less of an issue for *Tatort* viewers, but the mere knowledge that one could watch episodes on the go, in other countries through live streaming, or in someone else's household is regarded as comforting.

(c) **Temporal rhythm.** *Perry Rhodan* and *Tatort* recipients appreciate the weekly rhythm of publication/broadcasting. In both cases, the series' temporal connection to the weekend is important. Clearly, these narratives serve to mark leisure time. Often, the ritualized aspect of their reception is also associated with a transition from waking to sleeping: *Perry Rhodan* readers frequently read their booklets in bed, while *Tatort* viewers say they like to watch the show before falling asleep or even consider the weekly mystery as an aid to do so.

Both series are characterized by their extraordinary longevity; traditions of reception have been established over fifty years for *Perry Rhodan* and over forty years for *Tatort*. This includes generational linkages and "inheritances": Many new users found their way to the respective series through older relatives. Individual users may have a biographical connection, remembering their first time viewing or reading the series; or they may have gained expert knowledge over time, allowing them to see the key role of some installments for the series' overall development.

(d) Buying and collecting. There are interesting differences in the ways recipients experience and evaluate the materiality of each series' delivery technologies. *Perry Rhodan* subscriber Stefanie Waltz argues that "receiving *Perry Rhodan* as a (digital) newsletter would be like receiving a Christmas gift that is not wrapped." In the case of *Tatort*, the television set—its screen size and sound quality as well as the material aspects of the setting of reception—matters to viewers. Still, there is a strong difference between both groups of recipients concerning the desire to own installments. *Tatort* viewers collect episodes—if they do so at all—randomly or in connection with biographical memories. By contrast, *Perry Rhodan* readers are often collectors wishing to own the complete series or at least particular curiosities that embody *Perry Rhodan*'s history.

Clearly, the haptic immediacy of reading affects print-serial consumers in ways that watching a TV series does not. Viewing, like listening, is evanescent and takes on mediated form in DVDs, boxed sets, and so forth. The locus of immediacy here is the television set in its quotidian environs. The work entailed in collecting audiovisuals—recording, labeling, perhaps transferring from an outdated delivery technology such as VHS to DVD—is not concerned with revisiting content and the actual shape of its medium, as is the case with pulp booklets.

(e) On- and offline infomedia. Jason Mittell (2009, 2013) describes wikis and other digital platforms of information and exchange as a defining characteristic of serial storytelling in the convergence era. In this regard, the reception patterns of *Perry Rhodan* and *Tatort* increasingly come to resemble each other. There are websites administered by producers, blogs by authors and actors, fan pages, rankings, and social media pages, which in turn might reference all of the above. Yet before digital communication there already existed—and still exist—other information formats, such as encyclopedias and book publications that summarize narratives and production details. In the case of *Perry Rhodan*, fanzines, printed newletters, and even printed "easy entry" books remain important for the fan community. For *Tatort*, some of the most renowned national daily newspapers regularly offer previews and reviews (Hißnauer/Scherer/Stockinger 2014a).

Print and digital information co-reference one another, with print devices pointing to digital *Tatort* sites, which feature links to—or collect bibliographical data of—reviews and studies in print. In *Perry Rhodan* fandom, too, digital and print publications interrelate closely. In online fora, print information is presented and discussed, while print fanzines refer to online content.

Clearly, absorbing new narrative content is but one component of series attachment. Readers and viewers relish—or have at the very least habituated themselves to—major and minor everyday practices surrounding time and place of reception. Furthermore, series reception may, in the case of TV, anchor time spent with friends and significant others within the week; it may augment leisure activities with activities such as tending to a collection or participating in online and offline communications. All this is essential for fashioning the quotidian. We suggest that it is worthwhile to expand research further on the convergence of media effects and the continuous diversification of technologies in everyday life. Serial consumptions are an excellent realm for such work; in our last section, we present a few preliminary suggestions.

CENTRAL ISSUES REGARDING THE EFFECT OF MEDIA AND TECHNOLOGICAL DIVERSIFICATION

(a) **Conservatism: orientation along the habitual.** While audiences of *Tatort* and *Perry Rhodan* are generally open to nontraditional modes of reception, the majority is practicing habitualized, less participatory, and in this sense "conservative" modes of reception. Most people hold on to TV programming when it comes to *Tatort* and to print (pulp novels) when it comes to *Perry Rhodan*. Even when viewers shift away from *Tatort*'s Sunday-evening spot, they still look for a homelike feeling in watching the show; typically, bars that screen the cop show in a public setting try to draw in customers by advertising a "living-room atmosphere." In the case of *Perry Rhodan*, even e-book readers stick to a weekly reading rhythm, and they remain interested in the material and haptic aspects of the science fiction serial (for example, when they buy plush toys of their favorite characters or hang *Perry Rhodan* pictures on their walls).

(b) **Increasing individualization and decreasing face-to-face contact?** Not only has diversification in media and digital devices led to increasingly individualized types of consumption (Leder 2011: 38), but this process has also shaped the concerns of media scholarship. Autonomy, as opposed to dependency, has become a key term in studies of media reception (Kumpf 2011, Frizzoni 2012, and Gothe 2012). Conversely, buying or watching a series online might seem to reduce the necessity of personal interaction. But for recipients of *Tatort* and *Perry Rhodan*, online communication also spurs face-to-face exchange, with topics discussed in online fora coming up in personal conversations. For some fans, the online forum is even an opportunity to get in direct contact with other readers or viewers.

(c) Produsage as the future type of media reception? A predominant concept that sheds light on popular reception in the age of Web 2.0 is participation (Jenkins 2006). Axel Bruns, for example, describes a current "shift away from industrial modes of production and towards collaborative, user-led content creation" (2008: 8), with users taking an active role in the process of production and therefore becoming *producers*. As far as the reception of *Tatort* and *Perry Rhodan* is concerned, we could not observe such a far-reaching development. In both series, direct participation of readers and viewers is, first, limited to marked-off areas. Second, where processes similar to produsage can be witnessed, they have already existed before the introduction of the Internet. Due to the long run of both series, most of today's producers are former recipients, and even as producers they continue to read or view the stories as fans. Still, well-defined roles persist, not least because of culturally specific histories and patterns of both production and reception. Despite the importance of U.S.-American entertainment on the German (and generally European) market, these practices continue to follow long-established cultural habits.

With respect to *Tatort*, what we observe is better described as cocreativity than as coproduction. German viewers like to comment on the latest episode via e-mail and on various online fora, but rarely do they introduce conceptual ideas (perhaps assuming that they would not be heard anyway). In turn, *Tatort* producers, such as editor Melanie Wolber, tend to regard television as a one-way medium.

With respect to *Perry Rhodan*, we witness close linkages between producers and an active fandom. However, active fans make up a very small part of the entire readership. Most recipients see their role in reading and criticizing episodes, sometimes playfully generating ideas that may be communicated to writers and other producers. Direct participation in the series, however, consists mainly in contributing to subareas of the serial universe. Rarely do fans influence—or try to influence—the main storyline of the ongoing narrative.

CONCLUSION

Over an exceptionally long time span, viewers of *Tatort* and readers of *Perry Rhodan* have developed numerous ways of integrating these serial narratives into their everyday routines. Even under the conditions of digital media change, they have tended to conserve reception practices closely connected to the original delivery system of these series: appointment-based television in the case of *Tatort,* and pulp novels in the case of *Perry Rhodan*. Quite a few recipients are open to new media devices, but we observe a certain persistence in reception practices that is based not only on the aesthetics of the series but also on cultural logics of tradition, communities of communication, a sense of obligation toward the narrative, and an appreciation of comfort and homeliness in the act of watching and reading.

Long-running series such as the two we have examined also offer excellent opportunities to observe generational continuities with subtle changes in reception preferences. Younger viewers opt to watch *Tatort* with friends in their dorms, in student housing, or in "public viewings," in part because the Sunday program has been an integral part of their weekly routine; in part because it is something they share with new friends; and in part because keeping up with the series is an important ingredient, among many, in everyday communication. The specific narrative content is not irrelevant, but it is worthwhile asking why some, though by no means all, series achieve regular and persistent quotidian integration. Our study shows that it is not only interaction with textual features but also specific reception routines that the interviewees enjoy in their favorite series. These reception practices are always corresponding with delivery technologies, materialities, social relations, and viewers' and readers' sense of a comfortable environment. Ethnographic work on a microlevel that pays attention to the sociocultural setting and the specifics of mass-mediated serial reception can tell us much about the highly specific intertwining of serial narration and everyday life, not just in Germany, not just in the United States, but in settings around the globe.

BIBLIOGRAPHY

Bausinger, Hermann (1983). *Alltag, Technik, Medien.* Berlin: Guttandin & Hoppe.
Bruns, Axel (2008). *Blogs, Wikipedia, Second Life, and Beyond: From Production to Produsage.* New York: Peter Lang.
Dieterich, Claus-Marco (2009). "Viewing Public: Das Publikum im Zeitalter seiner medialen Inszenierbarkeit." *Bilder–Bücher–Bytes: Zur Medialität des Alltags.* Ed. Michael Simon et al. Münster: Waxmann. 273–82.
dpa (2013). news.de (April 25). March 5, 2014. http://www.news.de/technik/855413696/immer-mehr-mitmach-tv-der-trend-zum-second-screen/1/.
Forum Perry Rhodan. May 8, 2013. http://forum.perry-rhodan.net.
Frizzoni, Brigitte (2012). "Zwischen Trash-TV und Quality-TV: Wertdiskurse zu serieller Unterhaltung." *Populäre Serialität: Narration–Evolution–Distinktion. Zum seriellen Erzählen seit dem 19. Jahrhundert.* Ed. Frank Kelleter. Bielefeld: Transcript-Verlag. 339–51.
Gothe, Miriam (2012). "Die Abarbeitung (an) der Unterhaltung: Zuschauerpraktiken angesichts höchst optionalisierten (TV-)Serienkonsums." *Die vergnügte Gesellschaft: Ernsthafte Perspektiven auf ein modernes Amüsement.* Ed. Michael Heinlein and Katharina Seßler. Bielefeld: Transcript-Verlag. 209–23.

Hasebrink, Uwe and Jutta Popp (2006). "Media Repertoires as a Result of Selective Media Use: A Conceptual Approach to the Analysis of Patterns of Exposure." *Communications* 31.3: 369–87.
Hickethier, Knut (1995). "Dispositiv Fernsehen. Skizze eines Modells." *montage/av* 4.1: 63–83.
——— (2003). *Einführung in die Medienwissenschaft*. Stuttgart: Metzler.
Hißnauer, Christian, Stefan Scherer, and Claudia Stockinger (2014a). *Föderalismus in Serie: Die Einheit der ARD-Reihe Tatort im historischen Verlauf*. Paderborn: Fink.
———, eds. (2014b). *Zwischen Serie und Werk: Fernseh- und Gesellschaftsgeschichte im Tatort*. Bielefeld: Transcript-Verlag.
Jenkins, Henry (2006). *Convergence Culture: Where Old and New Media Collide*. New York: New York University Press.
——— (2011). "Imagining Television's Futures: An Interview with Intel's Brian David Johnson (Part Two)." henryjenkins.org (June 20). May 1, 2013. http://henryjenkins.org/2011/07/imagining_televisions_futures_1.html.
Kumpf, Sarah (2011). "'Es muss was geben, worüber man nachdenken kann': Die Aneignung von Quality-TV-Serien." *Die Aneignung von Medienkultur: Rezeption, politische Akteure und Medienakteure*. Ed. Monika Elsler. Wiesbaden: VS. 19–33.
Leder, Dietrich (2011). "Fernseh-Unterhaltung." *Gute Unterhaltung?!: Qualität und Qualitäten der Fernsehunterhaltung*. Ed. Gerd Hallenberger. Konstanz: UVK. 33–46.
Lovelybooks (2016). "Klaus N. Frick zum 50-jährigen Jubiläum von *Perry Rhodan*." March 28, 2016. http://www.lovelybooks.de/thema/LovelyBooks-nachgefragt-mit-Klaus-N-Frick-zum-50-jährigen-Jubiläum-von-PERRY-RHODAN-Buchverlosung-739184575/klassisch/?seite=2.
Maase, Kaspar (2008a). "Einleitung: Zur ästhetischen Erfahrung der Gegenwart." *Die Schönheiten des Populären: Ästhetische Erfahrung der Gegenwart*. Ed. Kaspar Maase. Frankfurt: Campus. 9–26.
——— (2008b). "Die Erforschung des Schönen im Alltag. Sechs Thesen." *Die Schönheiten des Populären: Ästhetische Erfahrung der Gegenwart*. Ed. Kaspar Maase. Frankfurt: Campus. 42–57.
Mittel, Jason (2009). "Sites of Participation: Wiki Fandom and the Case of Lostpedia." *Transformative Works and Cultures* 3. March 5, 2014. http://dx.doi.org/10.3983/twc.2009.0118.
——— (2013). "Wikis and Participatory Fandom." *The Participatory Culture Handbook*. Ed. Aaron Delwiche and Jennifer Jacobs Henderson. New York: Routledge. 35–42.
Perrypedia. August 25, 2013. http://www.perrypedia.proc.org.
Pool, Ithiel de Sola (1983). *Technologies of Freedom: On Free Speech in an Electronic Age*. Cambridge: Harvard University Press.
Röser, Jutta, ed. (2007): *MedienAlltag. Domestizierungsprozesse alter und neuer Medien*. Wiesbaden: VS.
Röser, Jutta, Tanja Thomas, and Corinna Peil, eds. (2010). *Alltag in den Medien—Medien im Alltag*. Wiesbaden: VS.
Schröder, Jens (2015). "'Tatort'-Ermittler-Ranking: Kiel und Berlin preschen nach vorn, Saarland nun Vorletzter. "*MEEDIA* (January 26). August 26, 2015. http://meedia.de/2015/01/26/tatort-ermittler-ranking-kiel-und-berlin-preschen-nach-vorn-saarland-nun-vorletzter/.
T-Online News (2009). T-Online.de (December 3). March 3, 2014. http://www.t-online.de/unterhaltung/tv/id_20716764/-tatort-endlich-gibt-es-die-krimi-reihe-auf-dvd-.html.

CHAPTER 14

Digital Seriality

On the Serial Aesthetics and
Practice of Digital Games

SHANE DENSON AND ANDREAS SUDMANN

INTRODUCTION

This chapter outlines a set of perspectives on the seriality of digital games and game cultures, that is, the aesthetic forms and cultural practices of game-related serialization, which we see unfolding against the background of media and sociocultural transformations in the wake of popular culture's digitization.[1] Seriality is a factor not only in explicitly marked game series, but also within individual games, as well as on the level of transmedial relations between games and other media. Particularly with respect to processes of temporal "collapse" or "synchronization" that, in the current age of digitization and media convergence, are challenging the temporal dimensions and developmental logics of predigital seriality, computer games are eminently suited for an exemplary investigation of a specifically *digital* type of seriality. In the following, we look at serialization processes in digital games and game series, seeking to understand how they relate to transformations of serially structured experiences and identifications on the part of historically situated actors. These transformations range from the microtemporal scale of players'

---

1. A different version of this chapter appeared in *Eludamos: Journal of Computer Game Culture* 7.1 (2013): 1–32. We thank the editors for granting permission to revise and reprint.

encounters with algorithmic computation processes all the way up to the macrotemporal level of collective brokerings of identities in the digital age. To account for this multilayered complexity, we argue for an interdisciplinary approach, combining media-aesthetic and media-philosophical perspectives with the resources of discourse analysis and cultural history. We approach the seriality of digital games in terms of both textual and aesthetic forms as well as the broader context of serialized game cultures and popular culture at large. An investigation of digital serial forms brings into view a phase of transformation in the experience and construction of seriality that impacts the contemporary practice and aesthetics of popular culture far more broadly than just in those areas directly affected by digitization. In our effort to identify specific differences between digital and nondigital forms of seriality, we seek to demonstrate how games are central to our experience of these changes and to show how the self-reflexive and self-historicizing impulses that have characterized serialized media throughout modernity are now crucially involved in shaping our experience of the contemporary world.

LOCATING DIGITAL SERIALITY

The history of digital games is above all a history of popular series: it is the story of countless sequels, prequels, remakes, hacks, mods, copies, updates, and franchises. This observation about the essential seriality of digital games may seem obvious in an age of quickly proliferating properties like *Bejeweled* and *Angry Birds*—game series that seem to spawn a new installment every time we turn around, spreading rapidly across platforms and into a variety of merchandising outlets and tie-ins with other media. But if it is true that we have become sensitive to the seriality of such games, the story of digital seriality has yet to be told in any systematic manner. This unwritten story would look beyond the endless stream of recycled physics engines and the birds they've launched to fame; it would survey the history of gaming and look at games themselves as part of larger serial networks, where they often mark a "before," an "after," or a "meanwhile" with respect to the popular-cultural practices of other media. Sometimes this takes place in the context of transmedial narratives, where serialized forms and formats of digital gaming find a natural home. But seriality is both more far-reaching in scope and more fundamentally anchored in the media, platforms, and practices of gameplay.

Serial forms and functions are not restricted to the level of diegetic representations, as expressed in the ongoing narratives and their recurring characters—like Mario—that constitute a "game series" proper. Much more basically, computer games themselves constitute their own internal structures of seriality, for example, through their segmentation into distinct levels or worlds, thus establishing a serial schema of repetition and variation at the very heart of gameplay. At an even deeper level, games are constructed from iterative and modularized scraps of code, so that seriality might be seen to be hardwired into games at their core. Back at the experiential level of our active interface with them as well, games employ a variety of structures and strategies of serialization. By the 1980s, a game like *Batman* (1986) was not only involved in transmedial relations with a heavily series-based character, but it had also begun introducing the mechanism of save points, thus ordering gameplay itself as an episodically segmented but continuing serial activity. On the side of production, add-ons, ports, mods, and so forth, can be seen as further serial forms by which digital games, their diegetic worlds, and their underlying source codes are all expanded or continued. Moreover, the seriality of digital games is not restricted to the level of software; it is also a hardware phenomenon, as is evidenced in the numbering of console generations: marking innovation serially, the first PlayStation (retroactively dubbed the "PSOne" or "PSX") is followed by the PS2, PS3, and PS4, for example. However, the dynamics of linear seriality is complicated by the fact that gaming systems like the Atari Flashback revive old or "classic" games and platforms (Atari 2600, 5200, 7800) for the purposes of retrogaming (Suominen 2008), while other systems like the new Xbox One, successor to the Xbox 360, refuse the additive logic of innovation (the would-be "Xbox 720") and perform a symbolic reboot instead.

The seriality of digital games is thus a multifaceted phenomenon that is complexly imbricated with the serial formats that have developed and proliferated across the media of modern popular culture since the nineteenth century (Kelleter 2012). Digital games therefore pose a challenge to research on popular seriality: Is it possible to account for the media specificity of digital gaming without overlooking the historical and cultural connections between serial forms across media? At stake, moreover, is the conceptual scope of the term *seriality* itself. As the examples above illustrate, digital games challenge us to expand the purview of the serial beyond more common, narrower conceptions; this expansion takes us beyond the confines of ongoing linear narratives and opens onto structures of code, interface, and hardware. At the same time, we must guard against an excessive inflation of the concept, according to which any and every instance of formal or media-technical repetition and variation might be deemed serial. By dulling the analytical value of the category, such an inflationary approach would have exactly the opposite effect of the limited expansion that we deem necessary. That is, the epistemic payoff of a limited expansion lies in the ability it opens up for us to recognize, sometimes unexpectedly, a range of contemporary and historical media as sharing characteristics and formal attributes associated with popular seriality. The challenge, then, is to find the proper limit for such an expansion.

In the following, we aim to negotiate between the need for conceptual limits and the demand, originating in the media of digital games themselves, to open up a merely formal concept of seriality. Our mission here is largely exploratory, as we seek to chart uncertain waters, in which existing conceptual instruments may lead us off course. We therefore set out from a relatively broad definition of seriality, approaching it in terms of those practice-oriented and media-based processes of repetition and variation that operate in such a way as to solidify chains of sociocultural continuity—chains or threads that are capable of being recognized as such and that can serve an orienting function with regard to trajectories of historical, cultural, or media-technological change. Repetition and iterativity are accordingly necessary but not sufficient conditions of seriality: to become serial in a meaningful sense of the term requires repetition and variation to come together in such a way as to lay the foundation for a recognition or feeling that something is not merely being repeated or varied but that it is, by virtue of this very repetition, part of something that is ongoing, continuing. This base definition allows us to call into question taken-for-granted distinctions between seriality and other terms, such as *transmediality* and *media convergence*. Our larger epistemic point is that, for all the useful work they accomplish, these other terms often obscure the operation of seriality, which is a fundamental force in modern popular culture and one which is instrumental in producing cultural continuities across industrial-era and digital media. An expanded understanding of seriality, based in the relatively blank definition provided above, will therefore help us to recognize these continuities and to see digital games as participating in them in important ways, articulating novel inflections on an ongoing, largely serial, process. We begin by considering three contexts for studying digital seriality as both continuous and discontinuous with popular seriality more generally.

CONTEXTUALIZING DIGITAL SERIALITY

(a) Digitality, media convergence, and seriality. With the emergence of digital media, structures and operations of popular seriality established across commercial media channels since the nineteenth century have been fundamentally problematized, particularly as regards their media-historical functions (Denson/Mayer 2012a and Jahn-Sudmann/Kelleter 2012). Novel forms of seriality in the digital age are closely related to the phenomenon of media convergence. Jenkins's notion of "convergence culture" (2006) describes a media landscape that privileges "transmedial" over monomedial formats, thus transforming the contexts and conditions in which serialization processes take place. Transmedial formats go beyond linear forms of sequential narration: these types of seriality are arranged around the construction and piecemeal exploration of singular, more or less coherent worlds that span the borders of various media—expansive worlds that open up to recipients through the medially discrete entry points of comics, film, games, and so forth—while simultaneously exhibiting a high degree of formal openness with regard to the narrative order of texts, thus allowing for a variable order of consumption. This flexible approach to the sequentiality, rhythm, and frequency of serial reception corresponds in many respects to the more general increase of interactive choices and activities available to media consumers in the digital age. Interactivity is therefore an important background for the seriality of digital games, but it also forms the medium's central appeal and purpose: digital games' processual screen events are generated foremost through the interaction between games and gamers. This activity is itself serially organized, as we shall see, and it is integrated into the serial articulations of transmedial narration and world-building.[2]

In this context, the apparent timelessness produced by digital-media convergence is crucial: in our "convergence culture," historically diverse media contents exist in a state of synchronicity, permanence, and random and repeatable accessibility. But while some critics see digital media portending the virtual end of (media) history (e.g., Kittler 1986), we see the phenomenon of seriality in digital games and game series as a continuation of both the history of popular seriality and modern media history generally. Nevertheless, digital seriality must also be understood as the expression of a transformation in modern media history. With the emergence of digital media, all media are digitally "remediated" (Bolter/Grusin 1999). Most pertinently in our context, the traditional media of serialized production (print, film, etc.) are affected in a variety of ways. Serial literature from the predigital era is increasingly transferred and archived in digital storage media (Mussell 2012). Classic, contemporary, and forgotten film and television series are bundled and released in elaborate DVD box sets (Mittell 2011). Meanwhile, comics, film, and television productions migrate to new online outlets, where they are available for download or streaming.

---

2. For more on world-building, see chapter 12 in the present volume.

As a result of these transformations, serial forms and processes are subject to radically new conditions of mediation. A "logic of the database" (Manovich 2001: 218) emerges, opening long-running, linear narratives to new forms of experience, as text-based searchability and nearly instant access to complete series frees their storyworlds from the publication and distribution frequencies that governed their consumption in the predigital era. Accordingly, media users have more power to decide when and how rapidly they will consume a series, and phenomena such as "binge viewing" become an option with digital infrastructures. Since consumers were previously more dependent on the periodical rhythms of a temporally unfolding distribution process, serial productions had to find ways to deal with the dynamics of remembering and forgetting (Engell 2010)—for example, by reminding the reader or viewer what had happened in previous installments or episodes. In contrast, however, digital networks such as the Internet tend not to forget. The developmental logic and historicity of serial installments is therefore constituted differently in a digital media environment, and the temporality of serial forms is open to new forms of experience.

(b) The serial aesthetics of digital games. It is against this background that we approach the aesthetic forms and cultural practices of seriality in digital games. Game studies provides an essential context for coming to terms with these phenomena, but research in the field has seldom dealt with seriality per se. Interestingly, however, game studies' formative debate over "narratological" and "ludological" approaches to digital gaming already touches upon issues that are important for an understanding of digital seriality—especially as regards the temporal impact of digital technologies on serially unfolding stories. Thus, while the generally formalistic parameters of the ludology-vs.-narratology debate are now widely disparaged, we believe that essential insights into the dialectics of digital seriality—that is, the dialectics of a specifically *digital* form of popular *seriality* in general—are to be gained from revisiting this episode in the history of game studies.

Narratologically oriented theorists like Janet Murray (1997) argue that with the introduction of interactivity, digital platforms generally and computer games in particular have significantly and lastingly changed the parameters of storytelling. But against narratologists' implicit claim that the telling of stories is one of the central functions of digital games, the ludologists (e.g., Juul 2001) argue that narrative elements are only marginal or secondary with respect to the primary "core" of gameplay, which involves the player in negotiations not with stories but with formal rule sets. Juul attributes the conflict between properly ludic and narrative elements to the media specificity of interactive games, which hold out spaces for action, movement, and decision rather than linear narration. Espen Aarseth (1999) describes these spaces in terms of "ergodic phenomena"; the concept of ergodicity describes digital games, in contrast to other textual forms, as types of a discourse "whose signs emerge as a path produced by a non-trivial element of work" (32). Thus, a game's narrative "script" is not preexistent, not just "there" for us to read like a novel, but it is instead generated at the moment of interaction, on the fly and in response to a recipient's input. As Juul (2001) argues, this implies a fundamental paradox with regard to the temporal levels distinguished by narratologists for traditional forms of storytelling: because of their ergodic form, digital games collapse the otherwise distinct levels of "story time," "plot time," and the time of actual media consumption. While classical narratology explored the gaps between these levels as essential to the phenomenon of narrativity (Genette 1994), Juul's early ludology is built on the premise of their indistinguishability in digital games.

This debate raises a number of interesting questions with respect to seriality. Are games able to complement and continue the serialized narratives articulated in transmedial assemblages? Or is the connection purely superficial, a marketing practice that exploits the contents of serial narratives as mere "packaging" (Juul 2001) for games? On an aesthetic level, it is necessary to approach these questions by way of the two previously sketched revisions of temporal structures in digital media, namely, the "synchronization" processes implied by digital media convergence on the one hand and the "collapsed" ergodic-interactive temporality of digital games on the other. The few existing studies of temporal structures in digital games generally either restrict themselves to proposing formalistic models or concentrate exclusively on the emotional and cognitive involvement of the player. A more historically attuned engagement with phenomena of temporality in digital games is largely lacking, as is the connection to larger discussions of digital media and time—or the nexus of temporality and seriality. This latter nexus in particular is overlooked in ludological characterizations of gameplay because proponents of this position generally focus more on the integral "flow" of present events in a continually updated "now" of ergodic play than on its segmentation into discrete gaming sessions. However, the relation between the game-immanent continuity of temporal experience and the empirically discontinuous sessions out of which it emerges would seem to be homologous to the relation between the diegetic continuity and discontinuous reception of episodes that we find in serialized literary, filmic, or televisual productions (O'Sullivan 2010). And just as serial forms more generally continue to thrive in today's popular culture—*despite* contemporary synchronization processes that work to "bundle" series into units (like DVD boxes) and to make their installments co-present in digital networks—so too do digital games continue to articulate a form of seriality that arises *despite* the collapse of temporal levels in the real-time interaction of gameplay. As a result, we believe that a successful theoretical account of seriality in digital games will be neither strictly narratological (because insufficiently sensitive to the temporal transformations introduced in ergodic interactivity) nor narrowly ludological (because unable to see beyond these transformations toward the persistence of serial segmentation). Instead, an adequate theory of digital seriality will adapt elements of both approaches in an effort to account for continuity and discontinuity, medial specificity and serial commonalities.

The relations between serial continuity and discontinuity that arise in interactive games correlate in various ways with the interplay of repetition and variation that might be seen to constitute the structural core of serial narration. The precise nature of these correlations remains to be determined, but they suggest the possibility of bridging the gaps between various media, between ludic and narrative forms, and between the specific case of digital games and the broader phenomenon of popular seriality in the digital age. Accordingly, we need a comparative methodology that will make these gaps visible. In order to understand how players are integrated *serially* into the diegetic world of a game or installments of a game series, we will have to revise and expand notions of immersion, identification, and participation by putting them in contact with recent studies of film, television, and literature conducted from within a more decidedly seriality-oriented research paradigm (Kelleter 2012). In this context, one of our particular interests is to understand the affective and phenomenological dimensions of such serialized engagement, and so it will be important to compare the findings of other affect-oriented studies of digital media environments (e.g., Hansen 2004); we believe that the latter, in turn, will profit from a careful consideration of seriality's functions in these environments. We begin to sketch these intermedial relations and consider their implications for a theory of digital seriality in the second half of this chapter.

(c) **The cultural practice of digital seriality.** Games and play have long been the subject of cultural anthropological investigation, and these approaches, familiar in the field of game studies, have been adapted to some extent for digital games (e.g., Wolf/Perron 2003). However, the largely formalistic reception of these works in game studies has compounded the field's blindness to seriality. Play itself, we must recall, is an essentially serial activity, characterized by ritualistic practices of repetition and variation (Schechner/Schuman 1976). This is true of the rule-governed actions executed inside the "magic circle" of gameplay (Huizinga 1955), but it also points us beyond that circle and reminds us that any such realm of immersion has its own cultural history, one in which the rules of play have been practiced before they could be tacitly assumed as the invisible background for action. The erection of a magic circle, in other words, is never so magical as to be completely integral and self-sufficient, for it always also represents a single episode in an ongoing series. Indeed, it is precisely the circle's serial iterability, its reproducibility as a realm of cultural practice that guarantees the magical integrity it seems to have when we are immersed in it.

For this reason, it is necessary to complement formalistic approaches to the serial aesthetics of digital games with another perspective, one that will highlight the cultural histories and practices of digital seriality. How do gamers interact with game series, and how do gaming cultures arise from collective serialized activities and discourses? There are many ways in which to approach these questions, including direct empirical observation or by way of discourse-analytical (Foucault 1972) and media-archaeological methods (Parikka 2012), as well as through the lenses of cultural studies and culturally oriented media studies. The goal, in any case, would be to move beyond text-based approaches, not merely to contextualize them, but to understand how games and game series are implemented in social contexts and how these contexts (gaming cultures, etc.) are themselves shaped by and around the serialized activity of digital gameplay.

Existing studies of race, ethnicity, or gender in games, game series, and gaming communities (e.g., Poor 2012) offer a good starting point, but they too have generally failed to account for aspects of seriality. How have such identifications and representations been imbricated into the serialized practices and discourses of a community? Under the heading of "imagined community," Benedict Anderson (1991) has theorized the collective and identity-forming functions of serialized media consumption in the predigital age, arguing that the seriality of newspapers and later photography were instrumental in instilling pre-twentieth-century notions of "national identity" (Kelleter 2014b and Mayer 2014). But if studies of game series and their characters (Lara Croft, Mario, etc.) generally focus on audiovisual developments within a series at the expense of social-contextual serial practices, studies of digital communities generally fail to correlate such practices sufficiently with the content-level serialities of serialized media. What is called for is a perspective that would encompass and correlate both of these aspects within a larger framework of popular seriality, relating one to another the iterative deployment of digital games and platforms, the formal qualities of their serialized contents, the practical serialization of individual and collective gameplay, and the serially ongoing negotiations of community that take place upon that basis. Such a perspective on the cultural practices and serial aesthetics of digital gameplay would allow for a critical reemployment of the parameters of "imagined" community-building in the age of digital synchronicity, while the significance of digital-era transformations would be discernible through a comparative recontextualization vis-à-vis the larger history of popular seriality. To understand the role that ludic serialities play in the construction of (trans)national and (sub)cultural identities today, we must place digital games within the longer history of serialized popular culture, which has played a central role in the commercialized lifeworlds originating in Europe and North America since the nineteenth century and has been embodied in a variety of media (Denson/ Mayer 2012a and Kelleter/Stein 2012).

Henry Jenkins's (2006) observations on transmedial seriality as an aspect of cultures of convergence offer one important point of reference for a comparative and historicizing investigation of digital seriality. Of particular relevance in this context is his discussion of the role of digital games within the transmedia franchise *The Matrix* (2006: 93–130). In looking at such examples, we will have to consider the transmedial roles of games and game series from a historical, social, and medial and material point of view. Especially useful for developing such a perspective are those moments when an established (predigital) serial figure—like Batman—is taken up and redeployed in a game-based serialization. Appearing as the protagonist in over twenty games for various platforms since 1986, Batman has undergone repeated revisions and modifications in appearance, ability, narrative/thematic framing, and interface potential with gamers. Such transitional phenomena between predigital and digital serial forms seem particularly significant for a cultural-historical perspective on digital seriality: already in a predigital media ecology, a plurimedial figure like Batman tends to react to media changes in a highly self-reflexive manner, hence highlighting its own conditions of mediation (Denson/Mayer 2012b and Stein 2012). In comics, television, film, and now digital games, Batman operates sophisticated technical media (e.g., the "Batcomputer") and reacts to threats mediated to him via televisual or digital media channels. Media, in other words, are an important focus of narrative conflicts, and computational media are especially central to Batman's role as a high-tech crime-fighter. Such a figure therefore provides an important index of both the continuities and the discontinuities between a specifically digital seriality and serial practices of the predigital era. Placed in the context of its reception, the figure promises to deliver richly detailed snapshots of our serial-media culture in transition. From this perspective, the recent series of *Arkham* video games may be queried for what they tell us not only about the serial figure Batman but about our own changing relations to a computational media environment.

As we come to embody the avatar of the caped crusader in these games, we operate his sophisticated diegetic machinery through the physical manipulation of our own computational devices (gamepads and other controllers). It is precisely here, in this convergence of physical and imaginary embodiments of technology, that we may seek the broadly ideological contours of our evolving relations to the digital.

Finally, what this example points to is the way that concrete serial practices, spanning the fields of production and reception, might be approached via the perspective of actor-network theory (ANT), as it has emerged in the writings of Bruno Latour and others, in order to better understand the cultural work of digital games and game series. While several ANT-oriented studies of videogames have appeared in recent years (e.g., Giddings 2007), the main focus has been limited to the interactions between individual players and the apparatuses of digital gaming platforms. Nor has seriality played a role in these investigations, although an ANT perspective is well suited to illuminate the complex articulations of seriality and collectivity that we have here been considering (Kelleter 2014a). With respect to series-oriented actions (i.e., actions related to or constitutive of series, as well as serially executed actions) within the commercial, technological, aesthetic, and social networks surrounding digital games, ANT's methodological focus on the concrete mediations of agency in assemblages that are "simultaneously real, discursive, and social" (Latour 1993: 64) offers a way to think about how games that are *textually* situated in the above-mentioned transmedial contexts can also mark, in terms of *cultural practice,* a "before," an "after," or a "meanwhile" with respect to other popular-cultural (media) practices and thus serve as nodes for networking and community-building processes.

LUDIC SERIALITIES

Having explored a number of contexts within which to study digital seriality, we turn now to the task of bringing these perspectives together in order to outline a program for a more detailed examination of the various levels of seriality informing digital games, game series, and gaming cultures. We distinguish three categories or levels of digital seriality that are pertinent in the context of digital games:

- *intra-ludic seriality,* which manifests itself *within* games (paradigmatic for this level are the structures of repetition and variation that characterize the various "levels" or "worlds" of a game);

- *inter-ludic seriality,* which emerges *between* games (paradigmatic for this level are the explicit continuations of games—sequels, prequels, and so on—that identify game series as such); and
- *para-ludic seriality,* which is constituted *outside* of the actual games (paradigmatic for this level are the transmedial narrativizations of game scenarios, for example, adaptations on film, television, or other media, often in connection with the merchandising of iconic game-related figures and/or the social practices of fan communities).

On the basis of these distinctions, we propose looking at serialization processes in digital games and gaming cultures from two distinct perspectives:

- From the perspective of a philosophically informed *media aesthetics*: An affective-phenomenological approach addresses, primarily, the significance of intra- and inter-ludic serialities that inform gameplay. Of particular interest here is the serialized negotiation and aesthetic mediation of the difference between human temporal experience and the nonhuman temporalities of digital media. The aim of this perspective is to deliver qualitative descriptions of the processes of temporal-serial experience that transpire at the interface between humans and digital technologies. The focus thus lies on what we call the phenomenon of *serial interfacing* between games and gamers.
- From the perspective of *media history/cultural history*: This sociocultural and media-ecological perspective aims to illuminate the serial practices of digital games, especially at the inter- and para-ludic levels, in the context of collective negotiations of community and of the broader sociopolitical imagination (e.g., categories of identity and difference such as nationality, gender, race, etc., as they are reinforced or opened to question through serialized gameplay and related practices of gaming communities). This analytical mode seeks to locate the practices and experiences of play in their concrete historical settings. The focus here lies on what we term phenomena of *collective serialization,* that is, processes of community formation in connection with the consumption of serialized media.

We position these two modes of approach against the background of the media-historical transformations taking place with the emergence of a digital-media ecology. These processes of change, according to our central hypothesis, are registered in the practices and experiences of the serial-temporal structures of digital gameplay. Of decisive importance for this hypothesis are

(1) a homology between the temporal "collapse" of real-time interaction in digital games and the "synchronization" processes that form an aspect of digital culture more generally, and (2) the integration of serial games and game series in the fabric of our contemporary convergence culture, where they serve important functions with regard to the changing parameters of digital-era community. On the basis of these two central relations between the serial structures of digital games and the larger ecology of our digital media environment, our complementary media-aesthetic and cultural-historical perspectives work together to illuminate not only the forms and processes of seriality in digital games but also the changing contexts and conditions of popular seriality in the twenty-first century—and with them the very conditions of practice in our increasingly digitally mediated lifeworlds.

The common ground for the two analytical perspectives is located in the forms and practices of serialization that emerge on the inter-ludic level, generating explicitly marked game series. Of the three levels of ludic seriality sketched above, it is certainly this inter-ludic form that most closely resembles the dominant types of popular series of the past two centuries (as in the ongoing tales of serialized novels, film and television serials, etc.). For example, by numerating their installments or otherwise signaling continuation among serial parts, videogame series highlight their sequential structures and present themselves on a narrative level as the continuing unfolding of a previously established storyworld. These series can therefore be analyzed with the help of categories developed in the growing body of research on other forms of seriality, for example, notions of "operational aesthetics" (Mittell 2006) or "serial outbidding" (Jahn-Sudmann/Kelleter 2012). More significantly, though, the comparison with other forms of seriality allows for the identification of specific *differences* that arise between digital and predigital serialities, thus pointing to the ongoing emergence of new forms of popular culture manifesting themselves in digital games and the practical contexts of gamers' serial activities. Branching out from the common denominator of inter-ludic seriality toward the intra- and para-ludic serialities of digital games and gaming cultures, a media-aesthetic focus on "serial interfacing" and a media-historical focus on "collective serialization" work to reveal these differences from two complementary perspectives, as illustrated in table 14.1.

(a) **Serial interfacing.** Early "ludological" positions offer a first glimpse of such differences. Unlike in film and television, framing stories in game series often turn out to be marginal in comparison to the serializing effects of players' engagement with games and their procedural logics. For example, the patterns of repetition and variation that organize gamers' interactions with hardware and software across the various levels of *Super Mario Bros.* (the eight "worlds,"

TABLE 14.1

	INTRA-LUDIC SERIALITY	INTER-LUDIC SERIALITY	PARA-LUDIC SERIALITY
Serial Interfacing (media-philosophical / media-aesthetic perspective)	X	X	
Collective Serialization (media-historical / cultural-historical perspective)		X	X

each subdivided into four "stages") are more significant from an intra-ludic point of view than the rudimentary narrative that is related over the course of the game: in order to rescue the kidnapped princess, our protagonist runs and jumps his way through the Mushroom Kingdom, fighting countless enemies—who have various abilities but absolutely no depth of character—along the way. Repeatedly, this culminates in a boss battle in the castle at the end of each "world." And repeatedly, Mario finds there a princess, but unfortunately—with the exception of the final castle—it is always the *wrong* princess, so he has to set out once more. This repetitive story is varied somewhat over the course of Mario's inter-ludic serialization, but from an intra-ludic perspective the narrative content remains clearly subordinate to the interactive gameplay that it frames. This hierarchy, which marks a significant difference from many predigital serial forms, accentuates an important aspect of digital media generally: their open processuality, which problematizes the discrete temporal dimensions of narration. The framing story about Mario's quest is static and predictable, but its instantiation in a concrete game session is subject to all sorts of eventualities because the player directly controls Mario and acts in real time. The comparison between digital inter-ludic and predigital narrative serialities must therefore be supplemented with a media-phenomenological investigation of serial interfacing in order for us to come to terms with the changed material and affective basis of digital seriality.

The significance, in this respect, of serial interfacing can be gleaned from the example of the so-called bullet time employed in games like *Enter the Matrix* or the *Max Payne* series. As an aesthetic operation in which an impossibly fast-moving (virtual) camera dolly revolves around actors and objects as they move in extreme slow-motion, bullet time was made famous, above all, through its use in the first installment of the popular *Matrix* film trilogy. On the basis of its spectacular and innovative character, the effect itself soon underwent a form of serial continuation and dissemination across a variety of media, not least of which was the videogame tie-ins to the transmedial universe of *The Matrix,* as well as narratively unrelated games and game series such as *Max Payne.*

In terms of visual execution, the bullet time of games like *Max Payne* or *Enter the Matrix* might not be able to compete with its spectacular staging as a special effect in the Wachowskis' films; in games, this quality of a spectacle is still there, but it is subordinated in some respects to the effect's foregrounded ludic functionality: bullet time is there to help the player master in-game events by slowing down the opponents'—and his or her own—movements, while the technical polling of input devices continues to take place in real time. With respect to the affective dimension of the gamer's experience, however, bullet time qua gameplay mode has consequences that are not altogether different from those of bullet time qua cinematic spectacle. Byron Hawk (2007) has argued that bullet time in the *Matrix* films corresponds to the "virtual" as described by Brian Massumi (2002): it depicts something that happens so fast that the human brain is incapable of perceiving it—"something that happens too quickly to have happened, actually" (30). Bullet time, as it is employed both in film and in digital games, makes visible the duration of what is not actually perceptible—what we could call, with Bergson (1911), the "rhythm of duration" itself or, with Deleuze (1989), the ineffable "interval" that gives rise to the revolutionary effect of the "time-image" in post–World War II cinema (Hawk 2007). In digital games, bullet time furthermore stands out for the way it aesthetically exposes or "mediates" *algorithmic time*—that is, it makes experientable exactly that level of digital microtemporality that a player does not and cannot perceive, especially when he or she is wrapped up affectively and responding quasi-automatically to the constant flow of challenges that the game presents. Against this blindness to computational temporality, bullet-time sequences put the player in a position to experience an otherwise unheard-of level of control over space via the manipulation of time, so that an algorithmically generated time is rendered—paradoxically—as a *haptically experientiable duration.* This transduction produces not so much a substantial as a relational duration, that is, a duration that *marks the difference between the time of conscious experience and the imperceptible time of microtemporal computation processes* taking place during each and every gameplay event.

And because bullet time is serially organized on the intra-ludic level— because, in other words, the effect is progressively but intermittently (i.e., with gaps between discrete episodes) reactivated, and not simply repeated but varied in a range of forms—the phenomenological implications sketched above are compounded over time: the perception of an otherwise invisible time of algorithmic computation, as mediated by digital games employing the bullet-time effect, is strengthened through repeated exposure. Over the course of these incidents, the bullet-time experience takes on the quality of an experimental configuration, a setting in which one can probe, aesthetically and ludically, the temporal parameters of a new form of "anthropotechnical interface" (Denson 2014). Moreover, the bullet time of digital games is serially organized not merely in the sense of being continually repeatable within a particular game; rather, the effect gains partial autonomy and becomes visible as part of a larger series of similar processes precisely when it is activated outside of an immediate gameplay challenge, that is, apart from the diegetic and functional motivation of the effect within the game. (For example, the bullet-time perspective may be activated in an empty hallway, where no opponent is threatening the player and where there is accordingly "no good reason" to employ the technique—except for the perhaps unconscious purpose of probing the temporal dimensions of interfacing with the computer.) From an inter-ludic perspective as well, it is precisely with respect to such moments of "gratuitous" experimentation that the aesthetic differences between implementations of bullet time—in different games and over the course of ongoing game series, as well as in various media and transmedial assemblages—become most clearly visible and open to critical scrutiny. Here we witness a culture testing, by means of its popular media, the aesthetic bounds and trajectories of its transition to a computational environment. It is therefore not without significance that we find, finally—at the level of para-ludic seriality—countless examples attesting to the "serial autonomy" of bullet time in contemporary social-network-driven online spaces, for instance, in the compilations of especially spectacular instances of the effect that gamers have uploaded to YouTube, thus making their individual experiences of serialized temporal-technical mediation available for comment, comparison, and community-building.

(b) **Collective serialization.** User-generated videos and related para-ludic practices lead us to the level of collective serialization, where materially "individual experiences" are subject to reproduction, collocation, and interchange. In short, experiences that were uniquely "mine" become open, at this level, to appropriation by "you," and they form a potential basis for the recognition and negotiation of "our" shared experience. Here, the individual turns collective, as the unique goes serial in digital environments. From a comparative cultural and media-historical perspective, Anderson's notion of "imagined community" facilitates a focus on these sociocultural dealings with intra- and inter-ludic serialities, including their tendency to generate para-ludic discourses and material practices of all sorts. But again we find differences that are owing to the specificities of digital seriality. To begin with, the expansive transmedia franchises into which games and game series are often integrated exhibit a level of narrative, material, and operational totality (Harrigan/ Wardrip-Fruin 2009) that is virtually unheard of in predigital forms of seriality. More significantly, though, digital "world-building" (Jenkins 2006: 114) gives rise to structures and formats of community-formation that presuppose a new flexibility in the temporal organization of serial consumption, which is now susceptible to nonlinear sequences and arbitrary rhythms.

It is precisely in this connection that the processual openness of games is significant, for the real-time interactivity of digital games puts the teleological "directedness" of narratives partly out of play and places gamers in the role of actors whose own subjectivities are open to negotiation and revision. This has consequences on the para-ludic level of imagined communities because not only diegetic identities (imagined identifications with fictional avatars) but also players' real-world social self-descriptions in terms of nation, class, gender, and so on—or simply their imagined inclusion in the class of gamers—are activated in serialized gameplay, reinforced through serial repetition or opened up to revision. Anderson has shown how the serialization of media like the daily newspaper was involved in the production of collectives— or "serialities" (Anderson 1991)—such as the nation. Setting out from the practices accompanying long-running inter-ludic series, we can now ask about the implications of serialized gameplay's negotiable agencies and identities for the social world of lived differences and hierarchies under digital conditions.

To approach such questions, we must attend to the complex imbrication of para- and intra-ludic serialities. As in the case of bullet time, which links aesthetic experiments to the serial proliferation of YouTube videos documenting those experiments, the prima facie isolated activities of individual gamers necessarily raise broader questions of community. Conversely, collective negotiations of gaming communities are inseparable from low-level interfaces with computational technologies and the temporalities they embody; the seriality of collective serialization is itself a temporal experimentation, one that concerns the larger temporalities of historical becoming in relation to their transformation at the molecular level of digital computation. In short, processes of collective serialization are intimately tied to the same basic transformations that are at stake in practices of serial interfacing, which we described earlier as mediating "the difference between human temporal experience and the nonhuman temporalities of digital media." Hence, with respect to gameplay's cultural and thematic framings, it is no surprise that space-age scenarios have occupied a central place in computer games from the start; sci-fi visions of the future offer one means of imaginative engagement with the historical estrangement of our sensorial capacities from the computerized processes and "alien" (i.e., nonhuman) temporalities that increasingly structure our environments. Moreover, these technology-centric scenarios foreground an operational aesthetic according to which early gamers (often computer scientists or programmers) could imagine themselves operating machinery from the future or from an advanced civilization. But whereas the relatively recent example of bullet time emphasizes the incredible speed of our contemporary technical infrastructure, which threatens at every moment to outstrip our phenomenal capacities, earlier examples often mediated something of an inverse experience: a mismatch between the futurist fantasy and the much slower pace necessitated by the technomaterial realities of the day.

The example of *Super Star Trek* (1978) illuminates this inverse sort of experience and casts a media-archaeological light on collective serialization by way of the early history of gaming communities and their initially halting articulation into prototransmedia worlds. A quick look at the game's source code (figure 14.1) is revealing. Here, the opening comment lines ("REM" indicates a nonexecutable "remark" in BASIC) mention not only the "Star Trek TV show" as an influence but also a serial trajectory of inter-ludic programming, modification, debugging, and conversion that begins to outline a serialized collectivity of sorts. Beyond those mentioned by name (Mike Mayfield, David Ahl, etc.), a diffuse community is invoked and, in fact, solicited: "comments, epithets, and suggestions" are to be sent personally to R. C. Leedom at Westinghouse Defense & Electronics. Reminiscent of a comic-book series' "letters to the editor" page (Kelleter/Stein 2012), this invitation promises, in conjunction with the listing of the game's serial lineage, that readers' opinions are valued and that significant contributions will be rewarded (or honored with a hat tip in the REMs). In these few preliminary lines, the program demonstrates its common ground with serialized production forms across media: since the nineteenth century, readers have written to the authors of ongoing series in order to influence the course of serial unfolding; authors dependent on the demands of a commercial marketplace were not at liberty simply to disregard their audience's wishes. From an actor-network perspective, popular series therefore operate to create feedback loops in which authors and readers alike are involved in the production of serial forms—which therefore organize themselves as self-observing systems around which serialized forms of (para-)social interaction coalesce (Kelleter 2014a).

The snippet of code below thus attests to the aspirations of a germinal community of hackers and gamers, which has tellingly chosen to align itself with one of the most significant and quickly growing popular-culture fan communities of the time: the Trekkie subculture, which can be seen to constitute a paradigmatic "seriality" in Anderson's sense—a nationlike collective (complete

Program Listing - The Game

```
10  REM SUPER STARTREK - MAY 16,1978 - REQUIRES 24K MEMORY
30  REM
40  REM ****             **** STAR TREK ****           ****
50  REM **** SIMULATION OF A MISSION OF THE STARSHIP ENTERPRISE,
60  REM **** AS SEEN ON THE STAR TREK TV SHOW.
70  REM **** ORIGIONAL PROGRAM BY MIKE MAYFIELD, MODIFIED VERSION
80  REM **** PUBLISHED IN DEC'S "101 BASIC GAMES", BY DAVE AHL.
90  REM **** MODIFICATIONS TO THE LATTER (PLUS DEBUGGING) BY BOB
100 REM *** LEEDOM - APRIL & DECEMBER 1974,
110 REM *** WITH A LITTLE HELP FROM HIS FRIENDS . . .
120 REM *** COMMENTS, EPITHETS, AND SUGGESTIONS SOLICITED --
130 REM *** SEND TO:   R. C. LEEDOM
140 REM ***            WESTINGHOUSE DEFENSE & ELECTRONICS SYSTEMS CNTR.
150 REM ***            BOX 746, M.S. 338
160 REM ***            BALTIMORE, MD  21203
170 REM ***
180 REM *** CONVERTED TO MICROSOFT 8 K BASIC 3/16/78 BY JOHN BORDERS
190 REM *** LINE NUMBERS FROM VERSION STREK7 OF 1/12/75 PRESERVED AS
200 REM *** MUCH AS POSSIBLE WHILE USING MULTIPLE STATEMENTS PER LINE
205 REM *** SOME LINES ARE LONGER THAN 72 CHARACTERS; THIS WAS DONE
210 REM *** BY USING "?" INSTEAD OF "PRINT" WHEN ENTERING LINES
215 REM ***
220 PRINT:PRINT:PRINT:PRINT:PRINT:PRINT:PRINT:PRINT:PRINT:PRINT:PRINT
221 PRINT"                            ,------*------,"
222 PRINT"                    ,------------- '---  ------'"
223 PRINT"                    '---------- --'         / /"
224 PRINT"            ,---' '--------/ /---,"
225 PRINT"                    '------------------'":PRINT
226 PRINT"                 THE USS ENTERPRISE --- NCC-1701"
227 PRINT:PRINT:PRINT:PRINT:PRINT
260 CLEAR 600
270 Z5=""
330 DIM G(8,8),C(9,2),K(3,3),N(3),Z(8,8),D(8)
370 T=INT(RND(1)*20+20)*100:T0=T:T9=25+INT(RND(1)*10):D0=0:E=3000:E0=E
440 P=10:P0=P:S9=200:S=0:B9=0:X5="":X0S=" IS "
470 DEF FND(D)=SQR((K(I,1)-S1)↑2+(K(I,2)-S2)↑2)
475 DEF FNR(R)=INT(RND(R)*7.98+1.01)
480 REM INITIALIZE ENTERPRIZE'S POSITION
```

FIGURE 14.1. Source code: *Super Star Trek* (Ahl/Leedom, 1978).

with its own language) organized around the serialized consumption of serially structured media. Operating in parallel to that community, early gamers serialized code as their organizing medium, but they circulated it in a crude, paperbound form that was in many ways out of step with the space-age fantasy embodied in *Super Star Trek*. In order to play the game, one had to go through the painstaking (and mistake-prone) process of keying in the code by hand. If, afterwards, the program failed to run, the user would have to search for a misspelled command, a missing line, or some other bug in the system. And God forbid there was an error in the listing from which one was copying! Moreover, early versions of the game were designed for mainframe and minicomputers that, in many cases, were lacking a video terminal. The process of programming the game—or playing it, for that matter—was thus a slow process made even slower by interactions with punch-card interfaces. How, under these conditions, could one imagine oneself at the helm of the *USS Enterprise*? There was a mismatch, in other words, between the fantasy and the reality of early 1970s-era computing. But this discrepancy, with its own temporal and affective dynamics, was a framing condition for a form of collective serialization organized along very different lines from contemporary dreams of games' seamless integration into transmedia worlds.

To begin with, it is quite significant that *Super Star Trek*'s functional equivalent of the "letters to the editor" page, where the ongoing serialization of the game is both documented and continued, is not printed in an instruction manual or other accompanying paraphernalia but embedded in the code itself. In contrast to the mostly invisible code executed in mainstream games today, *Super Star Trek*'s code was regarded as highly visible, the place where early gamers were most likely to read the solicitation to participate in a collective effort of development. Clearly, the reason is that they would have to read (and rewrite) the code if they wished to play the game—while their success in actually getting it to work was more doubtful. Gameplay is here subordinated to coding, while the pleasures of both were those of an operational aesthetic: whether coding the game or playing it, mastery and control over the machine were at stake. Unlike the bullet time of *The Matrix* or *Max Payne*, which responds to an environment in which gamers (and others) are hard-pressed to keep up with the speed of computation, *Super Star Trek* speaks to a somewhat quainter, more humanistic dream of getting a computational (or intergalactic) jalopy up and running in the first place. In terms of temporal affectivities, patience is tested more so than quick reactions. If bullet time slowed down screen events while continuing to poll input devices as a means for players to cope with high-velocity challenges, the tasks of coding and playing *Super Star Trek* turn this situation around: it is not the computer but the human user who waits for—hopes for—a response. As a corollary, however, relatively quick progress was observable in the game's inter-ludic development, which responded to rapid innovations in hardware and programming languages. This fact, which corresponded well with the basically humanistic optimism of the Star Trek fantasy (as opposed to the basically inhuman scenario of *The Matrix*), motivated further involvement in the series of inter-ludic developments (programming, modification, debugging, conversion, etc.), which necessarily involved coders/tinkerers in the para-ludic exchanges upon which a gaming community was being built.

Interestingly, in this case, the primary interfacing activities, revolving around coding as an act of "serial interfacing" in the sense outlined above, were themselves strictly para-ludic (rather than intra-ludic)—but this distinction seems to blur in the context of *Super Star Trek*'s inter-ludic career, which tellingly mediates low-level interfacing and high-level community-building as equally directed at the serialized task of building a better machine.

In contemporary gaming cultures, the latter task has since given way, for the most part, to professional game developers. Mainstream games still employ operational configurations for players to manipulate, but they tend to contain such elements within the diegetic fantasy world of the game—they certainly do not expect players to get their hands dirty with coding. What the example of *Super Star Trek* reminds us, however, is that even in the apparently more integral and contained spaces of contemporary gaming, there is still a deep realm of serial practice and collective seriality at stake in gameplay. The "magic circle" that gets ever more magically sealed off as the infrastructure of code is pushed out of view has a rich and deep history of material exchanges, inter-ludic genealogies, and para-ludic activities.

TO BE CONTINUED . . .

The study of digital seriality has just begun. The ideas presented here are designed to outline possible research perspectives and to offer preliminary theoretical distinctions that suggest themselves when we turn our attention to the seriality of digital games. We find it hardly necessary, however, to emphasize the cultural relevance of a seriality-oriented approach in connection with the digital or the medium of the computer game. The notorious efforts to habilitate popular culture as a worthy object of academic study have rarely been very productive anyway. The field of game studies may well have understood this fact more quickly than television studies. Nevertheless, in memoriam of a controversy that maybe never took place (or just possibly never should have taken place), perhaps we will be excused if we repeat, in this context, a line of argumentation that we seem to have heard somewhere before: a focus on seriality does not imply that the media specificities of the digital game should be ignored or that we can simply apply approaches from television studies or popular culture studies, without modification, to digital games and game series. On the contrary, we are calling for a serious consideration of both the specificities of game-based serialities *and* the common ground they share with other media-cultural practices and aesthetic forms. Our model of a media-philosophical, media-archaeological, and cultural-theoretical approach to serial interfacing and collective serialization does justice, we believe, to this basic idea that continuity and change are not essentially opposed but capable of complex interrelation. We have sought here to remain true to this thought both on an epistemic and on a quasi-ontological level. To reassert at the end of this volume a theme from its first chapter: What is a series, after all, if not the continuing production of the same in the guise of the new or, conversely, the constant production of the new in the guise of the same? The series has recently been called—and rightly so, we believe—the central "mark of modernity" (Beil et al. 2012). Thus, in the context of digital games as well, we should reappraise the significance of serial processes; we should regard them as nothing less than the media of an experimental aesthetics of modern life, at least to the extent that they offer a playful mode of access to the vicissitudes of the modern lifeworld—even, and perhaps especially, where the media-aesthetic processes of the digital elude our conscious experience.

BIBLIOGRAPHY

Aarseth, Espen (1999). "Aporia and Epiphany in *Doom* and *The Speaking Clock*: The Temporality of Ergodic Art." *Cyberspace Textuality: Computer Technology and Literary Theory*. Ed. Marie-Laure Ryan. Bloomington: Indiana University Press. 31–41.

Anderson, Benedict (1991). *Imagined Communities: Reflections on the Origin and Spread of Nationalism* [1983]. London: Verso.

Beil, Benjamin, Lorenz Engell, Jens Schröter, Herbert Schwaab, and Daniela Wentz (2012). "Die Serie. Einleitung in den Schwerpunkt." *Zeitschrift für Medienwissenschaft* 7.2: 10–16.

Bergson, Henri (1911). *Creative Evolution* [1907]. London: Macmillan.

Bolter, Jay David and Richard Grusin (1999). *Remediation: Understanding New Media*. Cambridge: MIT.

Deleuze, Gilles (1989). *Cinema 2: The Time-Image* [1985]. Minnesota: University of Minnesota Press.

Denson, Shane (2014). *Postnaturalism: Frankenstein, Film, and the Anthropotechnical Interface*. Bielefeld: Transcript-Verlag.

Denson, Shane and Ruth Mayer (2012a). "Grenzgänger: Serielle Figuren im Medienwechsel." *Populäre Serialität: Narration—Evolution—Distinktion. Zum seriellen Erzählen seit dem 19. Jahrhundert*. Ed. Frank Kelleter. Bielefeld: Transcript-Verlag. 185–203.

———(2012b). "Bildstörung: Serielle Figuren und der Fernseher." *Zeitschrift für Medienwissenschaft* 7.2: 90–102.

Engell, Lorenz (2010). "Erinnern/Vergessen: Serien als operatives Gedächtnis des Fernsehens." *Serielle Formen: Von den frühen Film-Serials zu aktuellen Quality-TV- und Online-Serien*. Ed. Robert Blanchet et al. Marburg: Schüren. 115–33.

Foucault, Michel (1972). *The Archaeology of Knowledge and the Discourse on Language*. New York: Pantheon.

Genette, Gérard (1994). *Die Erzählung*. München: Fink.

Giddings, Seth (2007). "Playing with Non-Humans: Digital Games as Technocultural Form." *Worlds in Play: International Perspectives on Digital Games Research*. Ed. Suzanne De Castell and Jennifer Jenson. New York: Lang. 115–28.

Hansen, Mark B. N. (2004). *New Philosophy for New Media*. Cambridge: MIT.

Harrigan, Pat and Noah Wardrip-Fruin, eds. (2009). *Third Person: Authoring and Exploring Vast Narratives*. Cambridge: MIT.

Hawk, Byron (2007). *A Counter-History of Composition: Toward Methodologies of Complexity*. Pittsburgh: University of Pittsburgh Press.

Huizinga, Johan (1955). *Homo Ludens: A Study of the Play Element in Culture* [1938]. Boston: Beacon.

Jahn-Sudmann, Andreas and Frank Kelleter (2012). "Die Dynamik serieller Überbietung: Zeitgenössische amerikanische Fernsehserien und das Konzept des Quality TV." *Populäre Serialität: Narration—Evolution—Distinktion. Zum seriellen Erzählen seit dem 19. Jahrhundert.* Ed. Frank Kelleter. Bielefeld: Transcript-Verlag. 205–24.

Jenkins, Henry (2006). *Convergence Culture: Where Old and New Media Collide.* New York: New York University Press.

Juul, Jesper (2001). "Games Telling Stories? A Brief Note on Games and Narratives." *Game Studies* 1.1. August 20, 2013. http://www.gamestudies.org/0101/juul-gts/.

Kelleter, Frank. (2012). "Populäre Serialität: Eine Einführung." *Populäre Serialität: Narration—Evolution—Distinktion. Zum seriellen Erzählen seit dem 19. Jahrhundert.* Ed. Frank Kelleter. Bielefeld: Transcript-Verlag. 11–46.

——(2014a). *Serial Agencies: "The Wire" and Its Readers.* Washington: Zero Books.

——(2014b). "Trust and Sprawl: Seriality, Radio, and the First Fireside Chat." *Media Economies: Perspectives on American Cultural Practices.* Ed. Marcel Hartwig, Evelyne Keitel, and Gunter Süß. Trier: wvt. 47–66.

Kelleter, Frank and Daniel Stein (2012). "Autorisierungspraktiken seriellen Erzählens: Zur Gattungsentwicklung von Superheldencomics." *Populäre Serialität: Narration—Evolution—Distinktion. Zum seriellen Erzählen seit dem 19. Jahrhundert.* Ed. Frank Kelleter. Bielefeld: Transcript-Verlag. 259–90.

Kittler, Friedrich (1986). *Grammophon Film Typewriter.* Berlin: Brinkmann & Bose.

Latour, Bruno (1993). *We Have Never Been Modern.* Cambridge, MA: Harvard University Press.

Manovich, Lev (2001). *The Language of New Media.* Cambridge: MIT.

Massumi, Brian (2002). *Parables for the Virtual: Movement, Affect, Sensation.* Durham: Duke University Press.

Mayer, Ruth (2014). *Serial Fu Manchu: Iconocity, Ideology, and the Logic of Global Spread.* Philadelphia: Temple University Press.

Mittell, Jason (2006). "Narrative Complexity in Contemporary American Television." *The Velvet Light Trap* 58: 29–40.

——(2011). "Serial Boxes: DVD-Editionen und der kulturelle Wert amerikanischer Fernsehserien." *Serielle Formen: Von den frühen Film-Serials zu aktuellen Quality-TV- und Online-Serien.* Ed. Robert Blanchet et al. Marburg: Schüren. 133–52.

Murray, Janet H. (1997). *Hamlet on the Holodeck: The Future of Narrative in Cyberspace.* Cambridge: MIT.

Mussell, James (2012). *The Nineteenth-Century Press in the Digital Age.* New York: Palgrave Macmillan.

O'Sullivan, Sean (2010). "Broken on Purpose: Poetry, Serial Television, and the Season." *StoryWorlds: A Journal of Narrative Studies* 2: 59–77.

Parikka, Jussi (2012). *What Is Media Archaeology?* Cambridge: Polity.

Poor, Nathaniel (2012). "Digital Elves as a Racial Other in Video Games: Acknowledgment and Avoidance." *Games and Culture* 7.5: 375–96.

Schechner, Richard and Mady Schuman, eds. (1976). *Ritual, Play, and Performance: Readings in the Social Sciences/Theatre.* New York: Seabury.

Stein, Daniel (2012). "Spoofin' Spidey—Rebooting the Bat: Immersive Story Worlds and the Narrative Complexities of Video Spoofs in the Era of the Superhero Blockbuster." *Film Remakes, Adaptations, and Fan Productions: Remake / Remodel.* Ed. Kathleen Loock and Constantine Verevis. Basingstoke: Palgrave Macmillan. 231–47.

Suominen, Jaakko (2008). "The Past as the Future? Nostalgia and Retrogaming in Digital Culture." *Fibreculture* 11. August 19, 2013. http://eleven.fibreculturejournal.org/fcj-075-the-past-as-the-future-nostalgia-and-retrogaming-in-digital-culture/.

Wolf, Mark J. P. and Bernard Perron, eds. (2003). *The Video Game Theory Reader.* London: Routledge.

CONTRIBUTORS

SUDEEP DASGUPTA is Associate Professor in the Department of Media & Culture, University of Amsterdam (Netherlands). He is the editor of *Constellations of the Transnational: Modernity, Culture, Critique* (2007) and coeditor of *What's Queer about Europe?* (2014). He has published in the fields of critical theory, aesthetics and visual culture, and postcolonial and queer theory.

SHANE DENSON is Assistant Professor of Film and Media Studies in the Department of Art & Art History at Stanford University. In the Popular Seriality Research Unit (PSRU), he collaborated with Ruth Mayer on the subproject "Serial Figures and Media Change" and codirected the subproject "Digital Seriality" with Andreas Sudmann. He is the author of *Postnaturalism: Frankenstein, Film, and the Anthropotechnical Interface* (2014) and coeditor of several collections, including *Post-Cinema: Theorizing 21st-Century Film* (with Julia Leyda 2016). He has published on transitional-era cinema, televangelism, comics and graphic narratives, and the philosophy of technology.

JARED GARDNER is Professor of English at The Ohio State University and director of the Popular Culture Studies program. He is the author of *The Rise and Fall of Early American Magazine Culture* (2012), *Projections: Comics and the History of 21st-Century Storytelling* (2012), and *Master Plots: Race and the Founding of an American Literature* (1998). He is coeditor of the book series Studies in Comics and Cartoons at The Ohio State University Press and editor of *Inks: The Journal of the Comics Studies Society*.

CHRISTINE HÄMMERLING is a Senior Teaching and Research Assistant at Zürich University (Switzerland). As Research Associate in the Popular Seriality Research Unit (PSRU), she worked with Regina Bendix at the University of Göttingen (Germany) on the subproject "Quotidian Integration and Social Positioning of Pulp Novels and Television Series." She is the author of *"Today is a Holiday": Freizeitbilder in der Fernsehwerbung* (2012) and *Sonntags 20:15 Uhr—"Tatort": Zu sozialen Positionierungen eines Fernsehpublikums* (2016).

SCOTT HIGGINS is chair of the Film Studies Department at Wesleyan University, where he teaches courses in film history, genre, and theory. His books include *Harnessing the*

Technicolor Rainbow: Color Design in the 1930s (2007), *Matinee Melodrama: The Art and Legacy of Sound Era Serials* (2015), and the edited volume *Arnheim for Film and Media Studies* (2011). He has published extensively on film color and is now researching and writing about 3-D cinema.

HENRY JENKINS is the Provost's Professor of Communication, Journalism, Cinematic Arts and Education at the University of Southern California. He arrived at USC in 2009 after spending a decade as the Director of the MIT Comparative Media Studies Program and the Peter de Florez Professor of Humanities. He is the author and/or editor of seventeen books on media and popular culture, including *Textual Poachers: Television Fans and Participatory Culture* (2004), *Convergence Culture: Where Old and New Media Collide* (2006), *Fans, Bloggers and Gamers: Exploring Participatory Culture* (2006), and *Spreadable Media: Creating Value and Meaning in a Networked Culture* (2013, with Sam Ford and Joshua Green).

FRANK KELLETER is chair of the Department of Culture and Einstein Professor of North American Cultural History at the John F. Kennedy Institute for North American Studies (Freie Universität Berlin). He is director of the Popular Seriality Research Unit (PSRU) and three of its subprojects. He is the author of *Die Moderne und der Tod* (1997), *Con/Tradition* (2000), *Amerikanische Aufklärung* (2002), *Serial Agencies: "The Wire" and Its Readers* (2014), and *David Bowie* (2016). He has published articles and coedited collections on early American culture, media history, and theories of the humanities.

KATHLEEN LOOCK is post-doctoral Research Associate in the Popular Seriality Research Unit (PSRU) at the John F. Kennedy Institute for North American Studies (Freie Universität Berlin), working with Frank Kelleter on the subproject "Retrospective Serialization." She is the author of *Kolumbus in den USA: Vom Nationalhelden zur ethnischen Identifikationsfigur* (2014), coeditor of *Film Remakes, Adaptations and Fan Productions: Remake/Remodel* (2012) and *Of Body Snatchers and Cyberpunks: Student Essays on American Science Fiction Film* (2011), and editor of a special issue on serial narratives for *LWU: Literatur in Wissenschaft und Unterricht* (2014). She is currently writing a cultural history of Hollywood remaking and coediting a special issue on film seriality for *Film Studies* journal (2017).

RUTH MAYER holds the chair of American Studies at Leibniz University Hannover (Germany) and is a member of the Popular Seriality Research Unit (PSRU), where she directed two subprojects. Her research focuses on modernity, serialization, and the practices and aesthetics of mass culture. Her books include *Artificial Africas: Colonial Images in the Times of Globalization* (2002) and *Serial Fu Manchu: The Chinese Super-Villain and the Spread of Yellow Peril Ideology* (2013).

CHRISTINA MEYER is Assistant Professor in American Studies and Research Associate in the English Department at Leibniz University Hannover (Germany). She is the author of *War & Trauma Images in Vietnam War Representations* (2008) and has published articles and coedited volumes on comic books and graphic narratives.

JASON MITTELL is Professor of American Studies and Film & Media Culture at Middlebury College. He is the author of *Genre and Television: From Cop Shows to Cartoons in American Culture* (2004), *Television and American Culture* (2009), *Complex TV: The Poetics of Contemporary Television Storytelling* (2015), and the blog *Just TV,* and coeditor of *How to Watch TV* (2013). For the 2011/12 academic year, he was a fellow-in-residence at Lichtenberg-Kolleg in Göttingen (Germany) and a fellow of the Popular Seriality Research Unit (PSRU) in Göttingen (2011/12) and Berlin (2014).

MIRJAM NAST is a Research Associate in the Popular Seriality Research Unit (PSRU) where she worked with Kaspar Maase at the University of Tübingen (Germany) on the subproject "Quotidian Integration and Social Positioning of Pulp Novels and Television Series." She is a coeditor of the collections *Unterhaltung und Vergnügung: Beiträge der Europäischen Ethnologie zur Populärkulturforschung* (2013) and *Macher—Medien—Publika: Beiträge der Europäischen Ethnologie zu Geschmack und Vergnügen* (2014).

SEAN O'SULLIVAN is an Associate Professor of English at The Ohio State University, where he is a Core Faculty member of Project Narrative. He is the author of *Mike Leigh* (2011), and his articles on serial narrative and television include such topics as *The Sopranos* and episodic storytelling; *Deadwood* and Charles Dickens; modernist structure in *Mad Men*; poetic design and serial television; and third seasons. In 2014, he was a fellow of the Popular Seriality Research Unit (PSRU) at the John F. Kennedy Institute for North American Studies (Freie Universität Berlin).

DANIEL STEIN is chair of North American Literary and Cultural Studies at Universität Siegen (Germany). In the Popular Seriality Research Unit (PSRU), he cooperated with Frank Kelleter on a subproject on the authorization of superhero comics and directed a subproject on antebellum urban mysteries. He is the author of *Music Is My Life: Louis Armstrong, Autobiography, and American Jazz* (2012) and has published numerous articles and coedited collections on comics and graphic narratives.

ANDREAS SUDMANN is post-doctoral Research Associate at the John F. Kennedy Institute for North American Studies (Freie Universität Berlin). He has directed the Media Studies division of the Center for Interdisciplinary Media Studies at the University of Göttingen and taught Media Studies at the University of Regensburg. He cooperated with Frank Kelleter in the Popular Seriality Research Unit (PSRU) on the subproject "The Dynamics of Serial Outbidding" and codirected the subproject "Digital Seriality" with Shane Denson. He is the author of books on American independent cinema (2006) and Dogma (2001) and has published on television series, film history, computer games, and media theory.

CONSTANTINE VEREVIS is Associate Professor in Film and Screen Studies at Monash University, Melbourne (Australia). He is the author of *Film Remakes* (2006), coauthor of *Australian Film Theory and Criticism* (2013), and coeditor of *Second Takes: Critical Approaches to the Film Sequel* (2010); *Film Trilogies* (2012); *Film Remakes, Adaptations and Fan Productions* (2012); *B Is for Bad Cinema* (2014); *US Independent Film after 1989* (2015); and *Transnational Television Remakes* (2016). In 2014, he was a fellow of the Popular Seriality Research Unit (PSRU) at the John F. Kennedy Institute for North American Studies (Freie Universität Berlin).

INDEX

24 (Fox), 175–76

Aarseth, Espen, 267
abduction-and-rescue pattern, 99
absorption, 184, 185, 201–2
actor-network theory (ANT), 25–26, 271, 278
Adorno, Theodor, 22–23, 195, 201
Adventures of Obadiah Oldbuck, The (*Brother Jonathan*), 40, 43–44, 46–51
aesthetic experience, theories of, 8, 24n25
agency: actor-network theory (ANT) and, 271; city mysteries and, 54; local agency of the novel, 61n18; the postauteur and authorial agency in millennial remakes, 156; recipients as agents of narrative continuation, 13, 22; self-observing systems and, 25; urban mysteries and political agency, 2
Alice in Wonderland (Burton), 225
Alien (Scott), 163
Allen, Robert, 173–74
All in the Family (CBS), 189
Alltagsintegration (quotidian integration), 249. *See also* reception and quotidian integration of *Perry Rhodan* and *Tatort*
All the Real Girls (Green), 154
Ally Sloper character, 82n22
Ames, Melissa, 199n8
Anderson, Benedict, 26–28, 37, 62, 131, 269–70, 276–77
antebellum era. *See* city mysteries, cultural work of; comics, American antebellum emergence of

Appadurai, Arjun, 27
Archer, Heil, 153
archontic literature, 245–46
Aristotle, 198
Arp, Bill, 50
articulation, serial, 175
Asmodeus; or, Legends of New York (Buchanan), 64
Aubert, Gabriel, 47
Auerbach, Nina, 111, 120
authorization conflicts, 19
authorization practice, 59
autonomy, 257

backstory, 130, 231, 239–40, 246. *See also* world-building and storyworlds
Back to the Future (Zemeckis), 137
Baker, Rick, 143
Bakhtin, Mikhail, 98
Balderston, John L., 116
Bates Motel (A&E), 138
Batman and Robin (Bennet), 99
Batman Begins (Nolan), 148
Batman figure, 270–71
Baum, L. Frank: authorization conflicts and, 19; authorized successors to, 235; *Dorothy and the Wizard in Oz*, 232; emergence of world of Oz and, 228; *The Fairylogue and Radio Play* lecture tour, 235; *The Marvelous Land of Oz*, 235, 237; *Ozma of Oz*, 237; *Tik-Tok of Oz*, 232, 233 fig. 12.2, 234 fig. 12.3; transmedia storytelling by,

235; *The Wonderful Wizard of Oz* (or *The Wizard of Oz*), 231, 233–34. See also Oz
Baum Bugle, The, 236
Beacham, Travis, 225
Benjamin, Park, 41, 43
Benjamin, Walter, 37, 195, 200
Bennett, James Gordon, 42
Bergson, Henri, 11n7, 275
Bernds, Edward, 138
B'hoys of New York (Buntline), 67
Birmingham School, 10, 24
blackface minstrelsy, 68
Blade Runner (Scott), 160
Block, Rudolph Edgar, 76
Blood Simple (Coen and Coen), 155
body politic and body politics, 69
Body Snatchers (Ferrara), 133–34, 133 fig. 7.1
Bordwell, David, 227
Börnstein, Heinrich: *Die Geheimnisse von St. Louis*, 55, 66; political activity of, 63–64
Boulle, Pierre, 140, 141
Bourdieu, Pierre, 188
Bourriaud, Nicolas, 149
box sets, VHS and DVD, 136–39
Bradbury, Osgood, 55, 63
Bram Stoker's Dracula (Coppola), 115n7, 120–22
Brand, Dana, 77
Branigan, Edward, 104, 105
Breaking Bad (AMC): cultural circulation and gender politics, 176–81; inevitability vs. surprise and, 209–18
Brenda Starr: Reporter (Fox), 104
Brooks, Noah, 50
Brother Jonathan (newspaper): *The Adventures of Obadiah Oldbuck*, 40, 43–44, 46–51; Day at, 43; "East India Sporting: Marvelous Adventures with a Tiger," 44–46, 45 fig. 2.1, 48; *Gaspar: the Pirate of the Indian Seas*, 46; launching of, 41; postal rate and, 43, 49; story paper format and, 39–40; *The Tempter and the Tempted*, 46
Brown, Bill, 194, 196, 202n10
Brownies characters, 82n22
Browning, Tod, 113, 116–19, 121

Bruns, Axel, 258
Brunsdon, Charlotte, 188
Buchanan, Harrison Gray, 64
bullet time, 274–76
Buntline, Ned (pseud. for Edward Zane Carroll Judson): *B'hoys of New York*, 67; *G'hals of New York*, 67; *The Mysteries and Miseries of New York*, 53, 55–57, 61–67; prefatorials of, 64, 66–67; verisimilitude claims, 65
Buonnano, Milly, 190, 200
Burroughs, Edgar Rice, 162
Burton, Tim: *Alice in Wonderland*, 225; *Planet of the Apes*, 136, 141–43, 162; as world builder, 227
Butler, David, 98

Cain, James M., 155
Cameron, James, 141, 163
Canyons, The (Schraer), 158–59
capitalism, 26–31, 125
cards, collectible, 229–30
Carpenter, John, 8n3, 157
Carrie (De Palma), 8n3
Carroll, Noël, 205n1
Carter, Nathalie, 157
Chambers, John, 142
Chapiron, Kim, 160
Charivari, Le, 47
Chirstenfeld, Nicholas, 103
chronotopes, 98
Cincinnati, oder Geimnisse des Westens (Klauprecht), 55, 60, 66
cinema. See Dracula as serial figure; Hollywood remaking; remakes, new millennial; sound serials; *specific titles*
cinephile culture, 132
City Crimes, or, Life in New York and Boston (Thompson), 53, 55, 55n5, 62–63
city mysteries: Börnstein's *Die Geheimnisse von St. Louis*, 55, 66; Buchanan's *Asmodeus; or, Legends of New York*, 64; Buntline's *B'hoys of New York*, 67; Buntline's *G'hals of New York*, 67; Buntline's *The Mysteries and Miseries of New York*, 53, 55–57, 61–67; character types, storylines, and narrative modes, 57–58; intertextual and intermedial references, 68; Klauprecht's *Cincinnati,*

oder Geimnisse des Westens, 55, 60, 66; Lippard's *Quaker City; or, The Monks of Monk Hall*, 39, 53–55, 59, 61–65, 68, 70–71; New England mysteries, 65–66; Reizenstein's *Die Geheimnisse von New-Orleans*, 55, 58–59, 61, 66, 70; satire and parody, 68; Sue's *Les Mystères de Paris*, 19, 39, 40, 48, 54, 59; Thompson's *City Crimes, or, Life in New York and Boston*, 53, 55, 55n5, 62–63; Thompson's *House Breaker; or, The Mysteries of Crime*, 67; transatlantic origins and American adaptation of, 54–55

city mysteries, cultural work of: American impact and imagined collectivization, 68–71; body politic and body politics, 69; competition for audience attention, 67–68; genre history and characteristics, 53–56; media ecology and political subjectivity, 59–62; paratexts and, 64, 66–67; popular seriality, cultural work, and serial politics, 56–62; specific time and climate of Antebellum, 55–56; tension between entertainment and political objectives, 31n32, 56, 62–68; verisimilitude claims, 65

Clark, George, 79

Clarke, Alan, 160

cliffhangers, 96–97, 101–6

closure: city mysteries and, 62, 70; cultural forum and, 176; Dracula and deferral of, 115; ideological, 176; inevitability vs. surprise and, 218; opacities and, 184, 199, 202; recursivity and, 17; reproduction and, 7–9; sound serials and, 94, 98; televisual seriality and, 189–90

cocreativity, 258

Coen, Ethan, 155

Coen, Joel, 155

collecting, 229–30, 256

collection sets, VHS and DVD, 136–39

collective serialization with digital games, 272, 276–81

Comic Almanack, 46–47

comics, American antebellum emergence of: *The Adventures of Obadiah Oldbuck* (*Brother Jonathan*), 40, 43–44, 46–51; "East India Sporting: Marvelous Adventures with a Tiger" (*Brother Jonathan*), 44–46, 45 fig. 2.1, 48; "first paperback revolution" and, 43; friendship albums, scrapbooking, and, 44, 46; *Gaspar: the Pirate of the Indian Seas* (*Brother Jonathan*), 46; graphic literature, advantages and challenges of, 47–48; *Happy Hooligan* (Opper), 51; *The Laughable Adventures of Messrs. Brown, Jones, and Robinson* (Doyle), 49; "meanwhile time" of the novel vs. serial time, 37–38; penny press and, 42–43; rise of the novel and, 38–39; serial-mania and, 39, 42; story paper format and competition with tradebook publishers, 39–40, 41–44; *The Strange Adventures of Bachelor Butterfly* (Wilson & Co.), 49; *The Tempter and the Tempted* (*Brother Jonathan*), 46; Tilt & Bogue and Wilson & Co., 47–48, 49; Töpffer's polyautography (lithography) and, 40, 45–46

computer-capture work, 142

computer games. *See* gaming and digital seriality

Conan (Nispel), 161

Constandinides, Costas, 150

Cook, Pam, 150

Cooper, James Fenimore, 38

Coppola, Francis Ford, 115n7, 120–22

Coquette, The (Foster), 38–39

Corneau, Alain, 157

Crafton, Donald, 116

Crazies, The (Eisner), 160

Crazies, The (Romero), 160

Creeber, Glen, 188–90

Crime d'amour / Love Crime (Corneau), 157

Crimson Ghost, The (Witney/Brannon), 99–100

critical transculturalism, 155

Cronenberg, David, 138, 139

cross-cultural interactions, 155

Cruikshank, George, 46–47, 48

Cruikshank, Robert, 46

cultural forum (Newcomb), 176

cultural-historical perspective, 272–73

cultural politics in television narratives. *See* television narratives, meaning, and cultural politics

cultural studies, 10, 170

cultural work of city mysteries. *See* city mysteries, cultural work of

culture industry paradigm (Horkheimer/Adorno), 22–23

Curtiz, Michael, 151

INDEX

Dallas (CBS), 17
Dark Knight Trilogy, 148
database, logic of, 266
Dawn of the Planet of the Apes (Reeves), 141, 142, 143
Day, Benjamin, 42, 43
Day the Earth Stood Still, The (Derrickson), 137
Deadwood (HBO), 207–9, 212–13, 215–19
Deane, Hamilton, 116
De Laurentiis, Dino, 151
Deleuze, Gilles, 11, 275
democracy and self-reflexivity, 29
Denning, Michael, 55, 56, 60, 63
Denslow, William Wallace, 233–34, 235, 243
Denson, Shane, 21n22, 105–6, 139
De Palma, Brian, 8n3, 157
Derecho, Abigail, 245
detective novels, popularity and repetition in, 8. *See also* city mysteries
Dewey, John, 8
Dick & Fitzgerald, 49
Dickens, Charles: London of, 228–29; *Oliver Twist*, 42, 46, 229; *The Pickwick Papers*, 37, 42; serial-mania and, 39
Dick Tracy (Witney), 98, 100
digital games. *See* gaming and digital seriality
digital media: DVDs and Hollywood remakes and box sets, 134–39; information and exchange platforms, 256–57; quotidian reception of *Perry Rhodan* and *Tatort* and, 251–55
digital seriality. *See* gaming and digital seriality
discontinuity, 104–6, 267–68, 270
disorientation, 201–2
dispotif, 251
Dog Pound (Chapiron), 160
double formal structure, 17
Doyle, Arthur Conan, 228
Doyle, Richard, 49
Dracula as serial figure: Browning's film *Dracula* (1931), 113, 116–19, 121; Coppola's film *Bram Stoker's Dracula* (1992), 115n7, 120–22; cultural contextualization, modernity, and, 111–13; flatness of, 21n22; Hammer film series (1950), 119; Herzog's film *Nosferatu, Phantom der Nacht* (1979), 120; medial dialectics and modernity in the novel, 113–16; as meta-medium, 115–16; Moore and O'Neal's *League of Extraordinary Gentlemen*, 115n7; Murnau's film *Nosferatu* (1922), 116; NBC's *Dracula* (2013), 115n7, 120; plays (London 1924 and Broadway 1927), 116; Polanksi's film *The Fearless Vampire Killers* (1967), 119–20; as self-reflexive embodiment of the in-between, 119–20; serial figures, 108–12; spectral logic and, 108, 109–10; Stoker's *Dracula* (1897), 112, 113–16, 117, 119, 121; as transitional medium, 116–20, 121; Universal Studios film series (1931–1948), 116
drillable text, 183–84, 193. *See also* opacity in televisual seriality
Dudley, Andrew, 228–30
Dumont, Frank, 82
DVD era, remakes and box sets in, 134–39
Dyer, James, 160

"East India Sporting: Marvelous Adventures with a Tiger" (*Brother Jonathan*), 44–46, 45 fig. 2.1, 48
e-books, 252–53
Eco, Umberto, 20, 29, 110, 229
Edelstein, David, 141
Eisner, Breck, 160
Either Way / Á Annan Veg (Sigurðsson), 154
Ellis, Bret Easton, 158
Elsaesser, Thomas, 113, 155–56
Emerson, Paul J., 61n18
emotions: articulation and emotional engagement, 175; city mysteries and reader control over, 63; imagined communities and emotional attachment, 27; immersion and, 236–37, 243; in melodramas, 100; passivity and, 215; production/reception nexus and, 24; in sound serials, 100–101; suspense and, 205, 205n1; TV melodrama and emotional excess, 193
Engell, Lorenz, 109, 266
Enter the Matrix, 274–75
Erb, Cynthia, 151
ergodicity, 267
EU cultural exemption, 154
evolving narratives, popular series as, 12–16
excessive images and opacity, 192–95
extras, 43, 46

Fairylogue and Radio Play lecture tour (Baum), 235
fan cultures: cinephile culture and, 132; DVD editions and, 138; forensic fandoms, 131, 183–84, 187, 201–2. *See also* reception and quotidian integration of *Perry Rhodan* and *Tatort*
Fantômas, 109, 110
Far from Heaven (Haynes), 150
Fargo (FX), 219–20
"fast" narratives, 13–14
Fearless Vampire Killers, The (Polanksi), 119–20
Federalist Papers (Hamilton, Madison, and Jay), 69
Federal Operator 99 (Bennet/Canutt/Grissell), 99
Feuer, Jane, 189, 190
Filippusson, Árni, 154
film serials. *See* Dracula as serial figure; Hollywood remaking; remakes, new millennial; sound serials; *specific titles*
Fincher, David, 153, 156, 163
Flash Gordon (Stephani/Taylor), 95–98
Fluck, Winfried, 57n9
Fly, The: Bernd's *Return of the Fly* (1959), 138; Cronenberg's *The Fly II* (1986), 138, 139; *The Fly Chamber Collection*, 138–39; Neumann's *The Fly* (1958), 138; Sharp's *Curse of the Fly* (1965), 138
folio editions of story papers, 41, 44
forensic fandoms, 131, 183–84, 187, 201–2
Foster, Hannah Webster, 38–39
Foucault, Michel, 111, 251
Franco, James, 239
Frankenstein (Shelley), 83
Frankenstein's monster, 109, 118
Frankfurt School, 10, 24
Freeman, Matthew, 235
Fried, Michael, 201
friendship albums, 44, 46
Frye, Northrop, 111
Fu Manchu, 3, 20n20, 21n22, 109, 110
function, concept of, 227

Gambone, Robert, 76
gaming and digital seriality: bullet time, 274–76; collective serialization, 272, 276–81; conceptual scope of seriality and, 263–64; cultural practice of digital seriality, 268–71; cultural relevance of, 281–82; digitality, media convergence, and seriality, 264–66; history of gaming and seriality, 262–64; levels of digital seriality (intra-, inter-, and para-ludic), 271–72, 273, 274 table 14.1, 276–77; ludology-vs.-narratology debate, 266–68; media-aesthetic and cultural-historical perspectives, 272–73; media-archaeological approach, 278; serial interfacing, 272, 273–76; *Super Star Trek*, coding, and present-future mismatch in temporality, 278–80
Gardner, Jared, 21n22, 77, 79–80, 85
Gaspar: the Pirate of the Indian Seas (Brother Jonathan), 46
Geheimnisse von New-Orleans, Die (Reizenstein), 55, 58–59, 61, 66, 70
Geheimnisse von St. Louis, Die (Börnstein), 55, 66
genre profusion and diversification, 19. *See also* proliferation
George Washington (Green), 154
German immigrant authors, 55, 66
Gerrig, Richard, 101
G'hals of New York (Buntline), 67
Gilligan, Vince, 179–80, 209, 213
Girl with the Dragon Tattoo, The, 153
Gitelman, Lisa, 252
Godfather series (Coppola), 137
Goethe, Johann Wolfgang von, 40, 47
Goodman, Nelson, 228–29
graphic culture, 43–44
graphic literature, advantages and challenges of, 47–48. *See also* comics, American antebellum emergence of
Gray, F. Gary, 160
Gray, Jonathan, 136n13, 139
Great Train Robbery, The (Porter), 48–49
Green, David Gordon, 154
Greenberg, Clement, 192
Greene, Eric, 141
Griswold, Rufus, 41, 43
Gundam, 229–30
Gunn, Anna, 180
Gunning, Tom, 98, 192, 202

habitualized modes of reception, 257
Haggard, H. Rider, 233

INDEX   293

Hall, Stuart, 175
Halloween (Carpenter), 8n3, 157
Halloween (Zombie), 157–58
Hansen, Miriam, 195, 201
Happy Hooligan (Opper), 51
Harper & Bros., 40, 41, 42
Harry Potter (Rowling), 20
Hasebrink, Uwe, 254
Hatfield, Charles, 78
Hawk, Byron, 275
Hawley, Noah, 204, 219–20
Haynes, Todd, 150–51
He, Hilary Hongjin, 155
Hearst, William Randolph, 75–76
Hediger, Vinzenz, 134–35, 134n12
Heinrich, Rick, 143
Herzog, Werner, 120
Heston, Charlton, 136
Hickethier, Knut, 17, 251
Hidden Hand (Southworth), 39
Higginson, Thomas Wentworth, 49
Hirsch, Paul, 176
historical poetics, 170
Hitchcock, Alfred: *Psycho*, 138; on surprise and suspense, 204–6, 216; *Vertigo*, 156
Hollywood remaking: cinematic artwork rhetoric and, 127; as cinematic formatting practice, 129–31; DVD era and box sets, 134–39; hostile attitudes toward, 127; media-specificity, popular seriality, and, 128–29; the non-remake, 149n2; *Planet of the Apes* and media-generational change, 139–43; retrospective serialization, cinematic self-historicization, and second-order observation, 131–34; scenography of Subject vs. Object and, 127, 132; terminology and categories, 125–26, 130. *See also* remakes, new millennial
Homeland (Showtime), 171–76, 181, 213n2
Horkheimer, Max, 22–23
horror films, repetition in, 8
House Breaker; or, The Mysteries of Crime (Thompson), 67
How I Met Your Mother (CBS), 213n2

iconic serialities: Burton's *Alice in Wonderland*, 225; digital games and, 272; Dracula, 108, 110–13, 116–20, 122; *The Italian Job*, 159; *Planet of the Apes*, 141; transmedial malleability, flatness, and, 21n22; *The Wizard of Oz*, 240, 241, 243–44; Yellow Kid, 82
ideology: city mysteries and, 60, 62; non-symptomatic model of, 28; popular narrative theory and ideological practice, 28–29
imaginary worlds. *See* world-building and storyworlds
imagined communities, 26–29, 69–70, 269–70, 276–77
inevitability and surprise and serial television: continuum of, 209; *Deadwood* and *The Wire*, compared, 218–19; *Fargo* and, 219–20; Hitchcock on surprise vs. suspense, 204–6; *Homeland*, *Lost*, *The Newsroom*, *Louie*, and *How I Met Your Mother*, 213n2; inevitability in *Deadwood* and *The Wire*, 207–9, 212–13; inevitability in *Six Feet Under*, 213–15; narrative arc and, 217–18; narrative design vs. storyworld environment and, 210; serial narrative and, 206; surprise and apparent inevitability in *Breaking Bad*, 209–11; surprise in *Mad Men*, 215–16; surprise in *The Sopranos* and *Breaking Bad*, compared, 215–18; validation of surprise, 206–7
Innis, Harold, 132
In Remembrance of Things Past (Proust), 237
intellectual property rights and constraints, 153, 241–43
interfacing, serial, 272, 273–76
inter-ludic seriality, 272, 274 table 14.1
interruption, 104–6. *See also* opacity in televisual seriality
intra-ludic seriality, 271, 274 table 14.1
Invasion of the Body Snatchers (Siegel), 131–32; Ferrara's 1993 *Body Snatchers*, 133–34, 133 fig. 7.1
investigatory dynamic of television, 183–84
Italian Job, The (Gray), 159–60
Ito, Mimi, 229

Jackson, Peter, 151
Jameson, Fredric, 200–201
Jaws (Spielberg), 138
Jaws Quadrilogy, 137–38
Jazz Singer, The (Crosland), 118
Jenkins, Henry, 22, 251–52, 265, 270

Jenkins, Jerry, 31n32
Jeunet, Jean-Pierre, 163
Johnson, Derek, 227, 230–31
Johnson, Steven, 11n7
Journal des Débats, 54
Judge Dredd (Cannon), 161
Judson, Edward Zane Carroll. *See* Buntline, Ned
Jurassic Park (Spielberg), 121
Just Imagine (Butler), 98
Juul, Jesper, 266

Kammerer, Paul, 11n7
Kapner, Mitchell, 238
Katzman, Sam, 99
Kelleter, Frank, 68–69, 226, 231
Kemble, E. W., 83n26
King, Stephen: *Misery*, 19n15
King Kong, 132, 151
Kittler, Friedrich, 113, 114
Klauprecht, Emil, 55, 60, 66
Kompare, Derek, 136
Kovács, András Bálint, 192n2
Kracauer, Siegfried, 195, 200
Krämer, Sybille, 109

LaHaye, Tim, 31n32
Larsson, Stieg, 153
Latour, Bruno, 25, 27, 28n30, 126n3, 271
Laughable Adventures of Messrs. Brown, Jones, and Robinson, The (Doyle), 49
League of Extraordinary Gentlemen (Moore and O'Neal), 115n7
Leavitt, Jonathan, 103
Lee, Christopher, 119
Lee, Nathan, 157–58
Left Behind series (LaHaye and Jenkins), 31n32
Lehuu, Isabel, 41
Lem, Stanisław, 156
Levine, Caroline, 205n1
Life, 46n7, 50
Lippard, George: as the "American" Sue, 59; conflicting voices created by, 62; *New York: Its Upper Ten and Lower Million*, 71; *The Quaker City; or, The Monks of Monk Hall*, 39, 53–55, 59, 61–65, 68,

70–71; story paper format and, 39–40; verisimilitude claims, 65
literacy, 77–78, 135–36
lithography, 40, 45–46
Looby, Christopher, 67
Lost (ABC), 21n22, 190, 213n2
Love Crime / Crime d'amour (Corneau), 157
Lucas, Tim, 161–62
ludic digital seriality, levels of (intra-, inter-, and para-ludic), 271–72, 273, 274 table 14.1, 276–77
ludology-vs.-narratology debate, 266–68
Lugosi, Bela, 113, 116
Luhmann, Niklas, 8n3, 23n24, 193n4
Lukács, Georg, 200
Luks, George Benjamin, 75, 80, 83–84, 85n29
Lütticken, Sven, 148n1

Maase, Kaspar, 255
Madison, James, 69
Mad Men (AMC): inevitability vs. surprise and, 215–16; opacity and, 185–88, 194, 195–99
makeup artistry, 142
Mandrake the Magician (Deming/Nelson), 97
Manning, Knox, 104
maps, 232–33
Martin, George R. R., 19n15
Martineau, Harriet, 49–50
Marx, Karl, 112
Massumi, Brian, 275
Matrix, The (Wachowskis), 270, 274–75
Max Payne, 274–75
Mayer, Ruth, 20n20, 21n22, 83n24
Mayhew, Henry, 47
McDougall, Walt, 81n19
meaning-making: drillable text, investigatory dynamic, and forensic fandom, 183–84, 193, 201–2; objects, meaning, and opacity, 194–97; politics of the text and, 189; temporality of TV serials and, 190–92. *See also* opacity in televisual seriality; television narratives, meaning, and cultural politics
"meanwhile time" of the novel, 37–38
Mecom, Benjamin, 38
media: as complex apparatuses of meaning-making and world building, 109; repertoire of, 254

media-aesthetics perspective, 272–73
media-archaeological approach, 109, 269, 278
media convergence, 252, 264, 265
media ecology: Antebellum comics and, 41, 51; city mysteries and, 60; digital, 272–73; predigital–digital transition and, 270; remakes and, 134; separation of film serials from feature films and, 128n5; serial figures and, 22
Milch, David, 219
Mildred Pierce (Curtiz), 151
Mildred Pierce (Haynes), 150–51
minstrel discourse, 68
Misery (King), 19n15
Mittell, Jason, 17, 131, 136n13, 138n15, 183–84, 193, 201, 216, 256
modernity: Art Deco in *Wizard of Oz* and, 241; Dracula and, 110, 112, 113–15, 122; evolving phenomenology of, 195; imagined communities and, 27; opacity and, 200; self-description of, 27–30; serial figures and, 108, 111; Yellow Kid and, 77
Monks of Monk Hall, The (or *The Quaker City*) (Lippard), 39, 53–55, 59, 61–65, 68, 70–71
Moore, Alan, 115n7
Moretti, Franco, 112, 114
Murnau, Friedrich, 116
Murray, Janet, 266–67
Mystères de Paris, Les (Sue), 19, 39, 40, 48, 54, 59
Mysteries and Miseries of New York, The (Buntline), 53, 55–57, 61–67

narration and narrators: comics as "graphic narrations," 48; Lippard's paratext and conflation of author and narrator, 64; in sound serials, 96, 102, 104–5
narrative arc, 190, 217–18
narrative remission, 211
narrative sprawl, 20, 226, 231, 245
narratology-vs.-ludology debate, 266–68
naturalism, 218–19
Neill, John R., 233, 235, 243
neo-Marxism, 9–10
neo-vitalism, 9–10
Neumann, Kurt, 138
Newcomb, Horace, 176, 190

New England Magazine, 38
Newman, Kim, 157
Newman, Robin, 191n1
new millennial remakes. *See* remakes, new millennial
New Romances, 233
Newsroom, The (HBO), 213n2
New World, 39–41, 48
New York: Its Upper Ten and Lower Million (Lippard), 71
New York Herald, 42
New York Journal, 75, 81, 81n19, 83n26
New York Sun, 42
New York World, 74–76, 74n1, 81n19. *See also* Yellow Kid
Nispel, Marcus, 157, 161
Nolan, Christopher, 148, 156
Nosferatu, Eine Symphonie des Grauens (Murnau), 116
Nosferatu, Phantom der Nacht (Herzog), 120
nostalgic return, 236–38
novel, rise of, 38–39

Obadiah Oldbuck (*Brother Jonathan*), 40, 43–44, 46–51
objects, meaning, and opacity, 194–97
octavo, oblong, 46
O'Hehir, Andrew, 143
Ohmann, Richard, 86
Oliver Twist (Dickens), 42, 46, 229
OmniCorp, 152
O'Neal, Kevin, 115n7
opacity in televisual seriality: absorption-expulsion dialectic, 185; absorption-theatricality dialectic, 184; disorientation and, 201–2; drillable text and investigatory dynamic, 183–84; the excessive image and, 192–95; forensic fandom and, 184, 201–2; *Mad Men*, opacity, and mediation of objects and images, 195–200; *Mad Men* and television as theory, 185–88; modernity, postmodernity, and, 200; nonsignifying opacities, 194–95, 201; perforated seriality, 185; serial form and, 188–92
Opper, Frederick Burr, 51
Otsuka Eiji, 229–31
outbidding, outdoing, and one-upmanship, serial practices of, 30, 59, 273

Outcault, Richard Felton, 75–76, 75nn2–3, 78, 78n10, 80, 83–84, 83n26, 85nn28–29, 86n30. *See also* Yellow Kid

overdesign, 227, 245

Oz: *The Art of Oz the Great and Powerful* (Curtis, 2013), 241; authorization conflicts and, 19; *The Baum Bugle*, 236; Baum's Broadway musical and stage productions, 235; canonical story, 226; Disney live-action musical, planned (1950s), 243; *Dorothy and the Wizard in Oz* (Baum, 1908), 232; *His Majesty, the Scarecrow of Oz* (Oz film, 1914), 243 fig. 12.6; illustrations and illustrators, 233–34; maps of Oz, 232–33, 233 fig. 12.2, 234 fig. 12.3; *The Marvelous Land of Oz* (Baum, 1904), 235, 237; narrative sprawl of Oz universe, 226, 231; *Ozma of Oz* (Baum, 1907), 237; *The Ozmapolitan* (faux newspaper), 235; "Ozness" as network of information, 226; *Oz the Great and Powerful* (Disney film, 2013), 225–26, 226 fig. 2.1, 236, 238–44, 242 fig. 12.5, 244 fig. 12.8, 246; *Return to Oz* (Disney film, 1985), 237–38, 240, 243, 243 fig. 12.7, 246; television series in development, 236; *Tik-Tok of Oz* (Baum, 1914), 232, 233 fig. 12.2, 234 fig. 12.3; *Wicked* (Broadway musical, 2003), 238–44; *The Wizard of Oz* (MGM musical, 1939), 127, 242 fig. 12.4, 245; *The Wonderful Wizard of Oz* (or *The Wizard of Oz*; Baum, 1900), 231, 233–34. *See also* world-building and storyworlds

paperback revolution, "first," 43

para-ludic seriality, 272, 274 table 14.1, 276–77

paratexts: city mysteries and, 64, 66–67; entryway paratexts, 139; television narratives and, 170

Passion (De Palma), 157

Patterson, Cynthia, 44

penny press, 42–43

"people vs. the power bloc, the," 22–23, 25

Perils of Nyoka (Witney), 101–2, 103, 105–6

Perry Rhodan: about, 248–49; alternative delivery technologies and devices, 252–53, 253–55; classical mode of reception, 249–50; conservatism and habitualized modes of reception, 257; feature film (1966), 253; individualization and face-to-face contact, 257; media, technologies, culture, and, 251–52; prevailing reception practices and comparison with *Tatort*, 253–57; produsage and, 258

Phantom Empire, The (Brower/Eason), 100

Philipon, Charles, 47

Photoplay, 135

Pickwick Papers, The (Dickens), 37, 42

piggybacking strategies, 136

Planète des singes, La (Boulle), 140, 141

Planet of the Apes: Boulle's book *La planète des singes* (1963), 140, 141, 162; Burton's *Planet of the Apes* (2001), 136, 141–43, 162; *Evolution Collection*, 139, 140 fig. 7.2; media-generational change and, 139–43; Reeves's *Dawn of the Planet of the Apes* (2014), 141, 142, 143; Schaffner's *Planet of the Apes* (1968), 140–41, 143; television and Broadway versions, 141; Wyatt's *Rise of the Planet of the Apes* (2011), 141, 142, 143

Platt, Thomas Collier, 81n19

play as serial activity, 268–69. *See also* gaming and digital seriality

Poe, Edgar A., 44

Polan, Dana, 199n8

Polanski, Roman, 119–20

political engagement: city mysteries and entertainment vs. political objectives, 56, 62–68; media ecology and political subjectivity, 59–62. *See also* television narratives, meaning, and cultural politics

polyautography, 40, 45–46

Pool, Ithiel de Sola, 252

Popp, Jutta, 254

popular culture: cultural reproduction and, 8–10; meaning of, 8, 22; penny press and, 42–43; self-descriptions of, 15, 18, 23; seriality as practice of, 15, 19

popularity and repetition, 8–9

popular seriality, theory of: actor-network theory (ANT) and, 25–26; capitalist self-reflexivity, 26–31; closure and repetition, 7–9; cultural work and, 56–62; evolving narratives, 12–16; neo-Marxist and neo-vitalist approaches, 10–11; popular culture, 9–10; poststructuralist and posthumanist approaches, 11; proliferation, 18–22; recursive progression, 16–18; self-observing systems, 18, 22–26; terminology, 9

Popular Seriality Research Unit (PSRU), Freie Universität Berlin, 9, 10, 20n20, 86n31, 249n1
Porter, Edwin S., 48–49
postauteur, 155–58
post-celluloid adaptation, 150
postmodernity/postmodernism: Dracula and, 113, 121; opacity and, 200–201; self-description, 7; television series and, 11
postproduction, 149, 156
poststructuralist and posthumanist approaches, 11
prefatorials, 64, 66–67
prequels as before, after, and alongside, 238–39. *See also* Hollywood remaking
Prince Avalanche (Green), 154
problem spaces, 101–3
Proctor, William, 161
produsage, 258
proliferation: city mysteries and, 58; commercial series as narratives of, 1–2, 18–22; digital games and, 263, 277; Dracula and, 108, 109–10, 113, 115; new millennial remakes and, 149, 153, 158–61; *Planet of the Apes* and, 141, 143; self-contained treatment and, 7; Yellow Kid and, 77, 81–84, 86n30
Prometheus (Scott), 163
Proust, Marcel, 237
Psycho: A&E's *Bates Motel* (2013), 138; Hitchcock's *Psycho* (1960), 138; *Psycho Collection*, 138; Van Sant's *Psycho* (1998), 134
Puck, 46n7, 50
Pulitzer, Joseph, 74, 81n19
Punch, 47

Quaker City; or, The Monks of Monk Hall, The (Lippard), 39, 53–55, 59, 61–65, 68, 70–71
Quaresima, Leonardo, 136
quarto editions of story papers, 41, 44
"quick" media, 128–29
quotidian integration (*Alltagsintegration*), 249. *See also* reception and quotidian integration of *Perry Rhodan* and *Tatort*

Radar Men from the Moon (Brannon), 99–100
Rancière, Jacques, 198n7, 201
Raymond, Alex, 96n6

RC2000 Project (OmniCorp), 152
rebooting, 110, 130, 149, 161–63. *See also* Hollywood remaking
reception: autonomy and, 257; cultural work and, 59; evolving narratives and entanglement of production with, 12–13; habitualized modes of, 257; proliferation and, 18–22; scenography of Subject vs. Object and, 127, 132; setting and aesthetic experience, 255
reception and quotidian integration of *Perry Rhodan* and *Tatort*: about *Perry Rhodan* and *Tatort*, 248–49; *Alltagsintegration* (quotidian integration), 249; alternative modes of reception, 251–53; buying and collecting, 256; classic modes of serial reception, 249–51; conservatism and habitualized modes of reception, 257; individualization and face-to-face contact, 257; on- and offline infomedia, 256–57; produsage and cocreativity, 258; "public viewing," 253; setting and aesthetic experience, 255; technological diversification and choices, 253–55; temporal rhythm and, 255–56
recipients: as agents of narrative continuation, 13, 22; self-observing systems and, 22–26. *See also* opacity in televisual seriality; *specific themes*
recursivity: city mysteries and, 58–59; popular seriality, recursive progression in, 16–18; Yellow Kid and, 79–80
Reizenstein, Ludwig von, 55, 58–59, 61, 66, 70
remakes, new millennial: as intermedial, 149–52; postauteur, embrace of, 155–58; proliferation and simultaneity, 158–61; reboots, 161–63; transformation and "valued added," 148–49; as transnational, 152–55
remakes as practice. *See* Hollywood remaking
remix culture, 152–53
repertoire of media, 254
repetition: digital gaming seriality and, 264; in sound serials, 96, 99, 103; Yellow Kid and, 79–80
retcon (retrospective continuity), 18, 109, 109n3
retromania, 159
retrospective continuity (retcon), 18, 109, 109n3
retrospective serialization, Hollywood remakes and, 132–34

Reynolds, David S., 68, 159
Rick, Klaus N., 253
Riley, Michael O., 232
Rise of the Planet of the Apes (Wyatt), 141, 142, 143
Robocop, 152
Romero, George A., 157, 160
Roth, Joe, 238
running times, 96, 99
Rushton, Richard, 201, 202n10
Ryan, Marie-Laure, 217, 229, 236–37

Saler, Michael, 233
Sartre, Jean-Paul, 11
Savini, Tom, 157
Schaffner, Franklin J., 140–41
Schraer, Paul, 158–59
Scott, Ridley, 163
scrapbooking, 44, 46
Scum (Clarke), 160
second-order observation: Hollywood remakes and, 128, 131–34, 139; self-awareness, second-order, 22
second-order seriality, 13n9, 144. See also Hollywood remaking
Seitz, Matt Zoller, 204, 206
self-description: of digital gamers, 277; evolution of cultural self-descriptions, 139; modes of existence and, 126, 126n3; of popular culture, 9, 23, 23n24, 26; of popular seriality, 29; postmodernist, 7; systems theory and, 10n4, 25
self-historicization, cinematic, 134
self-observing systems, 18, 22–26
self-reflexivity: capitalist, 26–31; Dracula and, 118, 119–20, 121–22; sound, self-reflexive foregrounding of, 118; Yellow Kid and, 80–81, 84
sequels, Hollywood. See Hollywood remaking
serial figures, 8, 21–22, 108–12. See also Dracula as serial figure; Yellow Kid
serialism, 7n1, 11
seriality. See *specific topics and themes*
serial-mania: and comics, emergence of, 39; story papers and, 42
serial narrative: first-order and second-order seriality, 13n9; rules and conditions in, 8–9. See also popular seriality, theory of; *specific themes*

Serial Queen films, 105–6
Serkis, Andy, 142
Sharp, Don, 138
Shelley, Mary, 83
Sherlock Holmes, 19, 22, 109, 110
Sigurðsson, Hafsteinn Gunnar, 154
silence, 117–18
Siljeström, Per Adam, 42
Simmel, Georg, 200
Simpsons, The (Fox), 141
Sirk, Douglas, 150
Six Feet Under (HBO), 213–18
Smith, Iain Robert, 155
Smith, Murray, 179
Snow White and the Seven Dwarves (Disney), 243, 244
Snyder, Zack, 157, 227
Sobchack, Vivian, 163, 193n4
Soderbergh, Steven, 156–57, 158
Solaris (Soderbergh), 156–57, 158
Sollors, Werner, 55
Song of Ice and Fire (Martin), 19n15
Sopranos, The (HBO), 215–18
sound and silence, 117–19
sound serials: abduction-and-rescue pattern, 99; *Batman and Robin* (Bennet), 99; *Brenda Starr: Reporter* (Fox), 104; circuitous, digressive arc and non-additive chapters in, 94–95; cliffhanger problem spaces, 101–3; cliffhangers and knowledge management, 102–3, 104–6; cliffhangers in narrative structure, 96–97; *The Crimson Ghost* (Witney/Brannon), 99–100; exposition and narrative compression, 97–99; *Federal Operator 99* (Bennet/Canutt/Grissell), 99; five-part structure (A b C d E), 95–97, 99–100; *Flash Gordon* (Stephani/Taylor), 95–98; formula and audience engagement, 103; history of, 93–94, 128n5; interruption and discontinuity in, 104–6; loss and emotion in, 100–101; *Mandrake the Magician* (Deming/Nelson), 97; narration in, 104–5; *Perils of Nyoka* (Witney), 101–2, 103, 105–6; *The Phantom Empire* (Brower/Eason), 100; *Radar Men from the Moon* (Brannon), 99–100; repetition in, 96, 99, 103; running times, 96, 99; *The Spider's Web* (Horne/Taylor), 97; *Spy Smasher* (Witney), 97, 100–101; *Superman* (Bennet/

Carr), 97; *The Three Musketeers* (Clark/Schaefer), 97, 100; travel scenes, 98; *Zorro's Fighting Legion* (Witney/English), 94–95, 97, 98

Southworth, E. D. E. N., 39

Spadoni, Robert, 116

Spider's Web, The (Horne/Taylor), 97

Spielberg, Steven, 138, 156

spoilers, 103

Spy Smasher (Witney), 97, 100–101

Star Wars: box sets, 137; renaming of *Episode IV: A New Hope*, 132; revised versions of *Episode IV: A New Hope*, 16n14; sequels, open use of, 131; *Star Wars: Empire at War* (Petroglyph Games/LucasArts), 23 fig. 1.2

Stein, Gertrude, 7

Sternberg, Meir, 104

Stewart, David, 60

St. Nicholas magazine, 82n22

Stoker, Bram, 112, 113–16, 117, 119, 121. *See also* Dracula as serial figure

story paper format: *The Adventures of Obadiah Oldbuck* (*Brother Jonathan*), 40, 43–44, 46–51; "East India Sporting: Marvelous Adventures with a Tiger" (*Brother Jonathan*), 44–46, 45 fig. 2.1, 48; emergence of, 39–40; extras, 43, 46; "first paperback revolution" and, 43; friendship albums, scrapbooking, and, 44; *Gaspar: the Pirate of the Indian Seas* (*Brother Jonathan*), 46; *The Laughable Adventures of Messrs. Brown, Jones, and Robinson* (Dick & Fitzgerald), 49; penny press and, 42–43; postal rate and, 43, 49; quarto and folio editions, 41, 44; *The Strange Adventures of Bachelor Butterfly* (Wilson & Co.), 49; *The Tempter and the Tempted* (*Brother Jonathan*), 46; Tilt & Bogue and Wilson & Co., 47–48, 49; Töpffer's polyautography (lithography) and, 40, 45–46; trade-book publishers, competition with, 41–42, 43

storyworld environment and the inevitability vs. surprise, 210, 214. *See also* worldbuilding and storyworlds

Stowe, Harriet Beecher, 39, 56, 57

Strange Adventures of Bachelor Butterfly, The (Wilson & Co.), 49

sub-creation, 230, 245

Subject vs. Object, scenography of, 127, 132

Sue, Eugène: Lippard as the "American" Sue, 59; *Les mystères de Paris*, 19, 39, 40, 48, 54, 59; read by other city mystery authors, 59

Sun Koh (Müller as Myler), 31n32

Superman (Bennet/Carr), 97

Superman figure and proliferation, 20–21, 21 fig. 1.1

Super Mario Bros., 273–74

Super Star Trek (Ahl and Leedom), 278–81, 279 fig. 14.1

surprise. *See* inevitability and surprise and serial television

surroundings, serial, 79

surveillance, vicarious, 205

suspense: Carroll and Levine on, 205n1; cliffhangers in sound serials, 96–97, 101–6; Hitchcock on, 204–5; sound serials and management of, 102; surprise vs. the inevitable and, 205–6

Swartz, Mark Evan, 235

synchronization processes, 267–68, 273

systems theory: actor-network theory (ANT) and, 10n4; on auto-referential operations, 15; cultural-ecological approach and, 2; of Luhmann, 8n2, 19n17; modes of existence and, 126n3; narrative closure and, 8; popular series as self-observing systems, 22–26, 28, 278; regime of continuation and, 29

Tarkovsky, Andrei, 156, 158

Tarzan, 3, 109, 110, 111, 118, 162

Tatort (ARD): about, 248–49; alternative delivery technologies and devices, 252–55; classical mode of reception, 250–51; cocreativity and, 258; conservatism and habitualized modes of reception, 257; individualization and face-to-face contact, 257; media, technologies, culture, and, 251–52; prevailing reception practices and comparison with *Perry Rhodan*, 253–57

Taubin, Amy, 157

Tebbel, John, 43n4

technological conditions and change: collecting and, 256; cultural practices and, 252; digital gaming and, 271, 272, 277–78; Dracula and modern technologies of communication, 113–14; DVD technology, 134–39, 256; media and technological diversification, effect of, 257–58; *Planet of the Apes* and, 142; "quick" media and film seriality, 128–29; quotidian reception of *Perry Rhodan* and *Tatort* and, 251–55; remakes and, 132, 149, 151–52, 160; serial figures as liminal and, 108–9; serial narrative, technological conditions, and self-observation, 18; story papers and, 42; Yellow Kid and, 79

television narratives, meaning, and cultural politics: *Breaking Bad,* cultural circulation, and gender politics ("how does it matter?"), 176–81; historical-poetic approach, 170; *Homeland* and challenges of political interpretation ("how does it mean?"), 171–76; interpretive analysis as problematic, 181; textual meanings, about, 169–70

television series: appointment-based vs. engagement-based television, 251; double formal structure of, 17. *See also* opacity in televisual seriality

temporalities: algorithmic time, 275; bullet time in digital games, 274–76; chronotopes, 98; cliffhanger problem spaces and, 101–3; converted into space in sound serial travel scenes, 98; digital-media convergence, apparent timelessness in, 265; Dracula and, 112, 114; Hollywood films and temporal continuity markers at culture-level, 132; inevitability vs. surprise and, 210–11; infinite futurity, sense of, 30; interruption and discontinuity in sound serials, 104–6; loss, emotion, and "in the nick of time" in sound serials, 100–101; narrative compression in sound serials, 97–99; novel's "meanwhile time" vs. serial time, 37–38; opacity in televisual seriality and, 190–92, 195–96, 198–99; prequels and, 238–39; "quick" media vs. Hollywood films, 128–29; reception of *Perry Rhodan* and *Tatort* and, 255–56; *Super Star Trek,* coding, and, 278–80; suspense and, 204–5; synchronization processes and, 267–68, 273

Tempter and the Tempted, The (Brother Jonathan), 46

theatricality vs. absorption, 184

theory of popular seriality. *See* popular seriality, theory of

Thompson, George: *City Crimes, or, Life in New York and Boston,* 53, 55, 55n5, 62–63; *House Breaker; or, The Mysteries of Crime,* 67; verisimilitude claims, 65

Thompson, Kecia Driver, 218n3
Thompson, Kristin, 227
Thompson, Ruth Plumly, 235
Three Musketeers, The (Clark/Schaefer), 97, 100
Tilt & Bogue, 47
time. *See* temporalities
Tolkien, J. R. R., 230
Tompkins, Jane, 56–58
Töpffer, Rodolphe, 40–41, 45–47, 49, 51
Total Recall (Verhoeven), 160
Total Recall (Wiseman), 160
Townsend, Edward Waterman, 76, 78n10, 80, 83, 83n26, 85n28
trade-book publishers: story papers, competition with, 41–42, 43
transmedial proliferation. *See* proliferation
typewriter as modern media, 114–15

Uncle Tom's Cabin (Stowe), 39, 56, 57
undisguised commodities, 9
Universal Studios: Dracula series, 116

Van Sant, Gus, 134, 138
Verevis, Constantine, 135, 141, 143
Verhoeven, Paul, 152
verisimilitude claims: in city mysteries, 65
Vertigo (Hitchcock), 156
vicarious surveillance, 205
Vieux Bois (Töpffer), 46, 47

Walas, Chris, 138
Walter, Isaac N., 65
Warhol, Andy, 7
Warner, Susan, 57
War of the Worlds (Spielberg), 156
Wenders, Wim, 154
White, Pearl, 94n7
Wide Wide World, The (Warner), 57
Willemen, Paul, 193
Williams, Linda, 100, 103
Wilson, James G., 41
Wilson & Co., 47, 48, 49
Winter, Ralph, 136

Wire, The (HBO), 175–76, 208–10, 212–13, 215–19
Wiseman, Len, 160
Witney, William, 101–2. *See also* sound serials
Wizard of Oz. See Oz
Wolf, Mark J. P., 228, 230, 239, 245
Woman, A Gun, and A Noodle Shop, A (Zhang), 155
Woods, Paul, 141
world-building and storyworlds: archontic literature, 245–46; assessment of, 244–46; digital gaming seriality and, 277; inventiveness, completeness, and consistency, 230, 245; legal and intellectual property constraints, 241–43; as overdesign, 227, 245; Oz, particularity of, 231–36; Oz and nostalgic return, 236–38; Oz as predecessor of transmedia storytelling, 235–36; *Oz the Great and Powerful* and the becoming of Oz, 238–44; shift toward world-building over storytelling, 226–27; sub-creation, 230, 245; world-making and world-sharing, 228–31, 241–44
Wyatt, Rupert, 141

Yaszek, Lisa, 78
Yellow Bird, 153
Yellow Kid (comic figure): consumerism, mass media, and, 86; copyright protection request, 82–83; heterogeneous readership of, 77–78; history of, 74, 75–76; identificatory choices, multiple, 78n10; intramedial competition, 80; modernity, seriality, and consumption practices, 77–81; proliferation and, 81–84; repetitive redundancy and recursive seriality, 79–80; serial logic of, 84–86; *The Yellow Kid* (magazine), 82; *The Yellow Kid in MacFadden's Flats* (Townsend and Outcault), 76n4, 79; "The Yellow Kid Who Lives in Hogan's Alley, A Burlesque" (Dumont), 82
youth serials. *See* sound serials

Zboray, Mary Saracino, 65
Zboray, Ronald J., 65
Zhang Yimou, 155
Zombie, Rob, 157–58
Zorro's Fighting Legion (Witney/English), 94–95, 97, 98

THEORY AND INTERPRETATION OF NARRATIVE

James Phelan, Peter J. Rabinowitz, and Robyn Warhol, Series Editors

Because the series editors believe that the most significant work in narrative studies today contributes both to our knowledge of specific narratives and to our understanding of narrative in general, studies in the series typically offer interpretations of individual narratives and address significant theoretical issues underlying those interpretations. The series does not privilege one critical perspective but is open to work from any strong theoretical position.

Media of Serial Narrative, Edited by Frank Kelleter

Suture and Narrative: Deep Intersubjectivity in Fiction and Film, George Butte

The Writer in the Well: On Misreading and Rewriting Literature, Gary Weissman

Narrating Space / Spatializing Narrative: Where Narrative Theory and Geography Meet, Marie-Laure Ryan, Kenneth Foote, and Maoz Azaryahu

Narrative Sequence in Contemporary Narratology, Edited by Raphaël Baroni and Françoise Revaz

The Submerged Plot and the Mother's Pleasure from Jane Austen to Arundhati Roy, Kelly A. Marsh

Narrative Theory Unbound: Queer and Feminist Interventions, Edited by Robyn Warhol and Susan S. Lanser

Unnatural Narrative: Theory, History, and Practice, Brian Richardson

Ethics and the Dynamic Observer Narrator: Reckoning with Past and Present in German Literature, Katra A. Byram

Narrative Paths: African Travel in Modern Fiction and Nonfiction, Kai Mikkonen

The Reader as Peeping Tom: Nonreciprocal Gazing in Narrative Fiction and Film, Jeremy Hawthorn

Thomas Hardy's Brains: Psychology, Neurology, and Hardy's Imagination, Suzanne Keen

The Return of the Omniscient Narrator: Authorship and Authority in Twenty-First Century Fiction, Paul Dawson

Feminist Narrative Ethics: Tacit Persuasion in Modernist Form, Katherine Saunders Nash

Real Mysteries: Narrative and the Unknowable, H. Porter Abbott

A Poetics of Unnatural Narrative, Edited by Jan Alber, Henrik Skov Nielsen, and Brian Richardson

Narrative Discourse: Authors and Narrators in Literature, Film, and Art, Patrick Colm Hogan

An Aesthetics of Narrative Performance: Transnational Theater, Literature, and Film in Contemporary Germany, Claudia Breger

Literary Identification from Charlotte Brontë to Tsitsi Dangarembga, Laura Green

Narrative Theory: Core Concepts and Critical Debates, David Herman, James Phelan and Peter J. Rabinowitz, Brian Richardson, and Robyn Warhol

After Testimony: The Ethics and Aesthetics of Holocaust Narrative for the Future, Edited by Jakob Lothe, Susan Rubin Suleiman, and James Phelan

The Vitality of Allegory: Figural Narrative in Modern and Contemporary Fiction, Gary Johnson

Narrative Middles: Navigating the Nineteenth-Century British Novel, Edited by Caroline Levine and Mario Ortiz-Robles

Fact, Fiction, and Form: Selected Essays, Ralph W. Rader. Edited by James Phelan and David H. Richter.

The Real, the True, and the Told: Postmodern Historical Narrative and the Ethics of Representation, Eric L. Berlatsky

Franz Kafka: Narration, Rhetoric, and Reading, Edited by Jakob Lothe, Beatrice Sandberg, and Ronald Speirs

Social Minds in the Novel, Alan Palmer

Narrative Structures and the Language of the Self, Matthew Clark

Imagining Minds: The Neuro-Aesthetics of Austen, Eliot, and Hardy, Kay Young

Postclassical Narratology: Approaches and Analyses, Edited by Jan Alber and Monika Fludernik

Techniques for Living: Fiction and Theory in the Work of Christine Brooke-Rose, Karen R. Lawrence

Towards the Ethics of Form in Fiction: Narratives of Cultural Remission, Leona Toker

Tabloid, Inc.: Crimes, Newspapers, Narratives, V. Penelope Pelizzon and Nancy M. West

Narrative Means, Lyric Ends: Temporality in the Nineteenth-Century British Long Poem, Monique R. Morgan

Understanding Nationalism: On Narrative, Cognitive Science, and Identity, Patrick Colm Hogan

Joseph Conrad: Voice, Sequence, History, Genre, Edited by Jakob Lothe, Jeremy Hawthorn, James Phelan

The Rhetoric of Fictionality: Narrative Theory and the Idea of Fiction, Richard Walsh

Experiencing Fiction: Judgments, Progressions, and the Rhetorical Theory of Narrative, James Phelan

Unnatural Voices: Extreme Narration in Modern and Contemporary Fiction, Brian Richardson

Narrative Causalities, Emma Kafalenos

Why We Read Fiction: Theory of Mind and the Novel, Lisa Zunshine

I Know That You Know That I Know: Narrating Subjects from Moll Flanders *to* Marnie, George Butte

Bloodscripts: Writing the Violent Subject, Elana Gomel

Surprised by Shame: Dostoevsky's Liars and Narrative Exposure, Deborah A. Martinsen

Having a Good Cry: Effeminate Feelings and Pop-Culture Forms, Robyn R. Warhol

Politics, Persuasion, and Pragmatism: A Rhetoric of Feminist Utopian Fiction, Ellen Peel

Telling Tales: Gender and Narrative Form in Victorian Literature and Culture, Elizabeth Langland

Narrative Dynamics: Essays on Time, Plot, Closure, and Frames, Edited by Brian Richardson

Breaking the Frame: Metalepsis and the Construction of the Subject, Debra Malina

Invisible Author: Last Essays, Christine Brooke-Rose

Ordinary Pleasures: Couples, Conversation, and Comedy, Kay Young

Narratologies: New Perspectives on Narrative Analysis, Edited by David Herman

Before Reading: Narrative Conventions and the Politics of Interpretation, Peter J. Rabinowitz

Matters of Fact: Reading Nonfiction over the Edge, Daniel W. Lehman

The Progress of Romance: Literary Historiography and the Gothic Novel, David H. Richter

A Glance Beyond Doubt: Narration, Representation, Subjectivity, Shlomith Rimmon-Kenan

Narrative as Rhetoric: Technique, Audiences, Ethics, Ideology, James Phelan

Misreading Jane Eyre: *A Postformalist Paradigm,* Jerome Beaty

Psychological Politics of the American Dream: The Commodification of Subjectivity in Twentieth-Century American Literature, Lois Tyson

Understanding Narrative, Edited by James Phelan and Peter J. Rabinowitz

Framing Anna Karenina: Tolstoy, the Woman Question, and the Victorian Novel, Amy Mandelker

Gendered Interventions: Narrative Discourse in the Victorian Novel, Robyn R. Warhol

Reading People, Reading Plots: Character, Progression, and the Interpretation of Narrative, James Phelan

www.ingramcontent.com/pod-product-compliance
Lightning Source LLC
Chambersburg PA
CBHW021847300426
44115CB00005B/43